Brilliant
Microsoft®
Windows 7

Steve Johnson

Perspection, Inc.

Prentice Hall
is an imprint of

Harlow, England • London • New York • Boston • San Francisco • Toronto
Sydney • Tokyo • Singapore • Hong Kong • Seoul • Taipei • New Delhi
Cape Town • Madrid • Mexico City • Amsterdam • Munich • Paris • Milan

Pearson Education Limited
Edinburgh Gate
Harlow
Essex CM20 2JE
England

and Associated Companies throughout the world

Visit us on the World Wide Web at:
www.pearsoned.co.uk

Original edition, entitled MICROSOFT WINDOWS 7 ON DEMAND, 1st edition, 0789742012 by JOHNSON, STEVE; PERSPECTION, INC., published by Pearson Education, Inc., publishing as Que/Sams, Copyright © 2010 Perspection, Inc.

The UK edition published by PEARSON EDUCATION LTD, Copyright © 2010

This edition is manufactured in the USA and available for sale only in the United Kingdom, Europe, the Middle East and Africa

The right of Steve Johnson to be identified as the author of this work has been asserted by him in accordance with the Copyright, Designs and Patents Act 1988.

ISBN: 978-0-273-72914-3

British Library Cataloguing-in-Publication Data
A catalogue record for this book is available from the British Library

10 9 8 7 6 5
13 12 11

Printed and bound in the United States of America

The publisher's policy is to use paper manufactured from sustainable forests.

Brilliant Guides

What you need to know and how to do it

When you're working on your computer and come up against a problem that you're unsure how to solve, or want to accomplish something in an application that you aren't sure how to do, where do you look?? Manuals and traditional training guides are usually too big and unwieldy and are intended to be used as an end-to-end training resource, making it hard to get to the info you need right away without having to wade through pages of background information that you just don't need at that moment – and helplines are rarely that helpful!

Brilliant guides have been developed to allow you to find the info you need easily and without fuss and guide you through the task using a highly visual, step-by-step approach – providing exactly what you need to know when you need it!!

Brilliant guides provide the quick easy-to-access information that you need, using a detailed index and troubleshooting guide to help you find exactly what you need to know, and then presenting each task on one or two pages. Numbered steps then guide you through each task or problem, using numerous screenshots to illustrate each step. Added features include "See Also…" boxes that point you to related tasks and information in the book, whilst "Did you know?…" sections alert you to relevant expert tips, tricks and advice to further expand your skills and knowledge.

In addition to covering all major office applications, and related computing subjects, the *Brilliant* series also contains titles that will help you in every aspect of your working life, such as writing the perfect CV, answering the toughest interview questions and moving on in your career.

Brilliant guides are the light at the end of the tunnel when you are faced with any minor or major task!

Acknowledgements

Perspection, Inc.

Brilliant Microsoft Windows 7 has been created by the professional trainers and writers at Perspection, Inc. to the standards you've come to expect from Que publishing. Together, we are pleased to present this training book.

Perspection, Inc. is a software training company committed to providing information and training to help people use software more effectively in order to communicate, make decisions, and solve problems. Perspection writes and produces software training books, and develops multimedia and Web-based training. Since 1991, we have written more than 100 computer books, with several bestsellers to our credit, and sold over 5 million books.

This book incorporates Perspection's training expertise to ensure that you'll receive the maximum return on your time. You'll focus on the tasks and skills that increase productivity while working at your own pace and convenience.

We invite you to visit the Perspection Web site at:

www.perspection.com

Acknowledgements

The task of creating any book requires the talents of many hard-working people pulling together to meet impossible deadlines and untold stresses. We'd like to thank the outstanding team responsible for making this book possible: the writer, Steve Johnson; the technical editor, Beth Teyler; the proofreader, Holly Johnson; the production team, James Teyler; and the indexer, Katherine Stimson.

At Que publishing, we'd like to thank Greg Wiegand and Loretta Yates for the opportunity to undertake this project, Cindy Teeters for administrative support, and Sandra Schroeder for your production expertise and support.

Perspection

About The Author

Steve Johnson has written more than 45 books on a variety of computer software, including Adobe Photoshop CS4 and CS3, Adobe Flash CS4 and CS3, Dreamweaver CS4 and CS3, Adobe InDesign CS4, Adobe Illustrator CS4, Microsoft Office 2007 and 2003, Microsoft Windows Vista and XP, Microsoft Expression 2, Microsoft Office 2008 for the Macintosh, and Apple Mac OS X Snow Leopard. In 1991, after working for Apple Computer and Microsoft, Steve founded Perspection, Inc., which writes and produces software training. When he is not staying up late writing, he enjoys playing golf, gardening, and spending time with his wife, Holly, and three children, JP, Brett, and Hannah. Steve and his family live in Pleasanton, California, but can also be found visiting family all over the western United States.

Contents

12 Managing Files Using a Network

Introduction

Welcome to *Brilliant Microsoft Windows 7*, a visual quick reference book that shows you how to work efficiently with Windows 7. This book provides complete coverage of basic to advanced Windows skills.

How This Book Works

You don't have to read this book in any particular order. We've designed the book so that you can jump in, get the information you need, and jump out. However, the book does follow a logical progression from simple tasks to more complex ones. Each task is presented on no more than two facing pages, which lets you focus on a single task without having to turn the page. To find the information that you need, just look up the task in the table of contents or index, and turn to the page listed. Read the task introduction, follow the step-by-step instructions in the left column along with screen illustrations in the right column, and you're done.

What's New

If you're searching for what's new in Windows 7, just look for the icon: **New!**. The new icon appears in the table of contents and throughout this book so you can quickly and easily identify a new or improved feature in Windows 7. A complete description of each new feature appears in the New Features guide in the back of this book.

Keyboard Shortcuts

Most menu commands have a keyboard equivalent, such as Ctrl+P, as a quicker alternative to using the mouse. A complete list of keyboard shortcuts is available on the Web at *www.perspection.com*.

Step-by-Step Instructions

This book provides concise step-by-step instructions that show you "how" to accomplish a task. Each set of instructions includes illustrations that directly correspond to the easy-to-read steps. Also included in the text are time-savers, tables, and sidebars to help you work more efficiently or to teach you more in-depth information. A "Did You Know?" provides tips and techniques to help you work smarter, while a "See Also" leads you to other parts of the book containing related information about the task.

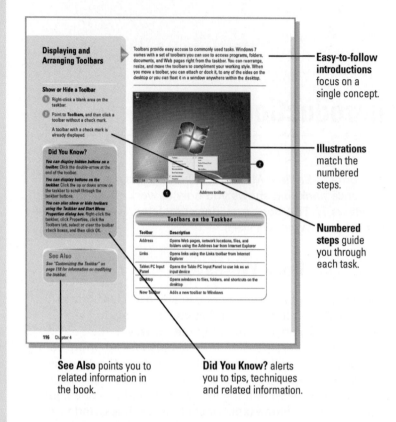

Easy-to-follow introductions focus on a single concept.

Illustrations match the numbered steps.

Numbered steps guide you through each task.

See Also points you to related information in the book.

Did You Know? alerts you to tips, techniques and related information.

Real World Examples

This book uses real world examples files to give you a context in which to use the task. By using the example files, you won't waste time looking for or creating sample files. You get a start file and a result file, so you can compare your work. Not every topic needs an example file, such as changing options, so we provide a complete list of the example files used through out the book. The example files that you need for project tasks along with a complete file list are available on the Web at *www.perspection.com*.

Real world examples help you apply what you've learned to other tasks.

Workshops

This book shows you how to put together the individual step-by-step tasks into in-depth projects with the Workshop. You start each project with a sample file, work through the steps, and then compare your results with a project results file at the end. The Workshop projects and associated files are available on the Web at *www.perspection.com.*

Workshops

Introduction

The Workshop is all about being creative and thinking outside the box. These workshops will help your right-brain soar, while making your left-brain happy; by explaining why things work the way they do. Exploring possibilities is great fun; however, always stay grounded with knowledge of how things work.

Getting and Using the Project Files

For Windows 7, only a few Workshops require project files. If one is needed, the project includes a start file to help you get started, and a final file to provide you with the results of the project so you can see how well you accomplished the project.

Before you can use the project files, you need to download them from the Web. You can access the files at *www.perspection.com* in the downloads area. After you download the files from the Web, uncompress the files into a folder on your hard drive where you'll have easy access from Microsoft Windows 7.

Project 1: Accessing the Control Panel

Skills and Tools: Search for and access Control Panel program items

Locating Control Panel program items and options can sometimes be difficult. Instead of using Classic View in the Control Panel, you can use the Search box on the Start menu or in the Control Panel window to quickly find the program item you want. In addition, you can also display Control Panel program items directly on the Start menu for easy access.

The Project

In this project, you'll learn different ways to search for and access Control Panel program items in Windows 7.

The Process

➤ **Search for Control Panel program items from the Start menu.**

1 In Windows 7, click the **Start** button.

The **Workshops** walks you through in-depth projects to help you put Windows 7 to work.

Microsoft Certified Applications Specialist

This book prepares you for the Microsoft Certified Applications Specialist (MCAS) exam for Microsoft Windows 7. Each MCAS certification exam has a set of objectives, which are organized into broader skill sets. To prepare for the certification exam, you should review and perform each task identified with a MCAS objective to confirm that you can meet the requirements for the exam. Information about MCAS appears in the back of the book. The MCAS objectives are available on the Web at *www.perspection.com.*

Microsoft Certified Applications Specialist

About the MCAS Program

The Microsoft Certified Applications Specialist (MCAS) certification is the globally recognized standard for validating expertise with the Microsoft Office suite of business productivity programs. Earning an MCAS certificate acknowledges you have the expertise to work with Microsoft Office programs. To earn the MCAS certification, you must pass a certification exam for Microsoft Windows 7. Additional exams are available for the Microsoft Office desktop applications of Microsoft Office Word, Microsoft Office Excel, Microsoft Office PowerPoint, Microsoft Office Outlook, or Microsoft Office Access. (The availability of Microsoft Certified Applications Specialist certification exams varies by program, program version, and language. Visit *www.microsoft.com* and search on *Microsoft Certified Applications Specialist* for exam availability and more information about the program.) The Microsoft Certified Applications Specialist program is the only Microsoft-approved program in the world for certifying proficiency with Microsoft Office programs.

What Does This Logo Mean?

It means this book has been approved by the Microsoft Certified Applications Specialist program to be certified courseware for learning Microsoft Windows 7 and preparing for the certification exam. This book will prepare you for the Microsoft Certified Applications Specialist exam for Microsoft Windows 7. Each certification level has a set of objectives, which are organized into broader skill sets. Throughout this book, content that pertains to a Microsoft Certified Applications Specialist objective is identified with the following MCAS certification logo and objective number below the title of the topic:

 WIN7-1.1.1
WIN7-2.2.1

Logo indicates a task fulfills one or more MCAS certification objectives.

Get More on the Web

In addition to the information in this book, you can also get more information on the Web to help you get up to speed faster with Windows 7. Some of the information includes:

Transition Helpers

◆ **Only New Features.** Download and print the new feature tasks as a quick and easy guide.

Productivity Tools

◆ **Keyboard Shortcuts.** Download a list of keyboard shortcuts to learn faster ways to get the job done.

More Content

◆ **Photographs.** Download photographs and other graphics to use in your Office documents.

◆ **More Content.** Download new content developed after publication. For example, you can download a complete chapter on Office SharePoint Server 2007.

You can access these additional resources on the Web at *www.perspection.com.*

Keyboard Shortcuts

Microsoft Windows 7

If a command on a menu includes a keyboard reference, known as a **keyboard short-cut**, to the right of the command name, you can perform the action by pressing and holding the first key, and then pressing the second key to perform the command quickly. For example, if you want to open a new document in Photoshop, you click the File menu, and then click New, or you can abandon the mouse and press Ctrl+N to use shortcut keys. In some cases, a keyboard shortcut uses three keys. Simply press and hold the first two keys, and then press the third key. Using shortcut keys reduces the use of the mouse and speeds up operations. Keyboard shortcuts provide an alternative to using the mouse and make it easy to perform repetitive commands.

Finding a Keyboard Shortcut

Photoshop contains keyboard shortcuts for almost every command and task in the program. To help you find the keyboard shortcut you're looking for, the shortcuts are organized in categories and listed with page numbers.

Internet Explorer, 7
Narrator, 16
Windows 7 (General), 2
Windows Explorer, 5
Windows Help Viewer, 7
Windows Login Screen, 5
Windows Mail, 11
Windows Media Center, 12
Windows Media Player, 15
Windows Photo Gallery, 6
Windows Security Screen, 5
WinKey, 17

New Keyboard Shortcuts

If you're searching for new keyboard shortcuts in Microsoft Windows 7, just look for the letter: **N**. The **N** appears in the Keyboard Shortcuts table so you can quickly and easily identify new or changed shortcuts.

1

Additional content is available on the Web. You can download a document of keyboard shortcuts.

Getting Started with Windows 7

Introduction

Microsoft Windows 7 introduces a breakthrough user experience that is designed to help you intuitively view, find, and organize information on your computer. Windows 7 delivers better personal productivity and digital entertainment on your computer. Before you get started with Windows 7, check out the new and improved features, which includes the Windows Aero user experience, Start menu and taskbar, Instant Searches, Explorers, gadgets, Internet Explorer, HomeGroups, Windows Live, media sharing in Windows Media Player, device management, and advanced security and protection in the Action Center. A complete description of each new feature appears in the New Features guide in the back of this book.

Microsoft Windows 7 is an **operating system**, a computer program that controls the basic operation of your computer and the programs you run. A **program**, also known as an **application**, is task-oriented software you use to accomplish a specific task, such as word processing, managing files on your computer, or performing calculations. Windows 7 displays programs in frames on your screen, called windows (thus the name of the operating system). A **window** can contain the contents of a file and the application in which it was created, **icons** (picture representations of a program or a file), or other usable data. A **file** is a collection of information (such as a letter or list of addresses) that has a unique name, distinguishing it from other files. This use of windows and icons is called a **graphical user interface** (GUI, pronounced "gooey"), meaning that you ("user") interact ("interface") with the computer through the use of graphics: icons and other meaningful words, symbols, and windows.

What You'll Do

Introduce Windows 7

Start Windows 7

Use Windows Aero

Explore the Windows Desktop

Use the Mouse

Use the Mouse for Quick Results

Use the Start Menu

Use the Taskbar

Use Desktop Gadgets

Manage Windows

Use Menus, Toolbars, and Panes

Choose Dialog Box Options

Use Windows Help and Support

Switch Users

Shut Down Your Computer

Introducing Windows 7

Windows 7 Editions

Windows 7 comes in four main editions: the Home Basic Edition for consumers; the Home Premium Edition for consumer power users; the Professional Edition for business and power users; and the Ultimate Edition for the complete package. Two other editions are available for specific needs: the Starter Edition and Enterprise Edition. The Starter Edition is for the beginning PC user and provides the most basic entry to Windows 7, which is targeted to emerging markets. The Enterprise Edition is for large corporations with advanced data protection, compatibility, and international support needs.

The **Home Basic** Edition provides a basic secure entry point for using Windows 7. The **Home Premium** Edition adds to the basic experience by providing the Windows Aero experience, the Mobility Center and Tablet PC support for laptops, Windows Meeting Space for sharing documents, and Windows Media Center for media entertainment.

The **Professional** Edition modifies the Home Premium Edition by adding advanced hardware protection, business networking and remote desktop access, and by removing the Windows Media Center. The **Ultimate** Edition combines every thing from all the editions into one complete package.

Windows 7 User Experience

Windows 7 provides two distinct user interface experiences: a basic experience for entry-level systems, and a more visually dynamic experience called **Windows Aero**. Both offer a new and intuitive navigation experience that help you more easily find and organize your applications and files, but Aero goes further

by delivering a truly next-generation desktop experience.

The basic experience has been updated and streamlined so you can find and work with your programs and files more easily than in previous versions of Windows. Some of the important new features include Explorer windows, Live icons, Search Folders, and Instant Search.

Windows 7 uses Explorer windows to give you more information and control while simplifying how you work with your files. Each Explorer window includes a Command Bar, Live icons, column headers, and a Navigation pane. Command Bars display only the tasks that are most appropriate for the files being displayed. Live icons are scalable thumbnails that display the first page of documents, the actual image of a photo, or the album art for individual songs in your music collection, making it easier to find exactly what you are looking for. The Navigation pane (**New!**) contains Libraries, HomeGroups, networks, disk drives, Search Folders and Favorites folders that you have created on your computer. A Search Folder is simply a search that you save. Opening a Search Folder instantly runs that saved search, displaying up-to-date results immediately.

With Windows 7, you no longer have to remember where you store every file. Instead, to find a file, you need only to remember something about it. The updated Start menu integrates the Instant Search box to help you quickly find and start any program or file on your computer. After you add or edit file properties or data associated with a file, such as a keyword on a document, you can use the Instant Search box to quickly find a file by the file property.

Start Menu   Library folders   Desktop gadget

Instant Search   Taskbar   Explorer window

Starting Windows 7

Windows 7 automatically starts when you turn on your computer. When you first start Windows 7, you see a Welcome screen that you use to log on to Windows. The Welcome screen displays all the user accounts on the computer. Unlike Windows XP, the Welcome screen can't be turned off. After you click a user name, and enter a password, you see the Windows 7 desktop and the Getting Started window (**New!**), which displays options to view information about new features in Windows 7, transfer files and setting, add new users, share files with homegroups, personalize Windows, change screen size, and get Windows Live Essentials.

Start Windows 7 Using the Welcome Screen

1. Turn on your computer, and wait while Windows 7 loads and displays the Welcome screen.

2. If prompted for added security, press and then release the Ctrl, Alt, and Delete keys at the same time.

3. Click your user name.

4. Type your password. Be sure to use the correct capitalization.

5. Click the arrow, or press Enter.

   The Windows 7 desktop appears and the Getting Started window (on first use) opens.

   ◆ To open the Getting Started window later, click the **Start** button, point to **All Programs**, click **Accessories**, and then click **Getting Started**.

Did You Know?

The Windows password is case-sensitive. Windows makes a distinction between uppercase and lowercase letters. Your password should be at least seven characters long, the optimal length for encryption, which is the process of logically scrambling data to keep a password secure.

Getting Started

Find Basic Information About Your Computer

1 Click the **Start** button, and then click **Computer**.

2 Click **System properties** button on the toolbar.

TIMESAVER *Click the Start button, right-click Computer, and then click Properties to display computer properties.*

3 Review the information about your computer, including:

- ◆ **Windows edition**
- ◆ **Computer processor name and speed**
- ◆ **Computer memory (RAM)**
- ◆ **Operating system type**
- ◆ **Computer name**
- ◆ **Workgroup or Domain name**

4 When you're done, click the **Close** button.

Did You Know?

You can activate Windows 7 or change the product key. Click the Start button, click Control Panel, click System And Security, click System, and then click the activation link or Change product key.

Activation information

Using Windows Aero

Introducing Windows Aero

Windows 7 provides two distinct user interface experiences: a "basic" experience for entry-level systems, and a more visually dynamic experience called **Windows Aero**. Windows Aero is an environment with an additional level of visual sophistication. Windows Aero provides spectacular visual effects, such as glass-like interface elements that you can see through, subtle window animations, window colors, live thumbnails that you can display on the taskbar, Windows Flip and Windows Flip 3D that you can use to graphically open windows, and Aero Peek or Aero Shake that you can use to minimize and restore open programs and windows.

Live Taskbar Thumbnails

When you rest the mouse pointer over a taskbar item, Windows Aero displays a Live thumbnail of the window, showing the content of that window. The **Live thumbnail** is displayed whether the window is minimized or not, and whether the content of the window is a document, photo, or even a running video or process.

Windows Flip and Windows Flip 3D

Windows Aero provides two ways to manage windows: Windows Flip and Windows Flip 3D. Flip allows you to flip through open windows, providing a Live thumbnail of each window, rather than just a generic icon and

Windows Aero

Windows Flip

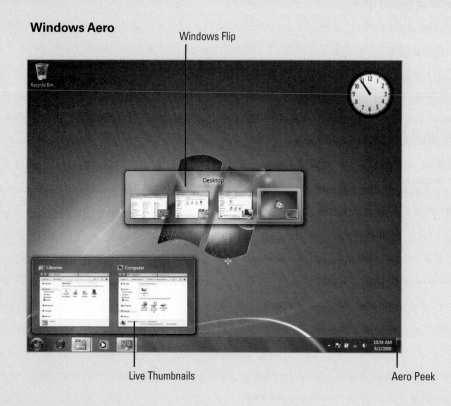

Live Thumbnails

Aero Peek

file name. By using the Alt+Tab keys, live thumbnails appear to make it easier to quickly identify the window you want, particularly when multiple windows of the same kind are open. The selected live thumbnail appears on the desktop and all other windows appear transparent (**New!**). Windows Flip 3D creates a view of your open windows in a three-dimensional stack on your desktop. By using the (Windows logo) ⊞+Tab keys, you can flip through the open windows to quickly locate and select the window you want. You can also use the scroll wheel on your mouse to flip through open windows in a stack and select the one you want.

Show the Desktop with Aero Peek

In Windows Basic, when you click the Show desktop button (the blank button on the right side of the taskbar next to the clock), it minimizes all open windows to display the desktop. In Windows Aero, the functionality changes a bit. When you point to the Show desktop button in Windows Aero, all open windows appear transparent (**New!**), which allows you to quickly peek at the desktop. If you prefer the Windows Basic functionality, you can turn off the peek transparency. Right-click the Show desktop button, and then click Peek At Desktop to turn it off and on (**New!**).

Minimize Windows with Aero Shake

With Aero Shake, you can minimize and restore all open windows except the one you're shaking, dragging back and forth (**New!**). Simply, click the menu bar of the window you want to keep open, and then drag (shake) the window back and forth. If you prefer using a keyboard shortcut, you can also press Windows logo key+Home to minimize or restore all windows except for the active window.

Preparing for Windows Aero

Windows 7 can display different features based on the hardware capabilities of the computer it is running on. Computers running Windows 7 Home Basic, Windows 7 Starter, or those without the hardware needed to run Windows Aero use the basic user interface. If your computer meets the minimal hardware requirements to be **Windows 7 PC Capability Ready**, you see the Windows 7 Basic user experience. If your computer meets the increased hardware requirements to be **Windows 7 PC Premium Ready**, you see the Windows Aero user experience. The increased requirements include:

- 1-gigahertz (GHz) 32-bit or 64-bit (x64) processor
- 1 GB of RAM
- 128 MB graphics card
- DirectX 9 class graphics processor
- 64, 128, or 256 MB of graphics memory (Recommended)

Running Windows Aero

Before you can run Windows Aero, you need to make sure Windows 7 contains the proper settings. Make sure your computer meets the increase hardware requirements and the Windows theme is set to a Windows 7 Aero theme in the Control Panel under Appearance and Personalization.

If you encounter a problem, the Aero troubleshooter opens to help you out. If the troubleshooter doesn't open, you can open it in Windows Help and Support. Click the Start button, click Help and Support, type *aero troubleshooter* in the Search box, press Enter, and then click Open The Aero Troubleshooter.

Exploring the Windows Desktop

When you first start Windows 7, you see the Windows desktop, or a Welcome screen (a way to identify yourself on the computer), depending on your installation. The **desktop** is an on-screen version of an actual desk, containing windows, icons, files, and programs. You can use the desktop to access, store, organize, modify, share, and explore information (such as a letter, the news, or a list of addresses), whether it resides on your computer, a network, a HomeGroup (shared home network) (**New!**), or the Internet. In addition to windows and icons, you can also add mini-programs, called **gadgets**, to the desktop, which provide easy access to frequently used tools, such as a clock or calendar, and information at a glance. The bar at the bottom of your screen is called the **taskbar**; it allows you to start programs and switch among currently running programs. At the left end of the taskbar is the **Start button**, which you use to start programs, find and open files, access the Windows Help and Support Center, and much more. Next to the Start button are program or taskbar buttons, which you can use to start programs and switch between open windows and programs. The default programs pinned to the taskbar include Internet Explorer,

Start menu

Background picture on desktop

Desktop icon

Desktop gadget

Explorer window

Start button

Taskbar

Windows Explorer, and Windows Media Player, however, you can customize it (**New!**) like the Start menu. At the right end of the taskbar is the **notification area**, which displays the time, the date, and program related icons. You can click an icon to display a window of options. For example, when you click the Volume icon, a window appears where you can adjust or mute the volume. If icons in the notification area are not used for a while, an arrow appears to hide the icons and reduce clutter. You can click the arrow to display hidden icons or click a link to customize the notification area to select which icons and notifications appear on the taskbar (**New!**). You can also quickly drag a hidden icon on or displayed icon off the notification area to add or remove it from the taskbar (**New!**). Next to the notification area is the Show desktop button (the blank button at the right end of the taskbar), which allows you to quickly show the desktop (**New!**). If you upgraded your computer to Windows 7 from a previous version of Windows, your desktop might contain additional desktop icons and toolbars.

Open program window

Start button

Similar open windows grouped on the taskbar

Program buttons

Notification icons

Show desktop button

Using the Mouse

A **mouse** is a handheld input device you roll across a flat surface (such as a desk or a mouse pad) to position the **mouse pointer**, the small symbol that indicates the pointer's relative position on the desktop. When you move the mouse, the mouse pointer on the screen moves in the same direction. The shape of the mouse pointer changes to indicate different activities. Once you move the mouse pointer to a desired position on the screen, you use the mouse buttons, right or left, to tell your computer what to do.

Dragging

Clicking   Mouse pointer

Basic Mouse Techniques

Task	What to do
Pointing	Move the mouse to position it over an item on the desktop.
Clicking	Press and release the left mouse button.
Double-clicking	Press and release the left mouse button twice quickly.
Dragging	Point to an item, press and hold the left mouse button, move the mouse to a new location, and then release the mouse button.
Right-clicking	Point to an item, and then press and release the right mouse button.

Using the Mouse for Quick Results

A typical mouse has two mouse buttons. You use the left one to click buttons, select text, and drag items around the screen. When you click an item with the right button, such as an icon, text, or graphic, a shortcut menu appears with a list of commands related to the selected item. For example, when you right-click a file icon, a shortcut menu appears with a list of file commands, such as Open, Explore, Search, Delete, and Rename. Instead of searching for commands on the main menus, you can save time and get quick results by using a shortcut menu.

Use the Shortcut Menu Command

1. Right-click an item.

2. Click a command from the shortcut menu.

Did You Know?

You can swap the functions of the right and left mouse buttons. Click the Start button on the taskbar, click Control Panel, click Hardware And Sound, click the Mouse link, click the Buttons tab, click the Right-handed or Left-handed option, and then click OK.

A mouse wheel can make scrolling fast and easy. If your mouse has a wheel between the two mouse buttons, you can roll it to quickly scroll a few lines or an entire screen at a time.

See Also

See "Changing Mouse Settings" on page 456 for information on changing the way the mouse works.

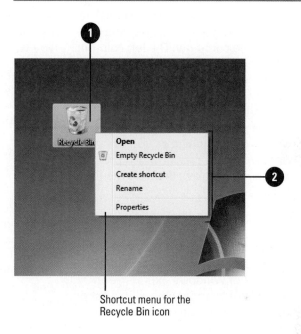

Shortcut menu for the Recycle Bin icon

For Your Information

Using the Mouse with the Web Style

Windows integrates the use of the Internet with its other functions. You can choose to extend the way you click on the Internet with the rest of your computer by single-clicking (known as the web style) icons to open them, or stay with the default by double-clicking (known as the Classic style). To change from one style to the other, click the Start button, click Control Panel, click Appearance And Personalization, click the Specify single- or double-click to open link under Folder Options, click the Single-click to open an item (point to select), or Double-click to open an item (Single-click to select) option, and then click OK.

Using the Start Menu

The key to getting started with the Windows desktop is learning how to use the Start button on the taskbar. Clicking the button on the taskbar displays the Start menu, a list of commands that allow you to start a program, open a document, change a Windows setting, find a file, or display support information. The top right of the Start menu indicates who is currently using the computer. The left column of the Start menu is separated into two lists: **pinned** items above the separator line and most frequently used items below. The pinned items remain on the Start menu, like a push pin holds paper on a bulletin board. The most frequently used items change as you use programs: Windows keeps track of which programs you use and displays them on the Start menu for easy access.

In addition to tracking frequently used programs, Windows also tracks recently opened files, known as **jump lists** (**New!**). When you point to a program—such as Microsoft Word, Internet Explorer or Windows Explorer—on the Start menu with a arrow next to it, a list of recently opened files or folders and related tasks appear for easy access. For example, Internet Explorer displays a jump list with recently visited web sites and commands for InPrivate browsing and New Tab. The arrow next to a menu item indicates a cascading menu, or submenu, which is a list of commands for that menu item. You can also pin recently opened files to the Start menu that you want to use on a regular basis.

The right column of the Start menu provides easy access to folders, Windows settings, devices and printers (**New!**), help information, and shutdown functionality. As you become more familiar with Windows, you might want to customize the Start menu to include additional items that you use most often.

As you continue to install programs on your computer, finding them on the Start menu can sometimes be difficult. Windows 7 makes it easy with the Instant Search box, which allows you to search the Start menu to find programs and other Windows items, such as Internet favorites, history, files, contacts,

Pinned items ——
Frequently used items

Point to display more programs

Instant search results

Instant Search box

e-mail messages, and appointments. To perform a search, click the Start menu, click in the Instant Search box and start typing the search text you want. As you type, the Start menu shows the possible results organized by type with the number of matches (**New!**). A priority given to the programs you use frequently. The search results continue to narrow as you continue to type. If you don't find what you are looking for on the Start menu during a search, you can click See More Results to see a complete listing of highlighted results (**New!**), or expand the search.

Start Menu Commands

Command	Description
All Programs	Opens a list of all the programs included on the Start menu
Search box	Locates programs, and other Windows items, such as Internet favorites, history, files, contacts, e-mail messages, and appointments
User name	Opens the personal folder, where you store files and information, such as Contacts, Desktop, Downloads, Favorites, Links, Document, Music, Pictures, Videos, Saved Games, and Searches
Documents	Opens the Documents folder, where you store and manage files
Pictures	Opens the Pictures folder, where you store and manage photos, images, and graphic files
Music	Opens the Music folder, where you store and manage sound and audio files
Games	Opens the Games folder, where you play Windows 7 games, such as Chess Titans, FreeCell, Hearts, Internet Backgammon, Internet Checker, Internet Spades, Mahjong Titans, Minesweeper, Purble Place, Solitaire, and Spider Solitaire
Computer	Opens the Computer window, where you access information about disk drives and other hardware devices
Control Panel	Provides options to customize the appearance and functionality of the computer
Devices and Printers (**New!**)	Opens the Devices and Printers window, where you can display and manage currently installed devices, such as monitors, printers, and faxes, and add new devices
Default Programs	Displays the Default Programs window, where you can choose default programs for web browsing, e-mail, playing music, and other activities
Help and Support	Displays Windows Help topics, tutorials, troubleshooting, support options, and tools
Power button (Shutdown) **New!**)	Exits Windows and turns off the computer; also customizable for other power/ shutdown options
Arrow (Shutdown menu)	Provides options to switch to a different users, log off the computer, lock the computer, restart the computer, or set the computer to sleep or hibernate mode

Using the Taskbar

The horizontal bar at the bottom of your screen is called the taskbar; it contains several important items: the Start button, program and taskbar buttons, notification area, and Show desktop button. The taskbar allows you to start programs, files, and windows, as well as switch among currently running programs or open windows. In addition to pinning programs and windows to the Start menu, you can now pin them to the taskbar (**New!**). The default programs pinned to the taskbar include Internet Explorer, Windows Explorer, and Windows Media Player, however, you can customize it. The Show desktop button minimizes all open windows to display the desktop. In Windows Aero, when you point to the Show desktop button, all open windows appear transparent, which allows you to peek at the desktop. In addition to tracking frequently used programs, Windows also tracks recently opened files, known as jump lists (**New!**), which you can open from the taskbar.

Use the Taskbar

- **Pin to the Taskbar**. Right-click an open program or taskbar button, and then click **Pin this program to taskbar.**

- **Unpin from the Taskbar**. Right-click a pinned item on the taskbar, and then click **Unpin this program from taskbar**.

- **Access a Jump List**. Right-click a taskbar button, and then click a recently opened item from the list.

- **Show desktop (minimize all windows)**. Click the **Show desktop** button on the taskbar (right side).

- **Show desktop (make all windows transparent)**. In Windows Aero, point to the **Show desktop** button. Right-click the **Show desktop** button, and then click **Peek at desktop** (**New!**) to turn it off and on.

- **Switch among open programs or windows**. Click in a window to make it active, or point to a taskbar button for an open program or window, and then click a name or icon. In Windows Aero, a live thumbnail appears when you point to an open program or window taskbar button. When you point to it, the program or window temporarily appears until you move the mouse (**New!**).

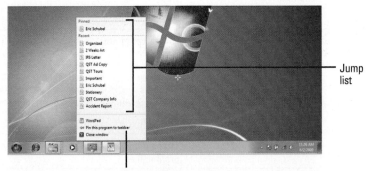

Jump list

Pin to taskbar

Switch among open windows

Show desktop button

Using Desktop Gadgets

Windows 7 gives you quick access to gadgets—such as news headlines and updates, slide shows, weather information, traffic maps, Internet radio streams, and slide shows of online photo albums—anywhere on your desktop (**New!**). **Gadgets** are mini-applications that can connect to web services, such as an RSS feed (which automatically delivers web content to your desktop), or integrate with many of your applications, such as viewing your calendar. Windows 7 comes with a set of gadgets to get you started, including the Windows Media Center gadget (**New!**). However, you can easily download more gadgets from an online gadget gallery.

Work with Desktop Gadgets

◆ **Add a Gadget**. Right-click a blank area of the desktop, click Gadgets, double-click the gadget you want, and then click the Close button.

◆ **Close a Gadget**. Point to the gadget you want to close, click the Close button, and then click Close Gadget (if requested).

◆ **Resize a Gadget**. Point to the gadget, and then click the Larger size or Smaller size button (toggles).

◆ **Change Gadget Options**. Point to the gadget you want to change, click the Options button (wrench icon), select the options you want, and then click OK.

◆ **Move a Gadget**. Point to the gadget, and then drag the Drag gadget (dot grid) to another location on the desktop.

Did You Know?

You can download more gadgets. Right-click a blank area of the desktop, click Gadgets, and then click Get More Gadgets Online to open the gadget web site and download more gadgets.

Windows Media Center gadget

Point to a gadget to display options

Gadget options

Drag to the desktop to add a gadget

Managing Windows

One of the most powerful things about Windows is that you can open more than one window or program at once. This means, however, that the desktop can get cluttered with many open windows for the various programs. Windows 7 groups similar types of windows under one button on the taskbar, which you can use to switch among open windows and programs (**New!**). If you prefer a keyboard shortcut, you can also press Alt-Tab or ⊞-Tab (Aero) to switch to an open window. You can identify a window by its name on the title bar at the top of the window, which you can also use to move or resize it (**New!**). Each window is also surrounded by a border and resize buttons in the upper-right corner that you can use to resize the window.

Switch Among Open Windows

1. Click anywhere in a window to make it active, or point to a taskbar button for an open program or window, and then click a name or icon. You can also press Alt-Tab to switch windows.

    ◆ In Windows Aero, a live thumbnail appears when you point to an open program or window taskbar button. When you point to the thumbnail, the program or window temporally appears until you move the mouse (**New!**). You can also press ⊞-Tab to switch windows.

Move or Resize a Window

1. Point to the window's title bar.

2. Drag the window to a new location, and then release the mouse button.

    ◆ **Maximize active window.** Drag the title bar to the top edge of the desktop (**New!**) or double-click the title bar.

    ◆ **Resize active window for side by side use.** Drag the title bar to the left or right edge of the desktop (**New!**).

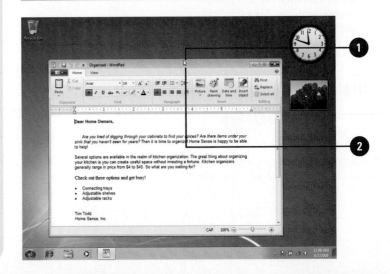

Use Buttons to Resize and Close a Window

All windows contain the same sizing and close buttons:

◆ **Maximize button.** Click to make a window fill the entire screen.

◆ **Restore Down button.** Click to reduce a maximized window.

◆ **Minimize button.** Click to shrink a window to a taskbar button.

◆ **Close button.** Click to close the window.

◆ **Show desktop button.** Click to minimize or restore all windows. In Windows Aero, point to the button to peek at the desktop through transparent windows (**New!**).

Maximize or Restore Down

Minimize

Close

Show desktop

Use the Mouse to Resize a Window

◆ **Resize a window using a border.** Move the mouse over a border in a non-maximized window until the mouse pointer changes into a two-headed arrow, and then drag until the window is the size you want.

◆ **Resize all open windows on the desktop.** Right-click a blank area of the taskbar, and then click a command:

  ◆ **Cascade windows.**

  ◆ **Show window stacked.**

  ◆ **Show windows side by side.**

◆ **Minimize or restore all open windows except active one.** In Windows Aero, drag the title bar back and forth (shake) to minimize or restore all open windows except the active one (**New!**).

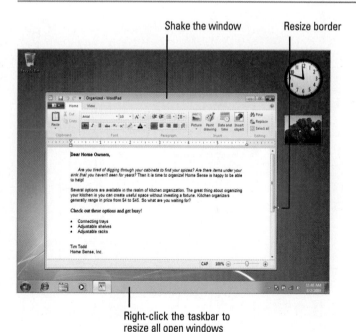

Shake the window

Resize border

Right-click the taskbar to resize all open windows

Using Menus, Toolbars, and Panes

A **menu** is a list of commands that you use to accomplish certain tasks, such as when you use the Start menu to open the Control Panel. A **command** is a directive that provides access to a program's features. Each Windows program has its own set of menus, which are on the menu bar along the top of the program window. The **menu bar** organizes commands into groups of related operations. Each group is listed under the name of the menu, such as File or Help. To access the commands in a menu, you click the name of the menu. If a command on a menu includes a keyboard reference, known as a **keyboard shortcut**, you can perform the action by pressing the first key, then pressing the second key to perform the command quickly. You can also carry out some of the most frequently used commands on a menu by clicking a button on a toolbar or

command bar. A **toolbar** or **command bar** contains buttons that are convenient shortcuts for menu commands. A **pane** is a frame within a window where you can access commands and navigation controls. You can use menus, toolbar buttons, and commands in a pane to change how the Control Panel window's contents appear. On a menu, a check mark or selected icons identifies a currently selected feature, meaning that the feature is enabled, or turned on. To disable, or turn off the feature, you click the command again to remove the check mark. A bullet mark also indicates that an option is enabled. To disable a command with a bullet mark next to it, however, you must select another command (within the menu section, separated by gray lines) in its place.

Pane

Menu bar   Command bar/Toolbar

Menu   Check mark or selected icon

Choosing Dialog Box Options

A **dialog box** is a window that opens when you choose a menu command followed by an ellipsis (. . .). The ellipsis indicates that you must supply more information before the program can carry out the command you selected. Dialog boxes open in other situations as well, such as when you open a program in the Control Panel. In a dialog box, you choose various options and provide information for completing the command.

Choose Dialog Box Options

All dialog boxes contain the same types of options, including the following:

◆ **Tabs.** Click a tab to display its options. Each tab groups a related set of options.

◆ **Option buttons.** Click an option button to select it. You can usually select only one.

◆ **Up and down arrows.** Click the up or down arrow to increase or decrease the number, or type a number in the box.

◆ **Check box.** Click the box to turn on or off the option. A checked box means the option is selected; a cleared box means it's not.

◆ **List box.** Click the list arrow to display a list of options, and then click the option you want.

◆ **Text box.** Click in the box and type the requested information.

◆ **Command buttons.** Click a button to perform a specific action or command. A button name followed by an ellipsis (...) opens another dialog box. OK executes the options and closes the dialog box. Cancel ignores the options and closes the dialog box. Apply executes the options and leaves the dialog box open.

◆ **Preview box.** Many dialog boxes show an image that reflects the options you select.

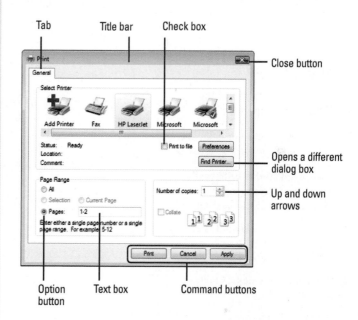

For Your Information

Navigating a Dialog Box

Rather than clicking to move around a dialog box, you can press the Tab key to move from one box or button to the next. You can also use Shift+Tab to move backward, or Ctrl+Tab and Ctrl+Shift+Tab to move between dialog box tabs.

Using Windows Help and Support

When you have a question about how to do something in Windows 7, you can usually find the answer with a few clicks of your mouse. Microsoft Help and Support is a resource of information, training, and support to help you learn and use Windows 7. Help and Support is like a book stored on your computer with additional links to the Internet, complete with a search feature, and a table of contents to make finding information easier. If you have an Internet connection, you can get online help from a support professional at Microsoft or from other users in Windows communities (an electronic forum where people share information), or you can invite a friend to chat with you, view your screen, and work on your computer to provide remote support.

Use Help and Support

1. Click the **Start** button, and then click **Help and Support**.

2. Click a toolbar button or link with the type of help you want to use:

   ◆ **How to get started with your computer.** Displays topics to help you set up your computer.

   ◆ **Learn about Windows Basics.** Displays topics to introduce you to Windows.

   ◆ **Browse Help topics.** Displays a table of contents.

3. Click the item of interest.

4. Read the information.

5. If you can't find the information you need, click the **Search Help** box, type a word or phrase, and then press Enter.

6. If you need additional help, click **More support options**, and then click an Internet resource link.

   ◆ **Windows Remote Assistance.** Click the link, and then follow the wizard instructions.

   ◆ **Microsoft Answers** or **Microsoft Customer Support.** Click the link to access the web site.

7. Click the **Close** button.

Home button   Browse Help button

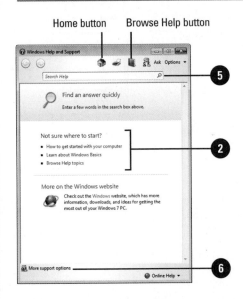

Click to go back   Click to print the current topic

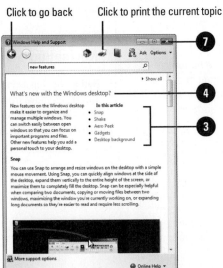

Use Dialog Box or Window Help

1. In a dialog box or window, click the Help button (? icon) or a Help link.

   ◆ In a dialog box, click the item you want information about.

2. Read the Help information.

3. Click the **Close** button.

Use Program Help

1. Click the program's **Help** button, or click the **Help** menu, and then click the Help command to open the Help program.

2. Click the main topic of interest. Click a subtopic, if necessary.

3. Read the Help information.

4. If you can't find the information you need, click the Search box, and get Help information using keywords.

5. Click the **Close** button.

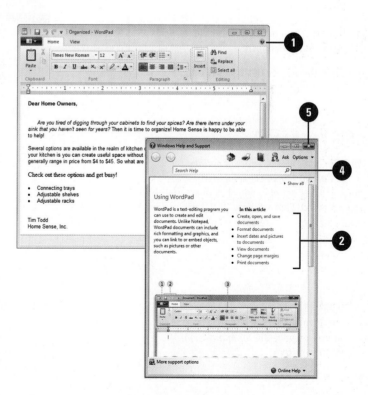

Switching Users

Many users are able to share the same computer. Their individual Windows identities allow them to keep their files completely private and to customize the operating system with their own preferences. Windows manages these separate identities, or accounts, by giving each user a unique user name and password. When a user selects an account and types a password (if necessary), Windows starts with that user's configuration settings and network permissions. When you want to change users, you can log off, (which closes all running programs, saves your settings, and signs you off the computer) or switch users, which quickly switches between users without having to close programs and saves your current settings.

Switch Users Quickly

1. Click the **Start** button, and then point to the arrow next to the Power button.

2. Click **Switch user** to change users without saving current settings.

    A Welcome screen appears, displaying user accounts.

3. Click your name.

4. If a box for a password appears, type your password.

5. Click the Arrow button or press Enter to log on to Windows.

Start button

Did You Know?

You can change user account options in the Control Panel. Click the Start button, click Control Panel, click User Accounts And Family Safety, click User Accounts, and then select the options you want.

See Also

See "Adding and Deleting User Accounts" on page 312 for information on switching users.

Log Off and Log On Your Computer

1. Click the **Start** button, and then point to the arrow next to the Power button.

2. Click **Log off** to close all your programs, save your settings, and sign off the computer.

   A Welcome screen appears, displaying user accounts.

3. Click your name.

4. If a box for a password appears, type your password.

5. Click the Arrow button or press Enter to log on to Windows.

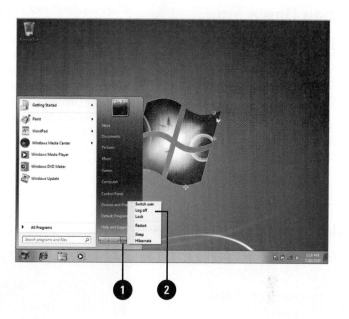

Log Off and Log On a Network Computer

1. Click the **Start** button, and then point to the arrow next to the Power button.

2. Click **Log off** to close all your programs, save your settings, and sign off the computer.

3. Press and then release the Ctrl, Alt, and Delete keys at the same time.

4. Click the **Switch User** button, and then click your name or **Other User**.

5. Type your user name. For example: *domain name\user name* or *computer name\user name*

6. Type your assigned password.

7. Click the Arrow button or press Enter to log on to Windows.

Shutting Down Your Computer

When you finish working on your computer, you need to make sure to turn off, or shut down, your computer properly. This involves several steps: saving and closing all open files, exiting all running programs, shutting down Windows itself, and finally, turning off the computer. However, if you shut down your computer before or while installing Windows updates (download must be complete), Windows will automatically complete the install before shutting down, so you don't have to wait around. Shutting down your computer makes sure Windows and all its related programs are properly closed and avoid potential problems in the future. If you turn off the computer by pushing the power switch while Windows or other programs are running, you could lose important data. In addition to the Shutdown option, you can put your computer in sleep or hibernate mode, or restart if problems occur.

Shut Down Your Computer

① Click the **Start** button, and then click the Power button (**New!**).

- ◆ **Shut Down.** Exits Windows 7 and prepares the computer to be turned off.

TIMESAVER *Right-click the Power button, and then click Properties to change the Power button action* (**New!**).

② Or click the **Start** button, point to the arrow next to the Power button, and then click the option on the menu you want:

- ◆ **Restart.** Exits Windows 7 and restarts the computer.

- ◆ **Sleep.** Saves your session to memory and switches to low-power mode; you can press the hardware power button to wake.

- ◆ **Hibernate.** Saves your session to memory and hard disk, and then exits Windows. Press the hardware power button to restore your session.

IMPORTANT *Options vary depending on Windows settings.*

Power button ① ②

Shut Down Options

Option	When to use it
Restart	When you want to restart the computer if problems occur and begin working with Windows again
Sleep	When you want to stop working for a few moments and conserve power (ideal for mobile computers); available when a power scheme is selected in Power Options
Hibernate	When you want to stop working for a while and safely save power; restores your session to work again later; available when a power scheme is selected in Power Options
Shut Down	When you finish working with Windows and you want to shut off your computer

Working with Windows Programs

Introduction

Now that you know how to work with the graphical elements that make Windows 7 work, you're ready to work with programs. A **program** is software you use to accomplish a specific task, such as word processing or managing files on your computer. This chapter shows you how to access your Windows programs (and to customize this access). It also shows you how to create and edit files in your programs, share information between programs, and what to do when a program is not responding.

Windows comes with several small programs, called **Accessories**, that are extremely useful for completing basic tasks, such as creating a written document or performing basic calculations. Windows 7 also provides a number of ways for you to resolve some common problems. For example, you can use older programs (designed to run on previous versions of Windows) on your Windows 7 computer by changing specific settings using the Accessories menu. You can run commands from a text-based interface (called a command line), and Windows provides an interface for quitting a program that has stopped responding without turning off your computer and losing information in other programs. Other special programs in Windows 7 are games. You can play games on your computer, or with other people over the internet.

What You'll Do

Start and Exit a Program

Change the Way a Program Starts

Use Windows Accessories

Create a Document

Edit and Format Text

Set Paragraph Tabs and Indents

Preview and Print a Document

Save and Close a Document

Share Information Among Programs

Insert and Edit Information

Link and Update Information

Insert Special Characters

Calculate Numbers

Run Commands

Play Games

Snip the Screen

Run Older Programs

Quit a Program Not Responding

Starting and Exiting a Program

The most common way to start a Windows program is to use the Start menu, which provides easy access to programs installed on your computer. Clicking the Start button on the taskbar displays the Start menu, which lists common and recently used programs and the All Programs submenu. The All Programs submenu is the master list of every program on your computer. In addition to tracking frequently used programs, Windows also tracks recently opened files, known as **jump lists (New!)**. When you point to a program—such as Microsoft Word—on the Start menu with a arrow next to it, a list of recently opened files or folders and related tasks appear for easy access. For example, Windows Media Player displays a jump list with recently played music files and commands to play all music and resume previous list (**New!**). When you're done working with a program, you should exit, or close it, to conserve your computer's resources.

Start a Program from the Start Menu

Windows provides several ways to start a program:

◆ Click the **Start** button, and then click a program.

◆ Click the **Start** button, point to a program, and then click a file name from the jump list (**New!**).

When a program on the Start menu displays a submenu, a jump list displays recently opened files.

◆ Click the **Start** button, point to **All Programs**, click a program group if necessary, and then click a program.

◆ Click the **Start** button, click **Computer** or **Documents**, navigate to the folder with the program or file associated with the program you want, and then double-click the icon.

◆ Click the **Start** button, point to **All Programs**, click **Accessories**, click **Run**, type the full path and file name of the program, and then click **OK**.

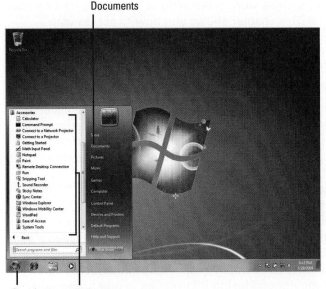

Documents

Start button   All Programs

Jump list for WordPad with pinned and recently used files

Exit a Program

Windows provides several ways to exit a program:

- Click the **File** menu, and then click **Exit**.

- Click the **Close** button on the program's title bar.

- Double-click the Control-menu on the program's title bar.

- Right-click the program's taskbar button, and then click **Close**.

Did You Know?

You can display the Programs list in a single column. Right-click the Start button, click Properties, click Customize, click the Advanced tab, select the Scroll Programs check box, and then click OK twice. Point to the black triangle arrows at the top and bottom to scroll through the list.

See Also

See "Using Windows Accessories" on page 29 for information on using Windows built-in programs.

Control menu   Close button

Taskbar button for WordPad

For Your Information

Starting a Program When You Start Windows

If you start a program, such as your e-mail program, every time you start Windows, you can save some time by adding the program to the Startup folder. The contents of the Startup folder appear on the Startup submenu on the All Programs menu. Sometimes a program installs a program to the Startup folder. Every time you start Windows, the programs in the Startup folder automatically start. Click the Start button, and then locate the program you want to add to the Startup submenu. Using the Ctrl key copies the program to the Startup submenu. Hold down the Ctrl key, and then drag the program on top of the Startup item on the All Programs submenu. When the Startup submenu opens, drag the program onto the submenu, and then release the mouse button and the Ctrl key. If you don't want the program automatically starting with Windows, you can remove it from the Startup folder. Click the Start button, point to All Programs, and then click Startup. Right-click the program you want to remove on the Startup submenu. Click Delete, and then click Yes to confirm the deletion.

Changing the Way a Program Starts

The left column of the Start menu is separated into two lists: pinned items above the separator line and most frequently used items below. The pinned items remain on the Start menu, like a push pin holds paper on a bulletin board, until you unpin them. In addition to pinning and unpinning programs and windows to the Start menu, you can now pin and unpin them to the taskbar (**New!**). The default programs pinned to the taskbar include Internet Explorer, Windows Explorer, and Windows Media Player, however, you can customize it. Windows also tracks recently opened files, known as jump lists, to programs on the Start menu and taskbar, which you can pin or unpin to the list (**New!**).

Pin or Unpin a Program or Items on the Start Menu or Taskbar

◆ **Pin a program on the Start menu.** Right-click a program on the Start menu, and then click **Pin to Start Menu**.

◆ **Unpin a program on the Start menu.** Right-click a pinned program on the Start menu, and then click **Unpin from Start Menu**.

◆ **Pin a program on the taskbar.** Right-click an open program on the taskbar, and then click **Pin this program to taskbar (New!)**.

You can also, right-click a program on the Start menu, and then click **Pin to Taskbar (New!)**.

◆ **Unpin a program on the taskbar.** Right-click a pinned program on the taskbar, and then click **Unpin this program from taskbar (New!)**.

◆ **Pin or unpin an item on a jump list.** Click the **Start** menu or right-click a taskbar program, point to jump list, point to an item, and then click the **Pin** or **Unpin** icon **(New!)**.

◆ **Remove an item on a jump list.** Click the **Start** menu or right-click a taskbar program, point to jump list, right-click an item, and then click **Remove from this list**.

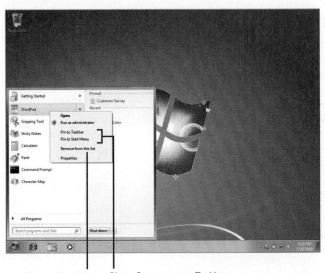

Remove from list   Pin to Start menu or Taskbar

Jump list for WordPad

Pin WordPad to taskbar   Click to pin to jump list

Using Windows Accessories

Windows comes with several accessories, built-in programs that are extremely useful for completing every day tasks.

One of the most useful features Windows offers is the ability to use data created in one file in another file, even if the two files were created in different Windows programs. To work with more than one program or file at a time, you simply need to open them on your desktop. A program button on the taskbar represents any window that is open on the desktop. When you want to switch from one open window to another, click the program button on the taskbar. If you tile, or arrange open windows on the desktop so that they are visible, you can switch among them simply by clicking in the window in which you want to work.

Frequently Used Windows Accessories

Program	Description
Calculator	Performs arithmetic calculations
Command Prompt	Executes MS-DOS commands
Internet Explorer	Displays web (HTML) pages
Notepad	Creates, edits, and displays text only documents
Paint	Creates and edits bitmap pictures
Snipping Tool	Captures different parts of the screen
Sound Recorder	Creates and plays digital sound files
Sticky Notes (**New!**)	Creates color notes on the screen
Windows DVD Maker	Burns pictures and videos to DVDs
Windows Fax and Scan	Sends and receives faxes or scanned pictures and documents
Windows Live Messenger (**New!**)	Sends and receives instant messages to online contacts; you need to download the program from the web (http://download.live.com)
Windows Live Mail (**New!**)	Provides e-mail, newsgroup, and directory services; you need to download the program from the web (http://download.live.com)
Windows Live Movie Maker (**New!**)	Creates movies using audio and video files; you need to download the program from the web (http://download.live.com)
Windows Live Photo Gallery (**New!**)	Views, edits, organizes, and shares photos and videos; you need to download the program from the web (http://download.live.com)
Windows Live Writer (**New!**)	Creates blogs with text, photos, and videos; you need to download the program from the web (http://download.live.com)
Windows Media Center	Provides entertainment options for digital and on-demand media
Windows Media Player	Plays sound, music, and video
WordPad	Creates, edits, and displays text, Rich Text Format, and Word documents

Creating a Document

A **document** is a file you create using a word processing program, such as a letter, memo, or resume. When you start WordPad, a blank document appears in the work area, known as the document window, along with a Ribbon (**New!**), similar to Microsoft Office 2007, at the top. The Ribbon with two tabs—Home and View—allows you to quickly select document related commands. You can enter information to create a new document and save the result in a file, or you can open an existing file and save the document with changes. As you type, text moves, or **wraps**, to a new line when the previous one is full.

Create a Document

1. Click the **Start** button, point to **All Programs**, click **Accessories**, and then click **WordPad**.

   If WordPad is already open, click the WordPad button, and then click **New**.

2. Type your text.

3. Press Enter when you want to start a new paragraph.

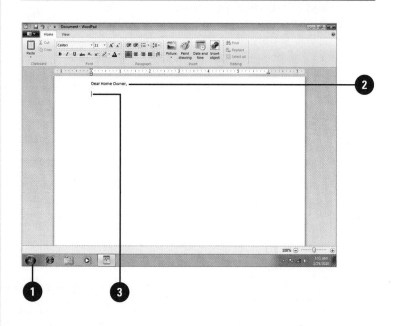

Change the Page Setup

1. Click the **Wordpad** button, and then click **Page setup**.

2. Specify the paper size and source.

3. Specify the page orientation, either portrait or landscape.

4. Specify the page margins.

5. Click **OK**.

Open an Existing Document from Within a Program

1 Click the **Wordpad** button, and then click **Open**.

2 Click the **Files name** list arrow, and then click the file type you want to open.

3 Use the Navigation pane to navigate to the folder from which you want to open the file.

4 Click the document you want to open.

5 Click **Open**.

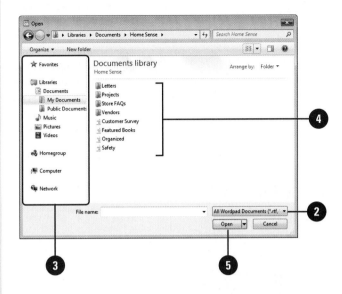

Open a Recent Document from the Start Menu or Taskbar

1 Click the **Start** button, and then point to the program or right-click the program on the taskbar.

2 Click the recently opened document you want to re-open.

Did You Know?

You can remove recently used documents from a jump list.. Right-click the Start button, click Properties, click the Start Menu tab, clear the privacy related check boxes, and then click OK.

Editing Text

One of the advantages of using a word processing program is that you can edit a document or change the contents without re-creating it. In the WordPad work area, the mouse pointer changes to the I-beam pointer, which you can use to reposition the insertion point (called navigating) and insert, delete, or select text. Before you can edit text, you need to highlight, or select, the text you want to modify. Then you can delete, replace, move (cut), or copy text within one document or between documents even if they're different programs. When you cut or copy an item, it's placed on the Clipboard, which stores only a single piece of information at a time. You can also move or copy selected text without storing it on the Clipboard by using drag-and-drop editing.

Select and Edit Text

1. Move the I-beam pointer to the left or right of the text you want to select.

2. Drag the pointer to highlight the text.

   TIMESAVER *Double-click a word to select it; triple-click a paragraph to select it.*

3. Perform one of the following editing commands:

   ◆ To replace text, type your text.

   ◆ To delete text, press the Backspace key or the Delete key.

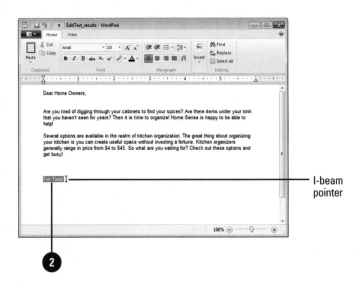

I-beam pointer

Insert and Delete Text

1. Click in the document to place the insertion point where you want to make the change.

   ◆ To insert text, type your text.

   ◆ To delete text, press the Backspace key or the Delete key.

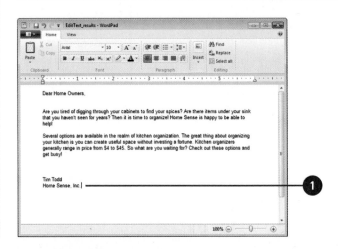

Move or Copy Text

1. Select the text you want to move or copy.

2. Click the **Cut** button or **Copy** button on the Home tab.

3. Click where you want to insert the text.

4. Click the **Paste** button on the Home tab.

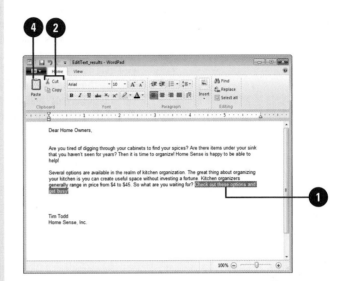

Move or Copy Text Using Drag and Drop

1. Select the text you want to move or copy.

2. Point to the selected text, and then click and hold the mouse button.

   If you want to copy the text to a new location, also press and hold the Ctrl key. A plus sign (+) appears in the pointer box, indicating that you are dragging a copy of the selected text.

3. Drag the selected text to the new location, and then release the mouse button (and the Ctrl key, if necessary).

4. Click anywhere in the document to deselect the text.

Dear Home Owners,

Are you tired of digging through your cabinets to find your spices? Are there items under your sink that you haven't seen for years? Then it is time to organize! Home Sense is happy to be able to help!

Several options are available in the realm of kitchen organization. The great thing about organizing your kitchen is you can create useful space without investing a fortune. Kitchen organizers generally range in price from $4 to $45. So what are you waiting for? Check out these options and get busy!

Tim Todd
Home Sense, Inc.

Dear Home Owners,

Are you tired of digging through your cabinets to find your spices? Are there items under your sink that you haven't seen for years? Then it is time to organize! Home Sense is happy to be able to help!

Several options are available in the realm of kitchen organization. The great thing about organizing your kitchen is you can create useful space without investing a fortune. Kitchen organizers generally range in price from $4 to $45. So what are you waiting for?

Check out these options and get busy!

Tim Todd
Home Sense, Inc.

Formatting Text

You can change the format or the appearance of text and graphics in a document so that the document is easier to read or more attractive. A quick and powerful way to add emphasis to parts of a document is to format text using bold, italics, underline, or color. For special emphasis, you can combine formats, such as bold and italics. In addition, you can change the font style and size. A **font** is a set of characters with the same typeface or design that you can increase or decrease in size. After formatting, you can create lists, and adjust text and line spacing.

Format Text

1. Select the text or click in the paragraph you want to format.

2. Use any of the formatting tools on the Home tab to style text:

   - Font list arrow
   - Font Size list arrow
   - Grow Text (**New!**)
   - Shrink Text (**New!**)
   - Bold button
   - Italic button
   - Underline button
   - Strikethrough button (**New!**)
   - Subscript button (**New!**)
   - Superscript button (**New!**)
   - Text Highlight button (**New!**)
   - Text Color button

3. Use any of the formatting tools on the Home tab to adjust text spacing:

   - Indent buttons (**New!**)
   - List button (**New!**)
   - Line Spacing button (**New!**)
   - Alignment buttons
   - Paragraph button (**New!**)

Did You Know?

Font size is measured in points. One point is 1/72 of an inch high.

Setting Paragraph Tabs

Tabs set text or numerical data alignment in relation to the edges of a document. A **tab stop** is a predefined stopping point along the document's typing line. Default tab stops are set every half-inch on the ruler, but you can set multiple tabs per paragraph at any location. Each paragraph in a document contains its own set of tab stops. The default tab stops do not appear on the ruler, but the manual tab stops you set do appear. Once you place a tab stop, you can drag the tab stop to position it where you want. If you want to add or adjust tab stops in multiple paragraphs, simply select the paragraphs first.

Create and Clear a Tab Stop

1. Select the text or click in the paragraph you want to format.

2. Click the ruler where you want to set the tab stop.

   ◆ **View ruler.** Click the **View** tab, and then select the **Ruler** check box.

3. To move a tab, drag the tab stop to position it where you want.

4. To clear a tab stop, drag it off the ruler.

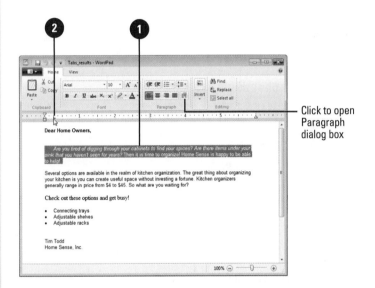

Click to open Paragraph dialog box

Did You Know?

You can insert the date and time in WordPad. Open a document in WordPad, click to place the insertion point, click the Date And Time button on the Home tab, select a format, and then click OK.

See Also

See "Setting Paragraph Indents" on page 36 for information on changing the text alignment.

For Your Information

Changing the Word Wrap Display

As you type a complete line of text, it wraps to the next line. Depending on your preference, you can change the Document window to display text wrapped to the window or ruler. To change word wrap options, click the View tab, click the Word Wrap button, and then click the word wrap option you want. The wrapping options affect only how text appears on your screen. When printed, the document uses the margin settings specified in Page Setup.

Setting Paragraph Indents

When you indent a paragraph, you move its edge in from the left or right margin. You can indent the entire left or right edge of a paragraph or just the first line. The markers on the ruler control the indentation of the current paragraph. The left side of the ruler has three markers. The top triangle, called the **first-line indent marker**, controls where the first line of the paragraph begins. The bottom triangle, called the **hanging indent marker**, controls where the remaining lines of the paragraph begin. The small square under the bottom triangle, called the **left indent marker**, allows you to move the first-line indent marker and the left indent marker simultaneously. When you move the left indent marker, the distance between the hanging indent and the first-line indent remains the same. The triangle on the right side of the ruler, called the **right indent marker**, controls where the right edge of the paragraph ends.

Change Paragraph Indents

Select the text or click in the paragraph you want to format.

◆ To view the ruler, click the **View** tab, and then select the **Ruler** check box.

◆ To change the left indent of the first line, drag the First-Line Indent marker.

◆ To change the indent of the second and subsequent lines, drag the Hanging Indent marker.

◆ To change the left indent for all lines, drag the Left Indent marker.

◆ To change the right indent for all lines, drag the Right Indent marker.

As you drag a marker, the dotted guideline helps you position the indent accurately.

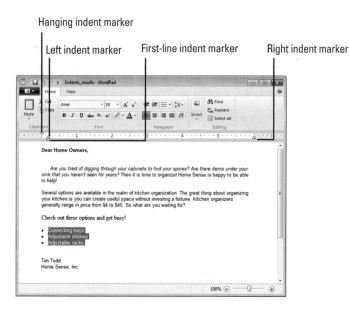

Hanging indent marker

Left indent marker   First-line indent marker   Right indent marker

Did You Know?

You can exact numbers for indents, line spacing, and tabs. Click the Paragraph button on the Home tab, specify the amounts you want, click Tabs if desired, and then click OK.

For Your Information

Creating Sticky Notes

A sticky note is an electronic postem note (**New!**). Click the Start button, point to All Programs, point to Accessories, and then click Sticky Notes. If a new sticky note appears, type the text you want in it. Click the Add (+) button to create a new note or click the Delete (x) button to remove a note. To change a note color, right-click a note, and then select a color. To exit, right-click the Sticky Note program on the taskbar, and then click Close Window.

Previewing and Printing a Document

Before printing, you should verify that the page looks the way you want. You save time, money, and paper by avoiding duplicate printing. Print Preview shows you the exact placement of your text on each printed page. Printing a paper copy is a common way to review and share a document. You can use the Print button on the toolbar to print a copy of your document using the current settings, or you can open the Print dialog box and specify the print options you want.

Preview a Document

1. Click the **WordPad** button, point to **Print**, and then click **Print preview**.

2. Use the toolbar buttons to preview the document:

   ◆ To change the view size, click the preview screen or **100%**.

   ◆ To view other pages, click **Next Page** or **Prev Page**.

   ◆ To view two pages at a time, click **Two Pages**.

   ◆ To print the document, click **Print**.

3. When you're done, click **Close**.

Print All or Part of a Document

1. Click the **WordPad** button, and then click **Print**.

2. Click a printer.

3. Specify the range of pages you want to print.

4. Specify the number of copies you want to print.

5. Click **Print**.

Saving and Closing a Document

Saving your files frequently ensures that you don't lose work during an unexpected power loss. The first time you save, specify a file name and folder in the Save As dialog box. The next time you save, the program saves the file with the same name in the same folder. If you want to change a file's name or location, you can use the Save As dialog box again to create a copy of the original file. To conserve your computer's resources, close any file you are not working on. WordPad saves a document by default in the **Rich Text document (RTF)**. In addition to RTF, you can also save documents in **Office Open XML document (DOCX)** (**New!**), which is for Microsoft Word 2007, **OpenDocument text (ODT)** (**New!**), which is for exchanging office documents, and **Plain Text Document (TXT)**, which is for plain text.

Save a Document

1 Click the **WordPad** button, and then click **Save as**.

◆ You can also point to Save as, and then select a specific file format (**New!**).

2 Use the Navigation pane to navigate to the drive or folder in which you want to save the file.

3 Type a name for the file, or use the suggested one.

4 To change the format of a file, click the **Save as type** list arrow, and then click a file format.

5 Click **Save**.

New folder button

Did You Know?

You can save a file in a new folder.
In the Save As dialog box, click the New Folder button, type the new folder name, press Enter, click Open, and then click Save.

You can close a document. Click the Close button in the program window or click the WordPad button, and then click Close. If necessary, click Yes to save your changes.

Sharing Information Among Programs

Windows makes it easy to insert a file or part of a file created in one program into a file created in a different program. The ability to share files and information among different programs is called **object linking and embedding (OLE)**. With OLE, you can work with a document in WordPad and at the same time take advantage of the specialized tools in another program, such as Paint or Microsoft Excel. By using OLE, you'll be able to access features from other programs, edit data easily, update to the latest information, and save space.

Information shared between two programs is an **object**, which can be a picture from a graphics program, a chart from a spreadsheet program, a video clip, text, or almost anything else you can create on a computer. The program that creates the object is called the **source program**; the program

that creates the file into which you want to insert the object is called the **destination program.** Likewise, the file that originally contained the object is the **source file**, and the file where you want to insert the object is the **destination file**. Both embedding and linking involve inserting an object into a destination file; they differ in where they store their respective objects. With **embedding**, a copy of the object becomes part of the destination file. If you want to edit the object, you make changes in the destination file, and the original file remains intact. With **linking**, a representation of the object appears in the destination file, but the object is stored in the source file. If you want to edit the linked object, you make changes in the source file or its representation in the destination file, and the other file will reflect the changes the next time you open it.

Destination program

Source program

Object

Embedded object

Inserting and Editing Information

Instead of switching back and forth between programs to copy and paste information, you can insert, or embed, the information. Embedding inserts a copy of one document into another. Once you embed data, you can edit it using the menus and toolbars of the source program without leaving the program in which it's embedded (that is, the destination program). For example, you can create a picture in a program, such as Paint, or select an existing picture and insert it into a WordPad document. In WordPad, you can use the Paint drawing button (**New!**) on the Home tab to embed a new Paint object. The inserted picture is an object you can resize.

Embed an Existing Object

1. Click where you want to embed the object.

2. Click the **Insert Object** button on the Home tab.

3. Click the **Create from File** option.

4. Click **Browse**, and then double-click the file with the object you want to embed.

5. Click **OK**.

Embed a New Object

1. Click where you want to embed the object.

2. Click the **Insert Object** button on the Home tab.

3. Click the **Create New** option.

4. Double-click the type of object you want to create.

5. Enter information in the new object using the menus and toolbars in the source program.

6. Click the **Program** button, and then click **Exit and return to document** to close the object.

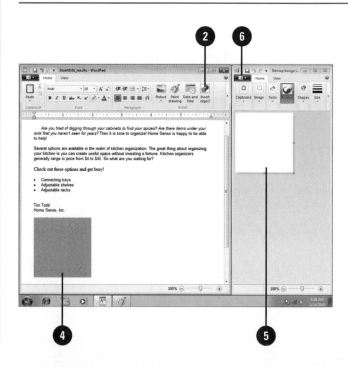

Edit an Object

1. Open the document with the object you want to edit.

2. Double-click the object.

3. Edit the object using the menus and toolbars in the source program.

4. Click the **Program** button, and then click **Exit and return to document** to close the object.

Did You Know?

You can use Paste Special to embed part of a file. Select and copy the information, click where you want to embed the copied information, click the Paste button arrow on the Home tab, click Paste Special, click the Paste option, select a format, and then click OK.

Resize an Object

1. Click the object to select it.

2. Drag a sizing handle to change the size of the object.

   - Drag a corner sizing handle to change height and width simultaneously.

   - Drag the top or bottom middle sizing handle to change height.

   - Drag the left or right middle sizing handle to change width.

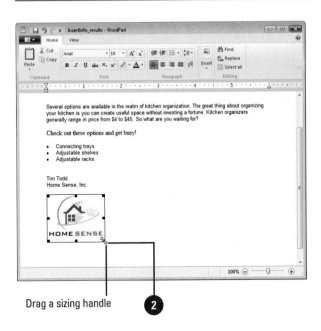

Drag a sizing handle

Linking and Updating Information

When you want to keep source and destination files in sync with each other, you can link the source file that created the object with the destination file that displays the object. Linking displays information stored in one document (the source file) into another (the destination file). You can edit the linked object from either file, although changes are stored in the source file. Only a representation of the object appears in the destination file; any changes made to the object are done in the source file, whether you access it by double-clicking the object in the destination file or by opening it in the source program.

Link an Object Between Programs

1. Click where you want to embed the object.

2. Click the **Insert Object** button on the Home tab.

3. Click the **Create from File** option.

4. Click **Browse**, and then double-click the file with the object you want to link.

5. Select the **Link** check box.

6. Click **OK**.

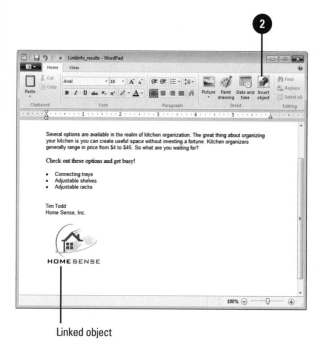

Linked object

Update a Linked File

① Open the file with the source program.

② Edit the file using the source program's commands.

③ Click the **Save** button on the toolbar.

④ Click the **Close** button to exit the source program.

⑤ Open the linked file with the destination program.

The object automatically updates.

⑥ Click the **Save** button on the toolbar.

⑦ Click the **Close** button to exit the destination program.

Did You Know?

You can change a link to update manually. In the destination program, right-click the linked object, click Links, click the Manual option button, and then click Close.

For Your Information

Finding, Changing, and Breaking a Linked Object

Instead of opening a linked object from the source file to make changes, you can open a linked object from the destination file using the Open Source button in the Links dialog box. The Open Source button finds the source file containing the linked object and opens that file. After making changes, you exit and return to the destination file. The Links dialog box keeps track of the source file location. You can change the linked source to a different file by using the Change Source button. If you want to disregard a link and change it to an embedded object, select the linked object in the destination file, right-click the object, click Object Properties, click the Link tab, click Break Link, click Yes in the message box, and then click OK. On the Link tab in the Object Properties dialog box, you can also open or change the source file, change update options, and update the source for the selected object.

Inserting Special Characters

When you need to insert special characters such as ©, ™, or ® that don't appear on your keyboard, you can use a special accessory program called Character Map to do the job. Character Map displays all the characters that are available for each of the fonts on your computer.

Insert a Special Character

① Click the **Start** button, point to **All Programs**, click **Accessories**, click **System Tools**, and then click **Character Map**.

② Click the **Font** list arrow, and then click a font.

③ Double-click the character you want to insert.

> **TIMESAVER** *Click a character to see an enlarged view of it.*

④ Click **Copy** to place the character on the Clipboard.

⑤ Click the **Close** button.

⑥ Click in the document to place the insertion point.

⑦ Click the **Paste** button on the Home tab.

> **TIMESAVER** *Press Ctrl+V to quickly paste the contents from the Clipboard.*

Did You Know?

You can create your own character. With the Private Character Editor program (**New!**), you can create your own characters, which you can insert into documents by using Character Map. Click the Start menu, point to All Programs, click Accessories, and then click Private Character Editor to create or edit a character. Click the Help menu, and then click Help Topics for detailed instructions.

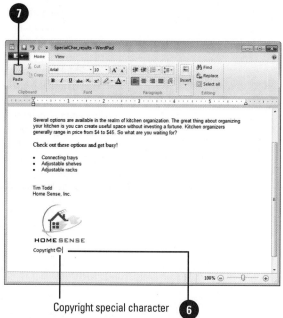

Copyright special character ⑥

Calculating Numbers

If you don't have a handheld calculator handy, you can use the Calculator program provided by Windows to perform standard calculations or even more complex ones. Calculator performs basic arithmetic, such as addition and subtraction, functions found on a scientific calculator, such as logarithms and factorials, programmer conversions (**New!**), such as Hex and Decimal, as well as functions for statistical analysis (**New!**). You can also change the display (**New!**) to perform functions, including unit conversion, date calculation, and worksheets, such as mortgage, vehicle lease, or fuel economy (mpg or L/100 km).

Use the Calculator

1. Click the **Start** button, point to **All Programs**, click **Accessories**, and then click **Calculator**.

2. Click the **View** menu, and then click **Standard**, **Scientific**, **Programmer**, or **Statistics**.

3. To change the view to display other functions, click the **View** menu, and then click **Basic**, **Unit conversion**, **Date calculation**, or point to **Worksheets**, and click an option.

4. Enter a number, or click the number buttons.

5. Click a function button, and then enter another number.

6. When you've entered all the numbers you want, click the equals (=) button.

7. Click the **Edit** menu, and then click **Copy** to copy the result to the Clipboard to paste in a document.

8. When you're done, click the **Close** button.

Worksheet for mortgage calculation

Did You Know?

You can use the numeric keypad on your keyboard with the Calculator. Press the number, +, -, *, /, and Enter keys to quickly enter numbers and use the calculator.

Running Commands

Besides running Windows programs, you can also enter commands and run programs written in MS-DOS. **MS-DOS** stands for Microsoft Disk Operating System. MS-DOS, or DOS, employs a **command-line interface** through which you must type commands at a **command prompt** to run different tasks. A character such as a > or $ appears at the beginning of a command prompt. Each DOS command has a strict set of rules called a **command syntax** that you must follow when expressing a command. Many commands allow you to include switches and parameters that give you additional control of the command.

Run a Command

1. Click the **Start** button, point to **All Programs,** click **Accessories**, and then click **Command Prompt**.

2. At the prompt, type a command including any parameters, and then press Enter.

3. When you're done, click the **Close** button, or type **exit**, and then press Enter.

Find a Command

1. Click the **Start** button, point to **All Programs**, click **Accessories**, and then click **Command Prompt**.

2. At the prompt, type **help**, and then press Enter.

3. Read the list of commands. Use the scroll bar or scroll arrows to display additional information.

4. When you're done, click the **Close** button, or type **exit**, and then press Enter.

prompt

Get Information About a Command

1. Click the **Start** button, point to **All Programs**, click **Accessories**, and then click **Command Prompt**.

2. At the prompt, type a command followed by a space and **/?**, and then press Enter.

3. Read the information about the command. Use the scroll bar or scroll arrows to display additional information.

4. When you're done, click the **Close** button, or type **exit**, and then press Enter.

Did You Know?

You can use a wildcard character to change more than one file. An asterisk is a wildcard and represents any number of characters. For example, the command *dir at*.doc* matches atback.doc, ati.doc, and atlm.doc.

You can change the appearance of the Command Prompt window. Right-click the Command Prompt window title bar, and then click Properties.

You can ping a connection to make sure it works and find out an IP address. Ping is a diagnostic network tool that verifies whether an IP address is accessible. To test a connection, type **ping *IP address*** at the command prompt, and then press Enter. To find an IP address, type **ipconfig /?** or type **ipconfig /all**, and then press Enter. To get a new IP address, type **ipconfig/release**, press Enter, type **ipconfig/renew**, and then press Enter.

Common DOS Commands

Command	Purpose
cd *foldername*	Changes to the specified folder
cls	Clears the screen
copy	Copies the specified files or folder
dir	Lists the contents of the current folder
c: (where c is a drive)	Switches to the specified drive
exit	Closes the Command Prompt window
rename	Renames the specified file or files
more *file name*	Displays the contents of a file, one screen of output at a time
type *file name.txt*	Displays the contents of the text file

Playing Games

If you have some free time, you can play some fun and exciting games. Windows Games Explorer (**New!**) provides tools to set up hardware, software and parental controls, options to get updates, and games you can play against the computer and other players online—Chess Titans, FreeCell, Hearts, Internet Backgammon, Internet Checkers, Internet Spades, Mahjong Titans, Minesweeper, Purble Place, Solitaire, and Spider Solitaire. When you start an Internet game, the game server finds players matched to your skill level and language from around the world. You can't select the players or locations of your opponents, but you can communicate with them by using the Chat controls.

Use Games Explorer

① Click the **Start** button, and then click **Games**.

② To access hardware and software tools to use with your games, click the **Tools** button on the toolbar, and then select a tool:

  ◆ **Hardware.** Opens Hardware and Sound options.

  ◆ **Display Devices.** Opens Screen Resolution options

  ◆ **Input Devices.** Opens Games Controllers dialog box.

  ◆ **Audio Devices.** Opens the Sound dialog box.

  ◆ **Windows Firewall.** Opens Windows Firewall options.

  ◆ **Programs and Features.** Opens Programs and Features options.

③ To access parental controls, click the **Parental Controls** button on the toolbar.

④ To set up game updates and options, click the **Options** button on the toolbar, select options to get game updates and news, or information.

⑤ To start a game, double-click the games icon.

Select options to get game updates and news, and other information

Play a Game

1 Click the **Start** button, and then click **Games**.

2 Double-click the game you want.

3 Play the game.

4 When you're done, click the **Game** menu, and then click a command to start a new game with the same or different players, or exit the game.

Get Help for each game

Did You Know?

You can get more information about playing each game in Help. Start the game, click the Help menu, and then click Contents or Help Topics.

You can access other Internet games online. Open your web browser, and then go to *www.zone.msn.com*. The MSN Games web site opens. Follow the online instructions and game Help to play the game you want.

Playing the Game

Game	Object is to
Chess Titans	Put your opponents' king in checkmate. Each player has one king. As you capture your opponent's pieces, strategize a way to capture the opposing king.
FreeCell	Stack the cards in the cells at the top in descending order, starting from any card, alternating the red and black cards.
Hearts	Score the lowest number of points, one point for each heart and 13 points for the Queen of Spades. You play a card to follow suit or a heart or the Queen of Spades when you can't follow suit.
Mahjong Titans	Remove all the tiles from the board by finding matching pairs of free tiles. Mahjong is a form of solitaire that is played with tiles instead of cards.
Minesweeper	Uncover all the squares that don't contain mines in the shortest amount of time. You use the numbers in the uncovered squares to determine which adjacent squares contain mines.
Purble Place	Teach colors, shapes, and pattern recognition.
Solitaire	Reveal all the cards that are turned face down by stacking them in descending order (alternating the red and black cards) on the lower piles, and stack them in ascending order from Ace through King by suit in the upper piles. You use the mouse to drag one card on top of another.
Spider Solitaire	Stack the cards by suit in one column in descending order.

Snipping the Screen

The Snipping Tool (**New!**) allows you to capture a screen shot of anything currently on your screen as an image file. After you capture the image, you can annotate, save and share it with others in an e-mail. You can capture the screen in different ways: draw a free-form shape around an object, draw a rectangle around an object, select a window, or take the entire screen.

Use the Snipping Tool

1. Click the **Start** button, point to **All Programs**, click **Accessories**, and then click **Snipping Tool**.

2. To change snipping options, click the **Options** button, select the options you want, and then click **OK**.

3. To capture a screen, click the **New Snip** button arrow, and then select a capture option:

   - ◆ **Free-form Snip.**
   - ◆ **Rectangle Snip.**
   - ◆ **Window Snip.**
   - ◆ **Full-screen Snip.**

4. Drag a free-form or rectangle shape, or click a window.

5. To annotate the image, use the **Pen**, **Highlighter**, and **Eraser** tools.

6. To share the image, use the **Send Snip** button.

7. Click the **Save** button, select a save location, and then select a file format (PNG, GIF, JPEG, or MHT). MHT is for a single page web page.

8. To copy it to the Clipboard to paste in a document, click the **Copy** button.

9. When you're done, click the **Close** button.

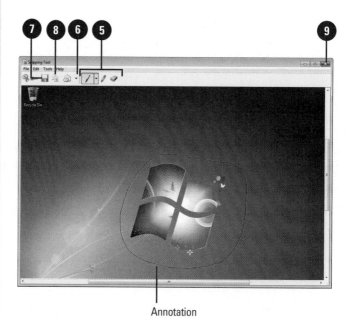

Annotation

Running Older Programs

Some older programs are designed to run on earlier versions of Windows and don't work properly on Windows 7. You can set the compatibility of Windows 7 to act like an earlier version of Windows to run an older program. In addition, you can also set display resolution and color settings, and user privilege levels to provide the best level of compatibility for the program and the Windows 7 operating system. You set options in the Compatibility tab in the program's Properties dialog box.

Set Compatibility for an Older Program

1 Click the **Start** button, and then locate the older program.

2 Right-click the program you want to run, and then click **Properties**.

3 Click the **Compatibility** tab.

4 Select the **Run this program in compatibility mode for** check box.

5 Click the list arrow, and then click the version of Windows in which the program was designed.

6 Select the check boxes for applying the appropriate settings to the display, based on the program's documentation.

7 Click **OK**.

Did You Know?

You can test your program using the Program Compatibility troubleshooter. Click the Start button, click the Control Panel, click Programs, and then click the Run Programs Made For Previous Versions Of Windows link to start the Program Compatibility troubleshooter. Follow the on-screen instructions.

Quitting a Program Not Responding

If a program stops responding while you work or freezes up, Windows provides you with the option to end the task. When you end a task, you'll probably lose any unsaved work in the problem program. If the problem persists, you might need to reinstall the program or contact product support to fix the problem. Pressing Ctrl+Alt+Delete or clicking the Close button closes the non responsive program and opens the Task Manager, where you can stop the program. You can also use the Task Manager to view system performance and log off users.

End a Task Not Responding

1. Right-click the taskbar, and then click **Start Task Manager**.

   If Windows doesn't respond when you right-click, press Ctrl+Alt+Delete, and then click **Task Manager**.

2. Click the **Applications** tab.

3. Select the program not responding.

4. Click **End Task**. If you're asked to wait, click **End Now**.

End a Program Not Responding

1. If a program is not responding, click the **Close** button on the program's title bar. Click several times, if necessary.

2. If you see a dialog box telling you the program is not responding, click **End Now**.

3. When a message appears, click **Send Information** to send information about the error over the Internet to Microsoft, or click **Cancel** to continue.

Managing Files and Folders

Introduction

File management is organizing and keeping track of files and folders, helping you stay organized, so information is easily located. A **folder** is a container for storing programs and files, similar to a folder in a file cabinet. As with a file cabinet, working with poorly managed files is like looking for a needle in a haystack—it is frustrating and time-consuming to search through irrelevant, misnamed, and out-of-date files to find the one you want. Windows allows you to organize folders and files in a file hierarchy, imitating the way you store paper documents in real folders. Just as a file cabinet contains several folders, each containing related documents with dividers grouping related folders together, so the Windows file hierarchy allows you to organize your files in folders, and then place folders in other folders. Windows 7 comes with four libraries: Documents, Pictures, Music, and Videos. Libraries (**New!**) are special folders that catalog folders and files in a central location. A library includes and displays folders that are stored in different locations on your computer, Homegroup, or network.

Using the file management tools, you can save files in folders with appropriate names for easy identification, quickly and easily create new folders so you can reorganize information and delete files and folders that you no longer need. You can also search for a file when you cannot remember where you stored it, create shortcuts to files and folders for quick and easy access, and even compress files and folders to save space.

A folder can hold different types of files, such as text, spreadsheets, and presentations. The Documents folder is the main location in Windows 7 where you store your files. However, there are some special folders, such as Pictures and Music, designed with specialized features to store specific types of files.

What You'll Do

Use the Explorer Window

Change the Explorer Window View

Open and View the Computer

Work with Libraries

Navigate Between Folders

View the Folders List

Customize the Navigation Pane

Organize Files by Headings

Search for Files and Folders

Perform an Instant Search

Add Properties and Tags to Files

Create and Rename Files and Folders

Copy and Move Files and Folders

Delete and Restore Files and Folders

Create a Shortcut to a File or Folder

Change Folder Options

Change File and Folder List Views

Customize Personal Folders

Share Folders or Files with Others

Compress Files and Folders

Manage Files Using a CD or DVD

Using the Explorer Window

The Explorer windows are powerful easy-to-use tools for working with files consistently across Windows 7. Explorers give you more information and control while simplifying how you work with your files. The experience is easy and consistent, whether you're browsing documents or photos or even using the Control Panel. Key elements of the Explorer windows in Windows 7 are designed to help you get to the information you need, when you need it. Each Explorer window includes the following elements:

◆ **Back and Forward buttons.** Use to navigate between previously viewed folders.

◆ **Address bar.** Use to navigate directly to a different location, including local and network disks, folders, and web locations.

◆ **Search box.** Use to perform instant searches, which show only those files that match what you typed in the Search box for the current folder and any of its subfolders.

◆ **Toolbar/Command bar.** Use to perform file related commands. Toolbar/Command bars display only the task buttons that are appropriate for the files being displayed. There are two consistent buttons on every Toolbar/Command bar: Organize and Views.

◆ **Navigation pane.** (**New!**) Use to display common folders, such as Favorites, Libraries, HomeGroup (a shared network), Computer, and Network, using a Folder list tree structure.

◆ **Libraries.** (**New!**) Use to access common folders, such as Documents, Music, Pictures, and Videos. A library is a collection of files and folders linked from different locations, including your computer, HomeGroup, or network, into a central place. A file or folder can be stored in one location, yet linked to a library for easy access. For example, your My Documents folder located in your personal folder (the one with your account name) is linked to the Documents library.

Back and Forward buttons

Address bar

Search box

Toolbar/Command bar

Navigation pane

Folder list

Changing the Explorer Window View

Windows 7 displays the contents of a drive or folder in different ways to help you find the information you are looking for about a file or folder. The available views include Extra Large, Large, Medium and Small Icons, List, Details, Tiles, and Content (**New!**).

Icons view displays icons in different sizes (Extra Large, Large, Medium, and Small), sorted alphabetically in horizontal rows with the name of the file or folder below each icon. When you view files using one of the Icon views, Live icons—thumbnails—display the first page of documents, the image of a photo, or the album art for individual songs, making it easier to find exactly what you are looking for.

List view displays small icons, sorted alphabetically into vertical columns with the name of the file or folder next to each icon.

Details view displays small icons, sorted alphabetically in a vertical column with the name of the file or folder and additional infor-

mation, such as file size, type, and date, in columns to the right.

Tiles view displays icons, sorted alphabetically into vertical columns, with information about the file next to each icon.

Content view (**New!**) displays medium icons in a vertical column with date modified information.

Switching Between Views

You use the Views button on the toolbar in an Explorer window to quickly switch between window views. When you click the Views button, the view switches between the following views: List, Details, Tiles, Content (**New!**), and Large Icons. If you want to select a different view, you can click the arrow next to the Views button to display a menu, where you can click a view or drag the slider. When you drag the slider, you can position it anywhere within the range, not just the main positions.

Live icons   Views button

Opening and Viewing the Computer

The Computer window is the starting point to access every disk, folder, and file on your computer. You can access the Computer window from the Start menu. The Computer window displays several types of local, removable, and network drives. Drives and folders are represented by icons. Each drive is assigned a drive letter, denoted with parentheses and a colon, such as Local Disk (C:), to make it easier to identify. Typically, the floppy is drive A, the hard (also known as local) disk is drive C, and the CD or DVD is drive D. If your computer includes additional drives, your computer assigns them letters in alphabetical order. Once you open more than one drive or folder, you can use buttons on the Command bar to help you move quickly between folders.

Open and View the Computer

1. Click the **Start** button, and then click **Computer**.

2. Click a drive to select it.

3. Review the drive details in the Details pane.

4. Double-click the drive to open it.

5. Click the **Back** button or **Forward** button on the toolbar to return or move to a previously visited window.

   TIMESAVER *You can press the Backspace key to go back to a previous folder you visited.*

6. When you're done, click the **Close** button.

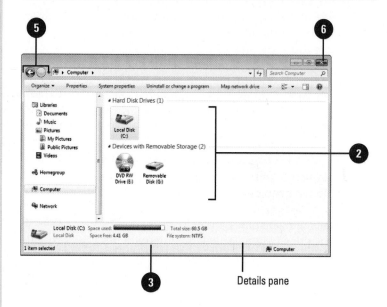

Details pane

Typical Disk Drives on a Computer

Icon	Type Description
Local	A hard magnetic disk (or hard disk) on which you can store large amounts of data. The Local Disk (C:) stores all the files on your computer.
Floppy	A soft removable magnetic disk that comes in a 3½-inch size, which stores up to 1.44 MB of data. Floppy disks are slower to access than a hard disk, but are portable and much less expensive.
Removable	A removable magnetic disk on which you can store computer data, such as a Zip disk (requires software). Another is a Flash memory card the size of a large stamp that holds128, 256, 512 MB or greater. Flash drives connect directly into a USB plug without software.
CD-ROM	**Compact Disc-Read-Only Memory** An optical disk on which you can stamp, or burn, up to 1 GB (typical size is 650 MB) of data in only one session. The disc cannot be erased or burned again with additional new data.
CD-R	**Compact Disc-Recordable** A type of CD-ROM on which you can burn up to 1 GB of data in multiple sessions. The disc can be burned again with new data, but cannot be erased.
CD-RW	**Compact Disc-Rewriteable** A type of CD-ROM on which you can read, write, and erase data, just like a hard disk.
DVD	**Digital Video Disc** A type of DVD-ROM that holds a minimum of 4.7 GB, enough for a full-length movie.
DVD-R	**Digital Video Disc-Recordable** A type of DVD-ROM on which you can burn up to 4.7 GB of data in multiple sessions. The disc can be burned again with new data, but cannot be erased.
DVD-RW	**Digital Video Disc-Rewriteable** A type of DVD-ROM on which you can read, write, and erase data, just like a hard disk.
HD-DVD DVD-ROM	**High Density Digital Video Disc** A type of high density on which you can read data; the disc appears as a high density drive.
Blu-ray	**High Density Blu-ray Disc** A type of high density DVD-ROM on which you can read data; the disc appears as a high density drive.

Viewing and Opening Documents

Windows makes it easy to manage the personal and business files and folders you work with every day. You can access your Documents folder from the Start menu, which displays the Documents library folder. The Documents library folder (**New!**) links and displays files and folders from different locations on your computer in a central place, which includes your My Documents folder located in your personal folder. In the folder, you can view file information, organize files and folders, and open files and folders. Once you open more than one folder, you can use buttons on the Command bar to help you move quickly between folders. Depending on previous installation, devices installed, or other users, your personal folders might differ.

View and Open Documents

1 Click the **Start** button, and then click **Documents**.

2 Click a file to select it.

3 Review the document details in the Details pane.

4 Double-click the file to open it.

5 Use the scroll bars to view additional documents. Drag the scroll box, or click the scroll arrows.

6 When you're done, click the **Close** button.

Did You Know?

Windows creates a separate Documents folder for each user.
When you share a computer, Windows creates a separate Documents folder and stores personalized settings for each user. Each user's Documents folder is located in the Documents And Settings folder under the user's name on the local hard disk.

Open Any Folder and Switch Between Folders

1. Click the **Start** button, and then click the user account name, or any other Explorer window, such as **Documents**, **Pictures**, or **Music**.

2. Double-click the folder to open it.

3. Click the **Back** button or **Forward** button to return or move to a previously visited window.

4. When you're done, click the **Close** button.

Did You Know?

Windows stores music and picture files in separate folders in your personal folder. Windows stores music files in the My Music folder and pictures in the My Pictures folder in your personal folder, which you can access from the Start menu or the Music and Pictures libraries.

See Also

See "Changing the Explorer Window View" on page 55 for information on changing the display of a folder's contents.

See "Working with Libraries" on page 60 for information on using and creating libraries.

See "Changing the Explorer Window View" on page 55 for information on changing the display of a folder's contents.

See "Working with Libraries" on page 60 for information on using and creating libraries.

For Your Information

Opening a Document with a Different Program

Most documents on your desktop are associated with a specific program. For example, if you double-click a document whose file name ends with the three-letter extension ".txt," Windows automatically opens the document with Notepad, a text-only editor. There are situations, though, when you need to open a document with a program other than the one Windows chooses, or when you want to choose a different default program. For example, you might want to open a text document in WordPad rather than Notepad so that you can add formatting and graphics. To do this, right-click the document icon you want to open, point to Open With, and then click the application you want to use to open the document, or click Choose Program to access more program options. Once you open a text file using WordPad, this option is automatically added to the Open With menu.

Working with Libraries

Libraries (**New!**) are special folders that catalog folders and files in a central location. A library includes and displays folders that are stored in different locations on your computer, Homegroup, or network. Windows 7 comes with four libraries: Documents, Pictures, Music, and Videos. The Documents library, for example, includes files and folders from your My Documents and Public Documents folders, which are actually stored in your Users folder. Instead of navigating to separate folders, you can quickly navigate to one central place, the Documents library. You can create additional libraries at any time and include folders from different locations or remove them. After you open a library, you can quickly arrange all files and folders included in a library by folder (the default) or other properties based on the library type (General Items, Documents, Music, Pictures, or Videos). When you save a file to a library, you can specify which folder it actually gets stored in.

Open and View a Library

1. Click the **Windows Explorer** button on the taskbar.

2. Double-click a library folder.

   ◆ To open a specific library, click the **Start** button, and then click **Documents**, **Pictures**, or **Music**.

3. To display the Library pane, click the **Organize** button on the toolbar, point to **Layout**, and then click **Library pane**, if necessary.

4. To change the library display, click the **Arrange by** button on the Library pane, and then click an option.

   ◆ **Folder.** File and folders.

   ◆ **General Items.** Date modified, Tag, Type, or Name.

   ◆ **Documents.** Author, Date modified, Tag, Type, or Name.

   ◆ **Pictures.** Month, Day, Rating, or Tag.

   ◆ **Music.** Album, Artist, Song, Genre, or Rating.

   ◆ **Video.** Year, Type, Length, or Name.

   ◆ **Clear changes.** Clears any arrange by modifications.

Create a New Library and Include or Remove Folders

1. Click the **Windows Explorer** button on the taskbar.

2. Click the **New library** button on the toolbar, type a library name, and then press Enter.

   ◆ To delete a library, right-click the library, click **Delete**, and then click **Yes**.

3. To include a folder in a library, navigate to the folder location, right-click the folder, point to **Include in library**, and then select the library you want.

4. To remove a folder from a library, open the library, click the **Locations** link on the Library pane, select the folder you want to remove, click **Remove**, and then click **OK**.

New library

Change the Save Location

1. Open the folder you want to change the save location.

2. Click the **Organize** button on the toolbar, and then click **Properties**.

3. Select the library location where you want to save files.

4. Click **Set save location**.

   A check mark appears to the left of the selected folder location.

5. Click **OK**.

Working with Personal Folders

Windows 7 comes with a personal folder that stores your most frequently used folders in one location. The personal folder appears on the Start menu with the name of the person logged on to the computer. The personal folder only contains files and folders associated with a user account and are unique for each user on the computer. The personal folder includes a variety of folders: Contacts, Desktop, Downloads, Favorites, Links, My Documents, My Pictures, My Music, My Videos, Saved Games, and Searches. You can access these folders using the personal folder on the Start menu. The My Documents, My Pictures, My Music, and My Videos folders are included in the Documents, Pictures, Music, and Videos libraries (**New!**) respectively, so you can also access them by name on the Start menu.

View and Open a Personal Folder

1. Click the **Start** button, and then click the user account name at the top of the right column on the Start menu.

2. Double-click a folder to open it.

3. When you're done, click the **Close** button.

Navigating Between Folders

The Address bar appears at the top of every Explorer window and displays the current location on your computer or network. The location appears as a series of links separated by arrows. You can change your current location by either typing a new location—even a web address on the Internet—or selecting one using the Address bar. You can also use the Back and Forward buttons to the left of the Address bar to switch between locations you have previously visited.

Navigate to a Location

◆ **Click a location**. Use either of the following methods:

  ◆ **Visible folder location**. To go directly to a location visible in the Address bar, click the location name.

  ◆ **Visible subfolder location**. To go to a subfolder of a location visible in the Address bar, click the arrow to the right, and then click the location name.

◆ **Type a location**. Click a blank space (to the right of text) in the Address bar, and then type the complete folder name or path to the location, and then press Enter.

You can type common locations and then press Enter. The common locations include: Computer, Contacts, Control Panel, Documents, Favorites, Games, Music, Pictures, Recycle Bin, and Videos.

If you type a web address (URL) in the Address bar, the Explorer window switches to Internet Explorer.

Address bar   Click a location

Navigation pane

Viewing the Folders List

Windows offers a useful feature for managing files and folders, called the **Folders list**, which is integrated under categories—Favorites, Libraries, Homegroups, Computer, and Network—into the Navigation pane (**New!**). The Folders list displays the window in two panes, or frames, which allows you to view information from two different locations. The Navigation pane displays the file hierarchy of all the drives and folders on the computer, and the right pane displays the contents of the selected drive or folder. This arrangement enables you to view the file hierarchy of your computer and the contents of a folder simultaneously making it easy to copy, move, delete, and rename files and folders. Using the non filled arrow and the filled arrow to the left of an icon in the Folders list allows you to display different levels of the drives and folders on your computer without opening and displaying the contents of each folder.

View the Folders List

1. Open any folder window.

2. In the Navigation pane, point to an item to display the navigation arrows.

3. Perform the commands you want to display folder structure and contents:

   ◆ To show the file and folder structure, click the non filled arrow.

   ◆ To hide the file and folder structure, click the filled arrow.

   ◆ To display the contents of a folder, click the folder icon.

Folder list tree structure

Did You Know?

You can quickly determine if a folder contains folders. When an arrow doesn't appear next to an icon in the Folders list, the item has no folders in it.

Changing the Explorer Layout

Windows 7 gives you the option to customize the layout for each Explorer window depending on the information the window contains. The layout for each Explorer window includes a Menu Bar, Details pane, Preview pane, and Navigation pane. The Details and Navigation panes appear by default. Some Explorer windows, such as a library folder, also include a Library pane (**New!**), which you can use to display the library name, includes link and Arrange by view options. The Organize menu shows or hides the layout elements. If you prefer working with menus like the previous version of Windows, you can show the menu bar and use traditional menus.

Change the Explorer Layout

1. Open the folder window you want to change.

2. Click the **Organize** button, and then point to **Layout**.

3. Select the layout item you want to show or hide: **Menu Bar**, **Details Pane**, **Preview Pane**, **Navigation Pane**, or **Library Pane (New!)**.

   Layout options vary depending on the type of Explorer window.

   TIMESAVER *To quickly display the Menu bar, press the Alt key, and then release it. Press the Alt key again to remove it.*

Customizing the Navigation Pane

The Navigation pane provides links to commonly used drives and folders to reduce the number of clicks it takes to locate a file or folder. Windows 7 provides a default list (**New!**) of favorites, libraries, homegroups, and networks in the Navigation pane. You can customize the list of favorites for your own purposes. You can move current links, add or rename folders, or remove an item. If the Navigation pane gets cluttered, you can restore it back to the original default items and start from there. You can also set Navigation pane options to show all folders (**New!**) like the Folder list in Windows Vista and automatically expand the folder list to the current folder (**New!**).

Customize the Navigation Pane

◆ **Move a link.** Drag an item in the Navigation pane to a higher or lower position in Favorites.

◆ **Add a link.** Drag an item from its original location to a position in the Navigation pane in Favorites.

◆ **Rename a link.** Right-click the link in Favorites, and then click **Rename**. Type a new name, and then press Enter. The original folder or search is not renamed, only the Navigation link.

◆ **Remove a link.** Right-click the link in Favorites, and then click **Remove**. The original folder or search is not removed, only the Navigation link.

◆ **Restore default links.** Right-click the Favorites link in the Navigation pane, and then click **Restore favorite links**.

◆ **Show all folders like the folders list. (New!)** Click the **Organize** button, click **Folder and search options**, select the **Show all folders** check box on the General tab, and then click **OK**.

◆ **Automatically expand the folder list to the current folder. (New!)** Click the **Organize** button, click **Folder and search options**, select the **Automatically expand to current folder** check box on the General tab, and then click **OK**.

Favorites in the Navigation pane   Remove and Rename a link

Navigation pane folder options

Organizing Files by Headings

In Explorer windows, files and folders appear in lists with headings at the top in Details view. You can use the headings to change how files are displayed in the window. You can use filtering and sorting to display the files and folders you want. Filtering displays only files and folders with the properties you select by heading type. For example, the A - H filter for file and folder names displays only files and folder that start with A - H. Sorting displays the files and folders in ascending or descending order by heading type. For example, the sort by name displays files and folders from A to Z or Z to A. You can apply a filter and sort a column to achieve the results you want.

Organize Files Using Filtering or Sorting

1. Open the folder that contains the files you want to sort or filter.

2. Click the **Views** button arrow, and then click **Details**.

3. To sort files by headings, click the heading title you want to sort by. An arrow in the middle of the heading indicates the sort direction, ascending and descending.

4. Point to the heading you want to filter by.

5. Click the arrow to the right of the heading you want to filter by.

6. Select the property check boxes you want to filter by.

7. Click in a blank area to close the search menu.

   A check mark replaces the arrow to indicates a filter is in place.

   ◆ To cancel the search, press Esc.

Searching for Files and Folders

Sometimes remembering precisely where you stored a file can be difficult. Windows 7 allows you to use Windows Search Explorer (by default) or a third-party search application, such as Google Desktop Search, to help you find and view all of your files or folders in one place. You start a search by using the Search box. As you type in a Search box, the search looks for matches in the file name, contents, and property tags, and displays the highlighted results (**New!**) in a Search Results folder. If you don't find the file or folders you're looking for, you can perform an advanced search using a menu (**New!**) from the Search box. An advanced search gives you the option to find files or folders by type, name, title, location, date (taken, modified, or created), size, or property tag. The search locates files and programs stored anywhere in indexed locations, which includes personal folders, e-mail, offline files, and web sites in your History list.

Create a Simple Search by Type

1. Start the default search application using any of the following:

   ◆ Open an Explorer window in the location where you want to search.

   ◆ Press Windows logo+F.

2. Click in the Search box or press Ctrl+F.

   A search menu appears. Disregard the menu for a simple search.

3. Type a word or part of a word.

   As you type, programs and files that match your text appear highlighted (**New!**) in the Search Results window. You don't have to press Enter.

   TROUBLE? *In the Search box, you must press Enter to start a search for non-indexed files.*

Highlighted search results

Search results

See Also

See "Setting Default Programs" on page 122 for information on using Windows Search Explorer (default) or a third-party search application.

Create an Advanced Search

① Start the default search application using any of the following:

◆ Open an Explorer window in the location where you want to search.

◆ Press Windows logo+F.

② Click in the Search box or press Ctrl+F.

A Search menu appears with advanced options.

③ Click the filter option you want on the Search menu. The filter options vary depending on the folder contents. Some of the filter options include:

◆ **Name.** Searches by file name.

◆ **Authors.** Searches by the document's author.

◆ **Tags.** Searches by a property tag.

◆ **Date modified.** Searches by date modified.

◆ **Size.** Searches by file size.

◆ **Type.** Searches by file type.

④ Type in the Search box or select from the menu the criteria you want based on the search option you selected.

◆ To add more search filter options, click back in the Search box at the end to display the Search menu.

⑤ To search again in other locations, click one of the following locations: **Libraries**, **Homegroup**, **Computer**, **Custom**, or **Internet**.

⑥ To clear and close the search, click the **Close** button (x) in the Search box.

Search results

Saving a Search

If you frequently perform the same search, you can save your search results like any file and perform or modify the search again later. When you save a search, the search is saved by default with Window Search Explorer in the Searches folder in your personal folder and added to the Favorites folder in the Navigation pane. Like any link, you can move a saved search from the Searches folder to the Favorites category in the Navigation pane to make it more accessible. To run a saved search, display the saved search link, and then click it.

Save a Search

1. Start the default search application using any of the following:
   - Open an Explorer window in the location where you want to search.
   - Press Windows logo+F.
2. Click in the Search box, specify the criteria you want, and then perform the search.
3. Click the **Save search** button on the toolbar.
4. Type a name for the search.
5. Click **Save**.
6. To use a saved search, click the saved search link in Favorites in the Navigation pane or double-click the saved search in the Searches folder in the personal folder.

Did You Know?

You can quickly perform a recent search. Click in the Search box to the display the Search menu. At the top of the Search menu displays recent searches, which you can select to quickly perform again. If the list gets cluttered, you can remove items. Point to the item on the menu, and then press Delete.

Changing Search Options

When you perform a search for files or folders, Windows 7 uses the search options to help customize the search results. You can specify whether you want to search for file names and content or just for file names and whether to include subfolders or find partial matches. For non-indexed searches, you can set options to include system directories or compressed files (ZIP, CAB...). The search options are available in the Folder Options dialog box under the Search tab.

Change Search Options

1. Click the **Start** button, and then click **Documents**.

2. Click the **Organize** button on the toolbar, and then click **Folder and search options**.

   TIMESAVER *After a search, click Search Tools on the toolbar, and then click Search Options.*

3. Click the **Search** tab.

4. Select the What to search option you want.

5. Select or clear the check boxes under How to search:

   ◆ **Include subfolders in search results when searching in file folders.**

   ◆ **Find partial matches.**

   ◆ **Use natural language search.**

   ◆ **Don't use the index when searching in file folders for system files (searches might take longer).**

6. Select or clear the check boxes under When searching non-indexed locations:

   ◆ **Include system directories.**

   ◆ **Include compressed files (ZIP, CAB, ...)**

7. Click **OK**.

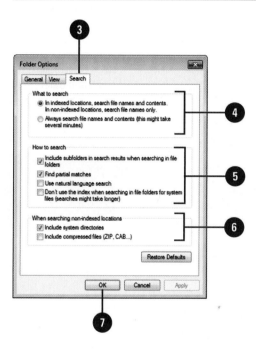

Performing an Instant Search

You can also find files and programs using the Search box at the bottom of the Start menu and at the top of every Explorer window. As you type, the Search box (**New!**) filters out items that don't match the text you type. The search results continue to narrow as you continue to type. The search includes text in the file name, text in the file, tags (a custom file property), and other file properties. The search locates files and programs stored anywhere in indexed locations, which includes personal folders, e-mail, offline files, and web sites in the History list for your web browser. If you don't find what you are looking for during a search, you can click See more results (**New!**) at the bottom of the Start menu search results to use additional Windows search capabilities. After you complete a search, you can use the Arrange by option to display your results the way you want (**New!**), which include Top Results and other properties, such as Date modified and Type.

Find a File or Program Using the Search Box on the Start Menu

1. Click the **Start** button.

2. Click in the **Search** box.

3. Type a word or part of a word.

   As you type, programs and files that match your text appear on the Start menu. You don't have to press Enter.

   TROUBLE? *In the Search box, you must press Enter to start a search for non-indexed files.*

4. If you don't find what you are looking for during a search, you can click **See more results** to use Windows search capabilities.

5. To clear and close the search, click the **Close** button (x) in the Search box.

Did You Know?

You can display search properties.
Right-click the heading in an Explorer window that you want to see properties for, and then click More.

Search results

Find a File or Folder Using the Search Box From a Folder

① Click the **Start** button, and then open the Explorer window where you want to start looking, such as **Documents**, **Pictures**, or **Music**.

② Click in the Search box.

A search menu appears. Disregard the menu for a simple search.

③ Type a word or part of a word.

As you type, programs and files that match your text appear highlighted (**New!**) in the Search Results window. You don't have to press Enter.

TROUBLE? *In the Search box, you must press Enter to start a search for non-indexed files.*

④ To change the results display, click the **Arrange by** button (**New!**), and then select an option: **Top Results** or other properties, such as **Author**, **Date modified**, **Tag**, and **Type**.

⑤ To search again in other locations, click one of the following locations (**New!**): **Libraries**, **Homegroup**, **Computer**, **Custom**, or **Internet**.

⑥ To clear and close the search, click the **Close** button (x) in the Search box.

Did You Know?

You can use wildcards to expand a search. Use the * (asterisk) wildcard symbol in a file name when you're unsure of the entire name. For example, type **S*rs** to find all files beginning with "S" and ending with "rs," such as Stars and Sports cars.

Search results

Performing an Advanced Search

The Search box at the bottom of the Start menu and at the top of every Explorer window filters out items that don't match the text you type. The search includes text in the file name, text in the file, tags (a custom file property), and other file properties. In the Search box, you can perform advanced searches by specifying properties and using boolean filters. For example, *Name:Agenda* finds only files that have the word *agenda* in the file name. In addition, you can use boolean filters, such as AND, NOT, OR, Quotes, Parentheses, >, or <. For example, *Agenda* AND *Report* find files that contain both words *agenda* and *report*. When you type boolean filters, you need to use all capital letters. You can also combine properties and boolean filters together to create a more specific search.

Find Files and Folders Using the Search Folder

1. Turn off natural language search. (default off).

   ◆ Click the **Start** button, click **Control Panel**, click **Appearance and Personalization**, click **Folder Options**, click the **Search** tab, clear the **Use natural language search** check box, and then click **OK**.

2. Click in the **Search** box at the bottom of the Start menu or at the top of an Explorer window.

3. Type an advanced search. See the table for some examples.

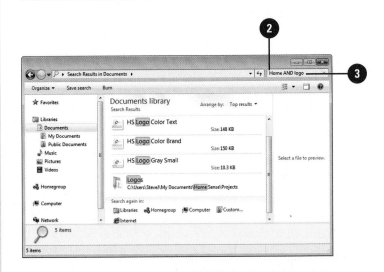

Search Examples

Example	Description
agenda AND report	Finds files that contain both *agenda* and *report*.
agenda NOT report	Finds files that contain agenda, but not *report*.
agenda OR report	Finds files that contain either *agenda* or *report*.
"Agenda Report"	Finds files that contain the exact phrase "Agenda Report" in quotes.
(agenda report)	Finds files that contain both words agenda and report in any order.
date: >10/10/08	Find files that are later than 10/10/08.
size: < 100 MB	Find files that are less than 100 MB.
subject: agenda AND report	Find files with the subject agenda and any files that contain the word report.

Performing Natural Language Searches

If using properties and boolean filters seems a little too much for you to handle, you can find files using natural language search, which allows you to perform the same property or boolean search, yet use a form that is easier to use. Instead of *kind: document author: (Steve AND Holly)*, you can type *documents by Steve and Holly*. Before you can use natural language in a Search box, you need to turn it on under the Search tab in Folder Options in the Control Panel.

Turn On Natural Language Search

1. Click the **Start** button, and then **Control Panel**.

2. Click **Appearance and Personalization**, and then click **Folder Options**.

   TIMESAVER *In an Explorer window, click the Organize button, and then click Folder and search options.*

3. Click the **Search** tab.

4. Select the **Use natural language search** check box.

5. Click **OK**.

Perform a Natural Language Search

1. Click in the **Search** box at the bottom of the Start menu or at the top of an Explorer window.

2. Type a natural language search. Some examples include:

   ◆ documents modified today

   ◆ e-mail from holly sent this week

   ◆ music by Mozart

   ◆ videos of family created December 2008

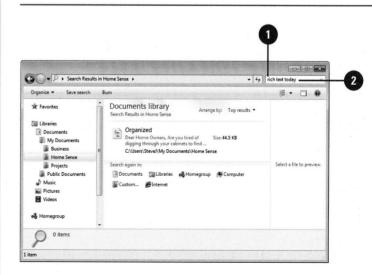

Modifying the Index to Improve Searches

Windows keeps track of files in indexed locations and stores information about them in the background using an index, like the one found in the back of this book, to make locating files faster and easier. You can use Indexing Options in the Control Panel to view, pause, add, remove, and modify indexed locations, indexed file types, and other advanced index settings. For example, if a file type is not recognized by the index, you can add it; if you want to stop indexing new content for 15 minutes to specify options, you can pause it; or if you're having problems with the search index, you can rebuild or restore it.

View, Pause, Add, or Remove Indexed Locations

1. Click the **Start** button, and then click **Control Panel**.

2. Click the **Indexing Options** icon in Small icons or Large icons view.

3. To pause new indexing for 15 minutes, click **Pause**.

4. Click **Modify**.

5. If you don't see all the locations, click **Show all locations**.

6. If a folder location contains subfolders, you can double-click the folder to expand it.

7. Select or clear the check box next to the folder locations you want to add or remove from the index.

8. Click **OK**.

9. Click **Close**.

Did You Know?

You can index file attributes for a folder. Right-click the folder, click Properties, click the General tab, click Advanced, select the Allow This File To Have Contents Indexed In Addition To File Properties check box, and then click OK twice.

Set Advanced Indexing Options

1 Click the **Start** button, and then click **Control Panel**.

2 Click the **Indexing Options** icon in Small icons or Large icons view.

3 Click **Advanced**.

4 Click the **Index Settings** tab.

5 Select or clear the following check boxes:

- ◆ **Index encrypted files.**

- ◆ **Treat similar words with diacritics as different words.**

6 For index troubleshooting, use either of these buttons:

- ◆ To re-index selected locations, click **Rebuild**.

- ◆ To restore your index to its original settings, click **Restore Defaults**.

7 If you need to change the Index Location, specify a new location or click **Select new**.

8 Click the **File Types** tab.

9 Select or clear the check boxes with the file types you want to include or exclude in the index.

10 For each selected file type, click the option to specify how the file should be indexed.

11 Click **OK**.

12 Click **Close**.

Adding Properties and Tags to Files

When you create a file, Windows automatically adds properties to the files, such as name, creation date, modified date, and size. These properties are important to Windows, however, they may not be useful when you are searching for a file. You can add or modify common file properties and create or modify custom tag properties to make it faster and easier to locate files in the future. You can add or modify properties for most files. However, there are some exceptions, such as plain text (.txt) or rich text format (.rtf) files. You can add or modify properties using the Details pane in an Explorer window, the Details tab in the Properties dialog box, or in the Save As dialog box. If you want to remove some or all of the property information in a file, you can quickly remove it using the Properties dialog box.

Add or Modify Properties

1. Click the **Windows Explorer** button on the taskbar.

2. Click the file you want to add or modify properties.

3. In the Details pane, click the tag you want to change, and then type the new tag.

    ◆ If you want to work with more properties and tags or the Details pane is not available, right-click the file, click **Properties**, and then click the **Details** tab. When you're done, click **Apply**.

4. To add more than one tag, separate each entry with a semicolon.

5. To rate a file using the rating property, click the star that represents the rating you want to give the file.

6. Click **Save**.

Add or Modify Properties While Saving a File

1. Click the **File** menu or Program button in the program you are using, and then click **Save A   s**.

2. Type tags and other properties in the boxes provides.

3. To add more than one property, separate each entry with a semicolon.

4. Type the name of the file.

5. Click **Save**.

Remove Properties

1. Click the **Windows Explorer** button on the taskbar, and then locate the file in which you want to remove properties.

2. Select the file you want to remove properties.

3. Click the **Organize** button on the toolbar, and then click **Remove properties**.

4. Click the **Create a copy with all possible properties removed** option or click the **Remove the following properties from this file:** option.

5. Select or clear the check boxes for each property.

6. Click **OK**.

Creating and Renaming Files and Folders

The keys to organizing files and folders effectively within a hierarchy are to store related items together and to name folders informatively. Creating a new folder can help you organize and keep track of files and other folders. In order to create a folder, you select the location where you want the new folder, create the folder, and then lastly, name the folder. You should name each folder meaningfully so that just by reading the folder's name you know its contents. After you name a folder or file, you can rename it at any time.

Create a Folder

1. Open the drive or folder where you want to create a folder.

2. Click the **Organize** button on the toolbar, and then click **New folder**.

   TIMESAVER *Right-click a blank area of the window, and then click New folder.*

3. With the New Folder name selected, type a new name.

4. Press Enter.

Did You Know?

File names can be up to 255 characters. You can use spaces and underscores in names, but you can't use the following characters: @ * : < > | ? " \ or /. Remember the best way to keep your files organized is with a consistent naming convention.

Rename a File or Folder

1. Click the file or folder to select it.

2. Click the **Organize** button on the toolbar, and then click **Rename**.

3. With the name selected, type a new name, or click to position the insertion point, and then edit the name.

4. Press Enter.

TIMESAVER *Right-click the file or folder you want to rename, click Rename, type a name, and then press Enter. You can also select the file, click the file name, type a name, and then press Enter.*

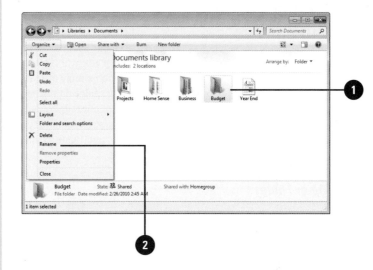

Did You Know?

You can rename a group of files. Select all the files you want to rename, right-click one of the selected files, click Rename from the shortcut menu, type a name, and then press Enter. The group name appears with numbers in consecutive order.

Copying and Moving Files and Folders

Sometimes you will need to move a file from one folder to another, or copy a file from one folder to another, leaving the file in the first location and placing a copy of it in the second. You can move or copy a file or folder using a variety of methods. If the file or folder and the location where you want to move it are visible in a window or on the desktop, you can simply drag the item from one location to the other. Moving a file or folder on the same disk relocates it whereas dragging it from one disk to another copies it so that it appears in both locations. When the destination folder or drive is not visible, you can use the Cut (to move), Copy, and Paste commands on the Edit menu to move or copy the items.

Copy a File or Folder

1. Open the drive or folder containing the file or folder you want to copy.

2. Select the files or folders you want to copy.

3. Click the **Organize** button on the toolbar, and then click **Copy**.

4. Display the destination folder where you want to copy the files or folder.

5. Click the **Organize** button on the toolbar, and then click **Paste**.

Did You Know?

You can arrange files and folders in an Explorer window by using Auto Arrange or Align to Grid. The Auto Arrange option keeps icons in a window organized so they don't overlap each other, while the Align to Grid option aligns icons in a window according an invisible grid to keep them organized. To turn either of these options on, click the View menu in folder you want to modify, and then click Auto Arrange or Align to Grid. To display the menu bar, click Organize on the toolbar, point to Layout, and then click Menu Bar.

For Your Information

Sending Files and Folders

When you right-click most objects on the desktop or in Computer or Windows Explorer, the Send To command, located on the shortcut menu, lets you send, or move, a file or folder to a new location on your computer. For example, you can send a file or folder to a removable disk to make a quick backup copy of the file or folder, to a mail recipient as an electronic message, or to the desktop to create a shortcut. You can also use the Send To command to move a file or folder from one folder to another. To send a file or folder, right-click the file or folder you want to send, point to Send To on the shortcut menu, and then click the destination you want.

Move a File or Folder

1. Open the drive or folder containing the file or folder you want to move.

2. Select the files or folders you want to move.

3. Click the **Organize** button on the toolbar, and then click **Cut**.

4. Display the destination folder where you want to move the files or folder.

5. Click the **Organize** button on the toolbar, and then click **Paste**.

Copy or Move a File or Folder Using Drag and Drop

1. Open the drive or folder containing the file or folder you want to copy or move.

2. Select the files or folders you want to copy or move.

3. In the Navigation pane, point to a folder list to display the expand and collapse arrows.

4. Click the arrows to display the destination folder, and then click the destination folder.

5. Right-click the selected files or folders, drag to the destination folder, and then click **Copy Here** or **Move Here**.

   TIMESAVER *To move the selected items, drag them to the destination folder. To copy the items, hold down the Ctrl key while you drag.*

Deleting and Restoring Files and Folders

When you organize the contents of a folder, disk, or the desktop, you might find files and folders that you no longer need. You can delete these items or remove them from the disk. If you delete a file or folder from the desktop or from the hard disk, it goes into the Recycle Bin. The **Recycle Bin**, located on your desktop, is a temporary storage area for deleted files. The Recycle Bin stores all the items you delete from your hard disk so that if you accidentally delete an item, you can remove it from the Recycle Bin to restore it. Be aware that if you delete a file from a removable disk, it is permanently deleted, not stored in the Recycle Bin. The files in the Recycle Bin do occupy room on your computer, so you need to empty it to free up space.

Delete Files and Folders

1 Select the files and folders you want to delete.

2 Click the **Organize** button on the toolbar, and then click **Delete**.

   TIMESAVER *Press the Delete key to delete selected items.*

3 Click **Yes** to confirm the deletion and place the items in the Recycle Bin.

4 On the desktop, right-click the **Recycle Bin** icon, and then click **Empty Recycle Bin**.

   Your computer permanently removes the items.

Recycle Bin icon

Restore Files and Folders

1 Double-click the **Recycle Bin** icon on the desktop.

2 Select the item or items you want to restore.

3 Click the **Restore this item** or **Restore all items** button on the toolbar.

4 Click **Yes** to confirm the restore or click **No** to cancel it.

Did You Know?

You can undo a deletion. If you accidentally delete a file, click Organize, and then click Undo Delete. Windows remembers your last three actions.

You can't open a deleted folder and restore selected items. When you've deleted a folder, you have to restore the entire folder.

For Your Information

Changing Recycle Bin Properties

You can adjust several Recycle Bin settings by using the Properties option on the Recycle Bin shortcut menu. For example, if you want to delete files immediately rather than place them in the Recycle Bin, right-click the Recycle Bin, click Properties, and then select the Don't Move Files To The Recycle Bin check box. Also, if you find that the Recycle Bin is full and cannot accept any more files, you can increase the amount of disk space allotted to the Recycle Bin by increasing the Maximum size (MB) amount.

Changing File and Folder List Views

You can display files and folders in a variety of different ways, depending on what you want to see and do. When you view files and folders in Details view, a default list of file and folder information appears, which consists of Name, Size, Type, and Date Modified. If the default list of file and folder details doesn't provide you with the information you need, you can add and remove any file and folder information from the Details view. If you need to change the way Windows sorts your files and folders, you can use the column indicator buttons in the right pane of Details view. Clicking one of the column indicator buttons, such as Name, Size, Type, or Date Modified, in Details view sorts the files and folders by the type of information listed in the column.

Change File Details to List

1. Open the folder you want to change in Details view.

2. Right-click a column title, and then click **More**, or click the **View** menu, and then click **Choose Details**.

   TIMESAVER *Right-click a column title in Details view, and then click the detail you want to show or hide.*

3. Select the check boxes with the details you want to include and clear the ones you don't.

4. Click the **Move Up** or **Move Down** buttons to change the order of the selected items.

5. Click the **Show** or **Hide** buttons to show or hide the selected items.

6. Specify the width in pixels of the column for the selected items.

7. Click **OK**.

Did You Know?

An ellipsis indicates information is hidden. To show the information, drag the edge of the column indicator button to resize the column.

Hiding Files and Folders

If you want to hide files and folders for added privacy purposes, you can do it by setting two separate options: one to set the option to hide specific files and folders, and the other to set a general folder option to show or hide files and folders. If you set the option to hide specific files and folders and the Show hidden files and folders option is set, the hidden files and folders appear transparent. If the general option is set to Do not show hidden files and folders, the hidden files and folders are actually hidden. The only way to view them again is to set the general option to Show hidden files and folders again. Anyone can show hidden files and folders, so it shouldn't be used for security purposes.

Show or Hide Hidden Files and Folders

1. Right-click the file or folder you want to hide or unhide, and then click **Properties**.

2. Select or clear the **Hidden** check box.

3. Click **OK**.

   The files or folders appear transparent or hidden.

Show or Hide Hidden Files and Folders

1. In an Explorer window, click the **Organize** button on the toolbar, and then click **Folder and search options**.

2. Click the **View** tab.

3. Click the **Do not show hidden files and folders** or **Show hidden files and folders** option.

4. To set the current view to all folders, click **Apply to Folders**.

5. Click **OK**.

Changing Folder Options

When you work with files and folders, Windows displays folder contents in a standard way, known as the **default**. The default folder view settings are as follows: Tiles view displays files and folders as icons; common task links appear in the left pane; folders open in the same window; and items open when you double-click them. Depending on previous installation or users, your folder view settings might differ. Instead of changing the folder view to your preferred view—Icons, List, or Details—each time you open a folder, you can change the view permanently to the one you prefer. In addition to the defaults, you can change options such as folder settings to show or hide file extensions for known file types, show or hide hidden files and folders, show or hide protected operating system files, and show pop-up descriptions of folders and desktop items. You can also set Navigation pane options to show all folders (**New!**) like the Folder list in Windows Vista and automatically expand the folder list to the current folder (**New!**).

Change Folder Options

1. In an Explorer window, click the **Organize** button on the toolbar, and then click **Folder and search options**.

2. Click the **General** tab.

3. Select a Browse folders option to display each folder in the same window or its own window.

4. Select a Click items as follows option to single-click or double-click items.

5. Select the Navigation pane (**New!**) check boxes option to **Show all folders** or **Automatically expand to current folder**.

6. Click **OK**.

Did You Know?

You can restore all folder options to default Windows settings. On the General tab in the Folder Options dialog box, click Restore Defaults.

Change the Folder View

① In an Explorer window, click the **Organize** button on the toolbar, and then click **Folder and search options**.

② Click the **View** tab.

③ To set the current view to all folders, click **Apply to Folders**.

④ Select the check boxes for the options you want, and clear the check boxes for the ones you don't. Some common options include:

♦ **Always show menus**.

♦ **Hidden files and folders**.

♦ **Hide extensions for known file types**.

♦ **Hide protected operating system files (Recommended)**.

♦ **Show encrypted or compressed NTFS files in color**.

♦ **Show pop-up description for folder and desktop items**.

⑤ Click **OK**.

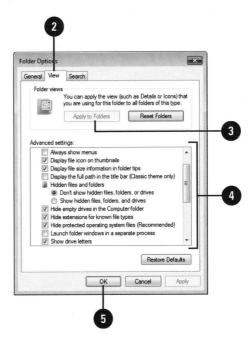

Did You Know?

You can reset folder views to original Windows settings. On the View tab in the Folder Options dialog box, click Reset Folders.

For Your Information

Understanding File Extensions

The program Windows uses to open a document depends on a three-letter extension to the document's file name, called a **file extension**. You might have never seen a document's file extension because your system might be set up to hide it. The file extension for simple text files is ".txt" (pronounced "dot t-x-t"), and many graphic files have the extension ".bmp". This means that the full name for a text file named Memo is Memo.txt. If you double-click a document whose file name ends with the three-letter extension ".txt," Windows automatically opens the document with Notepad, a text-only editor. If you want to display or change file extension settings, click the Start button, click Control Panel, click Appearance and Personalization, and then click Folder Options. If you want to display file extensions in dialog boxes and windows, click the View tab, and then clear the Hide Extensions For Known File Types check box in the Advanced settings list box. If you want to change the program Windows automatically starts with a given file extension, click the Start button, point to All Programs, click Default Programs, click Associate A File Type Or Protocol With A Program, select the file type, and then click Change Program to see the list of the file extensions Windows recognizes and the programs associated with each of them, and then make changes as appropriate.

Customizing Library Folders

In your library folders, you can customize view options based on the contents. In the toolbar of the Pictures and Music library folders, Windows provides buttons with file management activities specifically related to the contents of the folder, such as Slide Show in the Pictures library, or Play All in the Music library. The Arrange by options are also related to the folder contents, such as Rating in the Pictures library, or Artist in the Music library. When you create a new library folder, you can customize it for documents, pictures, music, and videos by applying a folder template (**New!**), which is a collection of folder tasks and viewing options. When you apply a template to a folder, you apply specific features to the folder, such as specialized tasks and viewing options for working with documents, pictures, music, and videos.

Customize a Library Folder

1 Open the library folder you want to change.

2 Click the **Organize** button on the toolbar, and then click **Properties**.

3 Click the **Optimize this library for** list arrow, and then select the type of folder you want: **General Items**, **Documents**, **Pictures**, **Videos**, or **Music**.

4 To show or hide the library in the Navigation pane, select or clear the **Shown in navigation pane** check box.

5 To restore library default settings for this folder, click **Restore Defaults**.

6 Click **OK**.

Customizing Personal Folders

In your personal folders, you can create your own folders and customize view options based on the contents. In the toolbar of the Pictures and Music folders, Windows provides buttons with file management activities specifically related to the contents of the folder, such as Slide Show in the Pictures folder, or Play All in the Music folders. When you create a new folder, you can customize it for documents, pictures, music, and videos by applying a folder template, which is a collection of folder tasks and viewing options. When you apply a template to a folder, you apply specific features to the folder, such as specialized tasks and viewing options for working with documents, pictures, music, and videos.

Customize a Folder

1. Open the folder you want to change.

2. Click the **Organize** button on the toolbar, and then click **Properties**.

3. Click the **Customize** tab for a folder.

4. Click the **Optimize this folder for** list arrow, and then select the type of folder you want: **General Items**, **Documents**, **Pictures**, **Videos**, or **Music**.

5. Select the **Also apply this template to all subfolders** check box to apply the option.

6. To select a picture for display on the folder icon, click **Choose File**.

7. To restore the default picture for the folder, click **Restore Default**.

8. Click **OK**.

> ### See Also
>
> See "Customizing the Taskbar" on page 118 for information on modifying the taskbar.

Sharing Folders or Files with Others

Windows 7 maintains a set of personal folders and options for everyone on your computer to make sure the contents of each user's personal folders remain private. The contents of your personal folders are private, unless you decide to share the contents with others who use your computer. If you want the other users on your computer to have access to files, you can place those files in a shared folder called the Public folder that each user can access. If you're connected to a network, the files in the public folder are available to network users. You can also share files from any folder on your computer that you want to designate as a shared folder to those connected to your network or Homegroup (**New!**), a shared network. When you specify a shared folder, you can also set access permission levels for a person or group. If you no longer want to share a folder, you can change the Share with option to Nobody (**New!**).

Share a File or Folders from the Public Folder

1. Open the drive or folder containing the files or folders you want to share.

2. Select the files or folders you want to share.

3. In the Navigation pane, point to a folder list to display the expand and collapse arrows.

   TIMESAVER *Click the Public link in the Navigation pane.*

4. Click the arrow next to the Public folder (Public Documents, Public Pictures, etc.) in a library to display the Public subfolders.

5. Drag the selected items onto the Public folder or subfolder where you want to share files.

See Also

See "Setting Network Sharing Options" on page 372 for information on controlling access to a public folder over a network.

Share or Unshare a Folder on Your Computer

1 Select the folders you want to share.

2 Click the **Share with** button on the toolbar, and then click **Specific people**.

◆ **Share with Homegroup.** Click the **Share with** button, and then click **Homegroup (Read)** or **Homegroup (Read/Write)**.

◆ **Unshare a folder.** Click the **Share with** button, and then click **Nobody**.

3 Do any of the following:

◆ Type the name of the person with whom you want to share files, and then click **Add**.

◆ Click the arrow to the right of the text box, click the person's name, and then click **Add**.

◆ Click the arrow to the right of the text box, and then click **Create a new user** to create a new user account.

4 Click the arrow next to the permission level for the person or group, and then select a sharing permission:

◆ **Read.** Allows viewing only.

◆ **Read/Write.** Allows viewing, adding, changing, and deleting all files.

◆ **Remove.** Deletes the current permission setting.

5 Click **Share**, and then wait while Windows sets up sharing.

6 If you want, click the e-mail or copy link to notify people you have shared this folder and files.

7 Otherwise, click **Done**.

Click to unshare a folder

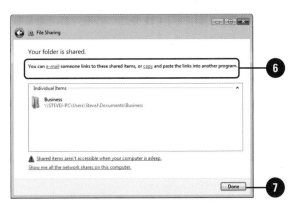

Compressing Files and Folders

You can compress files in special folders that use compressing software to decrease the size of the files they contain. Compressed folders are useful for reducing the file size of one or more large files, thus freeing disk space and reducing the time it takes to transfer files to another computer over the Internet or network. A compressed folder is denoted by a zippered folder icon. You can compress one or more files in a compressed folder by simply dragging them onto the compressed folder icon. When a file is compressed, a copy is used in the compression, and the original remains intact. You can uncompress, or extract, a file from the compressed folder and open it as you normally would, or you can open a file directly from the compressed folder by double-clicking the Compressed File icon. When you open a file directly, Windows extracts the file when it opens and compresses it again when it closes.

Compress Files and Folders

1. Select the files and folders you want to copy to a compressed folder.

2. Right-click one of the selected items, point to **Send to**, and then click **Compressed (zipped) folder**.

3. If you want, rename the compressed folder.

4. To copy additional files or folders to the compressed folder, drag the files onto the compressed folder.

Did You Know?

You can also compress file attributes in a folder. Right-click the folder, click Properties, click the General tab, click Advanced, select the Compress Contents To Save Disk Space check box, and then click OK twice.

Compressed folder

View Compressed Files

1 Double-click the compressed folder to open it.

2 Double-click an item in the folder to open it using its associated program.

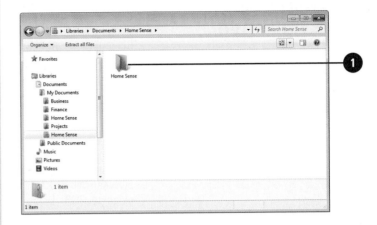

Uncompress Files and Folders

◆ **Individual files or folders.** Double-click the compressed folder to open it, select the files and folders you want to uncompress, and then drag the selection from the compressed folder to a new location in an uncompressed folder.

◆ **All files.** Right-click the compressed folder, and then click **Extract all**, and then step through the Extraction Wizard.

Double-click to open and decompress files and folders

Click to extract all files

Managing Files Using a CD or DVD

The low cost and large storage size of discs, either CD or DVD, makes creating and using CDs or DVDs an effective way to back up information or transfer large amounts of information to another computer without a network. Before you can create a CD or DVD, you must have a blank writable CD or DVD and a recorder (also known as a writer or burner) installed on your computer. You can copy, or write, files and folders to either a writable disc (CD-R or DVD-R) or a rewriteable disc (CD-RW or DVD-RW). With writable discs, you can read and write files and folders many times, but you can't erase them. With rewriteable discs, you can read, write, and erase files and folders many times, just like a hard disk. When you burn a disc, Windows needs disk space on your hard disk equal to the capacity of the disc. For a typical CD, this is between 650 and 740 megabytes (MB) and for a DVD, this is about 4.7 gigabytes (GB). Do not copy more files and folders to the CD or DVD than it will hold; anything beyond the limit will not copy. You can burn a disc using one of two formats: Live File System or Mastered. The **Live File System** format (*Like a USB flash drive* option) allows you to copy files to a disc at any time, while the **Mastered** format (*With a CD/DVD player* option) needs to copy them all at once. If you need a disc for Windows XP or later and want the convenience of copying files at any time, the Live File System is the best choice. When you need a compatible disc for older computers, the Mastered format is the better choice.

Burn a Disc Using the Mastered Format

1. Insert a writable CD or DVD into your CD or DVD recorder.

2. Click **Burn files to disc**.

3. Type a name for the disc.

4. Click the **With a CD/DVD player** option.

5. Click **Next** to continue.

6. Open the folder that contains the files you want to burn, and then drag the files onto the empty disc folder.

7. Click **Burn to disc** on the toolbar.

   The selected files are copied to the disc. The disc recorder tray opens when the disc is complete.

Burn a Disc Using the Live System Format

1. Insert a writable CD or DVD into your CD or DVD recorder.

2. Click **Burn files to disc**.

3. Type a name for the disc.

4. Click the **Like a USB flash drive** option.

5. Click **Next** to continue.

   Windows names, formats, and prepares the disc for use.

6. Upon completion, open the folder with the files you want to burn.

7. Drag the files into the disc folder.

   As you drag files into the disc folder, they are copied automatically to the disc.

8. To close the session and prepare the disc for use, display the disc folder, click the **Eject** button or **Close session** button on the toolbar.

   After you close a session, you can still add files to the disc. However, you need to close the session.

Did You Know?

You can erase some or all of the files on a disc. Insert the writable disc with the Live File System format, click the Start button, click Computer, click the writable drive, and then click Erase This Disc on the toolbar to erase all the files. Double-click the writable drive, select the files you want to delete, and then press Delete.

Live File System Versions

Version	Compatible with
1.02	Windows 98 and many Apple Computers; also works if you need to format DVD-RAM or MO (Magneto-optical) discs
1.5	Windows 2000, Windows XP, and Windows Server 2003
2.01	Windows XP and Windows Server 2003
2.5	The latest version of Windows; Windows Vista or Windows 7

Creating a Shortcut to a File or Folder

It could take you a while to access a file or folder buried several levels down in a file hierarchy. To save some time, you can create shortcuts to the items you use frequently. A **shortcut** is a link that you can place in any location to gain instant access to a particular file, folder, or program on your hard disk or on a network just by double-clicking. The actual file, folder, or program remains stored in its original location, and you place an icon representing the shortcut in a convenient location, such as in a folder or on the desktop.

Create a Shortcut to a File or Folder

1. Open the drive or folder containing the file or folder in which you want to create a shortcut.

2. Right-click the file or folder, and then click **Create shortcut.**

3. To change the shortcut's name, right-click the shortcut, click **Rename** from the shortcut menu, type a new name, and then press Enter.

4. Drag the shortcut to the desired location.

For Your Information

Placing Shortcuts on the Start Menu and Taskbar

You can place shortcuts to frequently used files, folders, and programs on the Start menu or toolbar on the taskbar. To do this, simply drag the shortcut file, folder, or program to the Start button, wait until the Start menu opens, drag to the All Programs submenu, wait until the submenu opens, and then drag the shortcut to the appropriate place on the menu. You can also drag a shortcut to a toolbar on the taskbar using the same method. When you release the mouse, the item appears on the menu or toolbar.

Customizing Windows Using the Control Panel

4

Introduction

Windows 7 gives you the ability to customize your work environment to suit your personal needs and preferences. You can adjust most Windows features through the Control Panel, a central location for changing Windows settings. From the **Control Panel** you access the individual programs for changing the **properties**, or characteristics, of a specific element of your computer, such as the desktop, the taskbar, or the Start menu. The Control Panel displays utilities in two different views: Category and Small or Large Icons (**New!**). Control Panel Category view displays utilities in functional categories based on tasks with some direct links, while Small or Large Icons view displays an icon for each utility program. Each icon in the Control Panel represents an aspect of Windows that you can change to fit your own working habits and personal needs. Some Control Panel settings are vital to how you work (such as the Date and Time, or the Language settings) and others are purely aesthetic (such as the background picture). This book uses the most efficient way to access Control Panel properties.

The Control Panel also includes icons to setup user accounts and maintain security (see Chapter 11), and setup and manage local-area, wide-area, and wireless networks (see Chapter 12). You can access printers and faxes (see Chapter 13), add and remove programs and automatically update Windows (see Chapter 14). You can also work with hardware, such as a scanner, digital camera, modem, audio and speakers, mouse, and keyboard (see Chapter 15).

If an option—typically in the Control Panel—displays the Security icon next to it (shown on page 110 in Step 4), you need to enter the administrator password or provide confirmation when prompted by the User Account Control (UAC). This adds an additional level of security to keep your computer secure. For more information, see page 310, "Securing a Computer."

What You'll Do

View the Control Panel

Change the Desktop Background

Customize the Desktop and Windows Sidebar

Use a Screen Saver

Change the Display

Use Multiple Monitors

Change the Desktop Appearance

Set the Date and Time

Change Regional and Language Options

Work with Fonts

Display and Arrange Toolbars

Customize the Taskbar and Start Menu

Change the Way a CD or DVD Starts

Use the Ease of Access Tools

Use the Ease of Access Center

Listen to the Computer

Recognize Your Speech

Viewing the Control Panel

The Control Panel is a collection of utility programs that determine how Windows 7 looks and works on your computer. The Control Panel displays utilities in two different views (**New!**): Category and Small or Large Icons. Control Panel Category view displays utilities in functional categories based on tasks with some direct links, while Small or Large Icons view displays an icon for each utility program as in previous versions of Windows. You can change views by using the View by button in the Control Panel. If you're not sure where an option is located, you can search for it by using the Search box in the Control Panel.

View the Control Panel

1. Click the **Start** button, and then click **Control Panel**.

2. Click the **View by** button, and then click a view: **Category**, **Small icons**, or **Large icons**.

3. Click a Control Panel link or icon.

4. Click the **Back** button (when available) on the toolbar to return to the previous Control Panel screen.

Search for Options in the Control Panel

1. Click the **Start** button, and then click **Control Panel**.

2. Click in the Search box.

3. Type a word or phrase related to the option you want.

4. Click a Control Panel link or icon in the list of results.

5. Click the **Back** button (when available) on the toolbar to return to the previous Control Panel screen.

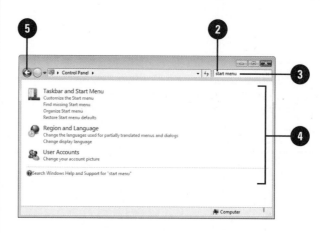

Changing the Desktop Background

The desktop **background**, or wallpaper, is a picture that serves as your desktop's backdrop, the basic surface on which icons and windows appear. You can select one or more background pictures (**New!**) and change how it looks using the Desktop Background dialog box. If you select more than one picture, you can set a change picture interval in to display them in order or shuffle them (**New!**). Once you select a background picture, you can display it on the screen five different ways: Fill, Fit, Stretch, Tile, or Center. Instead of selecting a background picture, which can sometimes make icons on the desktop difficult to see, you can also change the background to a color.

Select a Desktop Background

1. Right-click a blank area on the desktop, and then click **Personalize**.

2. Click **Desktop Background**.

3. Click the **Picture location** list arrow and select a location, or click **Browse**, select a picture in the location you want, and then click **Open**. The default picture locations include:

   ◆ **Windows Desktop Backgrounds.**

   ◆ **Pictures Library.**

   ◆ **Top Rated Photos.**

   ◆ **Solid Colors.**

4. Point to a pictures, and then select the check box next next to it.

5. If you select more than one picture, select a **Change picture every** interval, the **Shuffle** check box, or the **When using battery power, pause the slide show to save power** check box.

6. Select the **Picture position** button, and then select the option you want: **Fill**, **Fit**, **Stretch**, **Tile**, or **Center**.

7. Click **Save changes**.

8. Click the **Close** button.

Customizing the Desktop

The icons on the desktop provide easy access to programs, folders, and system related shortcuts. If your desktop is getting cluttered, you can quickly show or hide the desktop icons. In addition, you can customize the desktop to show or hide the familiar icons: Computer, User's Files, Network, Recycle Bin, or Control Panel. You can also quickly sort, resize, and rearrange desktop icons by right-clicking the desktop, and then using commands on the View and Sort By submenus.

Display or Hide Desktop Icons

1. Right-click a blank area on the desktop, and then click **Personalize**.

   TIMESAVER *To show or hide all desktop icons, right-click the desktop, point to View, and then click Show Desktop Icons.*

2. In the left pane, click **Change desktop icons**.

3. Select or clear the check boxes to show or hide desktop icons.

4. To change the appearance of an icon, select the icon, click **Change Icon**, select an icon, and then click **OK**.

5. Click **OK**.

6. Click the **Close** button.

Did You Know?

You can resize desktop icons. Right-click the desktop, point to View, and then click Large Icons, Medium Icons, or Small Icons.

You can arrange desktop icons. The Auto Arrange Icons option keeps icons organized so they don't overlap each other, while the Align Icons To Grid option aligns icons in a window according an invisible grid to keep them organized. Right-click the desktop, point to View, and then click Auto Arrange Icons or Align To Icons Grid.

Customize the Desktop Appearance

◆ **Resize desktop icons.** Right-click a blank area on the desktop, point to **View**, and then click **Large Icons**, **Medium Icons**, or **Small Icons**.

◆ **Auto arrange icons.** The Auto arrange icons option keeps icons organized so they don't overlap each other. Right-click a blank area on the desktop, point to **View**, and then click **Auto arrange icons**. (the option toggles on and off)

◆ **Align icons to grid.** The Align icons to grid option aligns icons in a window according an invisible grid to keep them organized. Right-click a blank area on the desktop, point to **View**, and then click **Auto arrange icons**. (the option toggles on and off)

◆ **Show or hide desktop icons.** Right-click a blank area on the desktop, point to **View**, and then click **Show desktop icons**. (the option toggles on and off)

◆ **Show or hide desktop gadgets.** (**New!**) Right-click a blank area on the desktop, point to **View**, and then click **Show desktop gadgets**. (the option toggles on and off)

◆ **Sort desktop items.** Right-click a blank area on the desktop, point to **Sort by**, and then select an option.

◆ **Show the next desktop background.** (**New!**) With multiple backgrounds selected, right-click a blank area on the desktop, and then click **Next desktop background**.

Desktop view options

Next desktop background   Sort by options

Using a Screen Saver

In the past, you needed a screen saver, a continually moving display, to protect your monitor from burn in, which occurs when the same display remains on the screen for extended periods of time and becomes part of the screen. Those days are gone with the emergence of new display technology. Screen savers are more for entertainment than anything else. When you leave your computer idle for a specified wait time, a screen saver displays a continuous scene, such as an aquarium, until you move your mouse to stop it.

Select a Screen Saver

1. Right-click a blank area on the desktop, and then click **Personalize**.

2. Click **Screen Saver**.

3. Click the list arrow, and then click a screen saver.

4. Click **Settings**.

5. Select the options you want for the screen saver, and then click **OK**.

6. Click **Preview** to see the screen saver in full-screen view, and then move your mouse to end the preview.

7. Specify the time to wait until your computer starts the screen saver.

8. Select or clear the **On resume, display logon screen** check box.

9. Click **OK**.

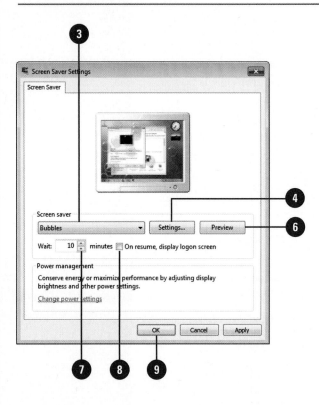

Did You Know?

You can turn off a screen saver. On the Screen Saver tab, click (None) from the Screen Saver list arrow.

Changing the Display

If you find yourself frequently scrolling within windows as you work or squinting to read small text, you might want to change the size of the desktop on your monitor. A monitor displays pictures by dividing the display screen into thousands or millions of dots, or pixels, arranged in rows and columns. The pixels are so close together that they appear connected. The **screen resolution** refers to the number of pixels on the entire screen, which determines the amount of information your monitor displays. A low screen resolution setting, such as 640 by 480 pixels (width by height), displays less information on the screen, but the items on the screen appear relatively large, while a high setting, such as 1024 by 768 pixels, displays more information on the screen, but the items on the screen appear smaller. You can also change the screen orientation (Landscape, Portrait, or flipped) (**New!**) and color quality. The higher the color quality, the more colors the computer displays, which requires greater system memory. The most common color quality settings are as follows: 16-bit, which displays 768 colors, and 24-bit and 32-bit, both of which display 16.7 million colors.

Change the Display Size

1. Right-click a blank area on the desktop, and then click **Screen resolution**.

2. Click the **Display** button, and then click a display.

3. Click the **Resolution** button, and then click a screen size.

4. Click the **Orientation** list arrow, and then click an orientation option (**New!**).

5. To change color quality, click the **Advanced settings** link, click the **Monitor** tab, select a color setting, and then click **OK**.

   ◆ To eliminate flicker, click the **Advanced settings** link, click the **Monitor** tab, increase the screen refresh rate, and then click **OK**.

6. Click **OK**.

7. If a message alert appears, click **Keep changes** or **Revert** to accept or decline the new settings.

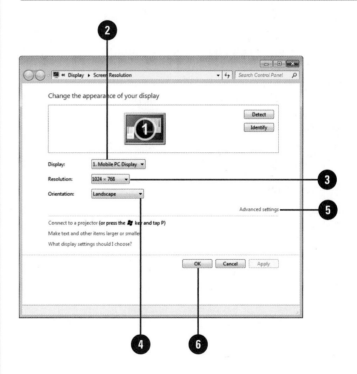

Using Multiple Monitors

You can increase the size of your workspace on the desktop and your productivity by adding another monitor to your computer. For example, you can work on a document in WordPad on one monitor and search for web content in your web browser on the other monitor. One monitor is the primary monitor, which displays the dialog boxes that appear when you start your computer and most programs; the other monitor is the secondary monitor, which displays windows, icons, and programs you drag to it from the primary monitor. Before you can use more than one monitor, you need to install another **display adapter**, a hardware device that allows a computer to communicate with its monitor, on your computer that supports multiple monitors. After you install the display adapter according to the manufacturer's instructions and restart the computer, Windows automatically detects the new device and applied the video settings best suited to the display. Right-click a blank area on the desktop, click Screen resolution, click Detect to discover the new monitor, click the Multiple displays button (**New!**), click a multiple display option, click the monitor icon that represents the primary monitor that you want to use, select the Make this my main display check box, click Apply, and then click Keep changes. To arrange multiple monitors, click the monitor icons and drag them in the preview window to the positions you want. You can set different screen resolutions and color settings for each monitor. See "Adding a Secondary Monitor" on page 462 for more information on using multiple monitors.

Using a Projector

If you're using a projector as an additional monitor, you can select display settings (**New!**) in the Screen Resolution window or on the Start menu. In the Screen Resolution window, click the Connect to a project link, and then select an option: Computer only, Duplicate, Extend, or Projector only, or click the Start menu, point to All Programs, click Accessories, and then click Connect to a Projector.

Selected monitor

Multiple monitors

Select to extend desktop

Changing Text Size on the Screen

If text and other items, such as icons, on the screen are not large enough for you to comfortably view, you can customize the screen to display items larger. Windows 7 allows you to increase the screen scaling option (**New!**), known as the Dots Per Inch (DPI) scale, which is the number of dots that a device can display or print per linear inch. The greater the number, of dots per inch, the better the resolution. DPI is a standard measurement used to specify screen and printer resolution. The Smaller - 100% option is the default screen scale setting (96 DPI). If you want to make items on the screen larger, select the Medium - 125% or Larger - 150% option. After you change the screen scale option, you need to log off and restart Windows to see the change.

Change the Screen Scaling Options

1. Right-click a blank area on the desktop, and then click **Screen resolution**.

2. Click the **Make text and other items larger or smaller** link.

3. Click the **Smaller - 100% (default)**, or **Medium - 125%**, or **Larger - 150%** option (**New!**).

4. To adjust the DPI setting, click **Set custom text size** in the left pane, specify a scale percentage with a DPI, and then click **OK**.

5. Click **Apply**.

   To see the changes, close all of your programs, and log off Windows.

6. If a message alert appears, click **Log off now** or **Log off later** to log off now or later.

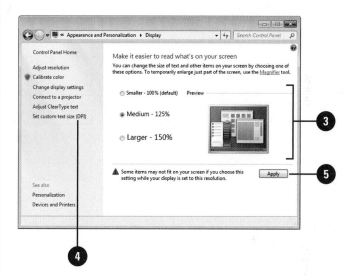

For Your Information

What's ClearType

ClearType is a font technology that improves the display on a computer monitor. ClearType makes on-screen text more clear, smooth, and detailed, which can reduce eye strain. ClearType is turned on by default in Windows. This is useful and most effective when you use LCD (Liquid Crystal Displays) devices, including flat-panel monitors, mobile computers, and smaller hand-held devices. ClearType is optimized for use with some fonts, including Constantia, Cambria, Corbel, Candara, Calibri, and Consolas. To set the ClearType setting, open the Control Panel, click Appearance and Personalization, click Make text and other items larger or smaller link, click Adjust ClearType text in the left pane, select the Turn On ClearType check box, click Next, and then follow the on-screen instructions.

Changing the Desktop Appearance

You can change the entire appearance of the desktop by using desktop themes. A desktop **theme** changes the desktop background, screen saver, mouse pointers, sounds, icons, and fonts based on a set theme, such as baseball, science, sports, travel, or underwater. You can even change your desktop to the classic Windows look. You can use one of the predefined desktop themes or create your own (**New!**). If a theme isn't exactly what you want, you can change the appearance of colors, fonts, and sizes used for major window elements such as title bars, icons, menus, borders, and the desktop itself. The theme options differ depending on the theme type, either basic or aero. An aero theme allows you to change color intensity and transparency.

Select a Desktop Theme

1. Right-click a blank area on the desktop, and then click **Personalize**.

2. Click a theme in the list.

   ◆ **Get more themes.** In the Theme list, click the **Get more themes online** link, and then follow the on-screen instructions to download the themes to your computer.

Did You Know?

You can save a theme. In the Theme list, create a custom theme by selecting a desktop background, Window color, sound, or screen saver, click Save theme (under My Themes), name the theme, specify a location, and then click Save.

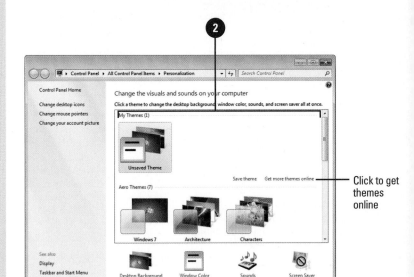

Click to get themes online

Customize the Desktop Appearance

1. Right-click a blank area on the desktop, and then click **Personalize**.

2. Select the theme you want to customize.

3. Click **Window Color**.

4. Make the changes you want based on the type of theme you selected:

   ◆ **Basic theme.** Select an item in the display, and then change the color, size, or font for individual items for a basic Windows color scheme.

   ◆ **Aero theme.** Select a color (**New!**), select or clear the **Enable transparency** check box, drag the **Color intensity** slider, and then use the color mixer to make any color adjustments.

5. Click **OK** or **Save changes**.

Basic theme options

5 Basic

Aero theme options

5 Aero

Setting the Date and Time

The date and time you set in the Control Panel appear in the lower-right corner of the taskbar. When you click or hover over the taskbar clock, the data appears. Programs use the date and time to establish when files and folders are created and modified. To change the date and time, you modify settings in the Date and Time dialog box. When you modify the time, it's important to also verify or update the time zone setting in the Time Zone Settings dialog box, which is used to accurately display creation and modification dates in a different time zone. With an Internet connection, you can set options on the Internet tab to make sure the time is accurate. If you need to know the time in other time zones, you can display additional clocks, which you can display by clicking or hovering over the taskbar clock.

Change the Date or Time

1 Click the time on the taskbar in the notification area, and then click **Change date and time settings**.

2 Click the **Date and Time** tab.

3 If needed, click **Change time zone**, click the list arrow, select a time zone, and then select or clear the **Automatically adjust clock for Daylight Saving Changes** check box, and then click **OK**.

4 Click **Change date and time**.

5 Click the date arrows to select the month and year.

6 Click a day, and then specify a time.

7 Click **OK**.

8 Click **OK**.

Keep the Time Accurate

1. Click the time on the taskbar in the notification area, and then click **Change date and time settings**.

2. Click the **Internet Time** tab.

3. Click **Change settings**.

4. Select the **Synchronize with an Internet time server** check box.

5. Click the **Server** list arrow, and then click a time server.

6. Click **Update now**, and then wait for the time to update.

7. Click **OK**.

8. Click **OK**.

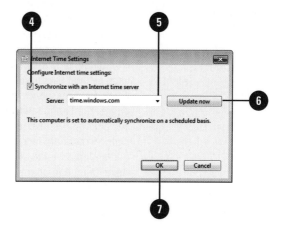

Add Clocks

1. Click the time on the taskbar in the notification area, and then click **Change date and time settings**.

2. Click the **Additional Clocks** tab.

3. Select the **Show this clock** check box.

4. Click the **Select time zone** list arrow, and then select a time zone.

5. Type a name.

6. If you want another clock, perform steps 3 through 5 for Clock 2.

7. Click **OK**.

Changing Language Options

You can also install multiple input languages on your computer and easily switch between them. An **input language** is the language in which you enter and display text. When you install additional languages on your computer, the language for the operating system doesn't change, only the characters you type on the screen. Each language uses its own keyboard layout, which rearranges the letters that appear when you press keys. When you install Text services or another language, the Language Bar toolbar appears on your desktop and in the Toolbars menu. Text services are text-related add-on programs for a second keyboard layout, handwriting recognition, speech recognition, and an Input Method Editor (IME), which is a system that lets you input Asian language characters with a standard 101-keyboard. You can switch between different language keyboard layouts using the Language bar or keyboard shortcuts.

Change Text Services and Input Languages

1. Click the **Start** button, click **Control Panel**, and then click the **Regional and Language** icon in Small icons or Large icons view.

2. Click the **Keyboards and Languages** tab, and then click **Change keyboards**.

3. Click the **Language** list arrow, and then click a language to use when you start your computer.

4. Click **Add** to add an input language.

5. Select an input language, and then click **Remove** to delete it, or click **Properties** to modify it.

6. Click the **Language Bar** tab to change the look and behavior of the Language bar.

7. Click the **Advanced Key Settings** tab to define keyboard shortcuts to switch between input language.

8. Click **OK**.

9. Click **OK**.

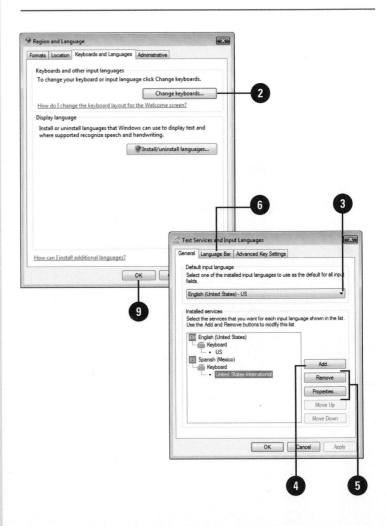

Change the Language Bar Settings

① Click the **Start** button, click **Control Panel**, and then click the **Regional and Language** icon in Small icons or Large icons view.

② Click the **Keyboards and Languages** tab.

③ Click **Change Keyboards**.

④ Click the **Language Bar** tab.

⑤ Select the options you want.

⑥ Click **OK**, and then click **OK** again.

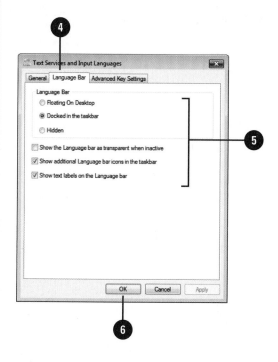

Use the Language Bar

◆ To switch languages, click the **Language bar**, and then click a language.

◆ To change Language bar settings, click the **Options** button (small white arrow) or right-click the **Language bar**, and then click an option, such as transparency, vertical (orientation), and minimize.

◆ To change Text Services and Input Languages, right-click the **Language bar**, and then click **Settings**.

Language bar options

Languages

Language bar

Changing Regional Options

For those who work in international circles, you can change the format of the date, time, currency, and number into almost any form. For example, you can change the decimal symbol and list separator, the format used for negative numbers and leading zeros, and the measurement system (U.S. or metric).

Change the Display for Dates, Times, Currency, and Numbers

1. Click the **Start** button, click **Control Panel**, and then click the **Regional and Language** icon in Small icons or Large icons view.

2. Click the **Formats** tab.

3. Click the **Format** list arrow, and then click a locale with the settings you want.

4. Click the buttons to select the date and time formats you want.

5. Click **Additional settings** to change individual settings.

6. Select the format options you want on the different tabs.

7. Click **OK**.

8. Click **OK**.

Did You Know?

You can change regional format by language and country. On the Location tab, click the Current language list arrow, and then click a language.

See Also

See "Changing Language Options" on page 112 for information on working with different languages.

x

Working with Fonts

Everything you type appears in a **font**, or typeface, a particular design set of letters, numbers, and other characters. The height of characters in a font is measured in points, each point being approximately 1/72 inch, while the width is measured by **pitch**, which refers to how many characters can fit in an inch. You might have heard common font names, such as Times New Roman, Arial, Courier, or Symbol. Windows comes with a variety of fonts for displaying text and printing documents. Using the Fonts window, you can view these fonts, see a sample of how a font appears when printed, and even install new fonts.

View or Install Fonts

1. Click the **Start** button, click **Control Panel**, and then click the **Fonts** icon in Small icons or Large icons view.

   The currently installed fonts on your computer appears in the Fonts window.

2. To install a font, drag the font into the Fonts window in the Control panel (**New!**).

   ◆ You can also right-click the font, and then click **Install**.

3. To delete a font, select the font, and then click the **Delete** button on the toolbar.

   ◆ To select more than one font, hold down the Ctrl key while you click each font.

4. To show and hide fonts based on language settings, install fonts using a shortcut, or restore default font settings, click **Font settings** in the left pane (**New!**).

5. Click the **Close** button.

See Also

See "Formatting Text" on page 34 for information on using fonts.

For Your Information

What's the Difference Between the Fonts?

Everything you type appears in a font, a particular typeface design and size for letters, numbers, and other characters. Usually, each typeface, such as Times New Roman, is made available in four variations: normal, bold, italic, and bold italic. There are two basic types of fonts: scalable and bitmapped. A **scalable font** (also known as **outline font**) is based on a mathematical equation that creates character outlines to form letters and numbers of any size. The two major scalable fonts are Adobe's Type 1 PostScript and Apple/Microsoft's TrueType or OpenType. Scalable fonts are generated in any point size on the fly and require only four variations for each typeface. A **bitmapped font** consists of a set of dot patterns for each letter and number in a typeface for a specified type size. Bitmapped fonts are created or prepackaged ahead of time and require four variations for each point size used in each typeface. Although a bitmapped font designed for a particular font size will always look the best, scalable fonts eliminate storing hundreds of different sizes of fonts on a disk.

Displaying and Arranging Toolbars

Toolbars provide easy access to commonly used tasks. Windows 7 comes with a set of toolbars you can use to access programs, folders, documents, and web pages right from the taskbar. You can rearrange, resize, and move the toolbars to compliment your working style. When you move a toolbar, you can attach or dock it, to any of the sides on the desktop or you can float it in a window anywhere within the desktop.

Show or Hide a Toolbar

1. Right-click a blank area on the taskbar.

2. Point to **Toolbars**, and then click a toolbar without a check mark.

   A toolbar with a check mark is already displayed.

Did You Know?

You can display hidden buttons on a toolbar. Click the double-arrow at the end of the toolbar.

You can display buttons on the taskbar. Click the up or down arrow on the taskbar to scroll through the taskbar buttons.

You can also show or hide toolbars using the Taskbar and Start Menu Properties dialog box. Right-click the taskbar, click Properties, click the Toolbars tab, select or clear the toolbar check boxes, and then click OK.

See Also

See "Customizing the Taskbar" on page 118 for information on modifying the taskbar.

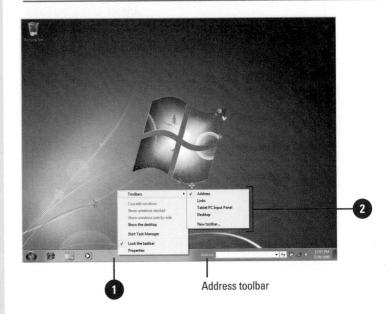

Address toolbar

Toolbars on the Taskbar

Toolbar	Description
Address	Opens web pages, network locations, files, and folders using the Address bar from Internet Explorer
Links	Opens links using the Links toolbar from Internet Explorer
Tablet PC Input Panel	Opens the Table PC Input Panel to use ink as an input device
Desktop	Opens windows to files, folders, and shortcuts on the desktop
New Toolbar	Adds a new toolbar to Windows

Unlock or Lock the Taskbar

1. Right-click a blank area on the taskbar.

2. Click **Lock the taskbar**.

   ◆ Toolbars on the taskbar are locked when a check mark is displayed.

   ◆ Toolbars on the taskbar are unlocked when a check mark isn't displayed.

Move a Toolbar

1. Right-click a blank area on the taskbar, and then click **Lock the taskbar** to remove the check mark, if necessary.

2. Point to the dotted bar or name of the toolbar, and then drag it to a new location on the desktop docked to the side or floating in the middle.

Did You Know?

You can resize a toolbar. Unlock the taskbar, and then drag the small vertical bar at the beginning of the toolbar.

You can expand or collapse a toolbar. Unlock the taskbar, and then double-click the small vertical bar at the beginning of the toolbar.

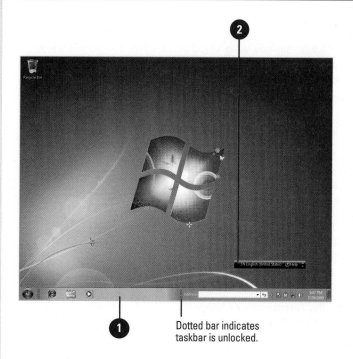

Dotted bar indicates taskbar is unlocked.

Customizing the Taskbar

The taskbar is initially located at the bottom of the Windows desktop and is most often used to switch from one program to another. As with other Windows 7 elements, you can customize the taskbar; for example, you can change its size and location, customize its display, or add or remove toolbars to help you perform the tasks you need to do. If you need more room on the screen to display a window, Auto-hide can be used to hide the taskbar when it's not in use. You can also combine similar windows (such as several WordPad documents) together on the taskbar to save space (**New!**). If icons in the notification area are hidden when you want to see them, you can customize the notification area to always show the icons and notifications (**New!**) you want to use. In addition, you can also choose whether to show or hide common system icons, including Clock, Volume, Network, Power, and Action Center (**New!**).

Customize the Taskbar

1. Right-click a blank area on the taskbar, and then click **Properties**.

2. Click the **Taskbar** tab.

3. Select the **Auto-hide the taskbar** check box to hide the taskbar when you're not using it.

   The taskbar appears when you move the mouse to where the taskbar would appear.

4. Select the **Use small icons** check box to display small icons on the taskbar.

5. Click the **Taskbar location on screen** button (**New!**), and then select a taskbar location: **Bottom**, **Left**, **Right**, or **Top**.

   ◆ You can also drag a taskbar. Unlock the taskbar, and then drag a blank area on the taskbar to a new location on any side of the desktop.

6. Click the **Taskbar buttons** button (**New!**), and then select a combine option: **Always combine, hide labels** (default), **Combine when taskbar is full**, or **Never combine**.

7. Click **OK**.

Customize the Notification Area

1. Right-click a blank area on the taskbar, and then click **Properties**.

2. Click the **Taskbar** tab.

3. Click **Customize**.

   ◆ You can also click the **Show hidden icons** button in the notification area, and then click **Customize**.

4. To shows all icons and notifications in the notification area, select the **Always show all icons and notifications on the taskbar** check box.

5. Specify the behaviors you want for the icons and notifications on the taskbar (**New!**):

   ◆ **Show icon and notifications.**

   ◆ **Hide icon and notifications.**

   ◆ **Only show notifications.**

6. To show or hide system icons on the notification area, click the **Turn system icons on or off** link, select **On** or **Off** for the system icons, and then click **OK**.

7. Click **OK**.

8. Click **OK**.

Did You Know?

You can show and hide icons by dragging them in the notification. (**New!**) To show hidden icons, click the Show Hidden Icons button in the notification area, drag a hidden icon to the notification area. To hide an icon, drag an icon to the Show Hidden Icons button, and then to the top of the menu.

Default desktop icons

Customizing the Start Menu

The left column of the Start menu is separated into two lists: pinned items above the separator line and most frequently used items below. The pinned items remain on the Start menu, like a push pin holds paper on a bulletin board, until you unpin them. The right column of the Start menu provides easy access to folders, Windows settings, help information, and search functionality. The Power button (**New!**) on the Start menu shuts down your computer by default. However, you can customize the button to another power option, such as switch user, log off, lock, restart, sleep, or hibernate. You can add shortcuts to programs, files, or folders to the Start menu or customize the way the Start menu looks and functions.

Pin or Unpin a Program on the Start Menu

1. Click the **Start** button, and then locate a program.

2. To pin a program, right-click the program, and then click **Pin to Start Menu**.

3. To unpin a program, right-click a pinned program on the Start menu, and then click **Unpin from Start Menu**.

4. To remove a program or item from the Start menu, right-click a program on the Start menu, and then click **Remove from this list**.

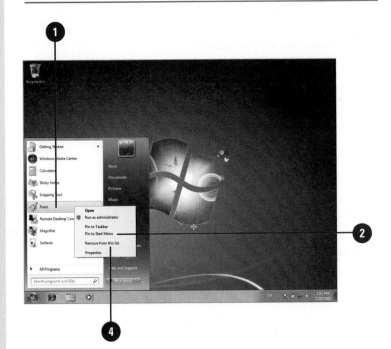

Did You Know?

You can rearrange Start menu items. Click the Start button, point to All Programs, locate the item you want to move, and then drag the item to a new location. A thick, black line indicates the new location of the item.

You can add a shortcut to an item to the Start menu. Right-click the item, point to Send To, and then click Desktop. Drag the shortcut from the Desktop onto the Start button, and then drag it to a new location on the All Programs submenu.

Customize the Start Menu

1 Right-click the **Start** button, and then click **Properties**.

2 Click **Customize**.

3 Select check boxes and click options to specify the items you want (as a menu or link) or don't want included on the Start menu.

4 Click the up or down arrow to specify the number of recently used programs on the Start menu.

5 Click **OK**.

6 To change the Power button, click the **Power button action** button, and then select an option (**New!**).

7 Select or clear the Privacy check boxes to store and display a list of recently opened files or programs.

When you clear these check boxes, Windows clears recently opened files or programs from the Start menu.

8 Click **OK**.

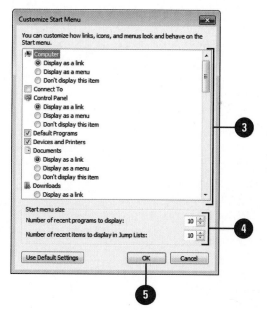

Setting Default Programs

When you double-click an audio or video file, or click a web link, a default program associated with that file type automatically starts and opens the file. The Default Programs icon in the Control Panel provides an easy way to change the default program used for specific file types. You can change file types, such as .bmp or .jpg, and set file associations for common activities, such as web browsing, sending e-mail, playing audio and video files, sending instant messaging, and using a search application, either Windows Search Explorer or a third-party one, such as Google Desktop Search. You can also specify which programs are available from the Start menu, the desktop, and other locations. To change default options, you need to have administrator privileges for your computer. The options you set apply to all users on your computer.

Set Your Default Programs

1. Click the **Start** button, point to **All Programs**, and then click **Default Programs**.

   ◆ You can also click the **Start** button, click the **Control Panel**, and then click **Default Programs** in Small icons or large icons view.

2. Click **Set your default programs**.

3. Select a program.

4. Click **Set this program as default**, or **Choose defaults for this program**.

5. If you select Choose defaults for this program, select the extension you want this program to open by default, and then click **Save**.

6. When you're done, click **Close**.

7. Click **OK**.

8. Click the **Close** button.

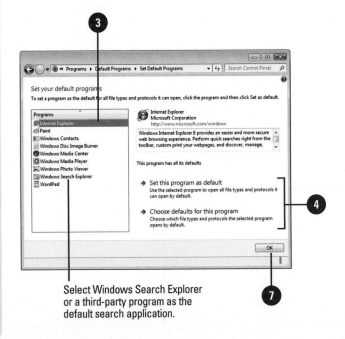

Select Windows Search Explorer or a third-party program as the default search application.

Set Program Access and Computer Defaults

1. Click the **Start** button, point to **All Programs**, and then click **Default Programs**.

2. Click **Set program access and computer defaults**, and then enter administrator permissions, if requested.

3. Click the option for the type of program you want to set: **Computer Manufacturer** (if available), **Microsoft Windows**, **Non-Microsoft**, or **Custom**.

4. Click the option or select from a list the defaults you want to set.

5. Click **OK**.

6. Click the **Close** button.

Change File Type or Protocol Association with a Program

1. Click the **Start** button, point to **All Programs**, and then click **Default Programs**.

2. Click **Associate a file type or protocol with a program**.

3. Click the extension.

4. Click **Change program**.

5. Select the program you want to use; click **Browse** if necessary to locate it.

6. Click **OK**.

7. When you're done, click **Close**.

8. Click the **Close** button.

Scroll down to the bottom of the list to display protocols including Windows Search Protocol.

Changing the Way a CD or DVD Starts

When you insert a CD or DVD into your computer disc drive or attach certain devices, such as digital cameras, to your computer, you can specify how you want Windows to respond. You can have Windows detect the type of content on the disc and automatically start, or prompt you each time to choose an action. If you have CDs or DVDs with music files, pictures, video files, or mixed content, you can change the action Windows takes when it detects the content on the disc. You can have Windows play or rip a CD or DVD using Windows Media Player, open the first folder to view files using Windows Explorer, or take no action. Windows 7 allows you to set AutoPlay options for a wide-variety of CDs and DVDs, including an audio or enhanced audio CD, DVD or enhanced DVD movie, Software and games, pictures, video and audio files, blank CD or DVD, mixed content, HD DVD or Blu-ray Disc movie, Video or Super Video CD.

Set AutoPlay Options

1. Click the **Start** button, and then click **Control Panel**, click the **Auto Play** icon in Small icons or Large icons view.

2. To display the AutoPlay dialog box every time you insert a CD or DVD. select the **Use AutoPlay for all media and devices** check box.

3. For each of the different media types, click the list arrow, and then select the default action you want; options vary depending on the type of CD or DVD.

   ◆ To turn off AutoPlay for a specific media type, click **Take no action**.

4. To reset defaults, click **Reset all defaults**.

5. Click **Save**.

Did You Know?

You can stop Windows from performing an action on a CD or DVD. Hold down the Shift key while you insert the CD or DVD.

Using Ease of Access Tools

If you have difficulty using a mouse or typing, have slightly impaired vision, or are deaf or hard of hearing, you can adjust the appearance and behavior of Windows 7 to make your computer easier for you to use. The Ease of Access Center helps you configure Windows for your vision, hearing, and mobility needs. You can also answer a few questions about your daily computer use that can help Windows recommend accessibility settings and programs for you. To open the Ease of Access Center, click the Start button on the taskbar, click Control Panel, click Ease of Access and then click Ease of Access Center. To use the Ease of Access questionnaire, click Get recommendations to make your computer easier to use. The Ease of Access Center provides utilities to adjust the way your keyboard, display, and mouse function to suit various vision and motor abilities. Some of the accessibility tools available include Magnifier (**New!**), On-Screen Keyboard, Narrator, and High Contrast. You can also set accessibility options, such as StickyKeys, FilterKeys, ToggleKeys, Sound-Sentry, ShowSounds, and MouseKeys, that automatically turn off accessibility features, provide warning sounds, and determine when to apply the settings. The accessibility tools in Windows are intended to provide a low level of functionality for those with special needs. If these tools do not meet your daily needs, you might need to purchase a more advanced accessibility program.

Ease of Access Center Tools

Option	Description
Magnifier	Displays a separate window with a magnified portion of the screen; this is designed to make the screen easier to read for users who have impaired vision. In Windows Aero, you can use full-screen and lens modes for added functionality (**New!**).
On-Screen Keyboard	Displays an on-screen keyboard; this is designed to use the computer without the mouse or keyboard.
Narrator	Use the computer without a display; this is a text-to-speech utility program designed for users who are blind or have impaired vision.
High Contrast	Sets the desktop appearance to high contrast to make the computer easier to see; this is designed to make the screen easier to read for users who have impaired vision.
StickyKeys	Enables simultaneous keystrokes while pressing one key at a time, such as Ctrl+Alt+Del.
FilterKeys	Adjusts the response of your keyboard; ignores repeated characters or fast key presses.
ToggleKeys	Emits sounds when you press certain locking keys, such as Caps Lock, Num Lock, or Scroll Lock.
SoundSentry	Provides visual warnings for system sounds.
ShowSounds	Instructs programs to provide captions.
MouseKeys	Enables the numeric keypad to perform mouse functions.

Using the Ease of Access Center

The Ease of Access Center allows you to check the status of and start or stop the Magnifier, Narrator, and On-Screen Keyboard accessibility programs. Magnifier (**New!**) is a utility that enlarges the full screen (Aero), the mouse area (Aero), or an area of the screen. Narrator is a text-to-speech utility that gives users who are blind or have impaired vision access to the computer. On-Screen Keyboard is a utility that displays a keyboard on the screen where users with mobility impairments can type using a mouse, joystick, or other pointing device. If you have administrator access to your computer, you can specify how the accessibility programs start when you log on, lock the desktop, or start the Ease of Access Center.

Use the Ease of Access Center

1. Press ⊞+U to start the Ease of Access Center.

   TIMESAVER *The Windows key* ⊞ *is located in the lower-left corner of the keyboard.*

   ◆ You can also start the Ease of Access Center in the Control Panel. Double-click the Ease of Access icon in Classic view.

2. To get recommendations on what to use, click **Get recommendations to make your computer easier to use**, and then follow the instructions.

3. To provide quick access to common tools, select the **Always read this section aloud** and **Always scan this section** check boxes.

4. Click the utility program or the settings you want to manage.

5. Select or clear the check boxes you want to specify how you want the selected program to start or a setting to be applied.

6. Click **Save** or exit the window.

7. When you're done with the Ease of Access Center, click the **Close** button.

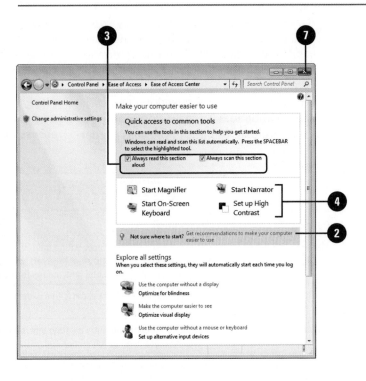

Use the Magnifier

① Click the **Start** button, point to **All Programs**, click **Accessories**, click **Ease of Access**, and then click **Magnifier**.

② Click the **Views** button (**New!**), and then select a view: **Full screen** (Aero), **Lens** (Aero), or **Docked**.

③ Click the **Options** button.

④ Drag the **Zooming** slider to adjust the view level.

⑤ Select or clear the **Turn on color inversion** check box.

⑥ Select or clear the check boxes with the tracking options to follow the mouse cursor, keyboard focus, or text editing (non Aero), or drag a slider to change the magnifier lens size (Aero) (**New!**).

⑦ Click **OK** to use the Magnifier program. When you're done, click the **Close** button to close the program.

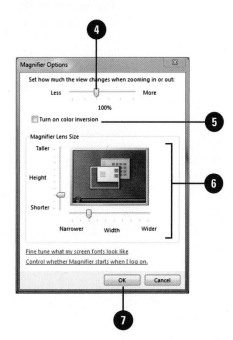

Use the On-Screen Keyboard

① Open the program in which you want to type.

② Click the **Start** button, point to **All Programs**, click **Accessories**, click **Ease of Access**, and then click **On-Screen Keyboard**.

③ Position the cursor, if necessary.

④ Type the text you want, or type keyboard commands.

⑤ When you're done, click the **Close** button.

Listening to the Computer

Windows 7 comes with an accessibility tool called Narrator that reads aloud what appears on your screen, such as window items, menu options, and typed characters. Windows uses Text-to-Speech (TTS) technology to recognize text and play it back as spoken words using a synthesized voice, which is chosen from several pre-generated voices. Narrator is designed for those who are blind or have impaired vision and works with the Windows desktop and setup, Control Panel, Notepad, WordPad, and Internet Explorer. Narrator supports only the English language and might not read words aloud correctly in other programs. You can adjust the speed, volume, or pitch of the voice in Narrator and change other Text-to-Speech options using Speech properties in the Control Panel.

Change Text-To-Speech Options

1. Click the **Start** button, click **Control Panel**, and then click the **Speech Recognition** icon in Small icons or Large icons view.

2. In the left pane, click **Text to Speech**.

3. Click the **Voice selection** list arrow, and then select a synthesized voice.

4. Drag the **Voice speed** slider to adjust the speed of the voice.

5. Click **Preview Voice**.

6. To set a preferred audio device as output for TTS playback, click **Advanced**, make a selection, and then click **OK**.

7. To adjust settings for your audio output devices, click **Audio Output**, specify the options you want on the Playback, Recording, or Sounds tabs, and then click **OK**.

8. Click **OK**.

See Also

See "Recognizing Your Speech" on page 130 for information on speech capabilities.

Use the Narrator

1. Click the **Start** button, point to **All Programs**, click **Accessories**, click **Ease of Access**, and then click **Narrator**.

2. Select the Narrator check box options you want:

   ◆ To hear what you type, select the **Echo User's Keystrokes** check box.

   ◆ To hear background events, select the **Announce System Messages** check box.

   ◆ To hear an announcement when the screen scrolls, select the **Announce Scroll Notifications** check box.

   ◆ Select the **Start Narrator Minimized** check box to minimize the Narrator dialog box.

3. Click **Voice Settings**.

4. Select a voice and adjust the voice speed, volume, and pitch.

5. Click **OK**.

6. Click the **Minimize** button to use the Narrator program or click **Exit** to close the program. (Restore the Narrator window, if necessary.) Click **Yes**, if necessary.

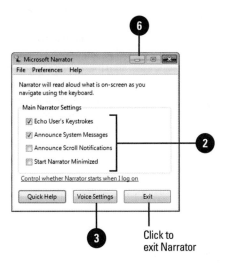

Click to exit Narrator

Common Narrator Shortcuts	
Action	**Result**
Ctrl+Shift+Enter or Alt+Home	Get information about the current item
Ctrl+Shift+Spacebar	Read the entire selected window
Ctrl+Alt+Spacebar	Read the selected window layout
Alt+End	Get a summary of the current item
Ctrl	Stop Narrator from reading text
Insert+F2	Select all of the text with the current text pattern
Insert+F3	Read the current character
Insert+F4	Read the current word
Insert+F5	Read the current line
Insert+F6	Read the current paragraph
Insert+F7	Read the current page
Insert+F8	Read the current document

Recognizing Your Speech

If you have a speech-enabled program, you can initialize and customize speech recognition options using Speech properties in the Control Panel. **Speech recognition** is the ability to convert a spoken voice into electronic text. Windows adapts to your speech, and speech recognition increases over time. You can use the speech recognition properties to select a language, create a profile to accommodate your speaking style and environment, and train your computer in as little as ten minutes to recognize and adapt to the sound of your voice, word pronunciation, accent, speaking manner, and new or distinctive words. Some programs use speech differently, so you need to check the speech-enabled program for details. Speech Recognition is not available in all languages.

Set Up Speech Recognition

1. Click the **Start** button, click **Control Panel**, and then click the **Speech Recognition** icon in Small icons or Large icons view.

2. Click **Set up microphone**, and then follow the wizard instructions to adjust the microphone.

3. Click **Take Speech Tutorial**, and then follow the instructions to take the 30 minute training tutorial to teach you the commands used with speech recognition.

4. Click **Train your computer to better understand you**, and then follow the wizard instructions to train your voice.

5. When you're done, click the **Close** button.

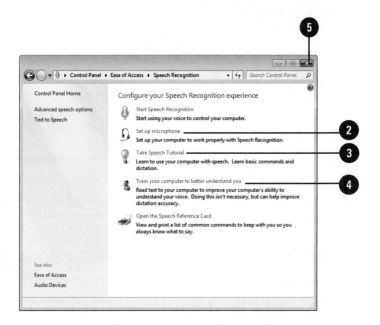

Did You Know?

You can view and print a Speech Recognition reference card. Click the Start button, click Control Panel, click the Speech Recognition Options icon in Small icons or Large icons view, and then click Open and Speech Reference Card.

Set Speech Recognition Options

1. Click the **Start** button, click **Control Panel**, and then click the **Speech Recognition** icon in Small icons or Large icons view.

2. In the left pane, click **Advanced speech options**.

3. Click the **Speech Recognition** tab.

4. Click the list arrow, and then select a language.

5. To start the Profile Wizard, click **New**, type your name, click **OK**, follow the wizard instructions to create a profile, adjust the microphone, and train your voice, and then click **Finish**.

6. Select or clear the User Settings check boxes you do or don't want.

7. Click **OK**.

Start Speech Recognition

1. Click the **Start** button, click **Control Panel**, and then click the **Speech Recognition** icon in Small icons or Large icons view.

2. Click **Start Speech Recognition**.

3. If requested, follow the wizard instructions to create a profile, adjust the microphone, and train your voice, and then click **Finish**.

4. Click the **Speech Recognition** button to toggle between Sleeping and Listening mode.

   TIMESAVER *Right-click the Speech Recognition button to select command options.*

5. When you're done, click the **Close** button.

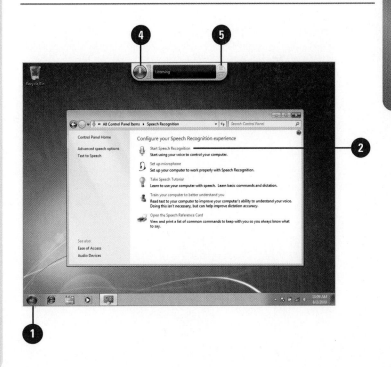

Exploring the Internet

5

Introduction

The **Internet** is a global collection of more than a billion computers (and growing) linked together to share information. The Internet's physical structure includes telephone lines, cables, satellites, and other telecommunications media. Using the Internet, computer users can share many types of information, including text, graphics, sounds, videos, and computer programs. The **World Wide Web** (also known as the web) is a part of the Internet that consists of web sites located on different computers around the world.

A **web site** contains web pages linked together to make searching for information on the Internet easier. **Web pages** are documents that contain highlighted words, phrases, and graphics, called **hyperlinks** (or simply **links**) that open other web pages when you click them. Some web pages contain frames. A frame is a separate window within a web page that lets you see more than one web page at a time. **Web browsers** are software programs that you use to "browse the web," or access and display web pages. Browsers make the web easy to navigate by providing a graphical, point-and-click environment.

Microsoft Internet Explorer 8 (**New!**) is a popular browser from Microsoft that is built-in to Windows 7. With a web browser, you can display web pages from all over the world, display web content on the desktop, view web feeds, use links to move from one web page to another, play audio and video clips, search the web for information, make favorite web pages available offline (when you're not connected to the Internet), and print text and graphics on web pages.

What You'll Do

Connect to the Internet

Create an Internet Connection

Set Up Windows Firewall

Start Internet Explorer

View the Internet Explorer Window

Change Your Home Page

Browse the Web

Browse Privately

Use Compatibility View

Use and Manage Accelerators

Get Updates with Web Slices

Add a Web Page to the Favorites List

View and Maintain a History List

Read and Subscribe to Feeds

Search the Web

Preview and Print a Web Page

Save Pictures or Text from a Web Page

Save a Web Page

Download Files from the Web or FTP

Download Windows Live Essentials

Connecting to the Internet

Universities and large companies are most likely connected to the Internet via high-speed wiring that transmits data very quickly. As the Internet continues to explode around the world, several high-speed connection options are becoming more available and affordable for business and home use: DSL (Digital Subscriber Lines), wires that provide a completely digital connection; and cable modems, which use cable television lines. DSL and cable modems, also known as broadband connections, are continually turned on and connected and use a network setup. If a broadband connection is not available, you need to establish a connection over a phone line using a dial-up modem. Data travels more slowly over phone lines than over digital lines and cable modems. Whether you use a phone line, a DSL line, or a cable modem, Windows can help you establish a connection between your computer and the Internet using the Connect to the Internet wizard. First, you need to select an ISP (Internet Service Provider), which is a company that sets up an Internet account for you and provides Internet access. ISPs maintain servers connected directly to the Internet 24 hours a day. You pay a fee, sometimes by the hour, but more often a flat monthly rate. To connect to the Internet, you need to obtain an Internet account and connection information from your ISP or your system administrator. For details, see "Creating an Internet Connection" on page 135. If you are working on a network, you can also share one Internet connection with everyone. For information on creating an Internet Connection Sharing (ICS), see "Sharing an Internet Connection" on page 378.

Protecting your Computer with a Firewall

When you connect to the Internet, you can access web sites on the Internet, but other users on the Internet can also access information on your computer and potentially infect it with harmful viruses and worms. For more information, see "Avoiding Viruses and Other Harmful Attacks" on page 330.

You can prevent this by activating Windows Firewall, another security layer of protection. A **firewall** is a security system that creates a protective barrier between your computer or network and others on the Internet. Windows Firewall monitors all communication between your computer and the Internet and prevents unsolicited inbound traffic from the Internet from entering your computer. Windows Firewall blocks all unsolicited communication from reaching your computer unless you specifically allow it (unblock) to come through, known as an exception. For example, if you run a program, such as Windows Live Messenger that needs to receive information from the Internet or a network, Windows Firewall asks if you want to block or unblock the connection. If you choose to unblock it, Windows Firewall creates an exception so the program can receive information. For details, see "Setting Up Windows Firewall" on page 136.

If you send and receive e-mail, Windows Firewall doesn't block spam or unsolicited e-mail or stop you from opening e-mail with harmful attachments. To protect your computer from these attacks, see "Protecting Against E-mail Attacks" on page 194. Windows Firewall helps block viruses and worms from reaching your computer, but it doesn't detect or disable them if they are already on your computer or come through e-mail. To protect your computer, you need to install antivirus software.

Creating an Internet Connection

Sometimes connecting your computer to the Internet can be the most difficult part of getting started. The Connect to the Internet wizard simplifies the process, whether you want to set up a new connection using an existing account or select an Internet service provider (ISP) to set up a new account. In either case, you will need to obtain connection information from your ISP or your system administrator.

Create an Internet Connection

1. Click the **Network Connection** icon on the taskbar, and then click **Open Network and Sharing Center**.

2. Click **Set up a connection or network**, click **Connect to the Internet**, and then click **Next**.

3. Click **Set up a new a connection**, or **Set up a new connection anyway** to set up a second connection.

4. Click the option with the way you want to connect: **Wireless**, **Broadband (PPPoE)**, or **Dial-up**.

   ◆ For the wireless option, select a network, and then go to Step 9.

5. Type the name and password from your ISP. For a dial-up connection, type a dial-up phone number.

6. For the password, select or clear the **Show characters** or **Remember this password** check boxes.

7. Type a connection name.

8. Select or clear the **Allow other people to use this connection** check box.

9. Click **Connect**.

See Also

See "Connecting to a Wireless Network" on page 364 for information on wireless Internet connection.

Setting Up Windows Firewall

If your computer is directly connected to the Internet, you need Windows Firewall (**New!**) to protect your computer from unauthorized access from others on the Internet. Windows Firewall is enabled by default for all Internet and network connections. However, some computer manufacturers and network administrators might turn it off, so you need to check it. When Windows Firewall is enabled, you might not be able to use some communication features, such as sending files with a messaging program or playing an Internet game, unless the program is listed on the Exceptions list in Windows Firewall. If you use multiple Internet and networking connections, you can enable or disable individual connections.

Set Up Windows Firewall

1. Click the **Start** button, click **Control Panel**, and then click the **Windows Firewall** icon in Small icons or Large icons view.

2. In the left pane, click **Turn Windows Firewall on or off**.

3. Select the **Turn on Windows Firewall** check box for each networks.

4. To set maximum protection, select the **Block all incoming connections, including those in the list of allowed programs** check box or clear it to make exceptions for each network.

5. Click **OK**.

6. To make program exceptions, click the **Allow a program or feature through Windows Firewall** in the left pane.

7. Select the check boxes with the exceptions you want; if necessary, click **Allow another program** to add it.

8. Click **OK**.

9. To restore default settings, click **Restore defaults** in the left pane, click **Restore defaults**, and then click **Yes**.

10. Click the **Close** button.

Windows Firewall Settings

Starting Internet Explorer

Internet Explorer is a web browser that you use to search the web. You can start Internet Explorer using the Start menu or the button on the taskbar. Internet Explorer 8 starts and loads pages faster than previous versions (**New!**). After you start Internet Explorer, you might need to establish a connection to the Internet by selecting a dial-up service and entering a user name and password. If you have problems running Internet Explorer—sudden crash—due to add-on programs, only that tab is affected while the other tabs remain stable (**New!**). The affected tab is automatically reloaded (**New!**). You can start Internet Explorer with no add-ons, and then turn off individual add-ons to determine the problem. The elements of the Internet Explorer window allow you to view, print, and search for information on the Internet.

Start Internet Explorer

① Click the **Internet Explorer** button, on the taskbar.

◆ To start Internet Explorer without Add-ons, click the **Start** button, point to **All Programs**, click **System Tools**, and then click **Internet Explorer (Non Add-ons)**.

② If necessary, click **Connect** to dial your ISP. You might need to type your user name and password before Internet Explorer will connect to the Internet.

The Internet Explorer window opens.

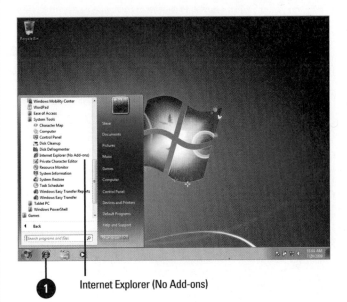

Internet Explorer (No Add-ons)

Did You Know?

You can work offline. If connection time is an issue, you can download and display a web page and then work offline to read it. Click the Tools button, and then click Work Offline. Internet Explorer stays in offline mode until you clear the check mark.

You can turn off the alert asking to make Internet Explorer the default. In Internet Options, click the Programs tab, clear the Tell Me If Internet Explorer Is Not The Default Web Browser check box, and then click OK.

For Your Information

Browsing with Protected Mode

Internet Explorer includes protected mode, which makes it difficult for hackers using a web site to install malicious software on your computer, yet makes it easy for you to install wanted software using the Standard user account (with security enabled) instead of the Administrator user account (with security disabled). Protected mode is turned on by default. When a web page tries to install unwanted software, a warning message appears on the Status bar. If you need to disable or enable it, click the Tools button, click Internet Options, click the Security tab, clear or select the Enable Protected Mode (requires restarting Internet Explorer) check box, and then click OK.

Viewing the Internet Explorer Window

Favorites bar
Displays favorite sites, RSS feeds, and web Slices.

Quick Tabs
Displays multiple web sites in a single browser window.

Address bar
Displays the address of the current web page or document you are viewing or trying to access.

Instant Search
Quickly search the web using different search providers to get the best results.

Explorer bar
Displays links to web pages from Search results, Favorites list, and History list. The Explorer bar is only visible when you click the corresponding button on the toolbar.

Browser pane
Displays the current web page, document, or folder contents.

Status bar
Indicates the progress of loading a web page, as well as other messages about selected actions.

Changing Your Home Page

Your **home page** in Internet Explorer is the page that opens when you start the program. When you first install Internet Explorer, the default home page is the Microsoft Network (MSN) web site. If you want a different page to appear when you start Internet Explorer and whenever you click the Home button, you can change your home page. With the introduction of tabbed browsing, you can display multiple home pages in tab sets. You can choose one of the millions of web pages available through the Internet, or you can select a particular file on your hard drive.

Change the Home Page

1. Open the web page or multiple web pages you want to be the new home page.

2. Click the **Home** button arrow, and then click **Add or Change Home Page**.

3. Click one of the following options:

   ◆ **Use this webpage as your only home page.**

   ◆ **Add this webpage to your home page tabs.**

   ◆ **Use the current tab set as your home page.**

4. Click **Yes**. Otherwise, click **No**.

5. To remove a web page as one of your home pages, click the **Home** button arrow, point to **Remove**, and then click the web page you want to remove, or click **Remove All**, and then click **Yes** to confirm.

Browsing the Web

A **Web address** (also known as a URL, which stands for Uniform Resource Locator) is a unique place on the Internet where you can locate a Web page. With Internet Explorer, you can browse sites on the Web with ease by entering a Web address or by clicking a link. Each method is better at different times. For example, you might type an address in the Address bar to start your session. Then you might click a link on that Web page to access a new site. When you type an Internet address in the Address bar, Internet Explorer uses **AutoComplete** to search for a recently visited page, favorite, and RSS feed that matches (**New!**) what you've typed so far. If Internet Explorer finds one or more matches, it displays a drop-down menu and highlights them in blue. You can also use AutoComplete to fill out forms on the Web, including single-line edits, and user names and passwords. When you visit a site, the Address bar highlights the domain name in black and leaves the remainder of the URL in gray (**New!**) to help you identify the site name, so you can avoid deceptive ones that try to mislead you.

View a Web Page

Use any of the following methods to display a Web page:

◆ In the Address bar, type the Web address, and then press Enter.

   If you have recently entered the Web page address, AutoComplete remembers it and tries to complete the address for you. The smarter Address bar searches your history, favorites, RSS feeds, displaying a drop-down menu with matches from any part of the Web site address (**New!**). The suggested matches are highlighted in blue (**New!**). Click the correct address or continue to type until the address you want appears in the Address list.

   If you want to get rid of suggestions in the drop-down menu, you can delete them. Point to a menu item, and then click on the Delete button (red X) (**New!**).

◆ Click any link on the Web page, such as a picture or colored, underlined text. The mouse pointer changes to a hand when it is over a link.

Type a Web address   Address bar arrow

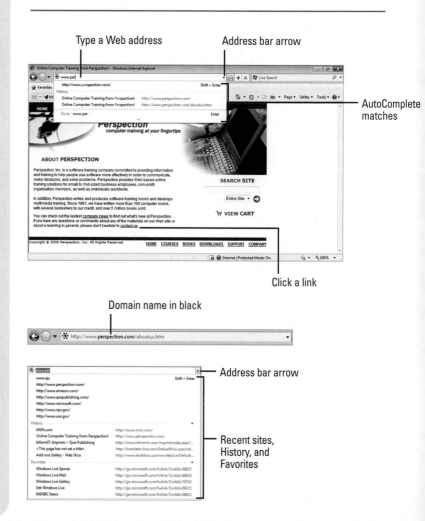

AutoComplete matches

Click a link

Domain name in black

Address bar arrow

Recent sites, History, and Favorites

Change AutoComplete Options

① Click the **Tools** button, and then click **Internet Options**.

② Click the **Content** tab.

③ Click **Settings**.

④ Select or clear the AutoComplete options you want to turn on or off.

⑤ To delete AutoComplete history, click **Delete AutoComplete history**, select the check boxes with the options you want, and then click **Delete**.

⑥ Click **OK**.

⑦ Click **OK**.

Did You Know?

You can have AutoComplete quickly complete a web address. In the Address bar, type the name of the web site, such as *perspection*, and then press Ctrl+Enter. AutoComplete adds the "www." and ".com".

You can use the Address bar to search for information. In the Address bar, type **go**, **find**, or **?** followed by a space and a word or phrase, and then press Enter. To turn off or change Address bar searches, click the Tools button, click Internet Options, click the Advanced tab, select options under Search from the Address bar, and then click OK.

You can display the menu bar and toolbars using the Tools button. If you want to display the menu bar and any toolbars, click the Tools button, point to Toolbars, and then click Menu Bar or a toolbar.

For Your Information

Understanding a Web Address

The address for a Web page is called a URL. Each Web page has a unique URL that is typically composed of four parts: the protocol (a set of rules that allow computers to exchange information), the location of the Web site, the name that maintains the Web site, and a suffix that identifies the type of site. A URL begins with a protocol, followed by a colon, two slashes, the location of the Web site, a dot, the name of the Web site, a dot, and a suffix. The Web site is the computer where the Web pages are located. At the end of the Web site name, another slash may appear, followed by one or more folder names and a file name. For example, in the web site address, http://*www*.perspection.com/downloads/main.htm, the protocol is *http* (HyperText Transfer Protocol), the location of the Web site is *www* (World Wide Web), the name of the Web site is *perspection*, and the suffix is *com* (a commercial organization); a folder at that site is called */downloads*; and within the folder is a file called *main.htm*.

Browsing with Tabs

As you open web sites, you can use separate tabs for each one, so you can view multiple web sites in a single window. You can open web pages on new tabs by using the redesigned New Tab page (**New!**) with links—use an Accelerator, browse with in Private, reopen closed tabs, and reopen your last browsing session—to make you get started. After you open a tab, you can click a tab to quickly switch between them or click the Close button on the tab to exit it. If you prefer a visual way to switch between tabs, you can use Quick tabs, which displays thumbnails, to open and close web pages. When you open a new tab from another tab, the new tab is grouped together and color coded (**New!**), which you can always ungroup later. You can right-click a tab to quickly perform a variety of operations, such as close a tab or tab group, ungroup a tab, refresh tabs, open a new tab, reopen the last tab closed (**New!**), or see a list of all recently closed tabs and reopen any or all of them (**New!**).

Use Tabbed Browsing

Use any of the following methods to use tabbed browsing:

◆ **Open a blank tab.** Click the **New Tab** button, or press Ctrl+T.

> **TIMESAVER** *In the Address bar, type a URL and then press Alt+Enter to open it in a new tab.*

◆ **Open or close Quick Tabs.** Click the **Quick Tabs** button, or press Ctrl+Q. To open the web page, click a thumbnail. To close a web page, click the **Close** button in the corner of the thumbnail.

◆ **Switch between tabs.** Click a tab, or press Ctrl+Tab.

◆ **Close a tab.** Click the **Close** button on the tab, or press Ctrl+W.

◆ **Close other tabs.** Right-click the tab you want open, and then click **Close Other Tabs (New!)**.

◆ **Reopen closes tabs. (New!)** Click the **New** tab button, and then click a site name link for a closed tab or click the **Open All** link. Click the **Reopen Last Browsing Session** link to reopen all tabs when Internet Explorer was last closed.

Quick Tabs   Close Tab   New Tab   Quick Tabs view

New Tab   Getting started links screen

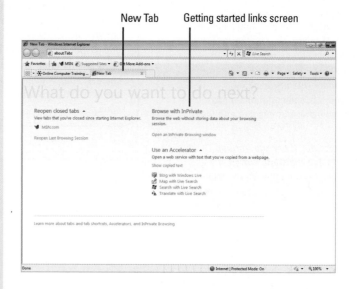

Group or Ungroup Tabs

◆ **Open a new tab in a group (in background). (New!)** Press Ctrl+click a link or right-click a link, and then click **Open Link in New Tab**.

◆ **Open a new tab in a group (in foreground). (New!)** Press Ctrl+Shift+click a link.

◆ **Ungroup a tab. (New!)** Right-click a tab in a group, and then click **Ungroup This Tab**.

Tabbed group in color

Click to close this tab group

Set Tabbing Options

① Click the **Tools** button, and then click **Internet Options**.

② Click **Settings** in the Tabs section on the General tab.

③ To enable or disable tabs, select or clear the **Enable Tabbed Browsing** check box.

④ If enabled, select the options that you want. Some options require you to restart Internet Explorer. Some common ones include:

◆ **Warn me when closing multiple tabs.**

◆ **When a pop-up is encountered.**

◆ **Open links from other programs in.**

⑤ To restore default settings, click **Restore defaults**.

⑥ Click **OK**.

⑦ Click **OK**.

Navigating Basics

As you browse the web or your local hard disk, you may want to retrace your steps and return to a web page, document, or hard disk you've recently visited. You can move backward or forward one location at a time, or you can jump directly to any location from the Back list or Forward list, both of which show locations you've previously visited in this session. When you go back, sometimes it takes you to the start of an application, such as a map. Now Internet Explorer takes you back to the right page (**New!**). After you start to load a web page, you can stop if the page opens too slowly or if you decide not to access it. If a web page loads incorrectly or you want to update the information it contains, you can reload, or **refresh**, the page. If you get lost on the web, you can start over with a single click of the Home button.

Move Back or Forward

◆ To move back or forward one web page or document at a time, click the **Back** button or the **Forward** button on the Address bar.

TIMESAVER *To move back, press Alt+left arrow. To move forward, press Alt+right arrow.*

◆ To move back or forward to a specific web page or document, click the list arrow next to the Back and Forward buttons on the Address bar, and then select the web page or document you want to visit.

Back button

Forward button

Back/Forward list arrow

Stop, Refresh, or Go Home

◆ Click the **Stop** button on the Address bar.

TIMESAVER *Press Esc.*

◆ Click the **Refresh** button on the Address bar.

TIMESAVER *Press F5.*

◆ Click the **Home** button on the toolbar.

Refresh button

Home button   Stop button

Browsing Privately

If you're using a computer at a friend's house, another office, hotel, or an Internet cafe and you don't want to leave any trace or evidence of your web activity, you can use InPrivate browsing (**New!**). InPrivate browsing doesn't retain or keep track of browsing history, searches, temporary Internet files, form data, cookie, and usernames and passwords. You can start InPrivate browsing from a new tab or using the Safety button on the Command bar. When you start InPrivate browsing, Internet Explorer opens a new browser window. An InPrivate indicator icon appears in the Address bar when the feature is turned on. When you're done, simply close the browser window to end the InPrivate browsing session.

Browse the Web Privately

1. Start an InPrivate browsing session using any of the following:

   ◆ **Safety button.** Click the **Safety** button on the Command bar, and then click **InPrivate Browsing**.

   ◆ **New tab.** Click the **New Tab** button to open a new tab, and then click **Open an InPrivate Browsing window**.

   ◆ **Shortcut.** Press Ctrl+Shift+P.

2. Browse the web.

   The InPrivate indicator appears in the Address bar.

3. To end InPrivate browsing, click the **Close** button to close the browser window.

New tab   Safety button

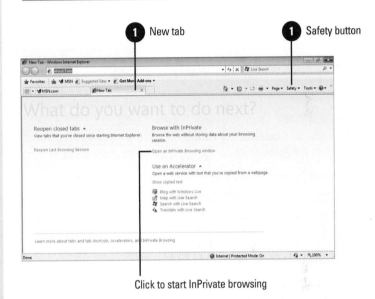

Click to start InPrivate browsing

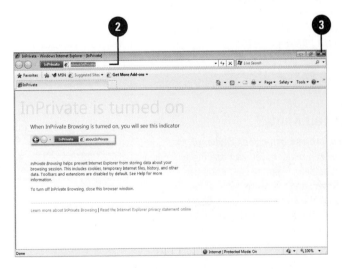

Using Compatibility View

If you visit an older web site that doesn't display correctly—misaligned text, images, and text boxes—in Internet Explorer 8, you can quickly fix it, in most cases, with Compatibility view (**New!**). When you open an older site that Internet Explorer recognizes, the Compatibility View button appears in the Address bar, near the Refresh button. The button appears on a per site basis. However, once you click the button for a site, you don't have to do it again. Internet Explorer maintains a list of sites with Compatibility view, which you can customize (**New!**).

Fix the Display of Older Web Sites

1. Open the older web page with the display you want to fix.

   If the Compatibility View button appears in the Address bar next to the Refresh button, the option is available (**New!**).

2. To fix the display of an older web site, click the **Compatibility View** button in the Address bar.

   A ScreenTip appears indicating Compatibility View is enabled.

3. To change Compatibility view settings, click the **Tools** button on the Command bar, and then click **Compatibility View Settings**.

4. To remove a site, select the site, and then click **Remove**.

5. To enable other options, select the check boxes you want.

6. Click **Close**.

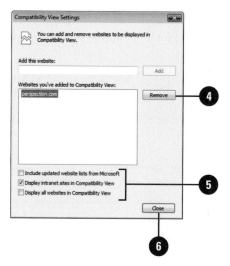

Did You Know?

You can browse using your keyboard. With caret browsing, you can use the navigation keys—Home, End, Page Up, Page Down, and the arrow keys. Press F7 or click the Page button, click Caret Browsing, and then click Yes.

Zooming the View In and Out

Working with the Zoom tools gives you one more way to control exactly what you see in a web page. Internet Explorer uses Adaptive Page Zoom tools (**New!**) that allow you to enlarge or reduce everything on the page, including text and images, by relaying out the page. You can adjust the zoom from 10% to 1000%. The Zoom tools are located in the bottom-right corner of the window or available on the Zoom submenu on the Page button. If you have a mouse with a wheel, hold down the Ctrl key, and then scroll the wheel to zoom in or out.

Change the View

1. Use any of the following zoom options available on the Status bar:

   ◆ **Zoom In or Out.** Click the **Change Zoom Level** button arrow on the Status bar, and then click a zoom percentage.

   TIMESAVER *Press Ctrl+(+) to zoom in by increments of 10%, or press Ctrl+(-) to zoom out by increments of 10%. Press Ctrl+0 to restore the zoom to 100%.*

   ◆ **Zoom Level.** Click the **Change Zoom Level** button on the Status bar to cycle through 100%, 125%, and 150%.

   ◆ **Zoom Custom.** Click the **Change Zoom Level** button arrow on the Status bar, click **Custom**, type a zoom value, and then click **OK**.

2. To change the view to full screen, click the **Tools** button, and then click **Full Screen**. To change back, press F11.

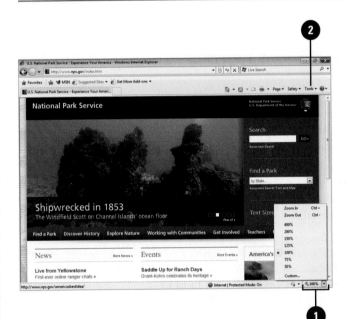

Did You Know?

You can change web page text size to make it easier to read. Click the Page button, click Text Size, and then click the size you want. When you change the text size, graphics and controls remain unchanged, so you can focus on the text.

Using and Managing Accelerators

An **Accelerator (New!)** allows you to perform everyday tasks without having to navigate to other web sites. Internet Explorer 8 comes with default Accelerators that make it easy to get driving directions on a map, translate and define words, e-mail information to others, and search for content. However, you can add more Accelerators from Bing, eBay, yahoo!, Wikipedia, Amazon and Facebook by adding them from the Internet Explorer Gallery. All you need to do is highlight text from any web page and then click the blue Accelerator icon that appears near your selection to obtain a window with the information you need. If you no longer want to use an Accelerator, you can use the Manage Add-ons dialog box to delete or disable it, or change defaults.

Use and Manage Accelerators

1. Select the text you want to use with an Accelerator, such as a word, phrase, paragraph, address, or e-mail address.

2. Click the blue **Accelerator** button, and then point an accelerator from the default menu or point to **All Accelerators**, and then point to an accelerator.

   The Accelerator displays a window with the results, such as a definition, translation, map, or search.

3. Click in the Accelerator window, if available, to open it.

4. To add an Accelerator, click the **Page** button, point to **All Accelerators**, and then click **Find More Accelerators**. Click **Add to Internet Explorer** for the Accelerator you want.

5. To manage Accelerators, click the **Page** button, point to **All Accelerators**, and then click **Manage Accelerators**, click Accelerators in the left pane, select an Accelerator, and then click **Set as default** or **Remove as default**, **Disable**, or **Remove**.

Manage Accelerators

Getting Updates with Web Slices

How many times a day do you visit a web site for updates to common items, such as e-mail, auctions, sports scores, weather reports, or stock quotes? With Web Slices (**New!**), you can check for updates directly from the Favorites bar in Internet Explorer instead of going to each site individually. If a Web Slice is available on a page, a green Web Slice button appears in the Command bar, similar to an RSS feed. Click on the button to subscribe and add the Web Slice to the Favorites bar. When an update happens, the Web Slice becomes highlighted in the Favorites bar. Click the Web Slice in the Favorites bar to preview the update, and then, if you want, click the preview to open the web page.

Get Updates with Web Slices

1. Point to an item on a web page that supports web Slices.

   ◆ To check a page for Web Slices, click the **Feeds/Web Slices** button arrow on the Command bar to display a list.

2. Click the green Web Slice button.

3. Click **Add to Favorites Bar**.

4. If the Web Slice in the Favorites bar is bold, click the button to display a preview of the updated Web Slice.

   ◆ To enable or disable the bold display, right-click the **Web Slice** button on the Favorites bar, and then click **Bold on Update**.

5. To visit the web site with the updated content, click the preview window.

6. To set update options for a web slice, right-click the **Web Slice** button on the Favorites bar, click **Properties**, and then select an update schedule option or click **Settings**.

7. To delete a Web slice, right-click the **Web Slice** button on the Favorites bar, and then click **Delete**.

For Your Information

Using Suggested Sites

If you're not sure what good sites are out there based on your own browsing history, then you might want to try Suggested Sites (**New!**), a free online service from Microsoft. To turn Suggested Sites on or off, click the Tools button on the Command bar, click Suggested Sites, and then click Yes or No. When enabled, Microsoft uses your browsing history to give you suggestions. Simply, click the Suggested Sites Web Slice (**New!**) on the Favorites bar to see a list of suggestions. The more places you visit, the better the suggested sites. You can also delete sites from your history. If you no longer want the service, you can choose to turn it off at any time.

Adding a Web Page to the Favorites List

Rather than memorizing URLs or keeping a handwritten list of web pages you want to visit, you can use the Favorites bar and Favorites Center to store and organize the addresses. The Favorites bar (**New!**) appears below the Address bar for easy access to favorites, RSS feeds and web slices. When you display a web page that you want to display again at a later time, you can add the web page to the Favorites bar with one click (**New!**) or to the Favorites Center, where you can also manage feeds and history. Once you add the web page to the Favorites bar or Center, you can quickly return to the page. To open all the favorites in a folder at the same time, click the blue arrow to the right of the folder. If your list of favorites grows long, you can delete favorites you don't visit anymore or move favorites into folders.

Add and Delete Favorites

1. Open the web site you want to add to your Favorites list.

2. To quickly add the web site to the Favorites bar, click the **Add to Favorites Bar** button (**New!**).

3. Click the **Favorites Center** button, and then click **Add to Favorites**.

4. Type the name for the site, or use the default name supplied.

5. Click **Create In** arrow, and then select a location on the Favorites menu to place the site.

6. If you want to create a new folder, click **New Folder**, type a folder name, and then click **OK**.

7. Click **Add**.

8. To remove an item from the Favorites bar or Favorites Center, right-click it, click **Delete**, and then click **Yes** to confirm.

Did You Know?

You can customize the title width of items on the Favorites bar. Right-click the Favorites bar, point to Customize Title Widths, and then click Long Titles, Short Titles, or Icons Only.

Access Favorites

1 Click the **Favorites Center** button.

The Favorites Center pane appears, displaying your current favorites list, like a menu. The pane is not pinned (locked) to the window.

2 To pin the pane to the window, click the **Pin the Favorites Center** button (green arrow).

When the pane is pinned, the Close button appears on the pane.

3 Click a folder, if necessary.

4 To open all the favorites in a folder at the same time, click the blue arrow to the right of the folder.

5 Click the page you want.

6 Click off the pane or click the **Close** button.

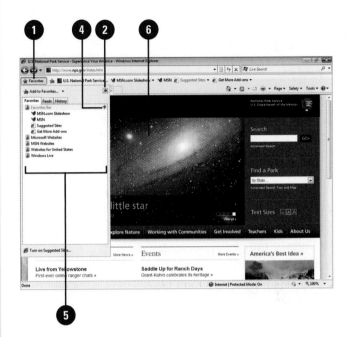

Organize Favorites

1 Click the **Favorites Center** button, **Add to Favorites** button arrow, and then click **Organize Favorites**.

2 Select one or more favorites from the list you want to work with.

3 Do any of the following:

◆ **New Folder.** Click **New Folder**, type the new folder name, and then press Enter.

◆ **Move.** Click **Move**, select a folder, and then click **OK**.

◆ **Rename.** Click **Rename**, type a new name, and then press Enter.

◆ **Delete.** Click **Delete**, and then click **Yes**.

4 When you're done, click the **Close** button.

Viewing and Maintaining a History List

Sometimes you run across a great web site and simply forget to add it to your Favorites list. With Internet Explorer there's no need to try to remember all the sites you visit. The History feature keeps track of where you've been by date, site, most visited, or order visited today, which you can now sort by (**New!**). To view the History list, click the History button in the Favorites Center, select a sort option (**New!**), and then click a link (if necessary) in the pane to expand the list of web sites visited. You can also search for pages in the History list by typing keywords (**New!**). Because the History list can grow to occupy a large amount of space on your hard drive, it's important to control the length of time you retain Web sites in the list. Internet Explorer deletes the History list periodically, based on the settings you specify. When you delete your History list, you can now protect and preserve your related data for trusted sites in your favorites list (**New!**).

View and Change the History List

1. Click the **Favorites Center** button on the toolbar.

2. Click the **History** button.

3. To change the history view, click the **Sort** button (**New!**), and then select the view option you want.

   - **View By Date.**

   - **View By Site.**

   - **View By Most Visited.**

   - **View By Order Visited Today.**

   - **Search History. (New!)** Type a keyword to search for a page, and then click **Search Now**. Click **Stop** to end the search.

4. If view By Date, click a week or day to expand or compress the list of web sites visited.

5. If necessary, click the folder for the web site you want to view, and then click a page within the web site.

6. Click off the pane or click the **Close** button.

Change the Number of Days Pages Are Saved

1. Click the **Tools** button on the Command bar, and then click **Internet Options**.

2. Click the **General** tab.

3. In the Browsing history section, click **Settings**.

4. Specify the total number of days you want to keep links listed in history.

5. Click **OK**.

6. Click **OK**.

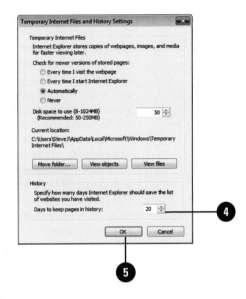

Clear the History List

1. Click the **Safety** button on the Command bar, and then click **Delete Browsing History**.

   ◆ You can also open this dialog by clicking **Delete** on the **General** tab in the Internet Options dialog box.

   ◆ To delete browsing history on exit, click the **Tools** button, click **Internet Options**, select the **Delete browsing history on exit** check box, and then click **OK**.

2. To preserve cookies and temporary Internet files for sites in your Favorites folder, which are trusted sites, select the **Preserve Favorites website data** check box (**New!**).

3. Select the **History** check box to clear the history list.

4. Click **Delete**.

Reading and Subscribing to Feeds

A **feed** delivers frequently updated web content to your browser on a continuous basis. A feed, also known as RSS (Really Simple Syndication) feed, XML feed, syndicated content, or web feed, is usually offered on a subscription basis and typically free of charge. A feed can deliver text content in the form of news headlines or blogs, or digital content in the form of pictures, audio, and video. When audio content is delivered usually in the MP3 format, it's referred to as a podcast. When you visit a web site, Internet Explorer checks for available feeds. If it discovers a feed, the orange Feeds button appears in the Command bar. You can view an individual feed or subscribe to one to get content automatically. When you subscribe to a feed, Internet Explorer checks the web site and downloads new content so you always stay updated with the latest site content. You can also add an RSS feed to your Favorites bar, making it easy to view updates (**New!**). Internet Explorer manages a common feeds list, which allows other programs, such as e-mail, to use them.

View and Subscribe to a Feed

1. Visit a web site with a feed.

    The Feeds button changes color and plays a sound.

    TIMESAVER *You can also press Alt+J to check for feeds.*

2. Click the **Feeds/Web Slices** button arrow (**New!**) on the Command bar, and then select an available feed.

3. If available, click the feed you want to see.

    A web page opens, displaying a lists of articles and other elements you can read and subscribe to.

4. Click the **Subscribe to this Feed** button, and then click **Subscribe to this Feed**, if necessary.

5. Type a name for the feed, and then select a location for the feed.

6. To add the feed to the Favorites bar, select the **Add to Favorites Bar** check box (**New!**).

7. Click **Subscribe**.

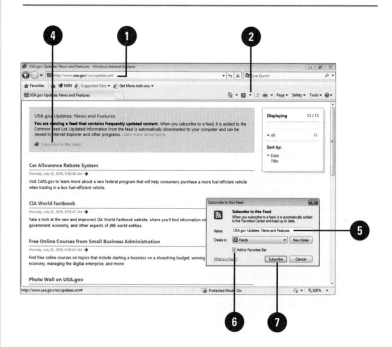

View Subscribed Feeds

1. If available, click the feed button on the Favorites bar, and then click a specific feed (**New!**).

   ◆ If the feed button on the Favorites button is bold, the feed has been updated.

2. Click the **Favorites Center** button.

3. Click the **Feeds** button.

4. If needed, click a folder to display related feeds.

5. Click the feed to visit the web site for the feed.

6. Click off the pane or click the **Close** button.

RSS feed on the Favorites bar

Searching the Web

You can find all kinds of information on the web using the Instant Search box from the Address bar. The best way to find information is to use a search engine. A **search engine** is a program you access through a web site and use to search through a collection of Internet information to find what you want. Many search engines are available on the web, such as Bing, Wikipedia, Google, and Yahoo, which you can add-on to Internet Explorer (**New!**). When performing a search, the search engine compares keywords with words that if finds on various Internet web sites. **Keywords** are words or phrases that best describe the information you want to retrieve. As you type in the Search box, the search engine displays a menu list of text and visual suggestions (**New!**) for the matched sites. These matched sites are sometimes called **hits**. The search results of different search engines vary. If you're looking for information on a page, you can use the Find toolbar (**New!**) to help highlight the text you want to find.

Search the Web

1 Click in the **Search** box.

> **TIMESAVER** *Press Ctrl+E to go to the Search box without using the mouse.*

2 To use a specific search provider for this session only, click the **Search** box arrow, and then click the provider you want.

3 Type the information you want to find. Use specific words, eliminate common words, such as "a" or "the", and use quotation marks for specific phrases.

As you type, a drop-down menu appears with text and visual suggestions (**New!**).

4 Click a suggestion (**New!**) or continue to type. Press Enter or press Alt+Enter to display the search results in a new tab.

Results

Add or Change Search Providers

1. Click the **Search** box arrow, and then click **Manage Search Providers**.

   ◆ To add more search providers, click the Search box arrow, click **Find More Providers**, and then follow the web site instructions.

2. Click the search provider you want to set as the default.

3. Click the button with the option you want to perform:

   ◆ To set as the default provider, click **Set as default**.

   ◆ To remove a provider, click **Remove**.

4. Click **OK**.

Available
search providers

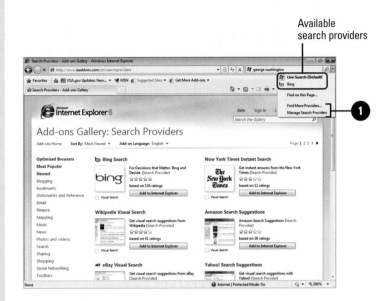

Find Text on a Page

1. Click the **Edit** menu or the **Search** box arrow, and then click **Find on this page** to display the toolbar.

   TIMESAVER Press Ctrl+F to find text on this page.

2. Click the **Highlight All Matches** button to turn highlighting in yellow on or off.

3. Click the **Options** button, and then click **Match Whole Word Only** or **Match Case** to turn them on or off.

4. Type text in the Find box. As you type, the search display the results on the page.

5. Click the **Previous** or **Next** button to go to the results on the page.

6. Click the **Close** button on the toolbar.

Highlighted results

Previewing and Printing a Web Page

Web pages are designed for viewing on a computer screen, but you can also print all or part of one. Before you print, you should verify that the page looks the way you want. You save time, money, and paper by avoiding duplicate or wasteful printing. Printing now scales web pages to fit the paper you're using. Print Preview shows you exactly how the web page will look on the printed page, and gives you more control over margins and scaling. This is especially helpful when you have multiple pages to print. When you are ready to print, Internet Explorer provides many options for printing web pages. For web pages with frames, you can print the page just as you see it, or you can elect to print a particular frame or all frames. You can even use special Page Setup options to include the date, time, or window title on the printed page. You can also choose to print the web addresses from the links contained on a web page.

Preview a Web Page

1. Click the **Print** button arrow on the Command bar, and then click **Print Preview**.

2. Use the Print Preview toolbar buttons to preview or print the web page:

   ◆ **Print the document.**

   ◆ **Portrait** or **Landscape.**

   ◆ **Page Setup.** Opens the Page Setup dialog box.

   ◆ **Turn headers and footers on and off.**

   ◆ **View Full Width** or **View Full Page.**

   ◆ **Show Multiple Pages.**

   ◆ **Change the Print Size.**

3. Use options at the bottom of the Print Preview to specify the page to display or switch between pages.

4. Drag a margin adjust handle to fine tune the page margins.

5. When you're done, click the **Close** button.

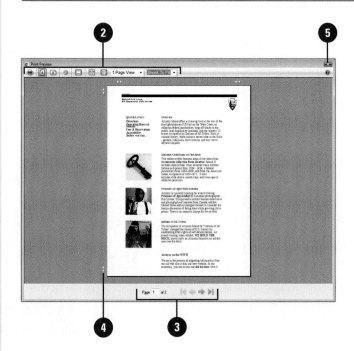

Print a Web Page

1. Click the **Print** button arrow, and then click **Print**.

   TIMESAVER *To print the current page with the current print settings, click the Print button.*

2. Click a printer.

3. Specify the range of pages you want to print.

4. Specify the number of copies you want to print.

5. Click the **Options** tab.

6. If the page contains frames, select the print frames option you want.

7. Select or clear the **Print all linked documents** and **Print table of links** check boxes.

8. Click **Print**.

See Also

See Chapter 14 "Printing and Faxing" on page 397 for information on installing and using a printer.

See "Previewing and Printing a Document" on page 37 for more information on using the Preview window and the Print dialog box.

For Your Information

Setting Up the Page Format

When you print a web page, you can use the Page Setup dialog box to control the printing of text and graphics on a page. To open the Page Setup dialog box, click the Print button arrow, and then click Page Setup. The Page Setup dialog box specifies the printer properties for page size, orientation, and paper source; in most cases, you won't want to change them. From the Page Setup dialog box, you can also change header and footer information. In the Headers and Footers text boxes, you can type text to appear as a header and footer of a web page you print. In these text boxes, you can also use variables to substitute information about the current page, and you can combine text and codes. For example, if you type **Page &p of &P** in the Header text box, the current page number and the total number of pages print at the top of each printed page. Check Internet Explorer Help for a complete list of header and footer codes.

Saving Pictures or Text from a Web Page

If you find information on a web page that you want to save for future reference or share with others, you can copy and paste it to another document or save it on your computer. When you copy information from a web page, make sure you're not violating any copyright laws.

Save a Picture from a Web Page

1. Open the web page with the picture you want to save.

2. Point to the picture you want to save to display a toolbar on the graphic, and then click the **Save** button.

   If the toolbar doesn't appear, right-click the picture, and then click **Save Picture As**.

3. Select the drive and folder in which you want to save the file.

4. Type a name for the file, or use the suggested name.

5. To change the format of a file, click the **Save as type** arrow, and then click a file format.

6. Click **Save**.

Did You Know?

You can save a page or picture without opening it. Right-click the link for the item you want to save, and then click Save Target As.

You can create a desktop shortcut to the current web page. Right-click in the web page, click Create Shortcut, and then click OK.

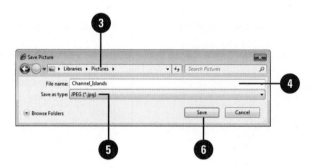

Set a Picture from a Web Page as the Background Picture

1. Open the web page with the picture you want to use.

2. Right-click the picture, and then click **Set As Wallpaper** or **Set As Background**.

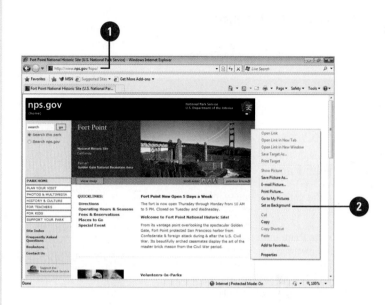

Copy Text from a Web Page

1. Open the web page with the text you want to copy.

2. Select the text you want to copy.

   TROUBLE? *The I-beam cursor may or may not appear. You can still select the text.*

3. Right-click the selected text, and then click **Copy**, or press Ctrl+C.

   ◆ You can also access an Accelerator from the shortcut menu where you can use the selected text in an e-mail, blog, search, or translate (**New!**).

4. Switch to where you want to paste the text.

5. Click the **Edit** menu, and then click **Paste**, or press Ctrl+V.

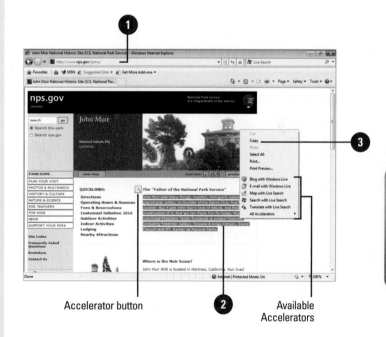

Accelerator button

Available Accelerators

Saving a Web Page

You can save a web page you want to view offline even if you don't need to share it with others or update its content, such as a published article whose content will not change. There are several ways you can save the web page, from saving just the text to saving all of the graphics and text needed to display that page as it appears on the web. When you save a complete web page, Internet Explorer saves all the graphic and text elements in a folder. If you need to send a web page to a friend or co-worker, you can save all the elements of the web page in a single file to make the process easier.

Save a Web Page

1. Open the web page you want to save.

2. Click the **Page** button arrow, and then click **Save As**.

3. Select the drive and folder in which you want to save the file.

4. Type a name for the file, or use the suggested name.

5. Click the **Save as type** arrow, and then click one of the following:

   - **Web Page, complete** to save the formatted text and layout with all the linked information, such as pictures, in a folder.

   - **Web Archive, single file** to save all the elements of the web page in a single file.

   - **Web Page, HTML only** to save the formatted text and layout without the linked information.

   - **Text File** to save only the text.

6. Click **Save**.

See Also

See "Saving and Closing a Document" on page 38 for more information on using the Save As dialog box.

Sending a Page or Link by E-mail

If you come across a web page that you want to share with a friend or co-worker, you can send the page or a link to the page directly from Internet Explorer using your default E-mail program. When you use the Send Page by E-mail and Send Link by E-mail commands on the Page button, Internet Explorer automatically opens your default E-mail program and creates a new message with the web page or link.

Send a Page or Link by E-mail

1. Open the web page with the picture you want to send.

2. Click the **Page** button arrow, and then click **Send Page by E-mail** or **Send Link by E-mail**.

   Internet Explorer opens your mail program, and creates a new message.

3. Address and send the message.

For Your Information

Accessing E-mail from Internet Explorer

If you installed the Windows Live Mail program from the Windows Live Essentials web site (*http://download.live.com*), you can access it directly from Internet Explorer. All you need to do is click the Read Mail button (**New!**) on the Command bar to access and open the mail program on your computer. If you want access e-mail with Windows Live through Internet Explorer, you can access it online. Click the Page button on the Command bar, and then click E-mail with Windows Live (**New!**) to access the web site, log in, and work with your mail.

Downloading Files from the Web

There are thousands of sites on the Internet offering all sorts of files you can download to your computer, from trailers to the latest game demos. You can download files from any web site by finding the file you want, right-clicking the link, and telling Internet Explorer where you want to save the file. Some web sites are designed with specific links to make it easier to download files. When you click a download link, a Security Warning dialog box opens, asking you to run or don't run the file from the Internet or save the file to your computer. Internet Explorer checks to see whether there are any irregularities with the file or a potential for harm based on the file type, and provides strong warning and guidance to help you understand more about the file you are downloading.

Download a File from a Web Page

1. Open the web page from which you want to download a file.

2. Click the download link, and then click **Save**, or right-click the link pointing to the actual file, and then click **Save Target As**.

3. Select the folder in which you want to save the file.

4. Type a name for the file, or use the suggested name.

5. Click **Save**.

   The File Download dialog box displays the estimated time to download the file, along with the estimated transfer time.

6. When the download is complete, click **Open** or **Run** to open or run the file, or click **Close**.

Did You Know?

You can access a site with lots of files to download. Try these sites to find plenty of files to download: *http://www.download.com* and *http://www.shareware.com*. Just beware of viruses which can come from downloaded files off the Internet.

Click to open
or save the file
download

Downloading Files from an FTP Site

Sometimes you'll need to connect directly to a File Transfer Protocol (FTP) site to download or transfer a file to a remote computer. Internet Explorer allows you to easily access and download files from any FTP site, public or private. Public FTP sites allow you to access files without requiring that you have an account on the server. Private FTP sites expect you to enter your user name and password in order to see the folders and files. When you are connected to an FTP site, Internet Explorer's view of the files is the same as looking at a folder on your local hard disk. Within this view you can drag onto your desktop or right-click to copy the file in a particular folder on your computer.

Download a File from an FTP Site

1. In the Address bar, type the address for the FTP site, and then press Enter.

2. If necessary, type your user name and password, and then click **Log On**.

> **IMPORTANT** *Before you download files, make sure your antivirus software is up-to-date.*

3. Click the **Page** button, and then click **Open FTP Site in Windows Explorer**.

4. Right-click the file or folder you want to download, click **Copy To Folder**, select a location, and then click **OK**.

> **TIMESAVER** *You can select the items you want to download, and then use the Copy and Paste commands. Select the files, press Ctrl+C, display the destination folder, and then press Ctrl+V.*

Folders on FTP site

Downloading Windows Live Essentials

Windows Live Essentials (**New!**) is a set of programs that allows you to communicate on the web and work with and share media. The Windows Live programs includes Windows Live Call, Windows Live Mail, Windows Live Messenger, Windows Live Movie Maker, Windows Live Photo Gallery, Windows Live Writer, and Windows Live Family Safety. Many of these programs came installed along with Windows Vista, however in Windows 7, you need to download and install them. Installing the programs separately allows you to get and use the latest versions of the software. After you install Windows Live Essentials, you can access the Windows Live programs from the Start menu.

Download and Access Windows Live Essentials

1. In Internet Explorer, visit the Windows Live Essentials web site at the following address:

   http://download.live.com

2. Click **Download**.

3. Click **Run** or **Save** to run the setup program or save it to your computer. If you click Save, select a location, click **Save**, and then click **Run**.

   The Windows Live setup program starts.

4. Select the check boxes with the Windows Live programs you want to install.

5. Click **Install**.

6. Follow the on-screen instructions to select additional tools and complete the installation.

7. When you're done, click **Close**.

8. To access the Windows Live programs, click the **Start** button, point to **All Programs**, point to **Windows Live**, and then click the programs you want to start.

Exchanging Messages and Information

Introduction

If you're like many people today who are using the Internet to communicate with friends and business associates, you probably have piles of information (names, e-mail addresses, phone numbers, etc.) that you need often. Unless this information is in one convenient place, and can be accessed immediately, the information becomes ineffective and you become unproductive. Microsoft Windows Live Mail (**New!**) solves these problems by integrating management and organization tools into one simple system. Windows Live Mail is a powerful program for managing **electronic mail** (known as e-mail), and contact information like names, and e-mail addresses. Windows Live Mail doesn't come installed with Windows 7; it's available for free online from Microsoft. You can download this program as well as other program tools from Windows Live at *http://download.live.com*.

Using Windows Live Mail with an Internet connection allows you to accomplish several tasks:

◆ Create and send e-mail messages

◆ Manage multiple e-mail accounts

◆ Use the contacts to store and retrieve e-mail addresses

◆ Create stationery or add a personal signature to your e-mail messages

◆ Attach a file to an e-mail message

◆ Set junk e-mail options and mark e-mail messages as block or safe

◆ Join any number of newsgroups, which are collections of e-mail messages on related topics

◆ Use the calendar to make and manage appointments and tasks

What You'll Do

Start Windows Live Mail and Set Up an Account

View the Windows Live Mail Window

Import and Export Information

Add a Contact to Windows Live Contacts

Compose and Send E-mail

Create E-mail Stationery

Read and Reply to E-mail

Send and Retrieve a File

Send a Photo File

Manage and Delete E-mail

Set Junk E-mail Options

Divert Incoming E-mail to Folders

Protect Against E-mail Attacks

Send Secure E-mail

Select and Subscribe to a Newsgroup

Read and Filter the News

Post a News Message

View Calendars

Schedule Appointments

Create and Use a Calendar

Create and View Feeds

Starting Windows Live Mail

Whether you want to exchange e-mail with colleagues and friends or join newsgroups to trade ideas and information, Windows Live Mail (**New!**) provides you with the tools you need. Windows Live Mail doesn't come installed with Windows 7; you need to download and install it from Microsoft Windows Live. This chapter describes version 2009; your downloaded version with updates may differ slightly; select About Microsoft Windows Live Mail on the Help menu for version information. The first time you start Windows Live Mail, you can set up an e-mail account using a wizard. If you already have Outlook Express 6 or Windows Mail on your computer, Windows Live Mail uses your existing accounts. You can set Windows Live Mail as your default e-mail program so that whenever you click an e-mail link on a web page or choose the mail command in your web browser, Windows Live Mail opens. You can also set Windows Live Mail as your default news reader. If you want to use other Windows Live services and additional features (**New!**) , such as Photo E-mail message, Windows Live Messenger, Windows Live Contacts, or Calendars, you need to sign in with Windows Live ID.

Download and Start Windows Live Mail

1. If you have not downloaded the program from Microsoft, open your browser, go to the Windows Live Essentials web site at *http://download.live.com*, and then click **Download** to download and install the program.

2. Click the **Start** button, and then point to **All Programs**.

3. Point to **Windows Live**, and then click **Windows Live Mail**.

   If the wizard opens, follow the step-by-step instructions to set up your e-mail account.

4. To use Windows Live services and additional features, click **Sign in** on the toolbar, type your Windows ID, and then click **Sign in**.

See Also

See "Setting Up an Account" on page 170 for information on creating an e-mail account.

Set Windows Live Mail as your Default Program

1 Click the **Start** button, point to **All Programs**, and then click **Default Programs**.

2 Click **Set your default programs**.

3 Click **Windows Live Mail** or **Windows Live Mail (News)**.

4 Click **Set this program as default**.

5 Click **OK**.

6 Click the **Close** button.

Did You Know?

You can set your e-mail and news program defaults in Windows Live Mail. In Windows Live Mail, click the Tools menu, click Options, click the General tab, click the Make Default button at the bottom of the Options dialog box, and then click OK. If the buttons are grayed out, the Windows Live Mail is already set as the default.

You can get Help in Windows Live Mail. In Windows Live Mail, click the Help menu, and then click Get Help With Mail. Your browser starts and displays the Windows Live Help web site for Mail.

See Also

See "Downloading Windows Live Essentials" on page 166 for information on downloading Windows Live programs.

Setting Up an Account

Before you can set up an e-mail account, you need your account name, password, e-mail server type, and the names of your incoming and outgoing e-mail servers from your ISP or network administrator. The Add an E-mail Account wizard helps you connect to one or more e-mail servers. However, if you already have Outlook Express 6 or Windows Mail on your computer, Windows Live Mail uses your existing accounts. Windows Live Mail allows you to send and retrieve e-mail messages from different types of e-mail servers, which are the locations where your e-mail is stored before you access it. Windows Live Mail supports three types of accounts: mail, newsgroups, and contacts directory services. A **newsgroup** is an electronic forum where people with a common interest can share ideas, ask and answer questions, and comment on and discuss any subject. **Contacts Directory** services are online address books that are typically provided by large organizations. You can set up multiple accounts in Windows Live Mail.

Set Up an Account

1. Click the **Tools** menu, click **Accounts**, and then click **Add**.

   TIMESAVER *Click the Add e-mail account link in the Folder pane.*

   ◆ If you can't see menus, click the **Menus** button, and then click **Show menu bar**.

   ◆ If Windows Live Mail starts for the first time, the Connect to the Internet wizard begins.

2. If prompted, click **E-mail Account**, and then click **Next** to continue.

   ◆ You can also set up an account for a newsgroup or Directory Service; the wizard steps vary depending on the account type.

3. In the Account wizard, type your E-mail address, password, and display name.

4. If you want to manually set up account options, select the **Manually configure server settings for e-mail account** check box. If you want to automatically set it up, clear the check box.

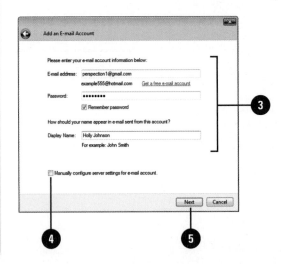

5 Click **Next**.

♦ For an automatic setup, go to Step 10 in order to finish.

6 Click the **Mail Server** arrow, and then select the incoming mail server type you want to use.

7 Enter the name of the incoming mail server, port number, and log on security settings from your ISP.

8 Enter the name of the outgoing mail server, port number, and security options from your ISP.

9 Click **Next**.

10 Click **Finish**, and then click **Close**.

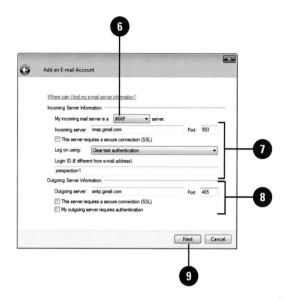

Did You Know?

You can remove a Windows Live Mail account. Click the Tools menu, click Accounts, click the account you want to remove, and then click Remove.

You can import or export Internet account settings. Click the Tools menu, and then click Accounts. To import account settings, click Import, select the Internet Account Files (.iaf), and then click Open. To export account settings, select the account you want to export, type a name, specify a location, and then click Save.

You can change account settings. Click the Tools menu, click Accounts, select the account you want to change, click Properties, use the tabs to display options, change the options you want, click OK, and then click Close.

You can choose an account as the default. Click the Tools menu, click Accounts, select the account you want to set, click Set As Default, and then click Close.

For Your Information

How Do I Choose an E-mail Server?

Windows Live Mail supports three types of incoming e-mail servers: **POP3** (Post Office Protocol), **IMAP** (Internet Message Access Protocol), and **HTTP** (Hypertext Transfer Protocol). A protocol is a set of rules and standards that control the transmission of content, format, sequencing, and error management for information over the Internet or network much like rules of the road govern the way you drive. POP3 servers allow you to access e-mail messages from a single Inbox folder, while IMAP servers allow you to access multiple folders. HTTP servers are used on web sites, such as online Windows Live Mail, and allow you to send and receive e-mail messages on a web site. When you use POP3 or IMAP e-mail servers, you also need to provide an outgoing e-mail server. **SMTP** (Simple Mail Transfer Protocol) is generally used to send messages between e-mail servers.

Viewing the Windows Live Mail Window

Menu bar
The Menu bar gives you access to all Windows Live Mail commands.

Toolbar
The Toolbar contains buttons for the most commonly used commands you need to work with mail messages.

Message list
The Message list displays e-mail messages.

Folder pane
The Folder pane contains all the folders in which Mail stores messages.

Programs
The Programs area contains all the programs in Windows Live Mail.

Status bar
The Status bar displays information about your Internet connection with a mail or newsgroup server.

Reading pane
The Reading pane displays the contents of the current message selected in the Message list.

Frequently Asked Questions

Showing the Menu and Customizing the Layout

If you don't see menus, click the Menus button on the toolbar, and then click Show Menu Bar. You can also use the Layout command on the View menu or Menus button to customize the Windows Live Mail window to suit your needs. You can show or hide different parts of the window, and customize the Folder and Reading pane display. To customize the toolbar, click the View menu or Menus button, and then click Customize toolbar.

Importing and Exporting Information

If you already have contact information in another e-mail program, you can import it into Windows Live Contacts. You can import information from Windows Address Book, Business Card, Microsoft Office Outlook, and Comma Separated Values. Windows Live Mail uses Windows Live Contacts to manage contact information. You can also export your contact information from Windows Live Mail to work with other programs. In Windows Live Mail, you can import and export messages and account information.

Import or Export Windows Live Contacts

1. Click the **Contacts** button in the Folder pane.

2. Click the **File** menu, point to **Import** or **Export**, and then click an import or export file type. Click CSV is a common text file type.

3. Click **Browse**, select the file with the contacts you want to import or export, click and then click **Open**.

4. Click **Next**.

5. Select the fields you want to import or export.

6. Click **Finish**, and then click the **Close** button to exit Windows Live Contacts.

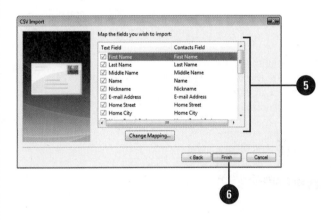

Import or Export Messages

1. Click the **File** menu, point to **Import** or **Export**, and then click **Messages**.

2. Select a message format.

3. Click **Next**.

4. Click **Browse**, select the location where you want to import or export, click and then click **Open**.

5. Click **Next**, follow the wizard instructions, and then click **Finish**.

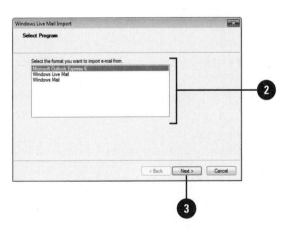

Adding a Contact to Windows Contacts

A **contact** is a person or company that you communicate with. One contact can often have several mailing addresses, phone numbers, or e-mail addresses. You can store this information in Windows Live Contacts along with other detailed information, such as job title, cell phone number, and web page addresses. You can organize your contacts into folders or into **contact category**, which are groups of related people with whom you communicate regularly.

Add or Edit a Contact

1. Click the **Contacts** button in the Folder pane.

2. Click the **New** button on the toolbar to create a new contact or select a contact, and then click **Edit** on the toolbar to edit one.

3. Enter the contact's name, e-mail address, and other quick information.

4. Click the other available categories in the left pane to enter additional information.

5. Click **Add contact**.

6. Click the **Close** button to exit Windows Live Contacts.

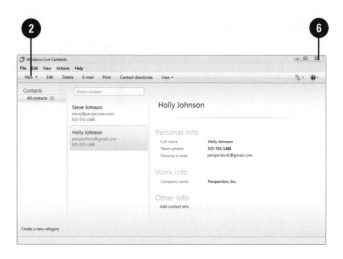

Did You Know?

You can add an address from an e-mail message. In the Inbox, open the message with the e-mail address you want, and then click Add contact.

You can automatically add a reply address to Windows Live Contacts. Click the Tools menu, click Options, click the Send tab, select the Automatically put people I reply to in my address book after the third reply check box, and then click OK.

Create a Contact Group

1. Click the **Contacts** button in the Folder pane.

2. Click the **New** button arrow on the toolbar, and then click **Category**.

   TIMESAVER *Click the Create a new category link at the bottom of the Contacts pane.*

3. Type a name for the new group.

4. Click each member in the list of contacts you want to add.

5. Click **Save**.

6. To add a contact to an existing category, drag the contact to the category in the Contacts pane.

7. To remove a contact from a category, click the contact in a category, click the **Delete** button on the toolbar, and then click **OK**.

8. Click the **Close** button to exit Windows Live Contacts.

Contact group

Did You Know?

You can edit or delete a category. In Windows Live Contacts, right-click a category, and then click Edit Category or Delete Category. To edit, make the change, and then click Save. To delete, click OK to confirm.

You can sort your Windows Live Contacts. In Windows Live Contacts, click the view menu, and then click List With Preview or List. In the contacts list, click the heading by which you want to sort. You can switch the sorting method from ascending to descending by clicking the same column heading again.

For Your Information

Printing Contacts from Windows Live Contacts

You can print your contact information in a variety of formats, such as Memo and Phone List. The Memo style prints all the information you have for a contact with descriptive titles. The Phone List style prints all the phone numbers for a contact or for all your contacts. To print contact information, open Windows Live Contacts, select the contacts you want to print, click Print on the toolbar, select a print range, print style, and the number of copies you want to print, and then click Print in the Print dialog box.

Composing and Sending E-mail

E-mail is becoming the primary form of written communication for many people. E-mail messages follow a standard memo format, with fields for the sender, recipient, date, and subject of the message. To send an e-mail, you need to enter the recipient's e-mail address, type a subject, then type the message itself. For a personal touch, you can also create an e-mail message with stationery designs. You can send the same e-mail to more than one individual, to a contact group, or to a combination of individuals and groups. Before you send the e-mail, you can set a priority flag (high, normal, or low) to convey the message's importance.

Compose and Send an E-mail

1. Click the **Mail** button in the Folder pane.

2. Click the **New** button on the toolbar.

3. Click the **To** button to select contacts.

   TIMESAVER *Type the recipient's name in the To box.*

4. Click a recipient or group.

5. Click one of the following:

   ◆ The **To** button if you want the recipient to receive the message and to see the addresses in the To and Cc fields.

   ◆ The **Cc** button if you want the recipient to receive a copy of the message and to see the addresses in the To and Cc fields.

   ◆ The **Bcc** button if you want the recipient to receive a copy of the message but not be listed as a recipient on any other copy of the message.

6. Click **OK**.

7. If you have multiple accounts, click the **From** button, and then select an account.

8. Click in the **Subject** box, and then enter a brief description of your message.

Or type the address here

9 Click in the **message** box, and then type the text of your message.

◆ If a red line appears under a word, right-click the misspelled word, and then click a suggested word or **Add to dictionary**.

10 If you want, use the commands on the Formatting toolbar to format your message.

◆ To add a stationery, click the **Stationery** button, click **More stationery**, select a file, and then click **OK**.

11 If you want, click the **High** or **Low** button on the toolbar to set a priority level. To set normal, click the **Tools** menu, point to **Set priority**, and then click **Normal**.

12 Click the **Send** button on the toolbar. Or click the **File** menu, click **Send later**, and then click **OK** to confirm that the message has been placed in your Outbox folder.

13 If you chose Send Later, click the **Sync** button on the toolbar to deliver your message.

◆ To send and receive e-mail from a specific account, click the **Sync** button arrow, and then click an account name.

TIMESAVER *Press F5 to send and receive e-mail for all accounts.*

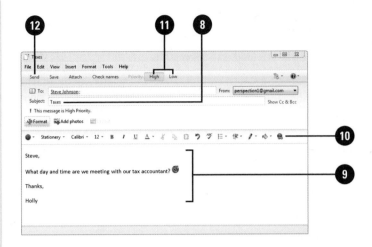

For Your Information

Checking the Spelling in E-mail

Before you send an e-mail message, you should spell check the text and read through the content to make sure your spelling is accurate and your content conveys the message you want to the recipient(s). To start the spell check, type an e-mail message, click the Spelling button on the Format toolbar or click the Tools menu, and then click Spelling. To have Windows Live Mail spell check all of your e-mail messages before sending them, display the Windows Live Mail window, click the Tools menu, click Options, click the Spelling tab in the Options dialog box, select the Always Check Spelling Before Sending check box, and then click OK. Additional options are turned on by default, which includes Automatically Correct Common Capitalization And Spelling Mistakes, Check My Spelling As I Type, and Check Spelling In Current Input Language. If you want to add or remove words from the custom dictionary, click Edit to make changes in the Edit Custom Dictionary dialog box.

Creating E-mail Stationery

If you're tired of the typical bland, unexciting look of e-mail, Windows Live Mail has the answer—Windows Live Mail stationery. This feature allows you to create e-mail messages with their own colorful background and font styles. You can also customize your messages with a signature or by attaching your business card. A **signature** is any file, text file with your signature, or photo of yourself that you choose. Several stationery styles are included with Windows Live Mail.

Create a Signature

1. Click the **Tools** menu, and then click **Options**.

2. Click the **Signatures** tab.

3. Click **New** to create a new signature.

4. Type the information for the signature. If available, select the file that contains your signature.

5. To enter more than one signature, repeat steps 3 and 4.

6. Select the signature you want to use most of the time, and then click **Set as Default**.

7. If you have multiple accounts, click **Advanced**, select the check boxes for the accounts you want to use, and then click **OK**.

8. If you want, select the **Add signatures to all outgoing messages** check box, or select the **Don't add signatures to Replies and Forwards** check box.

9. Click **OK**.

Advanced settings

Did You Know?

You can add your signature to e-mail quickly. In an e-mail message, click where you want the signature, click the Insert menu, and then click Signature. If you have more than one signature, point to Signature, and then click the signature you want to use.

Create Stationery Using the Stationery Setup Wizard

1 Click the **Tools** menu, and then click **Options**.

2 Click the **Compose** tab.

3 Click **Create New**, and then click **Next** to begin the Stationery Setup Wizard.

4 Select a picture and color, and then click **Next**.

5 Choose the font, font size, and color, and then click **Next**.

6 Choose the left and top margin, and then click **Next**.

7 Type a name for your stationery, and then click **Finish**.

8 Select the **Mail** check box to always include stationery with your e-mail messages.

9 Click **Select** to choose the standard stationery, and then click **OK**.

10 Click **OK**.

Did You Know?

You can create a message using other or new stationery. Click the New Mail button on the toolbar, click the Stationery button, click More Stationery, select a stationery file or click Create New to create one, and then click OK.

You can select a stationery for every new message. Click the Tools menu, click Options, click the Compose tab, select the Mail check box, click Select, click a stationery file, click OK, click the Send tab, click the HTML option, and then click OK.

Reading and Replying to E-mail

You can receive e-mail anytime—even when your computer is turned off. You can retrieve your e-mail manually or set Windows Live Mail to do so automatically. When you start Windows Live Mail, the program checks for new e-mail. It continues to check periodically while the program is open. New messages appear in boldface in the Inbox along with any messages you haven't moved or deleted. You can also view new messages for all accounts under Quick views (**New!**); after you read the e-mail, it's only available in the Inbox. Message flags may appear next to a message, which indicate a priority, the need for follow up, or an attachment. Windows Live Mail blocks images and other potentially harmful content from automatically downloading in an e-mail message from unknown people. Blocked items are replaced with a red "x". You can respond to a message in two ways: reply to it, which creates a new message addressed to the sender(s) and other recipients; or forward it, which creates a new message you can send to someone else. In either case, the original message appears in the response.

Open and Read an E-mail

1. Click the **Mail** button in the Folder pane.

2. Click the **Unread e-mail** icon under Quick views in the Folder pane, or click the **Inbox** icon for the mail account you want.

3. Open an e-mail message.

   ◆ Click an e-mail message to read it in the Reading pane.

   ◆ Double-click an e-mail message or press Enter for a selected message to open it in its own window.

4. To download blocked pictures and other content, click the Information bar at the top of the message, or click the **Delete and block** link in the heading of the message.

   ◆ To show the pictures, click the **Show images** link.

5. Click the **Previous** or **Next** button on the Message toolbar to read additional e-mail messages.

Reply to an E-mail

1. Open the e-mail message you want to reply to.

2. Click the **Reply** button to respond to the sender only, or click the **Reply all** button to respond to the sender and to all other recipients.

   TIMESAVER *Press Ctrl+R to reply to the message author.*

3. Add or delete names from the To or the Cc box.

4. Type your message.

5. Attach any files to send.

6. Click the **Send** button on the toolbar.

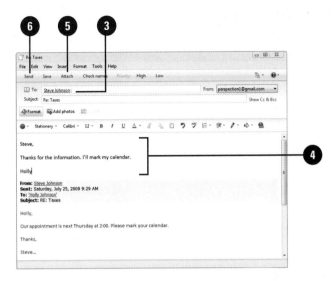

Forward an E-mail

1. Open the e-mail message you want to forward.

2. Click the **Forward** button on the toolbar.

3. Type the name(s) of the recipient(s), or click the **To** button, and then select the recipient(s).

4. Type your message.

5. Attach any files to send.

6. Click the **Send** button on the toolbar.

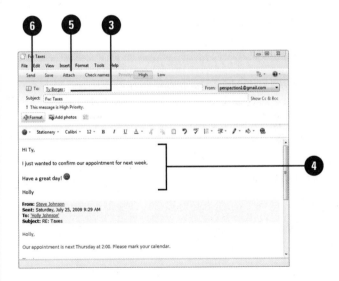

Did You Know?

Attachments aren't sent on replies. When you reply to a message that had an attachment, the attachment isn't returned to the original sender. You can forward the message to the original sender if you need to send the attachment back.

Sending and Retrieving a File

You can use e-mail to easily share a file, such as a picture or a document by attaching it to an e-mail. Upon receiving the e-mail, the recipient can open the file in the program that created it or save it. Make sure you know and trust the sender before you open it, because it might contain a virus or other security threat. It's important to keep your antivirus software up-to-date. The Attachment Manager provides security information to help you understand more about the file you are downloading. If an attachment is considered safe, Windows Live Mail makes it completely available to you. Examples of safe attachments are text files (.txt) and graphic files, such as JPEGs (.jpg) and GIFs (.gif). If an attachment is potentially unsafe, such as an executable program (.exe), screensavers (.scr) or script files (including .vbs), Windows Live Mail displays a notice on the Information Bar and blocks it so you will not be able to open it without taking explicit action. If Windows Live Mail can't determine the safety of an attachment, it displays a security warning (when you try to move, save, open, or print the file) with information about the file.

Send a File in an E-mail

1. Compose a new message or reply to an existing message.

   IMPORTANT *Some ISPs have trouble sending large attachments; check with your ISP.*

2. Click the **Attach** button on the toolbar.

3. Select the drive and folder that contains the file you want to attach.

4. Click to select the file.

5. Click **Open**.

6. Click the **Send** button on the toolbar.

Did You Know?

You can open an attachment from an e-mail message. Select the e-mail message in the Inbox, click the Attachment icon on the Reading pane, and then click the name of the file.

Attached file

Open a File in an E-mail

① Select the message with the attached file.

IMPORTANT *If you're not sure of the source of an attachment, don't open it, because it might contain a virus or worm. Be sure to use anti-virus software.*

② Right-click the **Attachment** icon.

③ Click **Open**.

See Also

See "Avoiding Viruses and Other Harmful Attacks" on page 330 for information on how to avoid getting a virus and other harmful threats.

See "Protecting Against E-mail Attacks" on page 194 for information on how to avoid getting a virus from an attached file in an e-mail.

Save Files in an E-mail

① Select the message with the attached file.

② Click the **File** menu, and then click **Save attachments**.

TIMESAVER *Right-click the attachment, and then click Save as or Save all.*

③ Select the attached file you want to save or click **Select All** to select all the attached files.

④ Click **Browse**, select the drive and folder where you want to save the file, and then click **Open**.

⑤ Click **Save**.

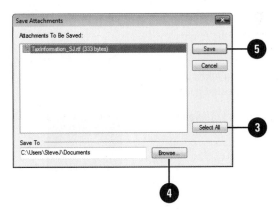

Sending a Photo File

In Windows Live Mail, you can add photos to an e-mail message as an inline image in the message area (**New!**) or as an attachment. With an inline photo, you can add formatting options to the image, such as frames, color borders, black and white, rotate, and captions. You can also correct exposure and color, change to black and white, rotate, and change image quality to reduce to size and increase the upload speed.

Send a Photo File in an E-mail

① Compose a new message or reply to an existing message.

IMPORTANT *Some ISPs have trouble sending large attachments; check with your ISP.*

② Click the **Add photos** button.

③ Select the drive and folder that contains the file you want to attach.

④ Select a photo file, and then click **Add**.

⑤ When you're done adding photos, click **Done**.

The photo images appears in the message area (inline) and the Photos toolbar appears.

⑥ To Add more photos, click the **Add more photos** button on the Photos toolbar.

⑦ Use the buttons on the Photos toolbar to modify a selected photo.

⑧ When you're done, click the **Send** button on the toolbar.

Format a Photo in an E-mail

1 Compose a new message or reply to an existing message.

2 Click the **Add photos** button, and then add the photos you want.

3 Select the photo you want to format.

4 Use the following buttons on the Photos toolbar to modify a selected photo:

◆ **Framing button.** Click a framing button to add matting, wood frame, instant photo, metal corners, pushpin, spotlight or brush edges.

◆ **Autocorrect.** Click to automatically adjust exposure and color.

◆ **Black & White.** Click to change the photo colors to black and white.

◆ **Rotate.** Click to rotate the photo.

◆ **Quality.** Click High, Medium, or Low to specify a quality level.

An upload time and size appears next to the quality selection.

5 To add a caption to a selected photo, click below the photo, and then type a caption.

6 To change the size and layout, click the **Layout** button, and then click an arrangement/size button on the toolbar.

7 When you're done, click the **Send** button on the toolbar.

Managing E-mail

A common problem with using e-mail is an overcrowded Inbox. To keep your Inbox organized, you should move messages you want to save to other folders and subfolders, delete messages you no longer want, and create new folders as you need them. Storing incoming messages in other folders and deleting unwanted messages make it easier to see the new messages you receive and to keep track of important messages. If you can't find a message, you can use the Search box to quickly find it. If you have not finished composing a message, you can save it in the Drafts folder and work on it later.

Create a New Folder

1. Click the **File** menu, point to **New**, and then click **Folder**.

2. Type a name for the new folder.

3. Click the folder in which you want to place the new folder.

   ◆ Click the account name to place the folder in the main folder list.

   ◆ Click one of the other folders in the list to make the new folder a subfolder.

4. Click **OK**.

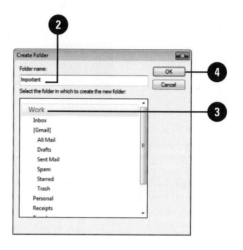

Organize E-mail in Folders

1. Select the e-mail message you want to move. If necessary, press and hold the Ctrl key, and click to select multiple e-mail messages.

2. Drag the e-mail message(s) to the new folder.

Did You Know?

You can sort messages quickly.
To sort messages by sender, subject, date, priority or flag, click a header in the Reading pane.

Find an E-mail or News Message

1 Click in the **Search** box.

2 Type a word or part of a word in the message.

As you type, the message list narrows and displays messages that match the search text.

3 Click the **Search in** button, and then click **Unread e-mail** or **All e-mail** to define the search.

Did You Know?

You can flag an important message that need attention later. Select the e-mail message, click the Actions menu, and then click Flag Message.

Search results

Work on a Draft E-mail

1 Open a new or a reply to an existing e-mail message, and then type a message.

2 Click the **Save** button on the toolbar, and then click **OK**.

3 Close the e-mail message.

4 Click the **Drafts** folder in the Folder pane.

5 Double-click the e-mail message to view it.

6 When you're done with the message, click the **Send** button on the toolbar.

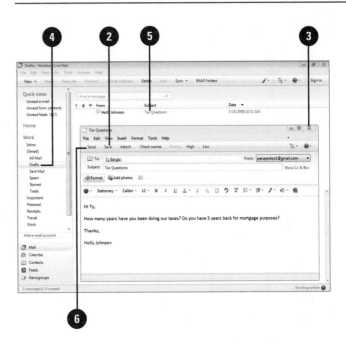

Deleting E-mail

When you delete an e-mail message, Windows Live Mail simply moves it into the Deleted Items folder. If you want to recover a deleted message, you just have to retrieve it from the Deleted Items folder. To get rid of a message permanently, you need to open the Deleted Items folder, select the message, and then click Delete. Windows Live Mail automatically places e-mail messages in the Sent Items folder every time you send them. You will want to periodically open the Sent Items folder and delete messages so your mail account doesn't get too large. You can also use maintenance options to help you clean up.

Delete Unwanted E-mail

1. Click a folder icon in the Folder pane with the e-mail you want to delete.

2. Click the e-mail you want to delete.

3. Click the **Delete** button on the toolbar.

   TIMESAVER *Press Delete or Ctrl+D to delete the selected message(s).*

Recover E-mail from the Deleted Items Folder

1. Click the **Deleted items** or **Trash** folder (depending on the account type) in the Folder pane to open the folder.

2. Select the e-mail message you want to retrieve.

3. Drag the e-mail message to another folder.

Change E-mail Maintenance Options

1. Click the **Tools** menu, and then click **Options**.

2. Click the **Advanced** tab.

3. Click **Maintenance**.

4. Select the maintenance options you want.

   ◆ Delete messages on exit or after a certain number of days.

   ◆ Compact messages to save space.

5. Click **Close**.

Setting Junk E-mail Options

Junk e-mail can seem like a never ending battle. It keeps piling up. Windows Live Mail provides the Safety Options dialog box to help you reduce the amount of junk e-mail you receive. You can set a junk e-mail protection level that makes sense to you, from no filtering to only the safe senders list. If you receive junk e-mail from international domains or languages, you can quickly and easily block them. E-mail has become the new way to commit fraud using spoof sites and addresses. These types of e-mail are called phishing. You can set options in Windows Live Mail that can help protect you again potential phishing attacks.

Change Junk E-mail Options

1 Click the **Tools** menu, and then click **Safety options**.

2 Click the **Options** tab.

3 Click the level of junk e-mail protection option you want.

4 Select or clear the **Permanently delete suspected Junk e-mail instead of moving it to the junk E-mail folder** check box.

IMPORTANT *You should only select this option if you selected the Low option above to avoid deleting regular e-mail.*

5 Click **OK**.

Windows Live Mail detects junk e-mail

Guard Against Phishing

1. Click the **Tools** menu, and then click **Safety options**.

2. Click the **Phishing** tab.

3. Select the **Protect my Inbox from messages with potential Phishing links** check box.

4. Select the **Move phishing E-mail to the Junk e-mail folder** check box.

5. Click **OK**.

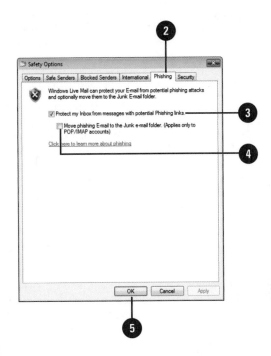

Block International Junk E-mail

1. Click the **Tools** menu, and then click **Safety options**.

2. Click the **International** tab.

3. Click **Blocked Top-Level Domain List**.

4. Select the individual check boxes with the domains you want to block or click **Select All**.

5. Click **OK**.

6. Click **OK**.

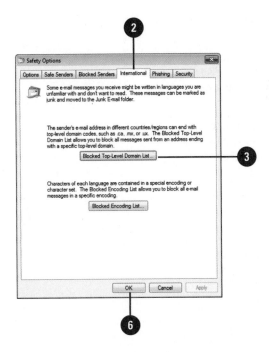

Marking an E-mail Blocked or Safe

If you receive unwanted e-mail from a specific address or domain, you can block all messages from that sender. You can also quickly mark an e-mail as junk. On the other hand, if you find a wanted e-mail in the Junk E-mail folder, you can mark it as safe and not as junk. When you mark a message as junk, Windows Live Mail moves the message into the Junk E-mail folder, where you can browser through or delete it later. You can mark individual or groups of messages as blocked or safe. If you want to add, edit, or remove addresses or domains from the Safe or Block Senders list, you can use the Safety Options dialog box, which you can access from the Tools menu.

Mark an E-mail Blocked or Safe from a Sender

1 Select the e-mail you want to block.

2 To mark the e-mail as junk and move it to the Junk E-mail folder, click the **Junk** button on the toolbar.

3 To mark blocked or safe, click the **Actions** menu, and then point to **Junk e-mail**.

4 Click the Junk E-mail option you want:

- ◆ **Block.** Click **Add sender to blocked senders list** or **Add sender's domain to blocked senders list**.

- ◆ **Safe. Add sender to safe senders list** or **Add sender's domain to safe senders list**.

5 Click **OK** to alert message.

Did You Know?

You can mark e-mail not as junk. In the Junk E-mail folder, select the e-mail you want to change, click the Actions menu, point to Junk e-mail, and then click Mark As Not Junk. The e-mail is moved back to the Inbox.

Diverting Incoming E-mail to Folders

Windows Live Mail can direct incoming messages for your POP account (IMAP and HTTP accounts not supported) that meet criteria to other folders in the Folder pane rather than to your Inbox. For example, your friend loves sending you funny e-mail, but you often don't have time to read it right away. You can set message rules to store any messages you receive from your friend in a different folder so they won't clutter your Inbox. When you are ready to read the messages, you simply open the folder and access the messages just as you would messages in the Inbox. If you receive unwanted e-mail from a specific address, you can block all messages from that sender.

Set Rules for Incoming E-mail

1. Click the **Tools** menu, point to **Message Rules**, and then click **Mail**.

   If no rules are set, skip to step 3.

2. Click **New** to create a new rule, or select a rule and the click **Modify** to edit an existing one.

3. Click the appropriate conditions and actions for your rule.

4. Click a link to enter the underlying information for that condition or action.

5. Specify the criteria for your rule in the Selection dialog box that appears, and then click **OK**.

6. Repeat steps 4 and 5 for each condition and action you have set.

7. Type a name for this rule.

8. Click **Save rule**.

9. Click **OK**.

Did You Know?

You can apply rules right now. Click the Tools menu, point to Message Rules, and then click Mail. Click Apply Now. Select the rule(s) you want to apply and the folder that contains the messages, and then click Apply Now.

Protecting Against E-mail Attacks

In Windows Live Mail, security zones allow you to determine whether or not to run active content, such as ActiveX controls, from inside HTML e-mail messages, which potentially can carry viruses and other harmful threats. You can adjust the security zone levels using Internet Options in the Control Panel. To provide further protection, you can set options to let you know when an program tries to send mail with your e-mail address to contacts in your address book (which is a common way to propagate a virus), to not allow attachments to be saved or opened that might contain a virus, and to stop pictures and other content from automatically downloading to your computer (which is a common way spammers confirm your e-mail address to send more spam) from contacts who are not in your address book until you have a chance to read the message.

Protect Against E-mail Attacks in Windows Live Mail

1. Click the **Tools** menu, and then click **Safety options**.

2. Click the **Security** tab.

3. Click the security zone option you want: **Internet zone (Less secure)** or **Restricted sites zone (More secure)**.

4. Select the **Warn me when other applications try to send mail as me** check box.

5. Select the **Do not allow attachments to be saved or opened that could potentially be a virus** check box.

6. Select the **Block images and other external content in HTML e-mail** and **Show images and external content sent from e-mail addresses in my Safe Senders list** (**New!**) check boxes.

7. Click **OK**.

See Also

See "Avoiding Viruses and Other Harmful Attacks" on page 330 for information on security threats in e-mail.

Sending Secure E-mail

In Windows Live Mail, you can set security options to send e-mail messages with a digital ID or encryption. A digital ID verifies your identity to your recipients in the same way a picture ID verifies your identify when you write a check. Before you can send a digitally signed e-mail, you need to get a digital ID from an independent certification authority, which you can access from Windows Live Mail. Encryption prevents others on the Internet from intercepting and reading your e-mail. Before you can send an encrypted e-mail, your Windows Contacts needs to contain a digital ID for each recipient, which allows them to decrypt the message for reading.

Set Options to Send Secure E-mail in Windows Live Mail

1. Click the **Tools** menu, then click **Safety options**.

2. Click the **Security** tab.

3. To get a digital ID, click **Get Digital ID**, and then follow the instructions.

4. To encrypt e-mail, select the **Encrypt contents and attachments for all outgoing messages** check box.

5. To digitally sign e-mail, select the **Digitally sign all outgoing messages** check box.

6. Click **Advanced**.

7. Select the check boxes to include my digital ID and add sender's certificates to my Windows Contacts.

8. To check for a revoked digital ID, click the **Only when online** option.

9. Click **OK**.

10. Click **OK** again.

Selecting a News Server

A newsgroup is an electronic forum where people from around the world with a common interest can share ideas, ask and answer questions, and comment on and discuss any subject. You can find newsgroups on almost any topic. Before you can participate in a newsgroup, you must select a news server. A **news server** is a computer located on the Internet, which stores newsgroup messages, also called **articles**, on different topics. Each news server contains several newsgroups from which to choose. The Internet Connection Wizard walks you through the process of selecting a news server. This wizard also appears the first time you use Windows Live Mail News. To complete the wizard process, you might need an account name and password, and you need to choose a news server that you want to use.

Set up a News Server Using the Connect to the Internet Wizard

1. Click the **Tools** menu, click **Accounts**, and then click **Add**.

2. Click the **Newsgroup Account**, and then click **Next** to continue.

3. Type your name, and then click **Next** to continue.

4. Read the information in each wizard dialog box, type the required information, and then click **Next** to continue.

5. In the final wizard dialog box, click **Finish**.

6. Click **Close**.

7. If prompted, click a Subscribe To Newsgroups option, and then click **OK**.

Did You Know?

You can change the news server. Right-click the news server in the Folder pane, click Properties, change settings, and then click OK.

You can remove a news server. Right-click the news server in the Folder pane, click Remove Account, and then click Yes.

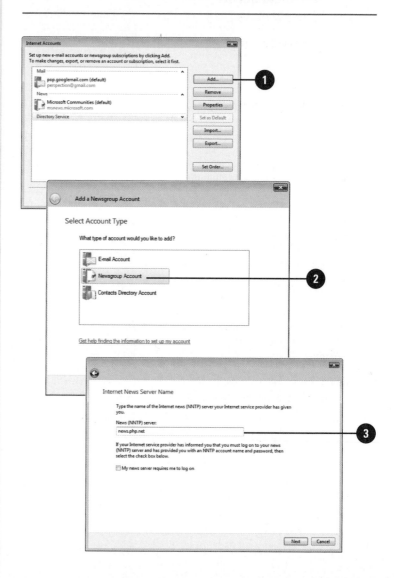

Subscribing to a Newsgroup

When you add a news server account, Windows Live Mail retrieves a list of newsgroups available on that server. Once you select a newsgroup, you can view its contents, or, if you expect to return to the newsgroup often, you can subscribe to it. Subscribing to a newsgroup places a link to the group in the Folder pane, providing easy access to the newsgroup. If you find that you are no longer interested in a newsgroup, you can unsubscribe from it. You can also view a newsgroup without subscribing to see if you might want to add it to your Folder pane.

Subscribe to a Newsgroup

1. Click the **Tools** menu, and then click **Manage Newsgroups**.

2. Type the word or phrase for which you want to search. As you type, the results appear in the Newsgroup list.

3. Scroll through the list of available newsgroups.

4. Click the newsgroup you want to subscribe to.

5. Click **Subscribe**.

6. Click **Go to** to see the posted messages.

Did You Know?

You can unsubscribe from a newsgroup. If you no longer want to see a newsgroup in your Folder pane, right-click the newsgroup name, click Unsubscribe on the shortcut menu, and then click OK.

Click to view subscribed newsgroups

Reading the News

Once you have subscribed to a newsgroup, you will want to view its messages. Click the newsgroup to display messages, and then click the message you want to read. Newsgroup messages appear in the Reading pane, just as e-mail messages do. If a plus sign (+) appears to the left of a newsgroup message, then the message contains a conversation thread. A **conversation thread** consists of the original message on a particular topic along with any responses that include the original message. Icons appear next to the news messages to indicate whether a conversation thread is expanded or collapsed, and whether or not it has been read.

Open and Read News Messages

1. Click the newsgroup in the Folder pane whose message you want to read.

2. Scroll through the list to see the posted messages.

3. Find the message you want to read using the following methods:

   ◆ To display all the responses to a conversation thread, click the plus sign (+) to the left of a message.

   ◆ To hide all the responses to a conversation thread, click the minus sign (-) to the left of a message.

   ◆ To view only unread messages, click the **View** menu, point to **Current View**, and then click **Hide Read or Ignored Messages**.

   ◆ To sort the messages based on type, click the column button you want to sort by. The column button toggles between sorting the column in ascending and descending order.

4. To read a message, click its header in the message list.

5. Read the message in the Reading pane.

News server

Filtering the News

After you become familiar with a newsgroup, you might decide that you don't want to retrieve messages from a particular person, about a specific subject, of a certain length, or older than a certain number of days. This is called **filtering** newsgroup messages.

Filter Unwanted Messages

1 Click the **Tools** menu, point to **Message Rules**, and then click **News**.

If no rules are set, skip to step 3.

2 Click **New** to create a new rule, or select a rule and click **Modify** to edit an existing one.

3 Select the conditions for your rule.

4 Select the actions for your rule.

5 Click any undefined value, such as the e-mail address you want to divert and the folder where you want to store the unwanted messages, and then provide information.

6 Type a name.

7 Click **Save rule**.

8 Click **OK**.

Did You Know?

You can ignore or watch a conversation. Select the conversation you want to ignore or watch, click the Actions menu, and then click Ignore Conversation or Watch Conversation.

Posting a News Message

Part of the fun of newsgroups is that you can participate in an ongoing discussion, respond privately to a message's author, or start a new thread yourself by posting your own message on a topic of interest to you. If you post a message to a newsgroup and then change your mind, you can cancel the message. Keep in mind that if someone has already downloaded the message, canceling the message will not remove it from that person's computer.

Post a News Message

1. Click the newsgroup in the Folder pane to which you want to post a message.

2. Click the **New** button on the toolbar.

3. Type a subject for your message.

4. Type your message.

5. Click the **Send** button on the toolbar.

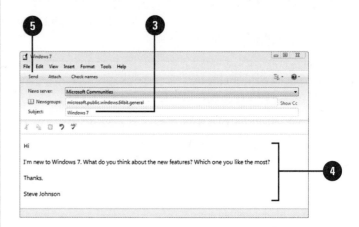

Cancel a Message

1. Select the newsgroup to which you posted the message in the Folder pane.

2. Select the message you want to cancel. You will need to wait until the newsgroup posts the message.

3. Click the **Actions** menu, click **Cancel Message**, and then click **OK**.

Did You Know?

You need to think before you post. Respond to personal questions posted to a newsgroup directly to the author, not to the entire newsgroup. Remember to click the Reply button.

Reply to a Message

1. Select the newsgroup to which you posted the message in the Folder pane.

2. Click the message to which you want to reply.

3. Select the appropriate command.

   ◆ Click the **Reply group** button on the toolbar to post your response to the newsgroup.

   ◆ Click the **Reply** button on the toolbar to send the message's author a private e-mail message.

   ◆ Click the **Forward** button to send an e-mail message to some other recipient.

4. Type your message, and if you want, delete parts of the original message that are unrelated to your reply.

5. Click the **Send** button on the toolbar.

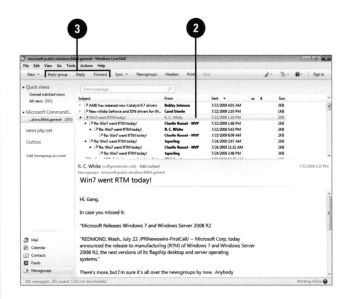

Did You Know?

You should name your messages carefully. When you compose a message, choose a subject that accurately reflects the content of your message so that people can decide whether they want to read it. When you reply to a message, don't change the subject line so that the conversation will remain threaded.

For Your Information

Deleting Old News Messages

Newsgroup messages are stored on your hard drive, so you should delete unneeded messages to free disk space. Windows Live Mail gives several clean-up options to help you optimize your hard drive space. You can delete entire messages (titles and bodies), compress messages, remove just the message bodies (leaving the title headers), or reset the information stored for selected messages, which allows you to refresh messages (download again). To clean up files on your local hard drive, select a news server in the Folder pane, click the Tools menu, click Options, click the Advanced tab, and then click Maintenance. You can select any of the clean-up options to delete or compress news messages at a specified time, or you can click Clean Up Now, and then click the button for the clean-up option you want to perform.

Viewing the Windows Calendar

Windows Calendar is an electronic version of the familiar paper daily planner. You can schedule time for completing specific tasks, meetings, vacations, holidays, or for any other activity with the Calendar. You can change the Calendar to show activities for the Day, Week (all seven days), or Month. The Appointment area serves as a daily planner where you can schedule activities by the day, week, or month. Appointments are scheduled activities such as a doctor's visit, and occupy a block of time in the Appointment area. Events are activities that last 24 hours or longer, such as a seminar, and do not occupy blocks of time in your calendar. Instead, they appear in a banner at the beginning of a day.

Open and Change the Calendar View

1. Click the **Calendar** button in the Folder pane.

2. You can change the Calendar view in several ways.

   ◆ Click the View buttons on the toolbar: **Day**, **Week**, or **Month**.

   ◆ Click the **View** menu, and then click the view option you want.

   ◆ Click the left arrow or right arrow on the Date Navigator to change the current month.

   ◆ Click a date on the Date Navigator to view that day's schedule. The date highlighted in red is today's date.

3. View and work with appointment or tasks associated with the current Calendar view.

Date Navigator   Use to change the view

Current calendar

Scheduling an Appointment

In Windows Calendar, an **appointment** is any activity you schedule that doesn't include other people or resources. An **event** is any appointment that lasts one or more full days (24-hour increments), such as a seminar, a conference, or a vacation. You enter appointment or event information in the same box; however, when you schedule an event, the *All day* check box is selected; the check box is cleared when you schedule an appointment. If an appointment or event recurs on a regular basis, such as a meeting, you can set the Recurrence option. If you need a reminder, you can also set the amount of time you need.

Schedule an Appointment

1. Click the **Calendar** button in the Folder pane.

2. To quickly add an event or appointment, select a time range in the primary calendar, and then start typing.

3. Click the **New** button on the toolbar to create a new one or double-click an existing one to edit it.

4. Type a subject and location.

5. Click the **Calendar** button, and then select the calendar where you want the appointment to appear.

6. To make an all-day appointment, select the **All day** check box.

7. Enter or select start and end times, as necessary.

8. To make an appointment recur, click the **Recurrence** button, and then select the option you want.

9. To set availability, click the **Availability** button, and then select an option: **Busy**, **Free**, **Tentative**, or **Away**.

10. Click the **Save & close** button on the toolbar.

Creating and Using Calendars

In Windows Calendar, you can create individual calendars for multiple people who use the program and share them with each other. When you have multiple calendars, you can view them individually or all at once, side-by-side, or overlaid to make it easier to compare one calendar with another and check for free time. Appointments for each calendar are displays in a different color to make them easier to tell whose schedule each item belongs to. If you want to add an appointment from another calendar to your calendar, you can drag appointments between the two calendars.

Create and View a Calendar

1. Click the **Calendar** button in the Folder pane.

2. Click the **Actions** menu, and then click **New calendar**.

   TIMESAVER *Click the Add Calendar link in the Calendar pane.*

3. Type the name you want for the calendar.

4. Click the color you want to use for the calendar.

5. Type a description for the calendar.

6. Select the **Make this my primary calendar** check box to make this your main calendar.

7. Click **Save**.

8. To view multiple calendars, select the check boxes next to the calendars you want. Clear the check boxes for the ones you want to hide.

Event on new calendar

Work with Calendars

- **Move an event.** Drag it to a new location.

- **New an event on a non primary calendar.** Click the **Calendar** button (calendar name), and then click **New event**, enter in information, and then click **Save & close**.

- **Hide calendar.** To hide a non-primary calendar, click the **Calendar** button (calendar name), and then click **Hide this calendar from list**.

- **Show hidden calendar.** To show a hidden calendar, click the **Calendar** button (calendar name) for the primary calendar, and then click **Add hidden calendars to list**.

- **Delete a calendar.** Click the **Calendar** button (calendar name) for the one you want, click **Delete**, and then click **Delete**.

- **Rename a calendar.** Click the **Calendar** button (calendar name), click **Properties**, change the name, and then click **Save**.

- **Change calendar properties.** Click the **Calendar** button (calendar name), click **Properties**, make the changes you want, and then click **Save**.

- **Print calendar.** To print a calendar, display the calendar you want to print, click the **Print** button on the toolbar, select a printer, the print style you want (**Day**, **Week**, or **Month**), and a print range (Start and End), and then click **OK**.

Click to print

Calendar options   Drag to move

Rename calendar

Calendar properties

Creating and Viewing Feeds

A feed, also known as RSS (Really Simple Syndication) feed, XML feed, syndicated content, or web feed, is usually offered on a subscription basis and typically free of charge. A feed can deliver text content in the form of news headlines or blogs, or digital content in the form of pictures, audio, and video. In Windows Live Mail, you create new feeds as well as view existing ones (**New!**). If you subscribed to feeds using Internet Explorer, those feeds also appear in Windows Live Mail.

Create and View a Feed

1. Click the **Feeds** button in the Folder pane.

2. To view a feed, select the feed in the Folders pane, and then select a specific article.

3. Click the **Manage feeds** button on the toolbar.

   TIMESAVER *Click the Add feed link in the Folder pane.*

4. To create a feed, click **Add Feed**, type a URL to the feed, and then click **OK**.

5. To edit a feed, select the feed, and then click **Edit**, select the options you want, and then click **OK**.

6. To delete a feed, select the feed, and then click **Delete**.

   ◆ Select the **When deleting a feed here, also delete it from your Internet Explorer feed list** check box.

7. Click the **Update feeds every** list arrow, and then select an interval.

8. Click **Close**.

Selected feed

Available feeds

Exchanging Instant Text and Video Messages

7

Introduction

Windows makes communicating with other computers over the Internet easier than ever with Windows Live Messenger (version 2009). This chapter describes version 2009 (v14); your downloaded version may differ slightly. You can talk to others over the Internet (like you do on a telephone), use video to see and be seen by others while you converse, share programs and files, collaborate on documents, share graphical content, and ask for or get remote online assistance from a contact.

You can use Windows Live Messenger to exchange instant messages with a designated list of contacts over the Internet. An **instant message** is an online typewritten conversation in real-time between two or more contacts. Unlike an e-mail message, instant messages require both parties to be online, and the communication is instantaneous. With Windows Live Messenger, you can send instant messages to any of your contacts who are online; have conversations with a group of friends; see the latest information about your contacts; see and hear your contacts; send and receive text messages with a mobile device; send a voice clip to express yourself personally; and save your conversations. In addition, you can make PC to telephone or PC to PC calls, share and update files with your friends using the Sharing folder, and connect with your friends who use Yahoo Messenger.

Windows Live Messenger uses different services to exchange messages, files, and other information. The default service is .NET Messenger Service, which individuals mostly use. For those working in a corporate environment, Windows Live Messenger supports Communications Service for networks that use SIP-server technology and Exchange Instant Messaging for networks that use Microsoft Exchange Server. You can set up Windows Live Messenger to access more than one type of messaging service.

What You'll Do

Prepare for Windows Live Messenger

Start and View Windows Live Messenger

Configure Windows Live Messenger

View Windows Live Messenger

Change My Status

Personalize Windows Live Messenger

Add Online Contacts

Manage Contacts and Categories

Send and Receive Instant Messages

Block a Contact

Send a File During an Instant Message

Make a Video and Voice Call

Send a Message to a Mobile Device

Get Remote Assistance

Customize Windows Live Messenger

Preparing for Windows Live Messenger

Windows Live Messenger is an instant messenging program that allows you to send and receive instant messages, hold video chats, and share files. Windows Live Messenger doesn't come installed with Windows 7, so you need to download and install it from the Microsoft Windows Live. This chapter describes version 2009; your downloaded version with updates may differ slightly; select About Live Messenger on the Help menu for version information. Before you can use Windows Live Messenger, you need to get an account ID. You use the ID to sign-in to Windows Live Messenger as well as other Windows Live services, such as Windows Live Mail and Windows Live Spaces. If you already have an Hotmail, Messenger, or Microsoft Passport account, you've already got a Windows Live ID.

Download and Start Windows Live Messenger

1. If you have not downloaded the program from Microsoft, open your browser, go to the Window Live Essentials Web site at *http://download.live.com*, and then click **Download** to download and install the program.

   ◆ During the installation process, you also have the opportunity to install other Windows Live online services and tools.

2. Click the **Start** button, and then point to **All Programs**.

3. Point to **Windows Live**, and then click **Windows Live Messenger**.

   The Windows Live Messenger Sign in window appears, along with the Windows Live Today window with information about Windows Live. You can turn off this window in the Sign in category of the Options dialog box.

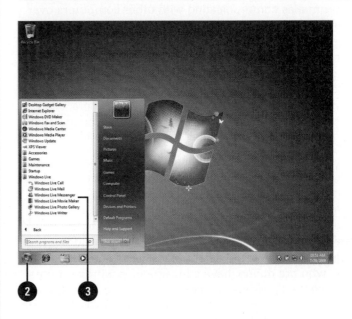

See Also

See "Downloading Windows Live Essentials" on page 166 for information on downloading Windows Live programs.

Click to close.

Welcome screen on first use; Windows Live Today appears on future use.

Create an Account

1. Click the **Start** button, point to **All Programs**, point to **Windows Live**, and then click **Windows Live Messenger**.

   The Windows Live Messenger sign-in windows opens.

2. Click **Sign up** in the Sign in window.

   Your web browser opens, displaying the Get your Windows Live ID web site.

3. Click the link to sign up for the Windows Live ID.

4. Follow the online instructions to create a Windows Live ID.

Forgot Your Password

1. Click the **Start** button, point to **All Programs**, point to **Windows Live**, and then click **Windows Live Messenger**.

   The Windows Live Messenger Sign-in windows opens.

2. Click **Forgot your password?** in the Sign-in window.

   Your web browser opens, displaying the Reset your password web site.

3. Type your Windows Live ID.

4. Type the security characters in the picture.

5. Click **Continue**.

6. Follow the online instructions to reset your password.

Starting Windows Live Messenger

Windows Live Messenger is an instant messaging program that allows you to exchange instant messages with a designated list of contacts over the Internet. An **instant message** is an online typewritten conversation in real time between two or more contacts. Instant messages require both parties to be online, and the communication is instantaneous. Before you can use Windows Live Messenger, you need a Windows Live ID, which you can get for no charge from Microsoft. After you start Windows Live Messenger, you sign in to let others online know you are connected. When you're done, you sign out.

Start Windows Live Messenger and Sign In and Out

1. Click the **Start** button, point to **All Programs**, point to **Windows Live**, point to **Windows Live Messenger**, and then click **Sign in**.

   TIMESAVER *Double-click the Windows Live Messenger icon in the notification area of the taskbar.*

2. If you're not automatically signed in, enter your user name and password. If you want to sign-in with a different ID, click the **E-mail address** list arrow, and then click **Sign in with a different Windows Live ID**.

3. Select or clear the **Remember me**, **Remember my password**, or **Sign me in automatically** check boxes and set your status.

4. Click the **Sign in** button.

5. If you want to stay signed in, yet still close it, click the **Close** button.

6. To sign out, select **Tools**, and then click **Sign out**.

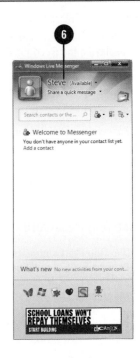

Did You Know?

You can stop signing in automatically. Click Tools, click Sign Out, and then clear the Sign Me In Automatically check box in the Sign-in window.

Configuring Windows Live Messenger

If you are having problems signing into Windows Live Messenger, you might need to add the program (MSNmsgr.exe) to your firewall exceptions list. If that doesn't help, you might need to check the Microsoft .NET Messenger Service status, which is the online service provided by Microsoft that makes it possible for you to use Windows Live Messenger or MSN Messenger. Microsoft is continually updating Windows Messenger with new functionality. When a software update is available, Windows Live Messenger displays a message, where you can download and install the upgrade.

Check the Connection Status

1. Select **Tools**, and then click **Options**.

2. In the left pane, click **Connection**.

3. Click **Refresh** to check the connection status.

4. If there are problems, click **Start**, and then follow the on-screen instructions.

5. Click **Advanced Settings** to check the connection status.

6. Click the **Test** buttons to check the connection settings.

7. Click **OK**.

8. Click **OK**.

Did You Know?

You might need to configure the firewall. Open the Control Panel, click the Windows Firewall icon in Small icons or Large icons view, click Allow A Program Or Feature Through Windows Firewall in the left pane , select the Windows Live Messenger check box, and then click OK.

You might need to check the .NET Messenger Service status. Click the Help menu, and then click Service status.

Viewing Windows Live Messenger

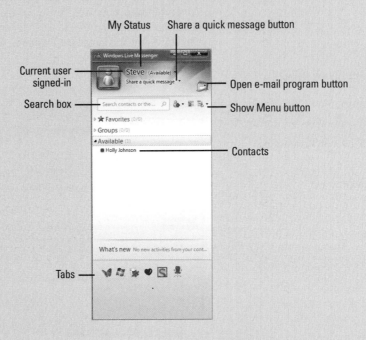

My Status

Share a quick message button

Current user signed-in

Open e-mail program button

Search box

Show Menu button

Contacts

Tabs

Conversation toolbar

Conversation with contact

Conversation participants

Type and send conversation text

Format conversation text

Changing My Status

When you sign in with Windows Live Messenger, the program notifies contacts currently online from your Contacts list that you are available to chat. While you're signed in, you might need to leave your computer for a meeting or lunch. Instead of signing out, you can change your online status to let your contacts know that you'll be right back, or that you're not available at the moment for other reasons.

Change My Status

1 Select **Tools**, and then click a status type:

♦ **Available**

♦ **Busy**

♦ **Away**

♦ **Appear offline**

♦ **Sign out from here**

Status types

Change Status Preferences

1 Select **Tools**, and then click **Options**.

2 In the left pane, click **Personal**.

3 Select or clear the **Show me as "Away" when I'm inactive for X minutes** check box, and then enter the number of inactive minutes you want, if necessary.

4 Select or clear the **Show me as "Busy" and block my alerts when I'm running a full-screen program or presentation settings are turned on** check box.

5 Click **OK**.

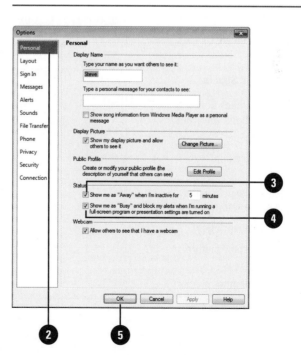

Personalizing Windows Live Messenger

Before you start using Windows Live Messenger, you can customize the program to show the menu bar if you prefer, automatically sign in, and display personalized information. You can change your display name, provide a personal message, and select a picture to represent you while you communicate with others online. Instead of selecting a regular static picture, you can select a dynamic display picture or character that provides animation, such as a WeeMee, MeeGos, Quebles, or Kiwee.

Access and Show or Hide Menus

◆ **Access and Show Menus.** Click the **Show menu** button on the toolbar to display menus, and then click **Show the menu bar**.

◆ **Hide Menus.** Click the **Show menu** button on the toolbar, and then click **Show the menu bar** again.

Show Menu button

Click to show menus in the window

Change Sign In Preferences

1 Select **Tools**, and then click **Options**.

2 In the left pane, click **Sign In**.

3 Select or clear the check boxes with the Sign In options you want to change:

◆ Run this program when Windows starts

◆ Allow automatic sign in when connected to the Internet

◆ Show Windows Live Today

◆ Use the same display picture and personal message

◆ Sign me out of all other places

◆ Show me all the other places

4 Click **OK**.

Change Personal Information

1 Select **Tools**, and then click **Options**.

2 In the left pane, click **Personal**.

3 Type the name you want others to see when you are online.

4 Type a personal message for your contacts to see.

5 To show a display picture, select the **Show my display picture and allow other to see it** check box, click **Change Picture**, select a picture, and then click **OK**.

6 Click **OK**.

Change Display Picture

1 Select **Tools**, and then click **Change display picture**.

2 Select the picture you want to use using one of the following:

- ◆ **Webcam Pictures.** Click to capture a picture.

- ◆ **Dynamic Display Pictures.** Click to select a dynamic picture, and then follow the online instructions.

- ◆ **Regular Pictures.** Click the picture you want.

- ◆ **Remove Pictures.** Select the picture, and then click **Remove**.

- ◆ **No Picture.** Click the (None) picture (a circle with a line).

3 Click **OK**.

TIMESAVER *In the Conversation window, click the Options for this person button arrow for you to change your display picture and other options.*

Adding Online Contacts

Before you can send instant messages to other people, they need to be in your Contacts list. You can add a person who has a Windows Live ID or a Yahoo member to your Contacts list by using the Add a contact button. If the person that you want to contact doesn't have Windows Live Messenger or an ID, you can send the person an e-mail with information about getting and installing Windows Live Messenger and obtaining an ID.

Add an Outline Contact

1. Click the **Add a contact or group** button, and then click **Add a contact**.

2. Type an instant messaging address.

3. Enter a mobile device number for sending IMs as text messages.

4. Specify a category to add the contact.

5. Click **Next**.

6. Type a message for an invitation to the contact.

7. Select or clear the **Also send this in e-mail in case this person doesn't have Messenger yet** check box.

8. Click **Send invitation**, add contact to your profile, if you want, or click **Close**.

Did You Know?

You can quickly delete a contact. Right-click a contact, click Delete Contact, select or clear the Also Block This Contact and Also Remove From My Windows Live Hotmail Contacts check boxes, and then click Delete Contact.

Managing Contacts and Categories

As your Contacts list grows, you may want to organize your contacts into categories (formally called groups) or remove the ones you no longer use. Windows Live Messenger makes it easy to organize them into predefined categories and categories that you create. Windows Live Messenger comes with predefined categories by default: Favorites, Groups, and Available. Once you have organized your categories, you can select or clear contact check boxes to modify it. You can use the Up and Down buttons next to the category name to hide and display contacts in a category.

Create a Contacts Category

1. Click the **Add a contact or group** button, and then click **Create a category**.

    TIMESAVER *Right-click a category, and then click Create new category.*

2. Type a name for the new category.

3. Select the contacts or type the e-mail addresses you want to add to the category.

4. Click **Save**.

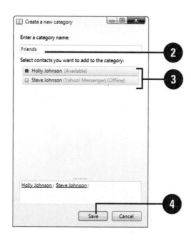

Modify Contacts and Contact Categories

◆ **Edit Contact.** Right-click the contact, click **Edit contact**, make changes, and then click **Save**.

◆ **Edit Contact Category.** Right-click the contact group, click **Edit category**, select or clear contact check boxes, and then click **Save**.

◆ **Rename Contact Category.** Right-click the contact group, click **Rename category**, type a name, and then press Enter.

◆ **Delete Contact Category.** Right-click the contact group, click **Delete category**, and then click **Yes**.

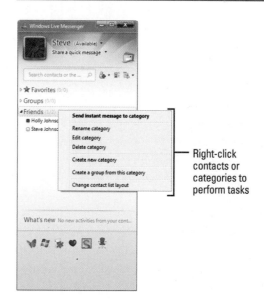

Right-click contacts or categories to perform tasks

Sending and Receiving Instant Messages

An instant message is an online typewritten conversation in real-time between two or more contacts. As you type an instant message, you can format your messages by changing fonts and text color and by inserting backgrounds and color schemes. Each message can contain up to 400 characters. If you have a writing input device and Microsoft Windows Journal Viewer installed, you can also draw or handwrite your messages. You cannot send an instant message to more than one person, but you can invite other people using the same messaging service to participate in an existing conversation; you can include up to five people in a conversation.

Send and Receive Instant Messages

① Double-click a contact or right-click a contact category and then click **Send an instant message to category**.

The Conversation window opens.

② Type your message in the box at the bottom of the window.

To start a new line while typing, press Shift+Enter.

③ If you want to handwrite your message, click the **Handwrite** tab, and then ink your message using the formatting buttons.

④ Press Enter, and then wait for a reply.

⑤ If you want to add another person to the conversation, click the **Invite** button on the toolbar, and then double-click the person you want to add.

◆ You can also click the **Show Menu** button, point to **Actions**, and then click **Invite a contact to join this conversation**.

⑥ When you're done, click the **Close** button to end the session.

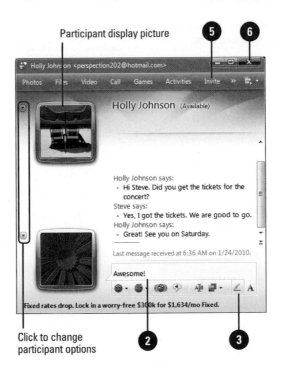

Participant display picture

Click to change participant options

Format Message Text

1. In the Conversation window, click the **Font** button.

2. Specify the font, font style, size, color, and effect you want, and preview the result in the sample box.

3. Click **OK**.

4. Type and send the formatted message.

Apply a Background to the Conversation Window

◆ **Background.** In the Conversation window, click the **Background** button, and then select a background.

    ◆ To set options or remove a background, click **Show all**.

    ◆ To view more featured backgrounds, click **More** to go online.

Did You Know?

You can search for contacts. Click in the Search box top of the main Messenger window, and then start typing to display results. Click the Clear search button (x) in the Search box to clear the search.

Background

Background button

Adding Symbols and Voice to an Instant Message

As you type an instant message, you can format your messages by inserting graphical symbols called **emoticons**, such as a happy face, which help convey your emotions, or graphical animations, such as as a wink. If your conversation needs a nudge to get people conversing, you can use the Nudge button. If you want to add a little audio to an instant message, you can record a voice clip and send it to others involved in the conversation. The voice clip appears in the conversation window and plays automatically. You need a microphone to record a voice clip and audio speakers to hear a clip.

Insert Emoticons

1. In the Conversation window, click the **Emoticons** button.

2. Click the icon you want to insert into the conversation.

   ◆ To create, modify, or remove an emoticon, click **Show all**.

   TIMESAVER *You can also type a sequence of characters to quickly insert emoticons as you type your message. To find out the characters, point to an icon on the Emoticons menu.*

Did You Know?

You can insert a nudge message to keep a conversation going. In the Conversation window, click the Nudge button.

You can create your own blog. A blog is short for web log, which is an online journal. In the main Messenger window, click the Get Your Own Space button. In the Create Your Windows Live Space web site, follow the online instructions.

You can save an instant message. In the Conversation window, click the File menu, click Save As, select a folder location, type a file name, and then click Save.

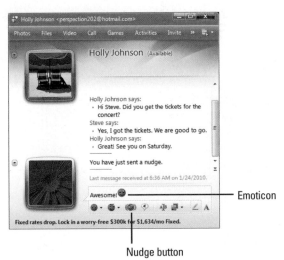

Emoticon

Nudge button

Insert a Wink

1. In the Conversation window, click the **Wink** button.

2. Click the wink icon you want to insert into the conversation.

   ◆ To preview or remove a wink, click **Show all**.

Record and Play a Voice Clip

1. In the Conversation window, point to the **Voice Clip** button.

2. Press and hold down the **Voice Clip** button or press F2, and then record your voice message.

3. Release the button or key to send the voice message.

4. To play or stop a voice clip, click **Play / Stop** in the Conversation window.

   TIMESAVER Press Esc to stop the voice clip.

Did You Know?

You can save a voice clip. In the Conversation window, click Save As or drag it from the conversation window onto your desktop or into a folder.

You can reuse a voice clip in another conversation. In the Conversation window, drag a voice clip to another another conversation window.

Recording in progress

Press and hold button

Click to save the clip

Blocking a Contact

If you no longer want to receive instant messages from a specific contact, you can block the contact from directly sending you instant messages. When you block a contact, you appear to be offline to the person, who doesn't know blocking is turned on. If another contact invites you and someone you blocked into a conversation, the blocked person can send you messages indirectly. Blocking a contact moves them from your Allow list to your Block list. Deleting a blocked contact from your Contacts list does not remove the block.

Block or Unblock a Contact

1 Select **Tools**, and then click **Options**.

2 In the left pane, click **Privacy**.

3 Select the contacts you want to block, and then click **Block**.

4 Select the contacts you don't want to block, and then click **Allow**.

5 To find out which users have added you to their Contacts list, click **View**, and then click **Close**.

6 Click **OK**.

Did You Know?

You can quickly block or unblock a contact. Right-click the contact, and then click Block Contact or Unblock Contact. You can also click the Block button during a conversation.

You can block a person not in your Contacts list. Click the Show Menu button, point to Actions, and then click Send An Instant Message, type the person's e-mail address in the results list box, click OK, and then click the Block button.

You can allow others to add you to their Contacts list without seeking your approval. Select Tools, click Options, click Privacy in the left pane, clear the Alert Me When Other People Add Me To Their Contact List check box, and then click OK.

Sending a File During an Instant Message

While you are conversing in Windows Live Messenger, you can send a contact a single file. You can send many different types of files, including documents, photos, and music. When you send a file, a request to transfer the file is sent to your contact. You are notified when your contact accepts or declines your request. Before you receive files over the Internet, make sure you have up-to-date virus protection software on your computer. When you receive a file, the Windows Live Messenger provides security information to help you understand more about the file. If your computer is located on a network behind a firewall, you might not be able to send files to those outside the firewall. If you want to send files to those behind the firewall, you need to manually open the connection; check with your network administrator for details.

Send a Single File

1. Click the **Show Menu** button, point to **Actions**, point to **Send other**, and then click **Send a single file.**

   TIMESAVER *If you're in a conversation, click the Photo button on the toolbar.*

2. If prompted, select the contact you want to send the file to, and then click **OK**.

3. Select the file you want to send.

4. Click **Open**.

5. To open a file, click the link in the Conversation window to start the transfer.

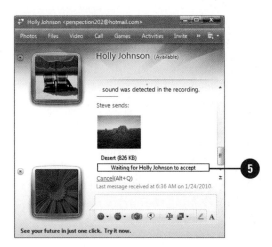

Creating and Using Groups

In addition to having conversations with individuals, you can also have a conversation with a group. A Windows Live Messenger group can have up to 20 members and you can only belong to 20 groups at any one time. As you create a group, you can invite people to join it; it's simple, a wizard walks you through the process. After you create a group, all you need to do is double-click the group in the Windows Live Messenger window.

Create a Group

1. Click the **Add a contact or group** button, and then click **Create a group**.

2. Type a group name, and then click **Next**.

3. Type your contacts or click the **Select from your contact list** link to add contacts, type a message, and then click **Next**.

4. Select the **When I drag a file onto a contact's name, automatically create a sharing folder if that contact doesn't already have one** check box.

5. Click **Done**.

6. When the recipient receives the invitation, click **Join**, **Decide later**, or **No thanks**.

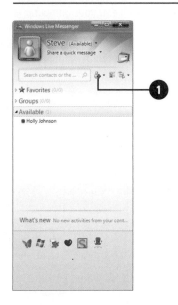

Did You Know?

You can follow up on a conversation with an e-mail. Right-click the contact, point to Send Other, and then click E-mail.

You can show or hide your display picture from contacts. Select Tools, click Options, click General in the left pane, select or hide the Show Display Pictures From Others check box, and then click OK.

You can search for contacts. Click in the Search box, and the type the name of the contact you want to find.

Send and Receive Instant Messages to a Group

① Double-click a contact group or right-click a contact group and then click **Send an instant message to group**.

The Conversation window opens.

② Type your message in the box at the bottom of the window.

To start a new line while typing, press Shift+Enter.

③ Use the **Font** button to format the text of the conversation as you want.

④ Use the **Emoticon**, **Wink**, or **Nudge** button during the conversation as you want.

⑤ If you want to handwrite your message, click the **Handwrite** tab, and then ink your message using the formatting buttons.

⑥ Press Enter, and then wait for a reply.

⑦ When you're done, click the **Close** button to end the session.

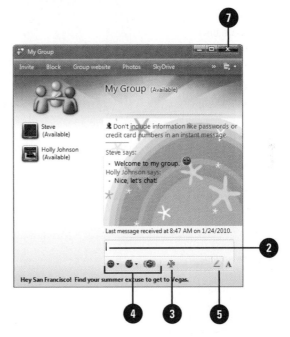

Making a Video Call with the Internet

When used with Windows 7 and the right hardware, Windows Live Messenger provides state-of-the-art computer communications features. With Windows Live Messenger, you can talk to others over the Internet as you do on a regular phone, and you can use video to see others and let others see you as you converse. Once you set up your computer hardware—Webcams, microphones and speakers— and related software, you're ready to communicate over the Internet. You have two communication choices: audio only, and audio and video. With audio only, you speak into a microphone and hear the other person's response over your computer's speakers. With audio and video, you send video to others so they receive live images as well as sound. If the contacts you call don't have a video camera, they will see you, but you won't see them.

Have a Video Conversation

1. Double-click the contact you want to send an instant message or right-click a contact group and then click **Send an instant message to group**.

2. Click the **Video** button on the toolbar, and then wait for the other person to accept the invitation.

3. Use the controls to adjust the volume of the speakers or microphone.

4. Start talking.

5. When you're done, click the **Close** button.

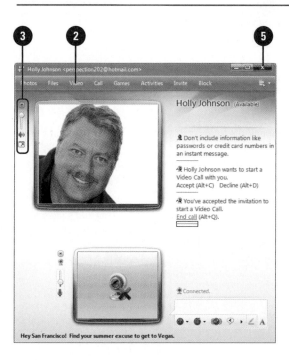

Did You Know?

You can set Webcam video options. In the Conversation window, click the Show Menu button, point to Actions, point to Video, and then select commands to show your Webcam or View a contact's Webcam.

Making a Phone Call with the Internet

Windows Live Messenger allows you to dial regular phones through a voice service provider using the Internet or a modem on your computer. Once the modem connects to the number you are dialing, called the remote party, you can pick up your phone and talk. This feature is useful for people who would otherwise be spending a fortune in long distance calling. It's also helpful for people who spent a lot of time on their computer. When you use Windows Live Messenger, having your modem's speakers on is helpful so you can hear what is actually happening with the connection. If your computer is located on a network behind a firewall, you might not be able to make phone calls; check with your network administrator for details.

Make a Phone Call With Windows Live Messenger

1. Click the **Show Menu** button, point to **Actions**, point to **Call**, and then select one of the following commands:

   ◆ **Call a contact's computer**.

   ◆ **Call a contact's phone**.

   ◆ **Call a phone**.

   TIMESAVER *If you're in a conversation, click the Call button on the toolbar, and then click Call computer or Call phone.*

2. If you need a voice service provider, follow the instructions to sign up.

3. Select a contact or type a phone number, including the area code (even for local calls), and then type a name after it for easy identification on your list.

4. Click **OK**.

   When you call a contact for the first time, click the link for the Windows Live Call web site to authenticate your ID.

5. Use the controls to adjust the volume of the speakers or microphone.

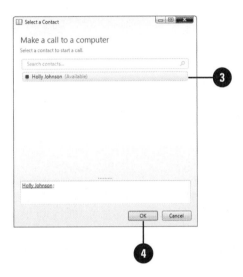

Click to start a call while in a conversation

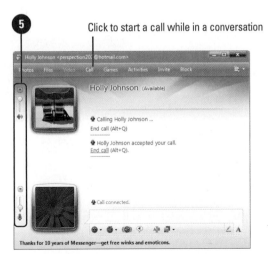

Sending a Message to a Mobile Device

If you have a wireless device, such as a web-enabled cellular phone, a pager, a Smartphone, Pocket PC Phone, or Pocket PC, you can set it up to receive instant messages using Windows Live Messenger. When you send a message to a contact's mobile device, the message includes your e-mail address and phone number unless the mobile device doesn't support the feature. If your contact's mobile device is not turned on, the message might be delayed or not arrive at all.

Set Up an Account for a Mobile Device

1. Select **Tools**, and then click **Options**.

2. In the left pane, click **Phone**.

3. Click **Mobile Settings**.

4. Follow the online instructions on the web site.

5. When you're done setting up a mobile account, close your browser, if necessary.

6. Select the **Allow people on my contact list to send messages to my mobile device** check box.

7. Click **OK**.

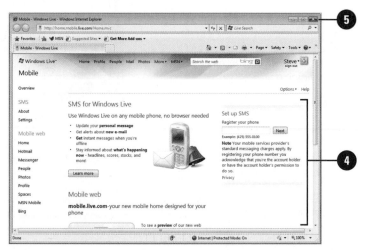

Send a Message to a Mobile Device

1. Double-click the Windows Live Messenger icon in the notification area of the taskbar, and then sign in, if necessary.

2. Right-click the contact you want to send a message, and then click **Send a mobile text (SMS)**.

   ◆ You can also click the **Show Menu** button, point to **Actions**, point to **Send other**, click **Send a message to a mobile device**, select a contact, and then click **OK**.

3. Type your message.

4. Press Enter, and then wait for a reply.

Conversation

Getting Remote Assistance

Sometimes the best way to fix a computer problem is to get help from a friend or colleague who knows how to solve it. If your friend or colleague lives too far away to help you in person, you can use Remote Assistance within Windows Live Messenger and an Internet connection to help you get the support and answers you need. You can ask a trusted contact in another location to connect to your computer over the Internet and provide support in real time. After connecting to your computer, you can invite a contact to view your desktop, chat online using instant messages, talk online using a microphone and speakers, and send files. Instead of simply talking about a solution, sometimes you need someone to show you how to perform the steps before you fully understand the procedure. With Remote Assistance, you can give a contact control of your computer whereby he or she can demonstrate how to perform the procedure using his or her mouse and keyboard while you watch in real time. If your computer is located on a network behind a firewall, you might not be able to use remote assistance; check with your network administrator for details.

Ask for Remote Assistance

1. Double-click the Windows Messenger icon in the notification area of the taskbar, and then sign in, if necessary.

2. Double-click the contact you want to send an instant message.

3. Click the **Activities** button on the toolbar, and then click **Request remote assistance**, and then wait for acceptance to the invitation.

4. Enter a password twice, and then click **OK**.

5. Click **Yes** to let this person connect to your computer.

6. To have a conversation, type a message to explain your problem, and then press Enter.

7. If the person asks to take control of your computer, click **Yes** or **No**.

8. To take back control of your computer, click **Stop sharing** on the toolbar.

9. When you're done, click **Disconnect**, and then click **Yes**.

Invitation for remote assistance

Provide Remote Assistance

1 Sign-in to Windows Messenger, and then wait for an invitation to provide remote assistance.

◆ To offer remote assistance, select a contact, click the **Show Menu** button, point to **Actions**, and then click **Request remote assistance**.

2 When you receive the invitation, click **Accept**, and then wait for the Remote Assistance window to open.

3 Wait, enter a password from the person asking for assistance, and then click **OK**.

4 To have a conversation, type a message to discuss the problem, and then press Enter.

5 Watch the screen of the person you want to help during the conversation.

6 To take control of the person's computer, click the **Request control** button on the toolbar, and then wait for the other person's response.

7 To give back control of the other person's computer, click the **Stop sharing** button on the toolbar.

8 When you're done, click **Disconnect**, and then click **Yes**.

9 If necessary, click **Cancel** to exit remote assistance and not connection to another person.

Controlling other computer

For Your Information

Sharing Games and Activities

If you need to share information in a specific program or document with others in a conference, you can use Windows Live Messenger to share your documents and programs. They cannot work with the document until you give them access to it. The user who clicks the program window "takes control" of the program and can then run any menu commands or make changes to the document. If you have a multi-player game, such as Age of Empires II, installed on both computers, you can play the game using Windows Live Messenger. To start an activity or game, start a conversation, click the Activities button on the toolbar, and then click an activity, and then follow the instructions.

Customizing Windows Live Messenger

Windows Live Messenger allows you to customize the program in many ways, including the display, layout, the sign in process, message delivery, alerts, sounds, file transfer, privacy, security, and connection status. To change program options, select a category in the left pane of the Options dialog box, and then select or specify the individual options you want. On the left side of the main Messenger window, tabs provide easy access to commonly used products and services. If the tabs at the bottom are in the way, you can hide them all together.

Customize Windows Live Messenger

1. Select **Tools**, and then click **Options**.

2. In the left pane, click **Messages**.

3. Select or clear the options to determine how you want messages to appear or be responded to.

4. In the left pane, click **Alerts**.

5. Select the alert check boxes you want to use.

6. Click the event you want to set the sound for, click **Browse**, select a sound, and then click **Open**.

7. In the left pane, click **Layout**.

   TIMESAVER *Click the Change Contact List Layout button on the toolbar in the Messenger window to open the Options dialog box, displaying the Layout pane.*

8. Select the layout check boxes you want to use.

9. In the Contact list area, select the icon size you want.

10. Select the options you want to label, organize, sort contacts, and display offline contacts.

11. Click **OK**.

Working with Pictures

Introduction

Windows 7 makes it easy to store and work with your pictures using the Pictures folder. You can quickly access the folder from the Start menu. From the Pictures folder you can view, organize, and share pictures with others on the Internet. When you download and save pictures from your digital camera or scanner to your computer, Windows stores the digital images in the Pictures folder by default. (You can specify an alternative location.) You can view your picture files as a slide show or in the Extra-Large view, which displays a larger image above thumbnail images of the pictures. The Pictures folder also contains links to specialized picture tasks that help you share pictures with others, such as sending pictures in an e-mail, publishing pictures and documents on the web, printing photographs, and ordering prints from the Internet. You can also create your own pictures or edit existing ones in Paint, a Windows accessory program designed for drawing and painting. Paint is useful for making simple changes to a picture, adding a text caption, or saving a picture in another file format.

Windows Live Photo Gallery (**New!**) allows you to view, locate, organize, open, and edit photos and pictures. Windows Live Photo Gallery shows all the pictures and videos located in the Pictures folder. In Windows Live Photo Gallery, you can also print photos, order photos through an online service, e-mail photos and pictures using your e-mail program, create CDs or DVDs, and make a movie using Windows Live Movie Maker (**New!**). Windows Live Photo Gallery and Windows Live Movie Maker don't come installed with Windows 7; they are available for free online from Microsoft. You can download the programs from Windows Live at *http://download.live.com*.

What You'll Do

Draw a Picture

Edit a Picture

View Pictures

Manage Pictures in the Photo Gallery

Fix Pictures in the Photo Gallery

E-mail a Picture

Format and Print Photos

Order Photo Prints from the Web

Publish Photos on the Web

Install a Scanner or Digital Camera

Scan a Picture

Download Digital Camera Pictures

Use Pictures as a Screen Saver

Use a Picture as a Desktop Background

Set Photo Gallery Options

Drawing a Picture

Paint is a Windows accessory you can use to create and work with graphics or pictures. Paint is designed to create and edit bitmap (.bmp) files, but you can also open and save pictures created in or for other graphics programs and the Internet using several common file formats, such as .tiff, .gif, or .jpeg. A **bitmap** file is a map of a picture created from small black, white, or colored dots, or bits. When you start Paint, a blank canvas appears in the work area, along with a Ribbon (**New!**), similar to Microsoft Office 2007, at the top. The Ribbon with two tabs—Home and View—allows you to quickly select document related commands. Paint comes with a set of tools on the Ribbon that you can use for drawing and manipulating pictures. A tool remains turned on until you select another tool. In addition to the drawing tools, you can also add text to a picture. When you create a text box and type the text, you can edit and format it, but once you deselect the text box, the text becomes part of the picture, which you can't edit.

Draw a Picture

1. Click the **Start** button, point to **All Programs**, click **Accessories**, and then click **Paint**.

   ◆ You can point to **Paint** on the Start menu to select a recently opened file.

2. If you want, drag a resize handle on the canvas to resize it.

3. Click a drawing tool.

   ◆ If available, use the **Outline**, **Fill**, and **Size** buttons for the selected tool.

4. Click **Color 1** to select the foreground color or click **Color 2** to select the background color.

5. Drag the shapes you want by holding down one of the following:

   ◆ The left mouse button to draw with the foreground color.

   ◆ The right mouse button to draw with the background color.

   ◆ The Shift key to constrain the drawing to a proportional size, such as a circle or square.

6. Click the **Paint** button, and then click **Exit**.

Curve tool · Polygon tool

Airbrush tool · Brush tool · Line tool · Rounded Rectangle tool

Add Text to a Picture

1. In Paint, create or open the picture you want to modify.

2. Click the **Text** tool on the Home tab.

3. Drag a text box.

4. Using the **Text** tab, select the font, font size, and any formatting you want to apply to the text.

5. Click in the text box, if necessary, and then type the text.

6. Drag a text box resize handle to enlarge or reduce the text box.

7. Edit and format the text.

8. Click outside the text box to deselect it and change the text to a bitmap.

   IMPORTANT *Once you click outside the text box to place the text in the picture, the text becomes part of the picture.*

Save a Picture in Different Formats

1. In Paint, create or open the picture you want to save in a different format.

2. Click the **Paint** button, and then click **Save As**. You can also point to Save as, and then select a format (PNG, JPEG, BMP, or BMP).

3. Select the drive and folder in which you want to save the file.

4. Type a name for the file, or use the suggested name.

5. Click the **Save as type** list arrow, and then click a file format.

6. Click **Save**.

Editing a Picture

After you create or open a picture, you can select all or part of the picture and use commands on the Image menu, such as rotate, stretch, and invert colors, to further modify it in Paint. In addition to the drawing tools, you can also use painting tools, such as Fill With Color, Airbrush, Brush, Pencil, and Pick Color, to transform the picture. The Fill With Color tool is useful if you want to color an entire item or recolor text letter by letter. If you need to remove part of a picture, you can use the Eraser tool, which comes in four different sizes.

Modify a Picture

1. In Paint, create or open the picture you want to edit.

2. Click the **Select** button arrow on the Home tab, and then click **Free-form selection** tool to select irregular shapes, or click the **Rectangular section** tool to select rectangle shapes.

3. Drag the selection area you want.

4. Click the **Select** button arrow, and then click **Transparent selection** to select it to use a transparent background or deselect it to use an opaque background.

5. In the Image area of the Home tab, click any of the following buttons:

   ◆ **Rotate or flip.**

   ◆ **Resize and skew.**

   ◆ **Crop.**

   ◆ **Invert colors.** Right-click the selection, and then click **Invert color**.

6. Click **OK**, if necessary.

7. Save the picture and exit Paint.

> ## Did You Know?
>
> *You can quickly copy a selection.*
> Hold down the Ctrl key, and then drag the selection.

Change picture resize and skew

Fill Part of a Picture

1. In Paint, create or open the picture you want to edit.

2. Click the color you want to fill, or click the **Color picker** tool and click a color from the picture.

3. Click the **Fill with color** tool.

4. Point the tip of the paint bucket to the area you want to fill, and then click.

Did You Know?

You can replace any color with the background color. Set the foreground color (Color 1) to the color to be replaced and the background color (Color 2) to the replacement color, and then hold down the right mouse button and drag the Eraser over the area you want to replace.

Erase Part of a Picture

1. In Paint, create or open the picture you want to edit.

2. To magnify an area of the screen, click the **Magnifier** tool, and then click the area you want to magnify.

   ◆ You can also drag the **Zoom** slider to change the view size.

3. Click the **Eraser** tool.

4. Drag the Eraser over the area you want to erase.

5. If you make a mistake, click the click **Undo** button on the Quick Access toolbar (on title bar) to restore your last action.

6. To restore the magnification, click the **Zoom (-)** or **Zoom (+)** buttons.

Zoom slider

Viewing Pictures

Windows gives you several ways to view pictures. In a folder with pictures, you can use Extra Large Icons view to see a larger view of the pictures. In the Pictures folder, you can use the slide show feature to display pictures in a full screen slide show. If you want to preview pictures or open a picture to edit, you can double-click the file icon to use the default program associated with the picture file type, or select the specific program—such as Paint, Windows Live Photo Gallery, Microsoft Office Document Imaging, or Microsoft Office Picture Manager—you want to use to make changes.

View a Picture

1. Click the **Start** button, and then click **Pictures**.

2. To view sample pictures, double-click the Sample Pictures folder.

3. Click a picture to view information about the picture in the Details pane.

4. Click the **Preview** button arrow, and then click the program you want to open the picture.

See Also

See "Understanding Faxes" on page 411 for information on working with faxes.

Details pane

Preview in Windows Photo Viewer

View Pictures as Extra Large Icons

1. Click the **Start** button, click **Pictures**, or open any other folder with pictures you want to view.

2. Click the **Views** button arrow, and then click **Extra Large Icons**.

   ◆ If the pictures are too large, you can also use **Large Icons** and **Medium Icons** to display pictures.

View Pictures as a Slide Show

1. Click the **Start** button, click **Pictures**, or open any other folder with pictures you want to view.

2. Select the pictures you want in the show, or click one picture to see all the pictures.

3. Click the **Slide show** button, and then watch the show.

4. To manually advance to the next slide, click anywhere in the picture.

5. To control the slide show, right-click the screen, and then click the control you want, including **Shuffle**, **Loop**, or a **Slide Show Speed (Slow, Medium, or Fast)**.

6. To exit the slide show, press Esc or right-click the screen, and then click **Exit**.

Managing Pictures in the Photo Gallery

Windows Live Photo Gallery (**New!**) is a program that allows you to view, locate, and edit pictures. Windows Live Photo Gallery doesn't come installed with Windows 7, so you need to download and install it from the Microsoft Windows Live. Windows Live Photo Gallery shows all the pictures and videos located in the Pictures libraries folder. However, you can add and view other folders on your computer. The left pane in Windows Live Photo Gallery displays a tree structure like the Folders list that allows you to display pictures by different criteria. To help you sort and search for pictures, you can add tags, ratings, and captions to pictures. The Find box is also available. You can also use the View button to change the icon thumbnail views, view a table of contents, or display groups and sorts.

View Pictures Using Windows Live Photo Gallery

1. If you have not downloaded the program from Microsoft, open your browser, go to the Window Live Essentials web site at *http://download.live.com*, and then click **Download** to download and install the program.

2. Click the **Start** button, point to **All Programs**, point to **Windows Live**, and then click **Windows Live Photo Gallery**. If prompted, Sign in.

3. Use the tree structure in the left pane to view the pictures:

   ◆ **All photos and videos.** Click a picture or video folder.

   ◆ **Date taken.** Click a date to display media.

   ◆ **People or Descriptive tags.** Click a tag to display media.

      ◆ **Add a new tag.** Click **Add a new tag**, type a tag name, and then press Enter.

4. Use the controls at the bottom of the window to change the display size, view details, play slide show, delete pictures, and rotate pictures.

Add Tags, Ratings, or Captions

① In Windows Live Photo Gallery, select the photo you want to add tags, a rating, or a caption.

② Click the **Info** button on the toolbar.

③ To add a tag, click a tag, type the tag you want, and then press Enter.

④ To add a rating, click the rating star you want.

⑤ To add a caption, click **Add caption**, type the caption you want, and then press Enter.

⑥ When you're done, click the **Close** button in the Info pane.

Find Pictures in Windows Photo Gallery

① In Windows Live Photo Gallery, click in the Search box.

② Type the work or phrase you want to find associated with the picture.

As you type, the pictures that match the criteria display in the gallery.

③ To clear the search, click the **Close** button in the Search box.

Search results

Fixing Pictures in the Photo Gallery

If you need to edit a picture, you can use Windows Live Photo Gallery (**New!**) to adjust brightness, contrast, and color, and to remove red eye. You can also crop a picture. If the colors in a picture don't look right, you can use Auto Adjust to enhance a picture by changing the brightness (light), contrast (dark), color temperature, tint, or saturation. Color temperature allows you to make the colors warmer (red) or cooler (blue); tint modifies the color cast (add or remove green); and saturation changes color vividness. If you don't like the changes made by Auto Adjust, you can use Adjust Color to change the individual color attributes.

Fix Pictures Using Windows Live Photo Gallery

1. In Windows Live Photo Gallery, select the photo you want to fix.

2. Click the **Fix** button on the toolbar.

3. Click **Auto adjust**.

4. To adjust brightness and contrast, click **Adjust exposure**, and then drag the sliders.

5. To adjust color temperature, tint, or saturation, click **Adjust color**, and then drag the sliders.

6. To straighten, click **Straighten photo**, and then drag slider.

7. To crop a picture, click **Crop Photo**, select a proportion or drag a selection, and move the selection, and then click **Apply**.

8. To adjust sharpness, click **Adjust detail**, and then drag the sliders.

9. To fix red eye, click **Fix red eye**, and then drag a rectangle around the eye you want to fix.

10. To add black and white effects, click **Black and white effects**, and then select an effect.

11. If you don't like the changes, use the **Revert** or **Undo** buttons.

12. When you're done, click the **Back to gallery** button.

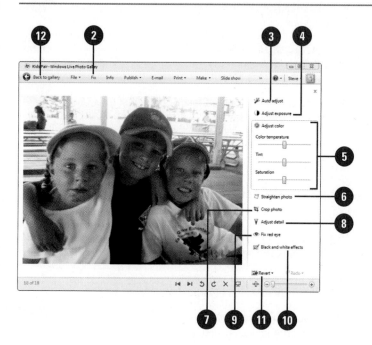

E-mailing a Picture

If you have one or more photos, pictures, or documents that you want to share with others, you can send them in an e-mail as attachments. Before you send photos or pictures in an e-mail as an attachment, you typically need to resize them in a separate graphics program so your recipient can view them with minimal scrolling, open your e-mail program, and then attach the files. With Windows you can send a photo or picture in an e-mail message without having to resize it in a separate graphics program, or even open your e-mail program. Using the E-mail button on the toolbar in Windows Live Photo Gallery or any Explorer window, Windows opens an e-mail message window with the attached files from your default e-mail program. All you need to do is address the message, add any message text, and then send it.

E-mail a Photo or Picture

1. In Windows Live Photo Gallery or an Explorer window, open the folder containing the picture or folder you want to e-mail.

2. Select the pictures or a folder with pictures you want to e-mail.

3. Click the **E-mail** button on the toolbar.

   Your e-mail program, displaying an e-mail message with a file attachment.

4. Type an e-mail address and a subject.

5. Click **Send** on the toolbar.

See Also

See "Sending and Retrieving a File" on page 182 for information on sending a file in an e-mail message.

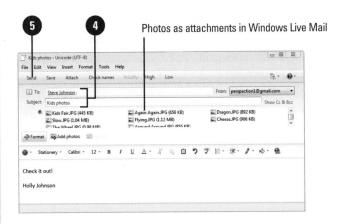

Photos as attachments in Windows Live Mail

Formatting and Printing Photos

Windows makes it easy to format and print photographs from Windows Live Photo Gallery, which allows you to print photographs. During the process, you can select the photo(s) to print, the paper type, and a page layout, such as full-page prints, contact-sheet prints, 4 x 6-inch prints, 5 x 7-inch prints, 8 x 10-inch prints, 3.5 x 5-inch prints, and wallet size prints. To print a photo from your computer, you need a color printer and special photo paper. In order to get the best results when you print photographs, set your printer resolution to the highest setting for the best quality output, and use high-quality glossy paper designed specifically for printing photographs. Check your printer documentation for the best resolution setting suited to print your photographs. When you print photographs with a high resolution setting, the printing process might take longer. Many printer manufacturers also make paper designed to work best with their printers; check your printer manufacturer's web site for more information.

Format and Print a Photo

1. In Windows Live Photo Gallery or an Explorer window, open the folder containing the photo or folder you want to print.

2. Select the photos you want to print.

3. Click the **Print** button on the toolbar, and then click **Print**.

4. Specify the printer options you want:

   ◆ Click the **Printer** arrow, and then select a printer.

   ◆ Click the **Paper size** arrow, and then select a paper size.

   ◆ Click the **Quality** arrow, and then click a resolution.

   ◆ Click the **Paper type** arrow, and then select a paper type.

5. Select the photo size you want.

6. Specify a number of copies.

7. Select or clear the **Fit picture to frame** check box.

8. Click **Print**, and then follow any printer specify instructions.

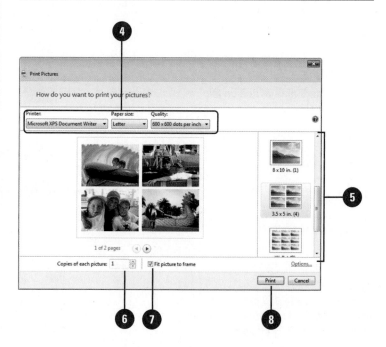

Ordering Photo Prints from the Web

If you have digital photographs taken from a digital camera or scanned into your computer, you can send your digital photographs to an online printing company where they create photo prints and send them to your mailing address. Windows makes the process easy from Windows Live Photo Gallery, which walks you through the ordering process. You'll need to provide print sizes, quantities, and billing and shipping information to complete the order.

Order Photo Prints from the Web

1. In Windows Live Photo Gallery, open the folder containing the photo or folder you want to print.

2. Select the photos you want to send to an online printing company.

3. Click the **Print** button on the toolbar, and then click **Order prints**.

4. Select the printing company you want to send your photos.

5. Click **Send Pictures**.

6. If necessary, click **Send**.

7. Follow the remaining steps to place an order with the specific printing company.

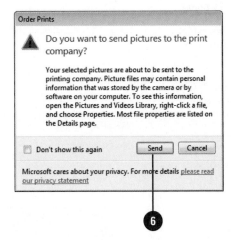

Publishing Photos on the Web

If you use Windows Live Photos on the web, you can use Windows Live Photo Gallery to publish your photos in online (**New!**). In order to publish photos, you need to be signed in to Windows Live. If you're not, click the Sign in button on the toolbar. You can publish your photos as an online, group, or event album. As an alternative, you can also publish your photos to Flickr, an online photo sharing web site.

Publish Photos on the Web

1. In Windows Live Photo Gallery, open the folder containing the photo or folder you want to publish.

2. Select the photos you want to publish in an album.

3. Click the **Publish** button on the toolbar, and then select a publishing option:

   ◆ **Online album.** A general photo album.

   ◆ **Group album** or **Event album.** A photo album for a group or event.

   ◆ **Flickr.** An online photo sharing service. Point to **More Services**, and then click **Flickr**.

4. For a group or event album, select an event or group, and then click **Next**.

5. Type an album name or select one, and then select the permission setting you want.

6. Click **Publish**.

   A message window appears as your photos are uploaded to the web.

7. To view your photos after they are published online, click **View album**.

Photos published on Windows Live Photos

Installing a Scanner or Digital Camera

Windows makes it easy to install a scanner or digital camera on your computer using plug-and-play. In most cases, all you need to do is turn off your computer, plug in the hardware device, and restart your computer. Windows recognizes the new hardware and installs it. If for some reason Windows doesn't recognize the hardware, you can start a wizard, which walks you through the installation process.

Install a Scanner or Digital Camera

1. Plug your scanner or camera into your computer to start the Scanner and Camera wizard.

   If the wizard doesn't open, click the **Start** button, click **Devices and Printers**, and then click the **Add a device** button on the toolbar.

2. Click **Next** to continue.

3. Click the manufacturer of the scanner or camera you want to install, click the device name, and then click **Next** to continue.

4. Connect your device to your computer, select a port, and then click **Next** to continue.

5. Type a name for the device, or use the suggested one, and then click **Next** to continue.

6. Click **Finish**.

Did You Know?

You can test a scanner or camera. Click the Start button, click Devices And Printers, right-click the scanner or camera icon, click Properties, click the General tab, and then click Test Scanner or Text Camera.

You can remove a scanner or camera. Click the Start button, click Devices And Printers, select the device icon, and then click the Remove Device button on the toolbar, and then click Yes.

Scanning a Picture

Windows 7 makes it easy to scan pictures with Windows Live Photo Gallery (**New!**) and Windows Fax and Scan (**New!**). A **scanner** is like a photocopy machine on which you can lay photographs, books, and other documents that you want to save in digital form on your computer. In addition to scanning photographs, many high resolution scanners also allow you to scan a negative from a film strip and enlarge it. You use Windows Live Photo Gallery to start the scanning process and store the scanned photo in the in Pictures folder. With Windows Fax and Scan, you can choose scanning preferences, such as picture type, resolution, (the number of dots per inch-dpi), preview the scanned picture, adjust the scan area, and select a graphic format. In order to use the scanner features of Windows, you need to have a scanner attached and installed on your computer.

Scan a Picture

1. Place the picture on the scanner.

2. Click the **Start** button, point to **All Programs**, point to **Windows Live**, and then click **Windows Live Photo Gallery**.

3. Click the **File** button, and then click **Import from a camera or scanner**.

4. Select the scanner you want to use.

5. Click **Import**.

   The New Scan dialog box from Windows Fax and Scan opens.

   ◆ You can also access this dialog box from Windows Fax and Scan. Click the **Start** button, point to **All Programs**, and then click **Windows Fax and Scan**.

   The default settings for scanning a document are automatically selected.

6. Specify the options you want for the new scan. Some important ones include:

   ◆ Click the **Profile** button arrow, and then click **Photo**.

   ◆ Click the **File type** list, and then click the file type you want.

◆ Click the **Resolution (DPI)** list, and then click the resolution you want.

◆ Adjust the brightness and contrast to the settings you want.

7 Select or clear the **Preview or scan images as separate files** check box.

8 To preview the scan, click **Preview**, and then make any adjustments you want before the final scan.

9 Click **Scan**.

10 Click the **Tag these pictures (optional)** list, type a tag name.

11 Click **Import**.

A new Explorer window with today's date opens within the Pictures folder, displaying the scanned picture.

Did You Know?

You can change where Windows Live Photo Gallery stores scanned pictures. In Windows Live Photo Gallery, click the File button, click Options, click the Import tab, click the Settings For List, and then click Scanners. Click Browse next to the Import To List, and then select the location you want.

For Your Information

Selecting the Appropriate File Format

Each file type has a different format and recommended use. JPG (Joint Photographic Experts Group; also known as JPEG) and PNG (Portable Network Graphics) are graphic file formats commonly used on web pages, while BMP (Bit-mapped) and TIF (Tagged Image File Format, also known as Tiff) are file formats used in documents. The format specifies how the information in the file is organized internally. JPG and PNG formats are compressible, which means that the file size is smaller and transfers over the Internet faster. Each file format uses a different compression method, which produces different results when you display the graphic files. JPG is designed for photographs and supports millions of colors, but loses some image quality by discarding image data to reduce the file size. PNG is designed for web graphics and supports millions of color without losing image quality, but not all web browsers fully support its capabilities without using a plug-in, which is a software add-on installed on your computer. TIF is designed for all graphics and colors and one of the most widely used graphic formats, but the file size is large. BMP is the standard Windows graphic format and is similar to TIF.

Downloading Digital Camera Pictures

A **digital still camera** stores pictures digitally rather than on film. The major advantage of digital still cameras is that making photos is fast and inexpensive. In order to use the digital camera features of Windows, you need to have a digital still or video camera attached and installed on your computer. When you connect a digital camera to your computer, Windows 7 displays the AutoPlay dialog, where you can choose to import or view files in the Camera window. When you import pictures, the files are stored and made available in Windows Live Photo Gallery. If you don't use AutoPlay, you can also use an Import command in Windows Live Photo Gallery or the Camera window. You can use the Camera window available from the Computer window to view pictures that you have already taken with the camera and copy them in a folder on your computer, or delete pictures from your camera.

Download Pictures from a Camera

1. Connect the digital camera to your computer, and follow instructions to install and recognize the camera.

2. If the AutoPlay dialog box opens, click **Import pictures and videos** (using Windows or using Windows Live Photo Gallery) to import the pictures.

   If the AutoPlay dialog box doesn't open, continue.

3. Click the **Start** button, and then click **Devices and Printers**.

4. Right-click the digital camera icon, and then click **Import pictures**.

   ◆ You can also click the **Start** button, point to **All Programs**, point to **Windows Live**, click **Windows Live Photo Gallery**, click the **File** button, and then click **Import from a camera or scanner**.

5. To change import settings, click the **Import settings** link, select the options you want, and then click **OK**.

6. Click **Import**.

Manage Pictures on the Camera

1. Connect the digital camera to your computer.

2. If the AutoPlay dialog box opens, click **Open this device to view files**, and then skip to Step 4.

   If the AutoPlay dialog box doesn't open, continue.

3. Click the **Start** button, and then click **Devices and Printers**, and then double-click the Camera icon associated with the digital camera.

4. Double-click the removable storage icon, and any folders to display the pictures stored on the digital camera.

5. Click a picture, and then perform any of the following commands:

   ◆ Click the **Preview** button on the toolbar or right-click the a picture, and then click **Preview** to display the picture in Windows Photo Viewer.

   ◆ Click the **Preview** button arrow on the toolbar, and then click **Windows Live Photo Gallery** to display the picture in Windows Live Photo Gallery.

   ◆ Right-click a picture, and then click **Open** to display the picture on the default program.

   ◆ Click the **Edit** menu, click **Copy to Folder**, select a folder, and then click **Copy**.

   ◆ Right-click a picture, and then click **Delete**.

Using Pictures as a Screen Saver

Instead of using standard screen savers provided by Windows, you can use your own pictures to create a slide show screen saver. Windows displays all the pictures, which you have designated in a folder, to create as a full screen slide show. You can add or remove pictures from the folder to modify the slide show.

Use Pictures as a Screen Saver

1. If you want to create a custom folder for pictures, create a folder, and then place the pictures you want to use in the slide show in the folder.

2. Right-click a blank area of the desktop, and then click **Personalize**.

3. Click **Screen Saver**.

   ◆ You can also click the **File** button in Windows Live Photo Gallery, and then click **Screen saver setting** to open this dialog box.

4. Click the **Screen Saver** list, and then click **Photos** or **Windows Live Photo Gallery**.

5. Click **Settings**.

6. Select the option to use pictures from Windows Live Photo Gallery or your own folder. If necessary, click **Browse**, select the folder with your pictures, and then click **OK**.

7. Click the **Slide show speed** list, select the speed you want, and then select or clear the **Shuffle contents** check box.

8. Click **Save**.

9. Click **Preview**, and then click the mouse to stop it.

10. Click **OK**.

Using a Picture as a Desktop Background

Instead of using one of the pictures provided by Windows, you can select a picture on your hard disk or from a web page as the desktop background. You can use Paint or any graphics program to create new background designs or change existing ones. Acceptable formats for background files are Bitmap (the format of a Paint file), JPEG (the format of an Internet graphic file), or HTM (the format of a web page). After you set a picture as the desktop background, Windows adds the picture to the Background list on the Desktop tab in the Display Properties dialog box. When you use a picture from a web page, Windows saves it in the Background list as Internet Explorer Background. Each new picture from a web page you set as a background replaces the previous one.

Set a Picture as the Background

1. Open the folder or the web page with the picture you want to set as the background.

2. Right-click the picture.

3. Click **Set as desktop background** for a picture file, or click **Set as background** for a web picture.

   If the picture doesn't appear on your desktop, continue.

4. Right-click a blank area of the desktop, and then click **Personalize**.

5. Click **Desktop Background**.

6. Click the picture you set as the background.

7. Click **Save changes**.

Setting Photo Gallery Options

Windows Live Photo Gallery allows you to set general, import, and publishing options. The general options allow you to show pictures and video previews in tooltips, specify how long to keep original photos that are fixed, and whether to get program update alerts. The import options allow you to specify import settings for cameras, CDs and DVDs, or Scanners. The import settings specify where Windows Live Photo Gallery import pictures based on date and tag criteria. In addition, you can set other options that allow you to rotate pictures, open the program, or erase pictures from the camera. The publish options allow you to specify which file details (metadata) you want to publish along with your photos (**New!**).

Set Windows Live Photo Gallery Options

① Click the **Start** button, point to **All Programs**, point to **Windows Live**, and then click **Windows Live Photo Gallery**.

② Click the **File** button, and then click **Options**.

③ Click the **General** tab, and then specify the options you want:

◆ **Tooltips.** Select to show picture and video previews in tooltips.

◆ **Save original pictures.** Select a delete option for original pictures.

◆ **Face detection.** Select to enable face detection.

④ Click the **Import** tab, and then specify the options you want:

◆ **Settings for.** Select Cameras, CDs and DVDs, or Scanners.

◆ **Import to.** Select a location.

◆ **Folder name.** Select a folder criteria based on date and tag.

◆ **File name.** Select an option to preserve tags and file names.

◆ **Other options.** Select or clear the check boxes you want.

⑤ Click the **Tags** tab, and then specify the publishing file details settings you want (**New!**).

⑥ Click **OK**.

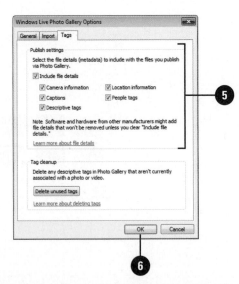

Working with Windows Media

Introduction

You can use Windows Media Player (WMP version 12) to play sounds, music, and digital movies on your computer and on the Internet, or listen to radio stations from all over the world. In addition, you can play and copy CDs, rip music from CDs, create your own CDs, play DVDs or VCDs, and copy music and videos to portable devices, such as portable digital audio players and portable PCs. If you have your media on another computer, you can use Remote Media Streaming to play it on your computer (**New!**). Using Windows Media Player requires a sound card, speakers, and an Internet connection to view the Media Guide and other online stores, look for music licenses, and listen to radio stations on the Internet.

Windows also comes with Sound Recorder, a sound recording utility program you can use to create and modify a sound. You can use the sound to indicate a Windows event, such as starting Windows or if an error has occurred. Using Sound Recorder requires a sound card, speakers, and a microphone.

In addition to Windows Media Player, you can also use Windows Media Center to play media files on your computer or on the web. Windows Media Center is an entertainment system integrated into your computer that lets you watch live or recorded TV, play video and watch pictures, listen to music and radio using an FM tuner or the Internet, play and burn CDs or DVDs, browse online media, and play games. You can also use Windows Media Center Extenders to add entertainment devices—such as a TV, DVD player, digital camera, or Xbox 360—to your system and control each one from Windows Media Center within a networked environment.

What You'll Do

Start, Update, and View Windows Media Player

Play a Music CD, DVD, or VCD Movie

Control the Volume

Browse the Media Guide and Online Stores

Listen to Radio Stations

Play Media Files and the Playlists

Rip CD Music

Copy Media Files to a CD or Portable Device

Stream Media

Enhance the Media Player Display

View and Play Music Files

Create a Sound File

Associate a Sound with an Event

Start, Navigate, and Customize Windows Media Center

Find and View Windows Media Center Files

Starting and Updating Windows Media Player

Before you can use Windows Media Player (WMP), you need to check to make sure you have the latest version (12 or later) installed on your computer using the About Windows Media Player command on the Help menu for the current player. If it's not, you can download and install it from the web at *www.microsoft.com/downloads*. You start Windows Media Player like any other Windows program. You can use the Start menu or a button on the taskbar (**New!**). After you start Windows Media Player, you should check for software updates on the Internet. Microsoft is continually adding features and fixing problems. You can use the Help menu in Windows Media Player to access the updates.

Start and Update Windows Media Player

1. Start Windows Media Player using any of the following:

   ◆ Click the **Windows Media Player** icon on the taskbar. Right-click the icon to start a task, such as Play all music.

   ◆ Click the **Start** button, point to **All Programs**, and then click **Windows Media Player**.

2. Click the **Help** menu, click **Check for updates**, and then follow the instructions to complete the upgrade. To show menus, see the DYK? below.

3. To use the player, click the toolbar button or task tabs. You can use the **Back** and **Forward** button to retrace previous steps.

Did You Know?

You can show and hide the menu bar. To show or hide the menu bar, click the Organize button, point to Layout, and then click Show Menu Bar.

You can automatically check for software updates. Click the Organize button, click Options, click the Player tab, and then click the Once A Day, Once A Week, or Once A Month option.

Viewing the Media Player Window

Now Playing View

Switch to Library

Playback controls

Library View

Search and layout options

Tabs

Library media

Music files

Create Playlist

Playback controls

Switch to Now Playing button

Playing Music from CDs

Windows allows you to play music on your computer in the background while you work. After you insert a music CD into your CD-ROM drive and the music starts to play, you can minimize Windows Media Player and continue to work with other programs on your computer. If you are connected to the Internet when you play a music CD, Windows Media Player tries to locate information about the CD from the Internet, such as the name of the artist and the songs on the album. If the information is not available, the track number of each song displays instead.

Play a Music CD

1 Insert a music CD into your CD-ROM drive.

2 If the Audio dialog box appears, click **Play audio CD** (using Windows Media Player).

The Windows Media Player window appears, and the CD starts to play.

3 To play the music, click the **Play** button.

4 To stop the music, click the **Stop** button.

5 To play a specific song, double-click the song in the list.

6 To play the previous or next song, click the **Previous** or **Next** button.

7 Click the **Minimize** button to continue to listen while you work, or click the **Close** button to exit.

Did You Know?

You can play CD songs in random order. Click the Turn Shuffle On button; click again to turn off.

You can stop a song from playing. Right-click the song in the list, and then click Remove From List.

You can play a CD continuously. Click the Turn Repeat On button; click again to turn off.

Shuffle

Repeat

Mute

Volume

Playing a DVD or VCD Movie

If you have a DVD drive and decoder hardware or software on your computer, you can play DVD movies with Windows Media Player. If you don't have a decoder, you can purchase one from a third party manufacturer. If you only have a CD player, you can play VCD movies. A VCD is similar to a DVD, yet the video quality is not as high. When you play a DVD or VCD movie, a list of titles appear with a section of content from the movie. You can use the titles to browse through the contents of the DVD or VCD.

Play a DVD or VCD Movie

1. Insert a DVD into your DVD drive or a VCD into your CD drive.

2. If the Audio dialog box appears, click the option to play the DVD or VCD, and then click OK.

   The Windows Media Player window appears, and the DVD or VCD starts to play.

3. To expand the contents list of the DVD or VCD click the plus sign (+).

4. To pause the movie, click the **Pause** button.

5. To stop the movie, click the **Stop** button.

6. To play a specific title, double-click it in the list.

7. To play the previous or next section of the movie, click the **Previous** or **Next** button.

8. Click the **Close** button to exit.

Did You Know?

You can display captions and subtitles for a DVD. Click the Play menu, point to Lyrics, Captions, and Subtitles, and then click Off (toggles on and off) or Defaults to select the language you want to use.

Controlling
the Volume

Windows comes with master volume controls that allow you to change the volume of all devices and applications on the computer at once. You can increase or decrease the volume, or you can mute (turn off) the sound on your computer. The volume control is available by default on the notification area on the taskbar. The Volume icon makes it easy to increase or decrease the volume or mute the sound on your computer. In addition to changing the master volume on your computer, you can also adjust the volume of specific devices, such as a CD or DVD player, without affecting the volume of other devices.

Change the Computer Volume

1 Click the **Volume** icon in the notification area on the taskbar.

2 Drag the slider to adjust the volume to the level you want.

TIMESAVER *Press F9 to increase the volume, press F8 to decrease the volume, or press F9 to mute the volume.*

3 To mute the sound, click the **Mute** button.

4 Press Esc or click off the menu to close the volume controls.

Mixer link

Did You Know?

You can display the Volume icon on the taskbar. Right-click the taskbar, click Properties, click Customize, click the Turn System Icons On or Off link, set the Volume Behavior to On, and then click OK.

You can quickly display the Volume. Point to the Volume icon in the notification area.

Troubleshooting

Testing Your Sound Hardware

If your are having trouble hearing the sound from Windows Media Player, the best place to start is to test your sound hardware. Click the Start button, click Control Panel, and then click the Sound icon in Small icons or Large icons view. Next, click the Playback tab, click Configure, click Test, click Next, and then follow the instructions to test the hardware. Once you have tested the hardware, click Finish, and then click OK.

Set Volume Levels for Specific Devices

1. Click the **Volume** icon in the notification area on the taskbar.

2. Click the **Mixer** link.

3. Drag the **Speakers** slider to adjust the settings for the sound level you want.

   The volume for the speakers is the main volume control.

4. Drag the other sliders to adjust the settings for the applications you want.

   The volume for the speakers is the main volume control.

5. When you're done, click the **Close** button.

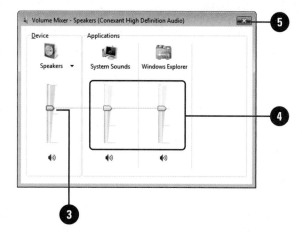

Did You Know?

You can set the recording volume. Right-click the Volume icon, click Recording Devices, click a device, click Properties, click the Levels tab, adjust the volume level, and then click OK twice.

You can set the playback volume for left and right speakers. Right-click the Volume icon, click Playback Devices, click a device, click Properties, click the Levels tab, adjust the volume level, click Balance (if available), adjust L and R levels, click OK, and then click OK twice.

Browsing the Media Guide and Online Stores

The Windows Media Player comes with a built-in Media Guide that is updated daily with the latest music, movies, and entertainment news from the Internet as well as access to your favorite online media stores, where you can download music and more. The Media Guide is a web page that provides links to a variety of media topics ranging from music to sports. Selecting a link opens a web page with more information about the topic, or plays music or movies. Links to media files, such as music or movies, appear with different speeds, which indicate the speed at which the file downloads and plays on your Internet connection.

Use the Media Guide and Online Stores

1. Start Windows Media Player and connect to the Internet, if necessary.

2. Click the **Media Guide** button arrow, and then click **Media Guide** or **Browse all online stores**.

   If necessary, follow the on-screen instructions to accept the license agreement and install any updates.

3. Click the links you want on the web page.

4. When you're done, click the **Close** button.

Listening to Radio Stations

You can use Windows Media Player to listen to radio stations around the world that broadcast on the Internet. When you listen to a radio station on the Internet, the audio continuously streams to your computer. The audio is partially downloaded and stored in a buffer, a temporary storage area, before it begins to play. As more audio streams, Windows Media Player continues to buffer it, which minimizes the interruptions to the radio broadcast. When you play a radio station, a web page for the radio station is displayed in your web browser behind Windows Media Player. While you listen to a radio station, you can browse the web or work in other programs.

Listen to the Radio on the Internet

1 Start Windows Media Player and connect to the Internet, if necessary.

2 Click the **Media Guide** button arrow, and then click **Media Guide**.

3 Click the link for **Internet Radio**.

4 To search for stations, click the **Search for radio stations** link.

5 Click the **Listen** link or name of the radio station you want to play.

TROUBLE? *If Play is not available, click Visit, and then play the radio station.*

6 To stop playing the radio station, click the **Stop** button.

7 To add the station to your playlist, click the **Play** tab, click **Save list**, type a name, and then press Enter.

8 When you're done, click the **Close** button.

Playing Media Files

With Windows Media Player, you can play sound and video files on your computer. You can find and download sound and video files from the Internet or copy media files from a CD or DVD. WMP now supports more audio and video formats, including 3GP, AAC, AVCHD, DivX, MOV, and Xvid (**New!**). The Library makes it easy to organize your media by category, such as Artist, Album, Genre, Rated Songs, or Year Released. You can quickly search for media by name or you can browse through the Library. If you want to do other things while you listen to media, you can switch to Now Playing view (**New!**) to use a smaller display.

Perform a Quick Search

1. Click a media library in the Navigation pane.

2. Click in the **Search** box.

3. Type the text that you want to search by.

   TIMESAVER *Click Search Results in the Library list to display it at any time.*

4. To clear the search, click the **Close** button in the Search box (x).

Results

Browse Media Files

1. Click a media library in the Navigation pane.

2. Click the **Select a Category** button on the address bar, and then select a category, such as Music, Pictures, Video, Recorded TV, or Other Media.

3. Select a view of that category in the Navigation pane.

4. To change the view:

   ◆ **View More**. Click the list arrow next to a button on the address bar, and then select a category.

   ◆ **View Less**. Click a button on the address bar to the left.

Play Media Files from the Library

1 Click a media library in the Navigation pane.

2 Click an arrow next to the category you want to view.

3 Click a category.

4 Double-click the media file to play it.

Play Media Files from a Playlist

1 Click a media library in the Navigation pane.

2 Click an arrow next to the **Playlists** category.

3 Double-click a playlist to play it.

Did You Know?

You can automatically add media files to the Library when played. Click the Organize button, click Options, click the Player tab, select the Add Local Media Files To Library When Played check box, and then click OK.

You can delete a file from the library. Click a media library in the Navigation pane, right-click the file you want to remove, click Delete, click the Delete from Library Only or Delete From Library And My Computer option, and then click OK.

Playing Media Using a Playlist

Instead of playing digital media files, such as music tracks, video clips, or DVD segments, one at a time or in sequential order from a CD or DVD, you can use Windows Media Player to create a **playlist**. A playlist is a customized list or sequence of digital media that you want to listen to or watch. A playlist allows you to group together media files and specify the order in which you want to play back the media. You can mix and match the media files on your computer, a network, a CD, or the Internet, creating a personal juke box. You can create an easy access general playlist called Play list, create one with a specific name, or specify criteria to create an Auto Playlist.

Create Playlist

1. Click a media library in the Navigation pane.

2. Click the **Play** tab.

3. To clear the Play list, click the **Clear list** button.

   ◆ To create a blank new playlist, click the **Create playlist** button, click **Create playlist**, type a name, and then press Enter.

4. Drag items from the details pane to the Play tab. Use the Ctrl or Shift keys to select multiple items.

   ◆ To rearrange items, drag them up or down the list.

5. To save the list, click the **Save list** button, type a name, specify a location, and then press Enter.

   ◆ To save a playlist in a another format, click the **List options** button, and then click **Save list as**.

6. To hide the List pane, click the **List options** button, and then click **Hide list**.

7. To add more items to the playlist, drag them to the playlist, or right-click the the media files, point to **Add to**, and then select the playlist name.

Create an Auto Playlist

1. Click a media library in the Navigation pane.

2. Click the **Create playlist** button, and then click **Create auto playlist**.

3. Type a name for the Auto Playlist.

4. Select the criteria options you want.

5. Click **OK**.

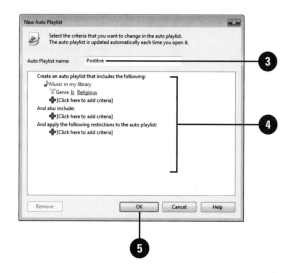

Add Media Files from Your Hard Disk to a Playlist

1. Open the folder window that contains the files or folders you want to add to a playlist.

2. Select the file(s) or folder(s) you want to include in the playlist.

3. Right-click the selection, and then click **Add to Windows Media Player list**.

Did You Know?

You can delete a playlist. Right-click the playlist in the Navigation pane you want to remove, click Delete, click the Delete From Library Only or Delete From Library And My Computer option, and then click OK.

You can edit playlist. Click the playlist in the Navigation pane you want to change, drag new items to the list or right-click items in the list, and then click Remove From List.

Ripping CD Music

Windows Media Player (WPM) allows you to **rip**, or copy, one music track or an entire album from a music CD to your computer. When you rip music from a CD or download music from the web to your computer, Windows copies music by the same artist into one folder in the Music folder and creates subfolders for each album. Windows gives you several ways to play the music on your computer.

Rip Tracks from a Music CD

1. Insert your music CD into the CD-ROM drive.

2. If the Autoplay dialog box appears, click **Play audio CD** (using Windows Media Player) to burn individual tracks, and then click the **Stop** button.

   The WMP window opens, and starts to play the CD.

3. Use default options, or click the **Rip settings** button, point to **Format** or **Audio Quality**, and then select the option you want.

4. Clear the check boxes next to the tracks you don't want to copy.

5. Click **Rip CD** (toggles with Stop Rip).

   The music is copied to the Music folder unless you specify a different location.

6. To stop the copy at any time, click **Stop Rip**.

Toggles to Start

Did You Know?

You can use error correction during a copy. Click the Tools menu, click Options, click the Devices tab, select the CD-ROM drive, click Properties, click Digital, select the Use Error Correction check box, and then click OK.

Select Rip Music Settings

1 Click the **Rip settings** button on the toolbar, and then click **More options**.

♦ You can also select Format and Audio Quality options directly from the Rip settings menu.

2 To change the location where Windows Media Player stores ripped music, click **Change**, select a new folder location, and then click **OK**.

3 Select the format and copy setting you want:

♦ **Windows Media Audio** or **Windows Media Audio Pro.** Most common WMA format with widest range of quality and file size.

♦ **Windows Media Audio (Variable Bit Rate).** High quality with variable file size.

♦ **Windows Media Audio Lossless.** Quality closest to the original with high file size.

♦ **MP3.** Common and flexible format.

♦ **WAV (Lossless).** Common alternate format.

4 Drag the slider to adjust audio quality.

5 Click **OK**.

Did You Know?

You can turn off music copy protection. Click the Tools menu, click Options, click the Rip Music tab, clear the Copy Protect Music check box, and then click OK.

For Your Information

Getting a License to Copy Music

Most CD music is secured with a license to prevent illegal distribution. A license is a legal agreement that specifies whether the license expires or how you can use the file. The terms of the license are entirely dependent upon the person or company that provided the file. Windows Media Player cannot play licensed files without a license. When you copy music from a CD with the Acquire Licenses Automatically option selected, Windows Media Player searches the Internet for the license and copies it to your computer. If the license is not available, you can still acquire a license by copying the music and selecting the Copy Protect music check box on the Rip Music tab in the Options dialog box. As you copy the music, the licenses are issued. The license allows you to copy the music to your hard disk, a portable device, or a CD. If you want to view the license information for a file, right-click the file, click Properties, and then click the Media Usage Rights tab. If you copy music without a license, you could be violating the music's copyright. You can avoid license problems by backing them up.

Copying Media Files to a CD or Portable Device

Windows Media Player makes it easy to burn (copy) music to a CD using a CD burner or copy the music and video you want to a portable device and keep it in sync. If you have a Portable Digital Media Player, such as an ipod or zune, you can download digital media from an online store and play it on the go. Windows Media Player verifies that there is enough space for the selected files on the portable device and then starts the copying process. As the music copies, the amount of used and free space on the portable device is displayed at the bottom of the Music On Device pane. You can synchronize music, video, and picture files to the device so you can bring your whole library with you. You can choose to automatically or manually sync your digital media between WMP and your device, known as a partnership. Set up sync once, and every time you connect your device to your computer, WMP updates the digital media between them, so devices that allow you to rate your music can automatically send them back to WMP.

Copy Music to a CD

1 Insert a blank CD or DVD in your CD recorder.

If the Autoplay dialog box appears, click **Burn an audio CD**. If the Autoplay dialog box doesn't appear, click the **Burn** tab.

If you need to erase your disc, right-click the drive in the Navigation pane, and then click **Erase disc**.

2 To select a disc type, click the **Burn options** button, and then click **Audio CD** or **Data CD or DVD**.

3 If you need to clear the List pane, click the **Clear list** button.

4 Drag the files you want to burn from the Details pane to the List pane.

5 To remove a file from the list, right-click the file, and then click **Remove from list**.

6 Drag the files in the list to arrange them in the order you want.

7 Click the **Start burn** button.

Copy Music to a Portable Device

① Start Windows Media Player, and then connect the portable device to your computer.

② If sync setup is needed for the device, follow the wizard instructions, and then click **Finish**.

③ If you set up Auto Sync, synchronization begins, click **Stop sync**.

④ Click a media library in the Navigation pane.

⑤ Click the **Sync** tab.

⑥ If you need to clear the List pane, click the **Clear list** button.

⑦ Display and drag the media files you want to the sync list.

⑧ To remove a file from the list, right-click the file, and then click **Remove from list**.

⑨ To change sync priority order, sync method, and other settings, click the **Sync options** button, and then click **Set up sync**, specify options, and then click **OK**.

⑩ Click the **Start sync** button.

⑪ If you want to stop the sync, click **Stop sync**.

Upon completion, status information appears next to files indicating success or failure.

Did You Know?

You can find a list of compatible portable devices on the Windows Media web site. Open your browser, go to *www.windowsmedia.com*, and then click the Music Players link.

For Your Information

Changing the Media Player Look

Windows Media Player gives you the freedom of expression to change the look, known as the **skin**, of the Media Player. Windows Media Player includes several skins from which you can select the one you like the best. When you select a skin, Windows Media Player changes from full mode to skin mode. You can use skins only when Media Player is in skin mode. Skin mode displays a smaller player, which provides more room on the screen for other programs. To apply a skin, click the View menu, click Skin Chooser, click a design, click Apply Skin, and then use the controls to play a media file. To delete a skin, click the Delete Selected Skin button, and then click Yes. Press Shift+F10 to display a shortcut menu of convenient commands in skin mode. To return to the full window, click the Return To Full Mode button. To switch back to skin mode, click the View menu, and then click Skin Mode.

Streaming Media

If you have a HomeGroup network, you can use Windows Media Player to stream music and video to another computer and media devices—such as a networked digital stereo receiver, Linksys or Xbox 360—in your home (**New!**). You can also stream your music library from a home computer over the Internet to another computer using remote media streaming (**New!**). Before you can start, you need to turn on home media streaming and enable options to allow devices to access, play, or control your media. In Windows Media Player, you can use the Navigation pane to access and play streamed media.

Prepare for Streaming Media

1. To turn on basic streaming, click the **Stream** button, and then click **Turn on home media streaming**. (If the command is not available, it's turned on.) Click **Turn on media streaming**, and then click **OK**.

2. Click the **Stream** button, and then click **More streaming options**.

3. Click **Allow All** to allow all computer to stream, click **Block All** to block all computers, or select **Allowed** or **Blocked** for each individual computer.

4. To select media types are streamed, click the **Choose default settings** link, select the options you want, and then click **OK**.

5. Click **OK**.

6. To enable streaming, click the **Stream** button, and then click any of the following:

   ◆ **Allow Internet access to home media.** Click to establish a link to an Online ID provider, such as Windows Live. Click the Link online ID link to sign in and use your Windows user account to share files.

   ◆ **Allow remote control of my Player.** Click to enable or disable.

   ◆ **Automatically allow devices to play my media.** Click to enable or disable.

Name of shared media

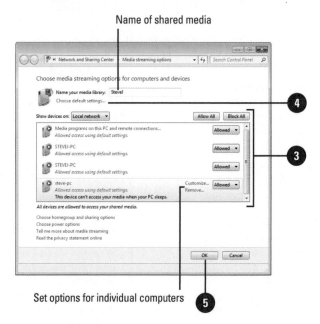

Set options for individual computers ⑤

Automatically allow devices to play my media; click on first use.

Play Media Streamed from the Another Computer

1. Click a media library in the Navigation pane.

2. Click an arrow next to the computer you want to view.

3. Click a category.

4. Double-click the media file to play it.

Did You Know?

You cannot modify the content of a Player library. The people accessing your media are only permitted to use your computer to play the items in your Player library and cannot add, remove, or modify any items.

You cannot access content outside of a Player library. The people accessing your media are not permitted to access any documents outside your Player library on your computer.

You may have problems on a public network. If you're on a public network, such as a coffee shop, Windows Firewall might block the streaming process to your Player library. Check your Windows Firewall settings to make sure Windows Media Player is an allowed program. You can also check the Enabled Network Protocols on the Network tab in the Options dialog box. Click the Organize button, and then click Options to open it.

See Also

See "Sharing with a Homegroup" on page 374-375 for more information on using a homegroup and stream media.

Networked computer on a HomeGroup

Music playing from networked computer

For Your Information

Adding Functionality to Media Player

Windows Media Player allows you to add functionality to the player using plug-ins. Plug-ins add or enhance the media experience with audio and video effects, new rendering types, and visualizations. Before you can use a plug-in, you need to download it from the web and add it to the Media Player. You can find lots of Media Player plug-ins at *www.wmplugins.com*. Before you download a plug-in, read the online information about the plug-in for additional instructions. Click the Organize button, click Options, and then click the Plug-ins tab. Select a plug-in category. Select a plug-in option, if available. To modify a plug-in, click Properties. To remove a plug-in, click Remove. Click OK.

Enhancing the Media Player Display

Visualizations are plug-ins that display geometric shapes and color on the Now Playing mode when you play music. Visualizations are grouped together into collections. You can add and remove visualizations or download additional collections from the web. You can also display special enhancement controls to change video settings, play speed, or audio levels with a graphics equalizer, choose color effects, and send a media link in an e-mail.

Select Visualizations

1. Click the **Switch to Now Playing** button.

2. Right-click the window, and then point to **Visualizations**.

3. Point to a category, and then click the visualization you want to display.

4. To go back to the library, click the **Switch to Library** button.

Select Enhancements

1. Click the **Switch to Now Playing** button.

2. Right-click the window, and then point to **Enhancements**.

3. Click the enhancement you want to display.

4. Adjust the enhancement controls.

5. When you're done, click the **Close** button in the control.

6. To go back to the library, click the **Switch to Library** button.

Viewing and Playing Music Files

You can view and play music files with relative ease in the Music folder. The Music folder is a folder specifically designated to play and manage music files. When you copy music files from a CD or download them from the Internet, the files are copied to the Music folder by default unless you specify a different location. The Music folder contains links to specialized music tasks that can help you play the music you store on your computer. In the Music folder, you can click Play All or Play on the toolbar or double-click an individual music file to open and play the music in Windows Media Player. If you click Play All in the Music folder, Windows Media Player opens and plays all the music in your Music folder and subfolder in random order. If you click Play All in a subfolder within your Music folder, Windows Media Player opens and plays all the music in the folder in consecutive order.

View and Play Music Files

1. Click the **Start** button, and then click **Music**.

2. Select the music files or folder you want to play.

3. Click **Play** or **Play all**.

Creating a Sound File

Using Sound Recorder and a microphone, you can record your own sound files. Sound Recorder creates Windows Media Audio files with the .wma file extension. If you are using Windows Vista Home Basic or Business, Sound Recorder saves files in the .wav format instead of .wma. Sound Recorder doesn't play sounds; you can play your recording in a digital media player, such as Windows Media Player. Before you can use Sound Recorder, you need to have a sound card, speakers, and a microphone installed on your computer.

Record a Sound

1. Click the **Start** button, point to **All Programs**, click **Accessories**, and then click **Sound Recorder**.

2. Click the **Start Recording** button, and then record the sounds you want.

3. When you're done, click the **Stop Recording** button.

4. Select a folder, type a name for the file, and then click **Save**.

5. Click the **Close** button.

Associating a Sound with an Event

Besides customizing the desktop appearance of Windows, you can also add sound effects to common Windows commands and functions, such as starting and exiting Windows, printing complete, opening and closing folders, or emptying the Recycle Bin. You can select a sound scheme (a collection of sounds associated with events), or you can mix and match sound files to create your own sound scheme for your computer. You need to use Wave files with the .wav file extension.

Create and Select a Sound Scheme

1. Click the **Start** button, click **Control Panel**, and then click the **Sound** icon in Small icons or Large icons view.

2. Click the **Sounds** tab.

3. Click an event to which you want to associate a sound.

4. Click the **Sounds** list arrow, and then select a sound, or click **Browse** and locate the sound file you want to use.

5. Click the **Test** button to preview the sound.

6. Click **Save As**, type a name for the sound scheme, and then click **OK**.

7. To select a sound scheme, click the **Sound Scheme** list arrow, and then select a scheme.

8. Click **OK**.

Did You Know?

You can add sounds to the list. If you put WAV files in the Media folder, located in the Windows folder, the sound files appear in the Sounds list.

You can remove a sound associated with an event. On the Sounds tab, click an event, click the Sounds list arrow, and then click (None).

Starting and Navigating Windows Media Center

Windows Media Center is an entertainment system integrated into your computer that lets you watch live or recorded TV, play video and watch pictures, create and play slide shows (**New!**), listen to music and radio using an FM tuner or the Internet, play and burn CDs or DVDs, and play games. When you start Windows Media Center, the program uses the entire screen and doesn't use menus or toolbars. You navigate by using the up and down arrows to specify a main category, and then left and right arrows to specify a subcategory using Turbo Scroll (**New!**). Play, Record, and other VCR/DVD type commands are available in the bottom right corner when you point to them. You can use your keyboard, mouse, a remote control, or touch screen (**New!**) to navigate the system. If you like using desktop gadgets, you can also play media using the Windows Media Center gadget (**New!**). Before you can play FM radio or watch TV, you need additional hardware installed on your computer, an FM tuner and a TV tuner card along with a remote control.

Start, Navigate, and Exit Windows Media Center

1. Click the **Start** button, point to **All Programs**, and then click **Window Media Center**.

   ◆ Right-click the desktop, click **Gadget**, and then double-click the **Windows Media Center** icon to add the gadget.

2. Press the Up or Down arrow keys to scroll the list of categories: **Extras**, **Pictures + Videos**, **Music**, **Movies**, and **TV.**

3. With the category you want, press the Left and Right arrow keys to display the subcategory you want, and then click the option icon.

4. Click the options you want to play music, movies, or videos, watch TV, display pictures, or create and display slide shows (**New!**).

5. To get back to the main screen, point to the upper-left corner, and then click the **Home** button. To go back to the previous screen, click the **Back** button.

6. To exit, point to the upper-right corner, and then click the **Close** button.

Click options

Windows Media Center desktop gadget

Changing Windows Media Center Settings

You can set up and customize Windows Media Center by selecting Tasks on the start screen, and then selecting Settings. In the Settings area, you can set general options for Windows Media Center and specific options for each of the media types, including TV, Pictures, Music, and DVD. You can also set options for extenders and libraries. A Windows Media Center Extender is a device you connect to your computer, such as a TV, DVD player, digital camera, or Xbox 360, that you want to control from Windows Media Center within a networked environment. Before you get started with Windows Media Center, it's a good idea to set general options, which include startup and window behavior, visual and sound effects, program library options, Windows Media Center set up, automatic download options, optimization, and privacy. You can also block access to objectionable TV shows and movies with parental controls in Windows Media Center (**New!**).

Change Windows Media Center Settings

1. On the Windows Media Center start screen, scroll to **Tasks**.

2. Display and click **settings**.

3. Click the type of settings you want to change: **General**, **TV**, **Pictures**, **Music**, **DVD**, **Start Menu and Extras**, **Extender**, or **Media Libraries**.

4. Click the setting type you want to change.

5. Specify the options you want. Use the up and down arrow to display option screens.

   Depending on the option, follow the on-screen wizard to complete the setup or settings.

6. When you're done, click **Save** or **Cancel**, if available.

7. Click the **Back** button to navigate back to the previous screen, or click the **Home** button to go back to the start screen.

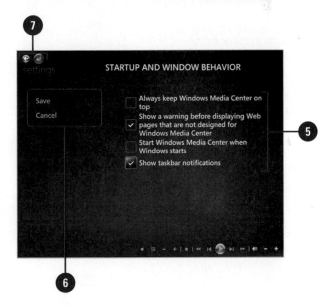

Finding and Viewing Windows Media Center Files

Windows Media Center uses all the media files you already have on your computer, HomeGroup (**New!**), and integrates it into an entertainment system. The same video and music files you use with Windows Media Player are available for use with Windows Media Center, which now supports more audio and video formats, including 3GP, AAC, AVCHD, DivX, MOV, and Xvid (**New!**). For example, when you rip music to your computer, you can play it using Windows Media Player and Windows Media Center. You can choose either one, the preference is yours. As you navigate to a media area, you can select options to find the media you want, and then use the media specific commands and controls to view, play, or change the media files.

Find and View Windows Media Center Files

1 On the Windows Media Center start screen, scroll to a media type: **Pictures + Videos**, **Music**, **Movies**, or **TV**.

2 Display and click the media type library you want, such as video library, music library, or picture library.

◆ If you know the library and want to play all the media, click **play all**.

3 Navigate to one of the sort criteria and find the file you want to view. You can sort by folders or date taken.

4 Use the available commands for the media you want to view, play or change.

5 Use the controls on the lower-right to pause, play, stop, and navigate through the media.

6 While you play media, you can navigate around; click the **Back** button to go back to the previous screen or click the **Home** button to return to the start screen.

◆ You can select **Now Playing** on the start screen to quickly access and play items.

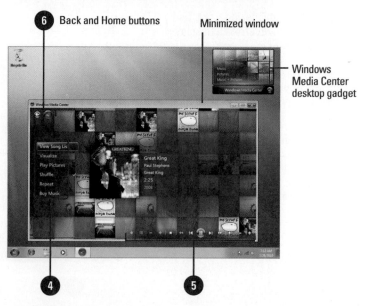

Continues to play video in the background while you navigate.

6 Back and Home buttons

Minimized window

Windows Media Center desktop gadget

Creating Movies and DVD Videos

Introduction

Windows Live Movie Maker (version 14) (**New!**) lets you combine video, audio, and image files with special effects to create movies and slide shows you can publish and show on your computer or CD/DVD, e-mail to others, or place on a web page or mobile device. Windows Live Movie Maker is a new program—built from scratch—that replaces Windows Movie Maker (installed by default in Windows Vista). Windows Live Movie Maker doesn't come installed with Windows 7; it's available for free online from Microsoft. You can download this program as well as other program tools from Windows Live at *http://download.live.com*.

In Windows Live Movie Maker, you create a project that contains the arrangement and timing information of audio and video clips, video transitions, video effects, and titles. You can drag video and audio clips from the storyboard. After you arrange the video and audio clips in the sequence you want, you can add video transitions, video effects, and text. After you preview your project using the monitor, you can publish it as a movie file to your computer, a recordable DVD, or send it to sharing sites on the web, such as Soapbox.

The movie you create can be watched in a media player, such as Microsoft Windows Media Player, or in a web browser. If you would rather create a DVD, you can output the movie in a DVD format (.wmv) from Windows Live Movie Maker, and then burn the file to a DVD or use it in Windows DVD Maker. In Windows DVD Maker, you can insert additional video, pictures, and audio, add DVD titles and menus, and specify publishing options before you burn the movie to a DVD.

What You'll Do

Plan a Movie Maker Project

Start Windows Live Movie Maker

View the Windows Live Movie Maker Window

Open an Existing Project

Use Photos and Videos from Photo Gallery

Add Photos and Videos

Add Slides to a Movie

Add a Soundtrack

Work with Clips

Add Text

Trim Clips

Add Transitions Between Clips

Add Photo and Video Effects

Save a Movie Project and a Movie

Add Functionality with Plug-ins

Publish a Movie

Create a DVD Video

Planning a Movie Maker Project

Windows Live Movie Maker lets you combine video, audio, and image files to create movies and slide shows you can publish and show on your computer or CD/DVD, e-mail to others, or place on a web page or mobile device. You save the movie you create as a file, just as you would save a word processing or spreadsheet file, and you can play and view it at any time. However, movies and their accompanying files are larger than most other documents you create—usually exceeding 5 MB. Before you begin, it's a good idea to plan your content.

Decide the purpose of the movie

Your movie might be a promotional piece or catalog for business use, or a vacation movie to share with family and friends. Your purpose determines the subject, type, and quality of the **source material**, which is the video and audio material you will use.

Determine how to share the movie with others

You might want to show your movie on a computer projection screen at a meeting, send it as an attachment in an e-mail message, or place it on a web site. When you place a movie on a web site, viewers might download it, which means to transfer it to their computers and store it for future viewing. If your movie is very long or has many high-quality images, the movie file will be large and will take a long time to download.

Choose source material

If you have a digital video or digital web camera, you can record or capture digital images, and then import them into Movie Maker. To use existing video or audio segments, called **clips**, you must import them, or bring them into Movie Maker.

Sketch the movie

Before putting your movie together in Movie Maker, it's important to make a sketch of your movie that shows the order of the audio and video components. What audio clips do you want to play with what video clips?

Review the process used to create a movie

First, you bring clips of source material into a Movie Maker project file. A **project file**, which is the working copy of your movie, is a Movie Maker document with the file name extension .mswmm. You then use the project file to do the following: set the order of your movie segments; **trim** (delete) portions of clips you don't want to use; specify how clips display from one to the next, called **transitions**; add a video special effect to clips; add titles and credits to the beginning and end of the movie or individual clips; and, lastly, preview your work. Finally, you save your project file as a movie with the file name extension .wmv and display the completed movie using the Windows Media Player program.

Starting Windows Live Movie Maker

Windows Live Movie Maker (**New!**) doesn't come installed with Windows 7, so you need to download and install it from the Microsoft Windows Live. This chapter describes version 14 beta; your down-loaded version with updates may differ slightly; select Options on the File menu for version information. Before you start Windows Live Movie Maker, use Display Properties in the Control Panel to make sure the screen resolution is set correctly. Windows Live Movie Maker is a program that you can start from the Start menu. You achieve the best results in Windows Live Movie Maker when the screen resolution is set to 1024 by 768 or higher. When you start Windows Live Movie Maker, a new untitled movie project is displayed. You can either create a new movie project or open an existing one.

Start Windows Live Movie Maker

1. Click the **Start** button, and then point to **All Programs**.

2. Point to **Windows Live**, and then click **Windows Live Movie Maker**.

3. If an alert appears, asking you to save changes to My Movie, click **Yes** or **No**.

   My Movie is the default movie file for Windows Live Movie Maker.

4. If you select Yes, select a location, and then click **Save**.

   A blank new movie (default My Movie) appears in the Windows Live Movie Maker window.

5. To exit Windows Live Movie Maker, click the **File** button, and then click **Exit**.

See Also

See "Changing the Display" on page 105 for information on changing the screen resolution.

Viewing the Windows Live Movie Maker Window

Ribbon
The Ribbon displays the File menu and tabs with button commands.

Storyboard
The Storyboard displays a sequence of clips and photos in your movie project.

Playback controls
The Playback controls allow you to playback the movie.

Monitor
The monitor displays individual clips or an entire project.

Opening an Existing Project

After you save a project in Windows Live Movie Maker, you can open it and continue to work on the project. A Movie Maker project file is saved with a .mswmm file name extension, which you can open using the Open command on the File menu. The project file's extension will change, once the project is finalized.

Open an Existing Project

1. Click the **Start** button, point to **All Programs**, point to **Windows Live**, and then click **Windows Live Movie Maker**.

2. Click the **File** menu, and then click **Open**.

3. Select the drive and folder that contains the project you want to open.

4. Select the project file.

5. Click **Open**.

Did You Know?

You can quickly reopen a recently opened movie. Click the Start button, point to Windows Live Movie Maker, and then click the movie you want to reopen.

You can create a new movie in Windows Live Movie Maker. Click the File button, and then click New.

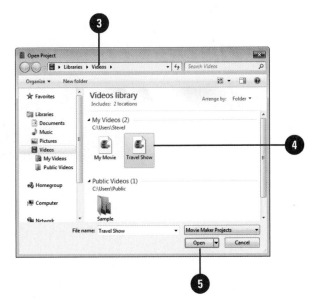

Using Photos and Videos from Photo Gallery

If you installed Windows Live Photo Gallery (**New!**) on your computer along with Windows Live Movie Maker, you can use the program to quickly import photos and video directly into Windows Live Movie Maker. Windows Live Photo Gallery comes with a Make a movie command on the Make menu, which connects the program with Windows Live Movie Maker. The command transfers selected photos and video to a new or open movie in Windows Live Movie Maker (**New!**).

Create a New Movie with Photos and Videos from Photo Gallery

1. Click the **Start** button, point to **All Programs**, point to **Windows Live**, and then click **Windows Live Photo Gallery**.

2. Select the photos and videos you want to use in a movie.

3. Click the **Movie** button on the toolbar, and then click **Make a movie**.

   Windows Live Movie Maker opens, displaying the photos and videos from Windows Live Photo Gallery in the Storyboard.

Photos from Windows Live Photo Gallery

Add Photos and Videos from Photo Gallery into a Movie

1. Click the **Start** button, point to **All Programs**, point to **Windows Live**, and then click **Windows Live Movie Maker**.

2. Click the **File** menu, and then click **Open**.

3. Select the drive and folder that contains the project you want to open.

4. Select the project file.

5. Click **Open**.

6. Click the **Start** button, point to **All Programs**, point to **Windows Live**, and then click **Windows Live Photo Gallery**.

7. Select the photos and videos you want to use in a movie.

8. Click the **Movie** button on the toolbar, and then click **Make a movie**.

   Windows Live Movie Maker appears, displaying the currently opened movie with the photos and videos from Windows Live Photo Gallery added into the Storyboard.

Video added from Windows Live Photo Gallery

Adding Photos and Videos

If you want to use existing video and audio clips in your movie instead of recording them yourself, you can obtain them from various companies that specialize in video processing, or you can download them from the web. Commercial CDs/DVDs are excellent sources for audio clips. You can import the video and audio clips into Windows Live Movie Maker from files on your computer, from your CD/DVD drive, or from the web. You can use the Add videos and photos button on the Home tab or drag photos and videos directly to the Storyboard. If you no longer want a photo or video in the Storyboard, you can remove it.

Add Photos or Videos to a Movie

1. Click the **Home** tab.

2. Click the **Add videos and photos** button on the Ribbon.

3. Select the folder that contains the photo or video files you want to use.

4. To select a specific media type, click the **Files of type** list arrow, and then select a file type.

5. Select the files you want to use.

    TIMESAVER *To import several files at one time, press and hold down the Ctrl key, and then click each file that you want to use.*

6. Click **Open**.

Movie Maker Import File Types

File Type	File Extensions
Video	.wmv, .avi, /dvr-ms, .mpg, .mod, .vod, .asf, .m1v, .m2ts, .mp2v, .mpe, .mpeg, .mpv2, .wm, .3g2, .3gp, .3gp2, .3gpp, .asx, .m2t, .m2v, and .m4v
Photos and Pictures	.jpg, .png, .bmp, .dib, .rle, .gif, .ico, .icon, .jpeg, .jpe, .jfif, . exif, .tiff, .tif, and .wdp

Drag Photos or Videos into a Movie

1. Open Windows Explorer and display the media files you want to use.

2. Start Windows Live Movie Maker, and then create or open the movie in which you want to add photos or videos.

3. Display the windows next to each other; right-click the taskbar, and then click **Show windows side by side**.

4. Drag the media files from Windows Explorer to the Storyboard in Windows Live Movie Maker.

Photos in Windows Live Movie Maker

Adding Slides to a Movie

Instead of using video clips, you can create slide shows in Windows Live Movie Maker with still images that you create using a digital camera, web camera, or scanner. You can import the clips into Windows Live Movie Maker and create transitions between them, just as you would in a movie. You can change the duration of individual photos. You can also add a sound clip to create a sound track that plays as your photos appear on the screen. Portrait-oriented pictures in Movie Maker are the same height as landscape-oriented pictures, and Movie Maker inserts a black background on either side of each one.

Create a Slide Show Movie

① Click the **File** button, and then click **New**.

② Click the **Add videos and photos** button on the Home tab.

③ Select the folder that contains the photo files you want to use.

④ To select a specific media type, click the **Files of type** list arrow, and then select a file type.

⑤ Select the files you want to use.

TIMESAVER *To import several files at one time, press and hold down the Ctrl key, and then click each file that you want to use.*

⑥ Click **Open**.

⑦ Click the **File** button, click **Save as**, navigate to a folder location, type a name, and then click **Save**.

Arrange Photos in a Slide Show

1. Create or open a slide show movie.

2. Select the photos you want to move.

3. Drag the selected photos to a new location in the order you want.

Set Photo Duration in a Slide Show

1. Create or open a slide show movie.

2. Select the photos you want to use in the movie.

3. Click the **Edit** tab.

4. Click the **Duration** list arrow, and then select the photo duration in seconds.

Adding a Soundtrack

If you have photos or video without sound, you can add a soundtrack to a movie. Windows Live Movie Maker allows you to add a single audio or music file to your movie. You can use audio or music with the WMA, MP3, or WAV file formats. If you want to use multiple audio or music files in a movie, use an external sound editing program to combine them together before you use it. You can use the Add music button on the Home tab to insert it. When you insert a soundtrack file when one already exists, the new one replaces the existing one. If you no longer want to use a soundtrack file, you can remove it. In addition, you can also set the soundtrack and video to play at the same volume or make one louder than the other, and adjust the duration of your movie to match your soundtrack.

Add an Audio or Music Soundtrack

1. Open the movie in which you want to fit the sound clip to the length of the movie.

2. Click the **Home** tab.

3. Click the **Add music** button on the Ribbon.

4. Select the folder that contains the audio or music file you want to use.

5. To select a specific media type, click the **Files of type** list arrow, and then select a file type.

6. Select the files you want to use.

7. Click **Open**.

Did You Know?

You can remove a soundtrack. Open the movie with the soundtrack you want to remove, click the Remove Music button on the Home tab.

Fit the Soundtrack to the Movie

1 Open the movie in which you want to fit the sound clip to the length of the movie.

2 Click the **Home** tab.

3 If not done, click the **Add music** button on the Ribbon to add a soundtrack file to the movie.

4 Click the **Fit** button to adjust the duration of your movie to match your soundtrack.

Mix the Soundtrack

1 Open the movie in which you want to adjust the sound clip.

2 Click the **Home** tab.

3 If not done, click the **Add music** button on the Ribbon to add a soundtrack file to the movie.

4 Click the **Mix** button.

5 Drag the slider to adjust the volume mix between the soundtrack and the video.

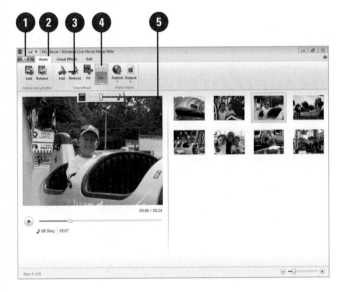

Working with Clips

After you capture or import a video clip or audio clip, you can preview the individual clips in the monitor. The monitor works similarly to a VCR/DVD. The Storyboard displays all the clips and photos in a movie. The order in which they appear in the Storyboard is the order it appears in the movie. You can rearrange the individual items by simply dragging them to a new location in the Storyboard. If you no longer want to use a clip, you can remove it.

Preview a Clip

1. Open the movie in which you want to work with clips.

2. Click the clip in the Storyboard you want to preview.

3. Right-click the selected clip, and then click **Play**.

   TIMESAVER *Press Spacebar to play or pause a clip quickly.*

4. To pause the clip, click the **Pause** button. Click the **Play** button again to continue.

   ◆ To adjust the start point, drag the **Seek** bar to the place you want.

Seek bar

Did You Know?

You can get ScreenTip information about a clip. Point to a clip in the Storyboard to display name and duration of the clip.

Arrange Clips in a Movie

1. Open the movie in which you want to work with clips.

2. Select the clips you want to move.

3. Drag the selected clips to a new location in the order you want.

Remove Clips from a Movie

1. Open the movie in which you want to remove clips.

2. Select the clips you want to remove.

3. Click the **Home** tab.

4. Click the **Remove** button.

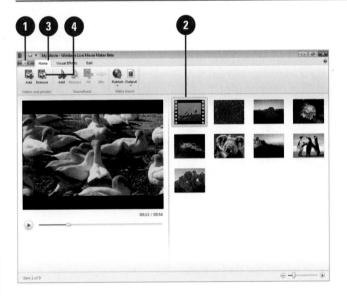

Did You Know?

You can cut and copy clips in Windows Live Movie Maker. Open the movie in which you want to work with clips, select the clips you want to cut or copy, right-click the selection, and then click Cut or Copy.

Adding Text

You can add text titles and credits to your movies. You can add any text you want, such as the title of your movie, your name, captions, and credits at the end. You can add a title at the beginning of a movie, before or after a clip, or overlapping a clip or credits at the end of a movie. You add text in Windows Live Movie Maker just like you would in Paint with a Text box. Like Paint, if you click outside the text box, you can't change it. It becomes part of the clip. When you insert text in a video, the text appears throughout the entire video. You can also change the appearance of the text using the font formatting options on the Edit tab.

Add and Edit Text to a Movie

1 Open the movie in which you want to add text.

2 Click the **Edit** tab.

3 Select the clip you to which you want to add a title.

4 Click the **Text box** button.

A blank text box appears on the monitor.

IMPORTANT *If you click outside the text box, you can't change it. It becomes part of the clip.*

5 To move the text box, point to the edged of the box (4-headed arrow), and then drag it.

6 Click in the box, if necessary, and then type the text you want to appear as the title.

7 To adjust the size of the text box, point to a size box in the corners or middle edges, and then drag it.

8 To edit the text, click in the text box, and then modify or format the text.

9 When you're done, click outside the text box.

Add and Format Text to a Movie

1. Open the movie in which you want to add text.

2. Click the **Edit** tab.

3. Select the clip to which you want to add a title.

4. Click the **Text box** button.

    A blank text box appears on the monitor.

    IMPORTANT *If you click outside the text box, you can't change it. It becomes part of the clip.*

5. Use the options under Font on the Edit tab to format the text:

    ◆ **Font Type.**

    ◆ **Font Size.**

    ◆ **Bold.**

    ◆ **Italic.**

    ◆ **Font Color.**

    ◆ **Grow Font.**

    ◆ **Shrink Font.**

6. Click in the box, if necessary, and then type the text you want to appear as the title.

7. To adjust the size of the text box, point to a size box in the corners or middle edges, and then drag it.

8. To move the text box, point to the edged of the box (4-headed arrow), and then drag it.

9. When you're done, click outside the text box.

Trimming Clips

Frequently, the clips you record or import into Windows Live Movie Maker run longer than you want them to in your final movie. You can easily trim clips on the Trim tab by playing the clip and setting the **trim beginning** point and **trim end** point. The portion between the trim points remains in your movie. The frames before and after the trim points are deleted from your movie, but the original clip is not affected and retains its original length. You can trim a clip as it plays, or you can pause and set the trim points. You can drag the **timeline trim handles** (sliders at the beginning and end of a selected clip).

Trim a Video Clip

① Open the movie in which you want to modify clips.

② Click the **Edit** tab.

③ Select the video clip you want to trim in the movie.

④ Click the **Trim** button.

⑤ Drag the **Seek** bar to the point where you want to start the clip.

⑥ Drag the left slider to the point where you want to start the clip.

⑦ Drag the **Seek** bar to the point where you want to end the clip.

⑧ Drag the right slider to the point where you want to end the clip.

⑨ Click the **Save and close** button to save and exit the Trim tab or click **Cancel** to exit without saving your work.

Adding Transitions Between Clips

A **transition** is an effect that provides a smoother, more gradual change between clips in a movie. A transition plays before one clip ends while another starts to play. You can add a transition between two video clips, pictures, or titles on the storyboard or timeline. Windows Live Movie Maker provides a variety of video transitions that you can quickly add to a movie project, such as Crossfade, Slide, and Roll. If you no longer want to use a transition, you can remove it.

Add or Remove a Transition

1. Open the movie in which you want to add transitions.

2. Click the **Visual Effects** tab.

3. Select one or more photo or video clips you want to add a transition in the movie.

4. Click a transition on the Ribbon.

   A gold border appears around the transition box on the Ribbon to indicate it is applied to the photo or video clip.

5. To remove a transition, click the **No transition** (first box) on the Ribbon.

6. To test out the transition, click the **Play/Pause** button.

7. To increase or decrease the transition duration, click the **Edit** tab, and then change the duration time in seconds.

Adding Photo and Video Effects

Windows Live Movie Maker offers a variety of Black and White effects that you can add to a movie project, such as orange filter, red filter, yellow filter, sepia tone, or cyan tone. An effect is applied for the entire duration of a clip, photo, or text in a movie project. If you no longer want to use an effect, you can remove it.

Add or Remove Effects

① Open the movie in which you want to apply an effect.

② Click the **Visual Effects** tab.

③ Select one or more photo or video clips you want to apply an effect in the movie.

④ Click an effect on the Ribbon.

A gold border appears around the effect box on the Ribbon to indicate it is applied to the photo or video clip.

⑤ To remove an effect, click the **No effect** (first box) on the Ribbon.

⑥ To test out the effect, click the **Play** button.

Saving a Movie Project

If you're still working on a project, you can save the project file and open it later to continue working with your movie. A saved project file in Windows Live Movie Maker has an .mswmm file name extension. In Windows Explorer, you can include general information using tags, like any other file, about the movie, such as the title, author, copyright, a rating, and a description, that is often displayed during playback by many media players.

Save a Movie Project

1. Create or open the movie you want to save in the default Windows Live Movie Maker format (.mswmm).

2. Click the **File** button, and then click **Save as**.

3. Select the folder where you want to save the project file.

4. Type a movie project name.

5. Click **Save**.

Movie Maker Project with the .mswmm format

Saving a Movie

A movie project is saved with the default .mswmm file format. However, if you want to use your movie on a DVD or portable device, you need to save it in a compatible format, such as Windows Media Video (.wmv) (**New!**). With the Output button on the Home tab, you can save a movie in the .wmv format: Windows Media DVD quality (640x480, 2.8Mbps, 30fps) or Windows Media portable device (320x240, 1.5Mbps, 30fps). After you save the movie, your next step is to burn it to a DVD or sync it to a portable device. After you save the movie in the .wmv format, you can play it in a media player, such as Windows Media Player, or in a web browser.

Save a Movie for Use on a DVD or Portable Device

1. Create or open the movie you want to save in the .wmv format for use on a DVD or portable device.

2. Click the **Home** tab.

3. Click the **Output** button arrow, and then select an output option:

   ◆ **Windows Media DVD quality (.WMV).**

   ◆ **Windows Media portable device (.WMV).**

4. Select the folder where you want to save the project file.

5. Type a movie name.

6. Click **Save**.

   Upon completion, an alert dialog box appears, displaying options to view the file in Windows Explorer or in Windows Media Player.

7. Click **View Folder**, **Open**, or **Close**.

Burn a Movie to a DVD

1. Click the Windows Explorer icon on the taskbar, and navigate to the location with the movie you want to burn to a DVD.

2. Select the movie that you saved using Windows Media DVD quality (.WMV) in Windows Live Movie Maker.

3. Click the **Burn** button on the toolbar.

4. Insert a writable DVD into your DVD recorder.

5. Click **Burn files to disc**.

6. Type a title for the disc.

7. Click the **With a CD/DVD player** option.

8. Click **Next** to continue.

9. Open the folder that contains the files you want to burn, and then drag the files onto the empty disc folder.

10. Click **Burn to disc** on the toolbar.

The selected files are copied to the disc. The disc recorder tray opens when the disc is complete.

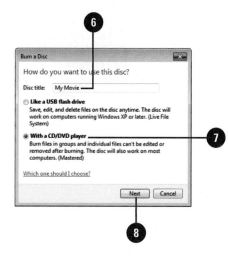

Adding Functionality with Plug-ins

Windows Live Movie Maker allows you to publish a movie to sharing sites on the web, such as Soapbox on MSN video (installed by default). Windows Live Movie Maker uses plug-ins (**New!**) to allow this functionality. Third-party developers have created additional plug-ins you can use to upload your movies to YouTube and SmugMug to name a few. You can open a web site from Windows Live Movie Maker that lists and provides access to a variety of plug-ins with more to come all the time. The plug-ins on the web site can be used in Windows Live Movie Maker and/or Windows Live Photo Gallery, such as upload to Facebook. Check the web site for details.

Add Functionality with Plug-ins

1. Create or open the movie you want to save in the .wmv format for use on a DVD or portable device.

2. Click the **Home** tab.

3. Click the **Publish** button arrow, and then click **Add a plug-in**.

   Your browser opens, displaying a web site with a list of available plug-ins.

4. To install a plug-in, click a link, and the click the download link for the plug-in.

5. Click **Run** or **Save** to run or save the setup program, and then follow the on-screen instructions.

6. Follow the on-screen instructions to complete the setup process, and then click **Finish**.

7. Click the **File** button, click **Exit**, and then restart Windows Live Movie Maker.

Installed plug-ins

Plug-ins web site

Publishing a Movie

After you preview the final project using the monitor, you can publish the project file as a movie file. Using a publishing plug-in (**New!**), you can publish the movie file to the web for use on sharing sites, such as Soapbox on MSN video, YouTube, or Pixelpipe. The Soapbox on MSN video plug-in is installed by default, while YouTube and other publishing plug-ins need to be downloaded and installed. You can open a web site from Windows Live Movie Maker that lists and provides access to a variety of plug-ins. Each publishing option uses a different process to publish your movie to the web site. In most cases, you need an account with the web site to continue. Get an account or sign in to your account.

Publish a Movie Using Plug-ins

1. Create or open the movie you want to save in the .wmv format for use on a DVD or portable device.

2. Click the **Home** tab.

3. Click the **Publish** button arrow, and then select a publishing options, such as LiveUpload to YouTube.

   Each publishing option uses a different process to publish your movie to the web site.

4. In most cases, you need an account with the web site to continue. Get an account or enter your user name and password.

5. Click **Sign In**.

6. Follow the on-screen instructions to complete the setup process.

Installed plug-ins

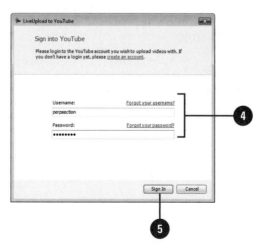

Creating a DVD Video

With Windows DVD Maker, you can insert video, pictures and audio, and combine it with titles and predefined menus to create a DVD video disc that you can play on a TV using a DVD player. To create a DVD, you add and arrange your media, add menu text, select a menu style, choose DVD playback options, and then burn it. If you have still photos, you can also create a slide show set to music.

Create a DVD Video Using Windows DVD Maker

1 Click the **Start** button, point to **All Programs**, and then click **Windows DVD Maker**.

2 Click the **Add items** button, locate and select the media you want to insert, and then click **Import**.

3 Select a media item, and then click the **Move up** or **Move down** button to arrange the media on the DVD.

4 Click the **DVD Burner** list arrow, and then select a DVD burner.

5 To set options, click the **Options** button, specify the options you want, and then click **OK**.

◆ **Choose DVD playback settings.** Select a playback option.

◆ **DVD aspect ratio.** Select a screen ratio, either the 4:3 or 16:9 option.

◆ **Video format.** Select the NTSC or PAL option. NTSC is common in the USA and PAL in Europe.

◆ **DVD burner speed.** Select the fastest possible for the DVD burner on your computer.

6 Type a disc title, and then click **Next** to continue.

DVD Options

7 Click the **Menu text** button, specify the text you want, and then click **Change Text**.

8 Click a menu style in the right pane.

9 To customize the menu, click the **Customize menu** button, specify the options you want, and then **Change Style**.

10 Click the **Slide show** button, specify picture length and music, and then **Change Slide Show**.

11 Click **Burn**.

12 Click the **File** menu, click **Save**, specify a location and name, and then click **Save**.

Change menu text options

Setting Up Accounts and Maintaining Security

11

Introduction

With user accounts, you can customize and personalize Windows for each user on your computer. Each user can have their own Documents folder and list of web favorites, customize computer preferences, and protect private files. When you set up a new user account, the account appears on the Welcome screen, where the new user can log on. You can use User Accounts in the Control Panel to add or delete user accounts, create a guest account, change a user's group or account type, change the way Windows starts, change the account picture, and set, change, and reset an account password.

Keeping your computer safe and secure is a continuing battle. With the Windows Action Center, you can manage computer security from one place. The Action Center makes it easy to find information about the latest virus or security threat, check the status of essential security settings, and quickly get support from Microsoft for a security-related issue.

While you're browsing the Internet or working in your e-mail program, you need to be aware of viruses and other harmful attacks so you can protect your computer from being infected by one. Internet Explorer and Windows Live Mail include security enhancements to help you make your computer more secure. In Internet Explorer, you can create security zones to designate trusted web sites, set web site ratings to restrict user access, clean up Internet files and information, and manage cookies to protect your personal identity from unauthorized access. If you're tired of closing unwanted pop-up ads, you can use Pop-up Blocker in Internet Explorer to prevent most pop-up windows from appearing. In Windows Live Mail, you can select a security zone, set options to prevent viruses in attachments and spam, and send secure e-mail using digital IDs and encryption.

What You'll Do

Secure a Computer

Add and Delete User Accounts

Change a User's Group or Account Type

Change the Start Up Screen

Set, Change, and Reset a Password

Lock the Computer

Manage Security in One Place

Defending Against Malicious Software

Set Parental Controls

Send Secure Information Using Windows CardSpace

Encrypt Files for Safety

Avoid Viruses and Other Harmful Attacks

Understand Security on the Internet

Create Security Zones and Set Ratings

Protect Internet Privacy and Identity

Block Pop-Up Ads with the Information Bar

Block Content with InPrivate Filtering

Manage Add-Ons

Securing a Computer

Windows 7 provides several ways to secure your computer.

Create User Accounts

For a shared or workgroup computer, there are two main types of user accounts: administrator and standard. For a domain network computer, different account types (administrator, standard user, restricted user) provide similar permissions as the ones on a shared or workgroup computer.

The **administrator** account is for the person who needs to make changes to anything on the computer as well as manage user accounts. An administrator account can install programs and hardware, make system-wide changes, access and read all non private files, create and delete user accounts, change other people's accounts, change your own account name, type and picture, and create, change, or remove your own password.

The **standard** account is for the person who needs to manage personal files and run programs. This account cannot install software or hardware, or change most computer settings.

The **guest** account doesn't have a password for easy access and contains more restrictions than the standard account. The guest account is disabled by default and needs to be turned on.

You can also create a **user group**, which is a collection of user accounts that all have the same security rights. The most common user groups are the standard user and administrator. A single account can be a member of more than one group.

Use Action Center

Use the Action Center (**New!**) to check your security settings— Window Firewall, Automatic Up-dates, and antivirus software— and learn how to improve the security of your computer.

If an option displays the Action Center icon next to it, you need to enter the administrator password or provide confirmation when prompted by the **User Account Control (UAC)**. This adds an additional level of security to keep your computer secure. If you don't need the security (not recommended), you can turn it off in User Accounts.

Icon indicates administrator privileges needed to access

Administrator account

Click to turn UAC on or off

UAC for administrators; click Continue for consent

UAC for standard users; enter credentials

Enable Windows Firewall

Windows Firewall is a security system that creates a protective barrier between your computer or network and others on the Internet. Windows Firewall monitors all communication between your computer and the Internet and prevents unsolicited inbound traffic from the Internet from entering your computer. For more information on Windows Firewall, see "Connecting to the Internet" on page 134 and "Setting Up Windows Firewall" on page 136.

Enable Automatic Updates

Windows Automatic Updates allows you to keep your computer up-to-date with the latest system software and security updates over the Internet. For more information, see "Updating Windows" on page 440.

Enable Internet Security Options

Internet Explorer provides security zones to browse secure web sites and a rating system to screen content, protects personal information and your privacy on the Internet, blocks pop-up ads, and displays information to help you make security decisions. For more information, see "Understanding Security on the Internet" on page 332.

Enable E-mail Security Options

Windows Live Mail provides security zones to help you determine whether or not to run potentially harmful content from inside an e-mail, prevents your e-mail program from sending mail with your e-mail address to contacts in your address book (which is a common way to propagate a virus), and stops pictures and other content from automatically downloading inside and e-mail to your computer (which is a common way spammers confirm your e-mail address to send more spam). For more information, see "Sending and Retrieving a File" on page 182, "Reading and Replying to E-mail" on page 180, and "Protecting Against E-mail Attacks" on page 194.

Protect Files and Folders

Another way to protect the files on your computer is to use the built-in security provided by the NTFS file system. The NTFS file system is available for Windows NT-based computers, which doesn't include Windows 95, Windows 98, or Windows Me. You can select your hard disk in the Computer window and display Details on the task pane to determine whether your computer uses the NTFS file system.

The NTFS file system provides additional security for your files and folders. You can make a folder private, use the advanced Encrypting File System (EFS) to protect sensitive data files on your computer. If someone tries to gain access to encrypted files or a folder on your computer, a unique file encryption key prevents that person from viewing it. While these security options are more advanced, they could be helpful for securing very sensitive information. For more information, see "Encrypting Files for Safety" on page 328.

Understand the Enemy

Knowing your enemy (harmful intruders) can help you make safe computing decisions that lead to a secure computer rather than unsafe ones that lead to potential disaster. For information, see "Avoiding Viruses and Other Harmful Attacks" on page 330.

Adding and Deleting User Accounts

If you have an administrator account or are a member of the Administrators group, you can create a new user account or delete an existing one. When you add a new user to your computer, Windows creates a separate identity, allowing the user to keep files completely private and customize the operating system with personal preferences. The name you assign to the user appears on the Welcome screen and the Start menu. The steps to add and delete user accounts differ, depending on whether your computer is part of a domain network or shared/workgroup computer.

Add an Account

1. Click the **Start** button, and then click **Control Panel.**

2. Click the **User Accounts** icon in Small icons or Large icons view.

3. Click **Manage another account**.

4. Click **Create a new account**.

5. Type an account name.

6. Click the **Administrator** option, or click the **Standard user** option.

7. Click **Create Account**.

8. Click the **Close** button.

Did You Know?

You can delete an account. In User Accounts, click the account you want to remove, click Delete The Account, click Keep Files To Save Account File To The Desktop or click Delete Files, click Delete Account, and then click the Close button.

You may need administrator access to make security changes. If a security option displays the Action Center icon next to it, you need to enter the administrator password or provide confirmation when prompted to make a change.

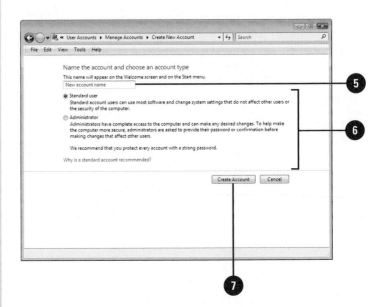

Add an Account on a Domain Network

1️⃣ Click the **Start** button, and then click **Control Panel**.

2️⃣ Click the **User Accounts** icon in Small icons or Large icons view, and then click **Manage User Accounts**.

3️⃣ Click **Add**.

4️⃣ Type a user name and domain, and then click **Next** to continue.

5️⃣ Click a user access level option: **Standard user**, **Administrator**, or **Other**.

6️⃣ Click **Finish**.

7️⃣ Click **OK**.

Did You Know?

You can delete an account on a domain network. In the User Accounts dialog box, click the Users tab, select the user you want to delete, click Remove, click Yes to confirm, and then click OK.

You can turn User Account Control on or off. In the User Accounts dialog box, click Turn User Account Control on or off, select or clear the User Account Control (UAC) To Help Protect Your Computer check box, click OK, and then click the Close button.

Creating a Guest Account

If you have an administrator account or are a member of the Administrators group, you can create a guest account. A guest account provides access to a computer for anyone who doesn't have a user account. The steps to create a guest account differ, depending on whether your computer is part of a domain network or shared/work-group computer.

Create a Guest Account

1. Click the **Start** button, and then click **Control Panel.**

2. Click the **User Accounts** icon in Small icons or Large icons view.

3. Click **Manage another account**.

4. Click the **Guest** icon.

5. Click **Turn On**.

6. Click the **Close** button.

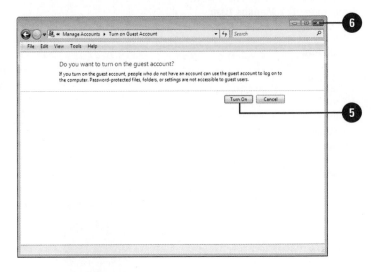

Create a Guest Account on a Domain Network

1. Click the **Start** button, and then click **Control Panel.**

2. Click the **User Accounts** icon in Small icons or Large icons view, and then click **Manage User Accounts**.

3. Click the **Advanced** tab, and then click **Advanced**.

4. Click **Users**.

5. Double-click the **Guest** icon.

6. Clear the **Account is disabled** check box.

7. Click **OK**, and then click the **Close** button.

8. Click **OK**.

Changing a User's Group or Account Type

If you have an administrator account or are a member of the Administrators group, you can change a user's account type or user group on a domain network. A user account or group grants permissions to a user to perform certain types of tasks based on the account type or user group (domain network). The steps to create a guest account differ, depending on whether your computer is part of a network domain or shared/workgroup computer.

Change a User's Account Type

1. Click the **Start** button, and then click **Control Panel**.

2. Click the **User Accounts** icon in Small icons or Large icons view.

3. If you want to change another account, click **Manage another account**, and then click the user's account name.

4. Click **Change your account type** or **Change the account type**.

5. Click an account type option.

6. Click **Change Account Type**.

7. Click the **Close** button.

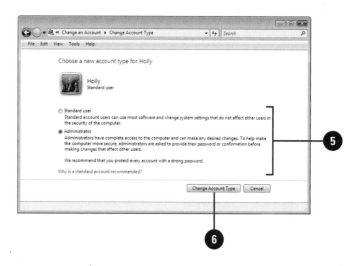

Change a User's Group on a Domain Network

1. Click the **Start** button, and then click **Control Panel**.

2. Click the **User Accounts** icon in Small icons or Large icons view, and then click **Manage User Accounts**.

3. Click the **Users** tab.

4. Select the user account name you want to change.

5. Click **Properties**, and then click the **Group Membership** tab.

6. Click the group you want.

7. Click **OK**, and then click **OK** again.

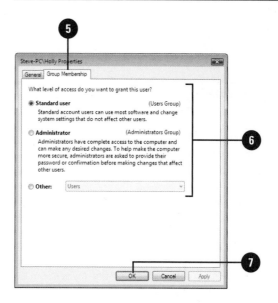

Changing the Start Up Screen

For added security, you can require users to use Ctrl+Alt+Delete (or Ctrl+Alt+Del) before they can select a user account and enter a password. This prevents other programs, such as spyware or a virus, from getting your user name and password as you enter it without your consent. When you lock your computer or switch users, the security option also requires users to press Ctrl+Alt+Delete.

Increase Logon Security on a Domain Network

1 Click the **Start** button, and then click **Control Panel**.

2 Click the **User Accounts** icon in Small icons or Large icons view, and then click **Manage User Accounts**.

3 Click the **Advanced** tab.

4 Select the **Require users to press Ctrl+Alt+Delete** check box.

5 Click **OK**.

Did You Know?

You can also change the logon security on a workgroup network. Open the User Accounts dialog box, click the Advanced tab, select the Require Users To Press Ctrl+Alt+Delete check box, and then click OK. To open the User Accounts dialog box, you can type *NetplWiz.exe* in the Run dialog box (click the Start button, point to All Programs, click Accessories, and then click Run), or click the link in the "Enable or disable secure logon" help topic in Windows Help and Support.

Changing an Account Picture

When you log on to Windows, the Welcome screen appears, displaying a list of user accounts with a picture next to each one. When you complete the logon process, the picture associated with your account appears at the top of the Start menu along with your user name. This identifies you as the current user of the computer. You can change the picture to suit your own personality. Changing your account picture is not available for computers on a domain network.

Change an Account Picture

1. Click the **Start** button, and then click **Control Panel**.

2. Click the **User Accounts** icon in Small icons or Large icons view.

3. If you want to change another account, click **Manage another account**, and then click the user's account name.

4. Click **Change your picture** or **Change the picture**.

5. Click the picture you want.

6. Click **Change Picture**, or click **Browse for more pictures** and double-click the picture you want.

7. Click the **Close** button.

See Also

See Chapter 8, "Working with Pictures" on page 233 for information on creating, scanning, and using pictures.

Changing and Setting a Password

If you don't have a password associated with your user account, anyone can access your files. A password controls who has access to your files. When you create a password, enter one that is easy for you to remember, yet difficult for others to guess. Good passwords are typically at least seven characters and include letters (uppercase and lowercase), numbers, and symbols. Once you create a password, you can always change it.

Change or Create a Password

1 Click the **Start** button, and then click **Control Panel.**

2 Click the **User Accounts** icon in Small icons or Large icons view.

3 If you want to change another account, click **Manage another account**, and then click the user's account name.

4 Click **Change your password** or **Change the password**, or **Create a password**.

5 Type a password, and then type it again.

6 Type a hint that reminds you of the password.

7 Click **Change password** or **Create password**.

8 Click the **Close** button.

Did You Know?

You can change a password. In User Accounts, click the account you want to change, click Change My Password, type your current password, if necessary, type a new password, type it again, type a hint, and then click Change Password.

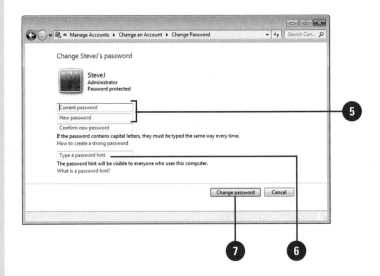

Change an Administrator Password on a Domain Network

1 Click the **Start** button, and then click **Control Panel**.

2 Click the **User Accounts** icon in Small icons or Large icons view, and then click **Manage User Accounts**.

3 Click the **Users** tab.

4 Click the administrator account.

5 Click **Reset Password**.

6 Type the new password, and then type it again.

7 Click **OK**.

8 Click **OK**.

Resetting a Password

If you have ever forgotten your password, you understand how important it is to write it down. However, writing down a password is not very secure. You can create a Password Reset disk, either a floppy disk or USB flash drive, to help you log on and reset your password. If you have any security credentials and certificates on your computer, the Password Reset disk restores them. If you have forgotten your password and don't have a Password Reset disk, you can ask your administrator to reset it for you. Resetting your password also erases any security credentials and certificates on your computer.

Create a Password Reset Disk

1. Click the **Start** button, and then click **Control Panel**.

2. Click the **User Accounts** icon in Small icons or Large icons view.

3. Insert a blank disk in the Floppy drive or USB Flash drive.

4. In the Tasks pane, click **Create a password reset disk**.

5. Follow the instructions in the Forgotten Password Wizard to create a password reset disk.

Did You Know?

You can reset your password at the Welcome screen. At the Welcome screen, click the Help button to see your password hint, and then type the password if you remember it. If you don't, click the arrow. Click Reset Password, and then follow the instructions in the Password Reset Wizard to create a new password. Type your new password, and then press Enter.

Type user account password

Locking the Computer

If you are working on sensitive material and need to leave your computer unattended for a while, you can lock it so that no one can use it without your permission. While your computer is locked, all your programs continue to run. When you return to your computer, you can access your computer in the same way you started Windows. If the Ctrl+Alt+Del security option is enabled, you are required to press Ctrl+Alt+Del before you can enter a password.

Lock and Unlock the Computer

1. Click the **Start** button, point to the arrow next to the Power button, and then click **Lock**.

   TIMESAVER Press ⊞+L to lock the computer. The Windows key ⊞ is located in the lower-left corner of the keyboard.

2. If the Ctrl+Alt+Del screen appears, press Ctrl+Alt+Del.

3. At the Welcome screen, click your name (if prompted), type your password, and then press Enter.

See Also

See "Starting Windows 7" on page 4 and "Switching Users" on page 22 for information on logging on to Windows 7.

Managing Security in One Place

The Action Center (**New!**) provides a single place to manage your four security essentials, Windows Firewall, Automatic Updating, Malware protection (virus and spyware) and Other security settings (Internet security and User Account Controls). If you're having computer problems, you can access troubleshooting (**New!**) and System Restore options. The Action Center recommends security settings that you can use to help protect your computer. It also provides links to important information about the latest virus or other security threat, or to get customer support from Microsoft for a security related issue. As you work, Windows 7 uses security alerts and icons in the notification area on the taskbar to help you recognize potential security risks, such as a new virus, out of date antivirus software or an important security option is turned off, and choose appropriate settings. If Windows requires your attention, the Action Center icon appears in the notification area (**New!**). Click the Action Center icon to view alerts and suggested fixes.

View Essential Security Settings Using the Action Center

1. Click the **Start** button, and then click **Control Panel**.

2. Click the **Action Center** icon in Small icons or Large icons view.

   TIMESAVER *Click the Action Center icon in the notification area (if available), and then click Open Action Center.*

   IMPORTANT *If you're part of a network, options might be grayed out; your security settings are managed by your network administrator.*

3. To find out information on a security area, click the down arrow next to it.

4. To set Action Center settings, click the **Change Action Center settings** link, select or clear check boxes to turn alert messages on or off, and then click **OK**.

5. When you're done, click the **Close** button.

Turn alert messages on or off

Act Upon Security Alerts

1. If Windows requires your attention, the Action Center icon appears in the notification area. Click the **Actions Center** icon in the notification area, and then click an issue.

   ◆ If the Action Center detects that your computer needs enhanced security, it displays an alert (if enabled) in the notification area, read the security alert, and then click it..

2. To find out information on a security option, click the down arrow next to it.

3. To find out how to address the problem, click a link or a button, and then follow the instructions.

4. When you're done, click the **Close** button.

Click to view and fix issues

Click to open Action Center

Did You Know?

You can change the way Automatic Updates alerts changes. Click the Start button, click Control Panel, click the Windows Update icon in Small icons or Large icons view, click Change Settings, select the alert option you want, click OK, and then click the Close button.

See Also

See "Troubleshooting Computer Problems" on page 466 for more information on using the troubleshooting wizards.

Security Icons	
Icon	**Description**
	Security Settings: Indicates important security information and settings that are available, such as the Windows Action Center.
	Potential Risk: Indicates your computer encountered a potential security risk; act upon the security alert.
	No Risk: Indicates your computer is more secure and using recommended security settings; no action needed.
	Security Warning: Indicates your computer encountered a warning alert, which is potentially harmful; consider adjusting security settings.
	Security Problem: Indicates your computer is not using recommended security settings; consider adjusting them.

Defending Against Malicious Software

Windows Defender helps you protect your computer from spyware and other potentially harmful software that attempts to install itself or run on your computer. Spyware is software that tries to collect information about you or change computer settings without your consent. Windows Defender alerts you in real-time when unwanted software tries to run on your computer. You can also use Windows Defender to scan your computer and set up a schedule to automatically scan on a regular basis. When you receive an alert of a potential problem, you can use the Microsoft SpyNet community to help you determine if the software is already to run. Windows Defender uses definitions to determine potential problems. Since software dangers continually change, it's important to have up-to-date definitions, which you can get online.

Use Windows Defender

1. If a real-time alert appears with an attempt to:

   ◆ **Install software.** Click **Ignore**, **Quarantine**, **Remove**, or **Always Allow**.

   ◆ **Change Windows settings.** Click **Permit** or **Deny**.

2. Click the **Start** button, and then click **Control Panel**.

3. Click the **Windows Defender** icon in Small icons or Large icons view.

4. To perform a scan, click the **Scan** button arrow, and then click **Quick Scan** or **Full Scan**.

5. To view or clear history, click the **History** button, and then click an item to view history or click **Clear History** to remove all activities.

6. To go backward and forward to the previously viewed screens, click the **Back** or **Forward** button.

7. When you're done, click the **Close** button.

Status information

Change Windows Defender Options

1. Click the **Start** button, and then click **Control Panel**.

2. Click the **Windows Defender** icon in Small icons or Large icons view.

3. Click the **Tools** button.

4. Click the links to the tools and settings you want to change:

   ◆ **Options.** Set up a scan schedule and choose default actions when alerts appear.

   ◆ **Microsoft SpyNet.** Allows you to join the SpyNet community.

   ◆ **Quarantined items.** Allows you to remove and restore items.

   ◆ **Allowed items.** Allows you to remove items from the list.

   ◆ **Windows Defender website.** Access the Windows Defender web site at Microsoft to get updates and definitions.

   ◆ **Microsoft Malware Protection Center.** Allows you to get information on definition updates and up to date information on Malware (**New!**).

5. To go backward and forward to the previously viewed screens, click the **Back** or **Forward** button.

6. When you're done, click the **Close** button.

4

Set Windows Defender options

Setting Parental Controls

Parental Controls help you manage how your children use the computer. Parental Controls allows you to set limits on your children's web access, the amount of time spent logged on the computer, and which games and programs they can use (**New!**). You can set different settings for each user account on your computer, so you can adjust the level you want for each child. You can also review activity reports on a periodic basis to see what your children are doing on the computer. You can also block access to objectionable TV shows and movies with Parental Controls in Windows Media Center (**New!**).

Set Parental Controls

1. Click the **Start** button, and then click **Control Panel**.

2. Click the **Parental Controls** icon in Small icons or Large icons view.

3. To select a games rating system, or an activity report reminder option, click an option in the Tasks pane.

4. Click the standard user account for which you want to set controls.

5. Click the **On, enforce current settings** option.

6. Click the links to the Windows Settings you want to change:

   ◆ **Time limits.** Click and drag the hours you want to block or allow.

   ◆ **Games.** Select options to block or allow games based on ratings or specific games.

   ◆ **Allow and block specific programs.** Select an option to use all programs or only the programs I use.

7. Click **OK**, and then click **OK** again.

Allow or block specific programs

Sending Secure Information Using Windows CardSpace

With Windows CardSpace you can securely send information in the form of online cards to web sites or online services. Windows CardSpace is a system for creating relationships with web sites and online services that provides a consistent way for you to review the identity of a site, manage your information, review information before sending it to a site and for sites to request information from you. Windows CardSpace can replace the user names and passwords that you use to register and log on to web sites and online services. You can create a personal card or have a business or organization issue you a managed card.

Use Windows CardSpace

1. Click the **Start** button, and then click **Control Panel**.

2. Click the **Windows CardSpace** icon in Small icons or Large icons view.

3. If necessary, click **OK** to dismiss the introduction screen.

4. To add a card, click the **Add a card** button, click **Add**, click a card type, enter information, and then click **Save**.

5. In the main screen, use task commands to duplicate, delete, back up, and restore cards.

6. To modify a card, double-click the card, and then click any of the following task commands:

   ◆ **Edit card.** Make changes, and then click Save.

   ◆ **View card history.** View the information, and then click OK.

   ◆ **Lock card.** Type a PIN code, type it again, and then click Lock.

7. To go back to the main screen, click the **Back** button.

8. When you're done, click the **Close** button.

Encrypting Files for Safety

If your computer uses NTFS, you can use the advanced Encrypting File System (EFS) to protect sensitive data files on your computer. If someone tries to gain access to encrypted files or a folder on your computer, a unique file encryption key prevents that person from viewing it. When you encrypt a file, you also need to decide whether you want to encrypt the folder, too. When you encrypt a folder, you need to decide whether you want to encrypt all files and subfolders within it. After you encrypt your files, you can use the Backup Wizard in the Backup and Restore Center to back them up for safe keeping.

Encrypt or Decrypt a File or Folder

1 Right-click the file or folder you want to encrypt, and then click **Properties**.

2 Click the **General** tab.

3 Click **Advanced**.

4 Select the **Encrypt contents to secure data** check box to encrypt the file or folder or clear the check box to decrypt it.

5 Click **OK**.

6 Click **OK**.

7 If necessary, click an option to apply changes to this folder only or to this folder, subfolders, and files.

8 Click **OK**.

Did You Know?

You can compress files and folders with NTFS. Right-click the file or folder, click Properties, click the General tab, click Advanced, select the Compress Contents To Save Disk Space check box, and then click OK twice.

For Your Information

Managing and Backing Up Encryption Certificate

When you encrypt a file or folder, Windows uses information from your Encrypting File system certificate. A certificate is a digital document that verifies the identify of a person, which is issued by a trusted Certification Authority. If you lost the certificate or it becomes corrupted, you will not be able to recover an encrypted file or folder. To avoid this problem, you should back up your Encrypting File System (EFS) certificate. To manage and back up your EFS certificate, click the Start button, click Control Panel, double-click the User Accounts icon, click Manage Your File Encryption Certificates, and then follow the Encrypting File System wizard.

Encrypting Files Using BitLocker

If you have a two NTFS drive partitions (also known as volumes)—one for the system boot volume and one for the operating system volume—and a computer with a compatible Trusted Platform Module (TPM) microchip and BIOS, you can use BitLocker to encrypt the operating system volume. If you have other internal volumes with data, you can also use BitLocker to encrypt it. BitLocker helps protect your system and blocks hackers from accessing sensitive information behind the scenes. With BitLocker To Go (**New!**), you can apply the same protection to portable storage devices, such as USB flash drives and external hard drives. When you add files to your computer, BitLocker automatically encrypts them. When you copy files to another location, the files are decrypted. After you turn on BitLocker, it's critical that you create a recovery password, because BitLocker locks up the entire drive if it detects a problem during startup. The encrypted data volume automatically unlocks when the system boots into the operating system volume.

Use BitLocker to Encrypt Files

1. Click the **Start** button, and then click **Control Panel**.

2. Click the **BitLocker Drive Encryption** icon in Small icons or Large icons view.

3. Click **Turn On BitLocker** on the volume you want.

4. Follow the wizard to save a recovery password, save or print the recovery key, click **Start Encrypting**, wait for BitLocker to encrypt the volume upon restart, and then click **Close**.

   When your computer starts up after the encryption, you won't see any change. If a problem occurs or someone tries to illegally access your operating system, your computer switches into recovery mode until you supply the recovery password.

5. To turn off BitLocker, click **Turn Off BitLocker**, and then click **Decrypt Drive**. To change or remove a password, save or print a recovery key, or automatically unlock a drive, click **Manage BitLocker**.

Avoiding Viruses and Other Harmful Attacks

Understanding Harmful Attacks

Using the Internet can expose your computer to a wide variety of harmful attacks, such as viruses, worms, and Trojan Horses. These attacks can come through e-mail, file transferring, and even possibly through Java and ActiveX, which are both programming languages used to enhance web pages.

A **virus** is an executable program whose functions range from just being annoying to causing havoc to your computer. A virus may display an innocuous warning on a particular day, such as Friday the 13th, or it may cause a more serious problem, such as wiping out your entire hard disk. Viruses are found in executable (.exe and .com) files, along with Microsoft Word and Microsoft Excel macro files. A **worm** is like a virus, but it can spread without human action across networks. For example, a worm might send e-mail copies of itself to everyone in your e-mail Address Book. A worm can consume memory causing your computer to stop responding or even take it over. A **Trojan Horse**, like its mythological counterpart, is a program that appears to be useful and comes from a legitimate source, but actually causes problems.

Spreading Harmful Infections

Many viruses and other harmful attacks spread through file downloads and attachments in e-mail messages. Virus writers capitalize on people's curiosity and willingness to accept files from people they know or work with, in order to transmit malicious files disguised as or attached to benign files. When you start downloading files to your computer, you must be aware of the potential for catching a computer virus, worm, or Trojan Horse. Typically, you can't catch one from just reading a mail message or downloading a file, but you can catch one from opening or running an infected program, such as a file attached to an e-mail message, or one you download for free. And even though most viruses and other harmful attacks take the form of executable programs, data files that have macros or Visual Basic code attached to them, such as Word or Excel files, can also be infected with viruses.

Avoiding Harmful Attacks

There are a few things you can do to keep your system safe from the infiltration of viruses and other harmful attacks.

1) Make sure Windows Firewall is turned on. Windows Firewall helps block viruses and worms from reaching your computer, but it doesn't detect or disable them if they are already on your computer or come through e-mail. Windows Firewall doesn't block unsolicited e-mail or stop you from opening e-mail with harmful attachments. For more information on Windows Firewall, see "Connecting to the Internet" on page 134 and "Setting Up Windows Firewall" on page 136.

2) Make sure Automatic Updates is turned on. Windows Automatic Updates regularly checks the Windows Update web site for important updates that your computer needs, such as security updates, critical updates, and service packs. Each file that you download using Automatic Update has a digital signature from Microsoft to ensure its authenticity and security. For more information, see "Updating Windows" on page 440.

3) Make sure you are using the most up-to-date antivirus software. New viruses and more virulent strains of existing viruses are discovered every day. Unless you update your virus checking software, new viruses can easily bypass outdated virus checking software. Companies such as McAfee and Symantec offer shareware virus checking programs available for download directly from their web sites. These programs monitor your system, checking each time a file is added to your computer to make sure it's not in some way trying to change or damage valuable system files.

4) Be very careful of the sites from which you download files. Major file repository sites, such as FileZ, Download.com, or TuCows, regularly check the files they receive for viruses before posting them to their web sites. Don't download files from web sites unless you are certain that the sites check their files for viruses. Internet Explorer monitors downloads and warns you about potentially harmful files and gives you the option to block them. For more information, see "Downloading Files from the Web" on page 164.

5) Be very careful of file attachments in e-mail you open. As you receive e-mail, don't open or run an attached file unless you know who sent it and what it contains. If you're not sure, you should delete it. The Attachment Manager provides security information to help you understand more about the file you're opening. To protect your computer from harmful attacks, see "Sending and Retrieving a File" on page 182, "Reading and Replying to E-mail" on page 180, and "Protecting Against E-mail Attacks" on page 194.

6) Make sure you activate macro virus checking protection in both Word and Excel. To do so, click the Tools menu, point to Macro on the expanded menu, click Security, and then make sure that the High Security Level option is selected. (In Office 2000, XP, or later, click the Tools menu, click Options, click the General tab, and then make sure the Macro Virus Protection option is selected.) And always elect not to run macros when opening a Word or Excel file that you received from

someone who might not be using proper virus protection.

Avoiding Other Intruders

Spyware is software that collects personal information without your knowledge or permission. Typically, spyware is downloaded and installed on your computer along with free software, such as freeware, games, or music file-sharing programs. Spyware is often associated with **Adware** software that displays advertisements, such as a pop-up ad. Examples of spyware and unauthorized adware include programs that change your home page or search page without your permission. To avoid spyware and adware, read the fine print in license agreements when you install software, scan your computer for spyware and adware with detection and removal software (such as Ad-aware from Lavasoft), and turn on Pop-up Blocker. For details, see "Blocking Pop-Up Ads" on page 342.

Spam is unsolicited e-mail, which is often annoying and time-consuming to get rid of. Spammers harvest e-mail addresses from web pages and unsolicited e-mail. To avoid spam, use multiple e-mail addresses (one for web forms and another for private e-mail), opt-out and remove yourself from e-mail lists, and turn on the Block Images And Other External Content In HTML E-mail option. For details, see "Protecting Against E-mail Attacks" on page 194.

Phishing is an e-mail scam that tries to steal your identity by sending deceptive e-mail asking you for bank and credit card information online. Don't be fooled by spoofed web site that look like the official site. Never respond to requests for personal information via e-mail; call the institution to investigate and report it.

Understanding Security on the Internet

No other web browser offers as many customizable features as Internet Explorer does, particularly advanced security features that are built into the program. To understand all the Internet Explorer security features, you first have to learn about security on the Internet in general.

When you send information from your computer to another computer, the two computers are not linked directly together. Your data may travel through multiple networks as it works its way across the Internet. Since your data is broadcast to the Internet, any computer on any of these networks could be listening in and capturing your data. (They typically aren't, but they could be.)

In addition, on the Internet it's possible to masquerade as someone else. E-mail addresses can be forged, domain names of sites can easily be misleading, and so on. You need some way to protect not only the data you send, but also yourself from sending data to the wrong place.

Furthermore, there is always the potential that someone (referred to as a "hacker") or something, such as a virus or worm, could infiltrate your computer systems. Once infiltrated, a hacker or virus can delete, rename, or even copy valuable information from your computer without your knowledge.

Security Zones

Through the use of **security zones**, you can easily tell Internet Explorer which sites you trust to not damage your computer and which sites you simply don't trust. In your company's intranet you would most likely trust all the information supplied on web pages through your company's network, but on the Internet you may want to be warned first of potential dangers a site could cause your system. You can set up different levels of security based on different zones.

Certificates

When shopping on the Internet, you want to do business with only those companies that offer a certain level of security and promise to protect your buying information. In turn, those companies want to do business with legitimate customers only. A **certificate** or **digital ID** provides both the browser and the company with a kind of guarantee confirming that you are who you say you are and that the site is secure and genuine, not a fraud or scam. When you send an e-mail message, it also verifies your identity to your recipients.

A digital ID is made up of a public key, a private key, and a digital signature. When you digitally sign an e-mail, Windows Live Mail adds your public key and digital signature (the two together is the certificate) to the message. When your recipients receive the e-mail, your digital signature verifies your identity and your public key is stored in their Address Book so they can send you encrypted messages, which only you can open with your private key.

An independent company, called a **credentials agency**, issues three types of certificates: personal, authority, and publisher. A **personal certificate** identifies you so that you can access web sites that require positive identification, such as banks that allow online transactions. You can obtain a personal certificate from a credentials agency called VeriSign using the Security tab of the Options dialog box in Windows Live Mail. An **authority certificate** ensures that the web site you are visiting is not a fraud. Internet Explorer automatically checks site certificates to make sure that they're valid. A **publisher certificate** enables you to trust software that you download, such as ActiveX controls. Internet Explorer maintains a list of software companies whose certificates are valid and trustworthy. You can view your certificate settings on the Content tab of the Internet Options dialog box.

Content Advisor

Just about everyone can find objectionable material on the Internet. Parents might not want to subject their children to some of this material, such as strong language, violence, and other adult themes. However, most parents cannot spend every online minute with their children, censoring objectionable sites. In such cases, you can employ Internet Explorer's **Content Advisor** to screen out inappropriate sites, preventing youngsters from seeing things they shouldn't.

The Content Advisor works with different rating bureaus, such as the Recreational Software Advisory Council (RSAC), to rate sites within certain ranges. The RSAC's rating system is based on research that compiled a rating system to reflect different levels of violence, strong language, and so on. You decide exactly what kind of sites that your children can access, what ratings systems are used, which ranges are available to users within those sites, and whether users of your computer can see unrated sites.

You can also assign a supervisor password to allow a user to view such sites. As long as the user supplies the password you specified when you initially set up the content rating systems, the user can view sites where the material rates above the level chosen. You can turn off the Content Advisor at any time, opening up all sites on the Internet for viewing by any user without having to enter a password.

In order for the rating system to work, sites must subscribe to the system so that their ratings are passed to your computer when you access the sites. Most sites that want to offer quality information for children and those adult sites interested in making sure only individuals 18 years old or older are accessing their sites subscribe to rating systems like the RSAC. A site that voluntarily rates itself usually displays the RSAC logo on its home page. This logo is your indication that the site has properly rated itself and offers only materials that are appropriate to its rating.

Cookies

When you browse the Internet, you can access and gather information from web sites, but web sites can also gather information about you without your knowledge unless you set up Internet security on your computer. You can set Internet privacy options to protect your personal identity from unauthorized access. When you visit a web site, the site creates a **cookie** file, known as a **first-party cookie**, which stores information on your computer, such as your web site preferences or personal identifiable information, including your name and e-mail address. Not all cookies are harmful; many first-party-cookies save you time re-entering information on a return visit to a web site. However, there are also **third-party cookies**, such as advertising banners, which are created by web sites you are not currently viewing. Once a cookie is saved on your computer, only the web site that created it can read it. The privacy options allow you to block or permit cookies for web sites in the Internet zone; however, when you block cookies, you might not be able to access all the features of a web site. When a web site violates your cookie policy, a red icon appears on the status bar.

Creating Security Zones

Internet Explorer lets you create security zones based on where information comes from. For example, you might want to restrict access to web pages that can be viewed from the Internet, but not to those sites within your company's intranet. You can specify the level of security for each of the four available security zones: Local Intranet, Trusted Sites, Restricted Sites, and Internet. When you access a web page or download content from the site, Internet Explorer checks its security settings and determines the web site's zone. Internet Explorer displays a padlock icon in the status bar to indicate the web site is secure. All Internet web sites are assigned to the Internet zone until you assign individual web sites to other zones.

Select a Security Zone and Its Security Level

1. Click the **Start** button, click **Control Panel**, and then click the **Internet Options** icon in Small icons or Large icons view.

2. Click the **Security** tab.

3. Click the zone to which you want to assign security options.

4. If you want, click **Default level** to reset the settings to Microsoft's suggested level.

5. Move the slider to the level of security you want to apply.

   TROUBLE? *If the slider is not available, click Default Level to change the security level to Medium and display the slider.*

6. If you want to specify individual security options, click **Custom level**.

7. Scroll to a settings area, and then click the **Enable**, **Prompt**, or **Disable** option button.

8. Click **OK**.

9. Click **OK**.

Add Sites to Your Restricted Sites Zone

1 Click the **Start** button, click **Control Panel**, and then click the **Internet Options** icon in Small icons or Large icons view.

2 Click the **Security** tab.

3 Click **Restricted Sites**.

4 Click **Sites**.

5 Type the full URL for the site.

6 Click **Add**.

7 Click **Close**, and then click **OK**.

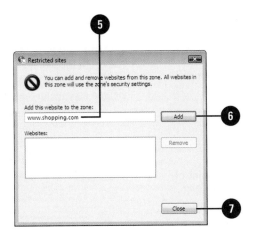

Security Zones

Zone	Description
Internet	Contains all web sites that are not assigned to any other zone; default is Medium
Local intranet	Contains all web sites that are on your organization's intranet and don't require a proxy server; default is Medium
Trusted sites	Contains web sites that you trust not to threaten the security of your computer; default is Low (allows all cookies)
Restricted sites	Contains web sites that you believe threaten the security of your computer; default is High (blocks all cookies)

For Your Information

Setting a Stronger Zone Defense

Internet Explorer also uses another zone called Local Machine, which provides security for your hard disk, but doesn't appear on the Security tab. In earlier versions of Internet Explorer, hackers were using low security levels to attack your computer. This is now stopped.

Setting Ratings Using the Content Advisor

If you have children who surf the Internet and you don't want to subject them to strong language, violence, or sexually explicit material, you can use the Content Advisor to restrict their access to inappropriate web sites. If a rated site matches your ratings specifications, the site can be viewed. If the site is rated above the level you've set, or if the site is not rated and you've restricted access to unrated sites, the site can be viewed only when the supervisor password is supplied.

Enable the Content Advisor Ratings

1. Click the **Start** button, click **Control Panel**, and then click the **Internet Options** icon in Small icons or Large icons view.

2. Click the **Content** tab.

3. Click **Enable**. This button toggles between Enable and Disable.

   The first time you use Content Advisor, set your initial settings.

4. Click **OK**, type a supervisor password twice, and then click **OK**.

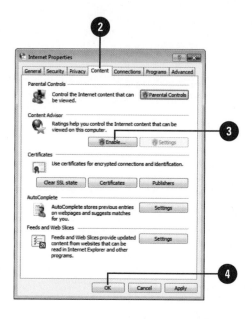

Set the Content Advisor Ratings

1. Click the **Start** button, click **Control Panel**, and then click the **Internet Options** icon in Small icons or Large icons view.

2. Click the **Content** tab.

3. Click **Settings**. If necessary, type the supervisor password, and then click **OK**.

4. Click the category for which you want to set the rating.

5. Move the **Rating** slider to the rating level you want.

6. Click **OK**, and then click **OK** again.

Cleaning Up Internet Files and Information

As you browse the web, Internet Explorer stores information relating to what you have provided to web sites when you log on (passwords) or fill out a form, the location of web sites you have visited (history), and preference information used by web sites (cookies). When you visit a web site, Internet Explorer saves web pages, images, media (temporary Internet files), and InPrivate filtering (**New!**) information for faster viewing and protection in the future. You can clean up the Internet files and information, which will also improve your computer performance. You can now save web page data (cookies and temporary files) from your trusted favorites (**New!**), so you don't have to restore them.

Delete Internet Files and Information

1 Click the **Start** button, click **Control Panel**, and then click the **Internet Options** icon in Small icons or Large icons view.

2 Click the **General** tab.

3 Click **Delete**.

4 Click the check boxes you want to clean up your computer:

- ◆ **Preserve Favorites website data.** Keeps cookies and temporary files from your trusted favorites (**New!**).

- ◆ **Temporary files.** Deletes files created while browsing.

- ◆ **Cookies.** Deletes information gathered by using web sites.

- ◆ **History.** Deletes list of web sites you have visited.

- ◆ **Form data.** Deletes saved information you have enter into forms.

- ◆ **Passwords.** Deletes password used for automatic logon to web sites.

- ◆ **InPrivate Filtering data.** Deletes saved data used by InPrivate filtering (**New!**).

5 Click **Delete**.

6 Click **OK**.

Select to delete browsing history on exit in IE

Protecting Internet Privacy

You can set Internet privacy options to protect your personal identity from unauthorized access. The privacy options allow you to block or permit cookies for web sites in the Internet zone; however, when you block cookies, you might not be able to access all the features of a web site. When a web site violates your cookie policy, a red icon appears on the status bar. To find out if the web site you are viewing in Internet Explorer contains third-party cookies or whether any cookies have been restricted, you can get a privacy report. The privacy report lists all the web sites with content on the current Web page and shows how all the web sites handle cookies.

Control the Use of Cookies

1. Click the **Start** button, click **Control Panel**, and then click the **Internet Options** icon in Small icons or Large icons view.

2. Click the **Privacy** tab.

3. Drag the slider to select the level of privacy you want.

4. Click **OK**.

Did You Know?

You can get a privacy report in Internet Explorer. Open the web page you want to view a privacy report, click the Page button on the toolbar, then click Web Page Privacy Policy.

Delete All Cookies

1. Click the **Start** button, click **Control Panel**, and then click the **Internet Options** icon in Small icons or Large icons view.

2. Click the **General** tab.

3. Click **Delete**.

4. Select the **Cookies** check box.

5. Click **Delete**.

6. Click **OK**.

Protecting an Internet Identity

To further protect your privacy, you can use certificates to verify your identity and protect important information, such as your credit card number, on the Internet. A **certificate** is a statement verifying the identity of a person or the security of a web site. You can obtain your personal security certification from an independent Certification Authority (CA). A personal certificate verifies your identity to a secure web site that requires a certificate, while a web site certificate verifies its security to you before you send it information. When you visit a secure web site (one whose address may start with "https" instead of "http"), the site automatically sends you its certificate, and Internet Explorer displays a lock icon on the status bar. A certificate is also known as a Digital ID in other programs, such as Windows Live Mail, or the Windows Live Contacts.

Import a Certificate

1. Click the **Start** button, click **Control Panel**, and then click the **Internet Options** icon in Small icons or Large icons view.

2. Click the **Content** tab.

3. Click **Certificates**.

4. Click the tab with the type of certificate you want.

5. Click **Import**.

6. Follow the instructions in the Certificate Import Wizard to import a certificate.

7. Click **Close**.

8. Click **OK**.

Click to find out about site certificate problems

Did You Know?

You can let e-mail recipients know a message is from you with a certificate. Click the Start button, point to All Programs, point to Windows Live, click Windows Live Mail, click the Tools menu, click Options, click the Security tab, select the Digitally Sign All Outgoing Messages check box, then click OK.

Protecting Against Phishing

Phishing is a technique people use to trick computer users into revealing personal for financial information. Typically, a phishing scam starts with an e-mail message that appears to come from a trusted source, such as a bank or credit card company, but actually directs recipients to provide information to a fraudulent web site. Windows and Internet Explorer provide the SmartScreen Filtering (**New!**) to increase security to help protect you from phishing schemes. You can set SmartScreen filtering options on the Safety menu in Internet Explorer. You can check web sites for phishing and report them to Microsoft if you think they are fraudulent.

Protect or Unprotect Against Phishing

1. In Internet Explorer, click the **Safety** menu, and then point to **SmartScreen Filter**.

2. Click **Turn On SmartScreen Filter** or **Turn Off SmartScreen Filter**.

3. Click the **Turn on SmartScreen Filter (recommended)**, or **Turn off SmartScreen Filter** option.

4. Click **OK**.

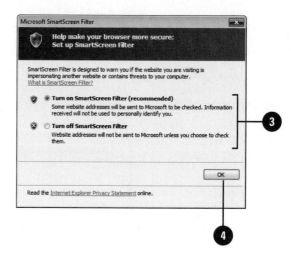

Check and Report a Web Site for Phishing

1 In Internet Explorer, click the **Safety** menu, and then point to **SmartScreen Filter**.

2 Click the command you want to perform:

◆ **Check This Website.** Click **Check This Website**, click **OK**, and then respond to the alerts as needed.

◆ **Report Unsafe Website.** Click **Report Unsafe Website**, specify the website language, select the **I think this is a phishing website** check box, and then click **Submit**.

Did You Know?

You can display security information in the Security Status bar. While you browse the web, Internet Explorer 7 automatically checks for valid web site certificates and any irregularities that might indicated a possible phishing site or any unwanted or malicious programs. If Internet Explorer detects a potential problem, it displays a color warning in the Address bar with text in the Security Status bar on the right indicating the problem type. The Address bar displays red for certificate errors and known phishing sites, green for sites with high security (connected to the certificate), and yellow for suspected phishing sites. You can click the security icon in the Security Status bar to find out more information and possible solutions.

Results of check this web site

Web site to submit a possible phishing site

Blocking Pop-Up Ads

The Pop-up Blocker prevents most unwanted pop-up windows from appearing. When Internet Explorer blocks an ad, a new window appears with an alert message in the Information Bar at the top. Blocked items are replaced in the window with a red "x". The Information Bar in Internet Explorer lets you temporarily or permanently open pop-ups, change Pop-up Blocker settings, and get Information Bar help. With the Pop-up Blocker Settings dialog box, you can allow or disallow pop-ups from specific sites, play a sound or show the Information Bar when a pop-up is blocked, and set a filter level to block pop-ups.

Set Options to Block Pop-Up Ads

1. Click the **Start** button, click **Control Panel**, and then click the **Internet Options** icon in Small icons or Large icons view.

2. Click the **Privacy** tab.

3. Select the **Turn on Pop-up Blocker** check box.

   TIMESAVER *In Internet Explorer, click the Tools button, point to Pop-up Blocker, and then click Turn Off Pop-up Blocker.*

4. Click **Settings**.

   TIMESAVER *In Internet Explorer, click the Tools button, point to Pop-up Blocker, and then click Pop-up Blocker Settings.*

5. To add a pop-up exception, enter a web site address, then click **Add**.

6. Select or clear check boxes to play sound or show on Information Bar when an ad is blocked.

7. Click the **Filter level** list arrow, then click a pop-up filter: **High**, **Medium**, **Low**.

8. Click **Close**.

9. Click **OK**.

Using the Information Bar

Security Information Bar for Browsing

The Information Bar in Internet Explorer makes it easier for you to make informed decisions about potentially harmful content entering your computer. Internet Explorer displays the Information Bar below the address bar where you can view important security information about blocked pop-ups, downloads, security risks, and other harmful threats. When Internet Explorer blocks a pop-up ad or program from running on your computer, the Information Bar appears at the top of the window with information and options. If the default settings in Internet Explorer are turned on, the Information Bar appears when a web site tries to install an add-on, such as an ActiveX control, open a pop-up window, or download a file to your computer. A pop-up window typically display annoying ads. ActiveX controls provide added functionality to Internet Explorer, which makes using the Internet more enjoyable. However, it also opens the door for Spyware and Adware to invade your computer and privacy. When an outsider tries to enter your computer, the Information Bar appears, where you can click the message to take an action, such as block or unblock the content, or get more informa-

tion. See "Blocking Pop-Up Ads" on page 342 for information on turning on the Information Bar.

Security Information Bar for E-mail

Windows Live Mail adds a security option to stop pictures and other content from automatically downloading to your computer from contacts who are not in your address book. Spammers commonly use automatic picture download to confirm your e-mail address and send you more spam. Blocking the picture download provides a faster display, and reduces spam e-mail. When Windows Live Mail blocks images and other potential harm content in an e-mail message from downloading to your computer, the Information Bar appears at the top of the e-mail message with status information. Blocked items in e-mail are replaced with a red "x". You can follow the instructions on the Information Bar to view the blocked content. However, when you edit, print, forward, or reply to an e-mail message with blocked items, the blocked content is downloaded. See "Protecting Against E-mail Attacks" on page 194 for information on setting e-mail security options.

Information Bar alert

Information Bar for a pop-up window

Information Bar menu

Blocking Content with InPrivate Filtering

Many web sites display and use content—such as maps and advertise-ments—supplied from other third-party web sites. These content providers can gather and track information about you and your browsing habits without your knowledge. With InPrivate filtering (**New!**), you can block this from happening. InPrivate filtering analyzes the web sites you visit looking for third-party content trying to track your movements, and the gives you the option to allow or block the content. You can also have InPrivate filtering automatically block any invasive content from a third-party that it detects. InPrivate filtering is off by default and needs to be turned on each time you use Internet Explorer. When you close Internet Explorer, InPrivate filtering is turned off. However, you can also turn it off in the InPrivate Filtering Setting dialog box.

Use InPrivate Filtering to Block Third-Party Content

1. In Internet Explorer, click the **Safety** button on the Command bar, and then click **InPrivate Filtering** to enable or disable InPrivate filtering.

   ◆ **On First Use.** Click **Block for me** to block web sites automat-ically or **Let me choose which providers receive my information**.

2. To set InPrivate filtering settings, click the **Safety** button on the command bar, and then click **InPrivate Filtering Settings**.

   ◆ **Block content.** Click the **Automatically block** option.

   ◆ **Choose content to block or allow.** Click the **choose content to block or allow** option, select a content provider, and then click **Allow** or **Block**.

   ◆ **Determine content sharing.** Set the number of sites you visit that share content before you can block or allow it.

   ◆ **Turn off.** Click the **Off** option.

3. When you're done setting options, click **OK**.

InPrivate filtering settings

Set Options for InPrivate Filtering and Browsing

1. Click the **Start** button, click **Control Panel**, and then click the **Internet Options** icon in Small icons or Large icons view.

2. Click the **Privacy** tab.

3. Select or clear the **Do no collect data for use by InPrivate Filtering** check box.

4. Select or clear the **Disable toolbars and extensions when InPrivate Browsing starts** check box.

5. Click **OK**.

Managing Add-Ons

Add-ons are programs that extend the functionality of Internet Explorer to perform a unique task, such as provide search toolbars or display Flash content. In most cases, add-ons are useful, but sometimes poorly built or old ones can slow down your computer, cause system crashes, or invade your privacy (such as Spyware or Adware that are sometimes deceptively installed). To help you work with add-ons, Internet Explorer includes the Add-on Manager, which provides a list of add-ons currently loaded or used by Internet Explorer. You can use the Add-on Manager to individually enable, disable, or update add-ons. The Add-on Manager can also detect add-ons related crashes in Internet Explorer and displays an option to disable it.

Manage Browser Add-Ons

1. Click the **Start** button, click **Control Panel**, and then click the **Internet Options** icon in Small icons or Large icons view.

2. Click the **Programs** tab.

3. Click **Manage add-ons**.

   TIMESAVER *In Internet Explorer, click the Tools menu, and then click Manage Add-ons.*

4. Click the type of add-ons you want to display.

5. Click the **Show** list arrow, and then click the option with the type of add-ons you want to display.

6. Click the add-on you want to manage.

7. Click **Enable** or **Disable**.

8. Click **Close**.

9. Click **OK**.

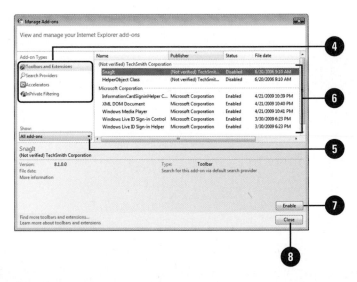

Managing Files Using a Network

Introduction

Windows 7 comes with many tools for managing files and folders across multiple computers. One of the more powerful tools is the Network and Sharing Center. A **network** is a system of two or more computers connected together to share resources. It consists of at least one host and one client. Using the Network folder, you can view the entire network (hosts and clients), share files and folders with people from other parts of the network, and create and manage your network connections to these other computers. This chapter helps you set up your host and client computers so they can easily share files across your network.

If you have two or more computers connected together in a local network running Windows 7, you can create a homegroup (**New!**), which makes it easy to share music, pictures, video, and document libraries. You can join a Homegroup in any edition, but you can only create one in Windows 7 Home Premium, Professional, or Ultimate editions. With a network, you can use the Share with button on the toolbar in a Windows Explorer window to easily share files and folders.

In addition, Windows provides tools for sharing files and folders with computers that are not located in your home or in the same office (commonly referred to as remote computers). You can connect your computer to a network in a different location via modem, or via the Internet using the Communications accessory provided. With wireless technology, such as laptop computers or Bluetooth-enabled devices (keyboards, cell phones and PDAs), you can seamlessly setup, discover and connect to wireless networks. You can also share and synchronize files between your laptop and your desktop computers.

What You'll Do

Understand Network Services

View a Network

View the Network and Sharing Center

View Network Computer and Connection Properties

Join a Workgroup Network

Join a Domain Network

Connect to a Network Using a Modem

Connect to a Network over the Internet

Connect to a Wireless Network

Set Up a Wireless Network

Set Up a Wireless Computer Connection

Manage a Wireless Connection

Map and Disconnect a Network Drive

Create a Shortcut to a Network

Set HomeGroup Sharing Options

Share with a Homegroup

Control a Remote Computer

Share an Internet Connection

Change a Dial-Up Connection

Understanding Network Services

Windows is a secure, reliable network operating system that allows people using many different computers to share resources, such as programs, files, folders, printers, and an Internet connection. A single computer on the network, called a **server**, can be designated to store these resources. Other computers on the network, called **clients** or **workstations**, can access the resources on the server instead of having to store them. You can share resources using two or more client computers, or you can designate one computer to serve specifically as the server. If the workstation computers are close together in a single building or group of buildings, the network is called a **local area network (LAN)**. If the workstation computers are spread out in multiple buildings or throughout the entire country using dial-up or wireless connections, the network is called a **wide area network (WAN)**. To set up a network with multiple computers, you need to install a network adapter for each computer on your network and connect each computer to a network hub using network cable or wireless technology, known as Wi-Fi. Network adapters are usually hardware cards, called **network interface cards**, or **NICs**, inserted in a slot, or **USB (Universal Serial Bus)**, port in the back of your computer that connects it to the network. A **network hub** is a hardware device that connects multiple computers at a central location. When data arrives at one port of the network hub, it is copied to the other ports so that all connected network devices see the data. If you have two LANs or two sections of the same LAN on different floors of the same building with different network adapter types, you can connect them together with a hardware device called a **bridge**. If you have any number of LANs, you can connect them together with a hardware device called a **router**. If you want to share a printer or Internet connection with the computers on a network, you simply connect the printer or modem to the server, a computer on the network, or directly to a network hub, router, or bridge.

Share central resources through client/server networking

Windows offers a network configuration called **client/server networking**. Under this arrangement, a single computer is designated as a server, allowing access to resources for any qualified user. Client/server networking provides all users on a network a central location for accessing shared files. In a client/server network, individual computers are often grouped into domains. A **domain** is a collection of computers that the person managing the network creates in order to group together the computers to simplify the set up and maintenance of the network. The network administrator defines the domains that exist on the network and controls access to computers within those domains.

Domain

Share resources through peer-to-peer networking

Windows also offers a network configuration called **peer-to-peer networking**. Peer-to-peer networking enables two or more computers to link together without designating a central server. In a peer-to-peer network, individual computers are often organized into workgroups. A **workgroup** is a group of computers that perform common tasks or belong to users who share common duties and interests. In this configuration, any computer user can access resources stored on any other computer, as long as those resources are available for sharing. Peer-to-peer networking allows individual computer users to share files and other resources, such as a printer, with other users on the network without having to access a server. Workgroups are available on all Windows computers.

Share resources through network connections

Windows provides connectivity between your computer and a network, another computer, or the Internet using **Network Connections**. Whether you are physically connected using a direct cable or connected remotely using a dial-up or cable modem, you can connect securely to a network over the Internet using a **Virtual Private Network (VPN)** connection or set up your computer to let other computers connect to yours using an **incoming network connection**. VPN and incoming network connection are examples of WANs.

Share designated files and folders on your computer with other network users

Windows provides support for security, so even though your computer is connected to a network, you can designate which resources on your computer you want to share with others. Before network users can use any resources on your computer, they must be granted the required permission.

Workgroup

Wireless

Viewing a Network

The key to managing files and folders in a network environment is understanding the structure of your particular network. Most networks consist of multiple types of computers and operating systems. The Network folder available in Windows Explorer lets you view the entire network or just your part of the network, to give you access to the servers, domains, and workgroups on the network. The Network folder also displays shared folders available on your network. If you're working on a domain network, you can use Active Search Directory to help you find network resources, such as computer and printers.

View a Workgroup or Domain Network

1. Click the **Start** button, and then click **Computer**.

2. Click **Network** in the Navigation pane.

   ◆ If a Network discovery and file sharing information bar appears, click the bar to enable it and display a network.

3. Double-click a network computer icon to display the shared files, folders, and devices on the computer.

4. To open the Network and Sharing Center, click the **Network and Sharing Center** button on the toolbar.

5. When you're done, click the **Close** button.

Click to display network

Did You Know?

A domain network and a workgroup are different. A domain network is a group of computers connected together to share and manage resources by an administrator from a central computer called a domain controller. A workgroup is a network of computers connected together to share resources, but each computer is maintained and shared separately.

View a Shared Folder

1 Click the **Start** button, and then click **Computer**.

2 Click **Network** in the Navigation pane.

3 Double-click a network computer icon.

◆ If prompted, enter a username and password.

4 Double-click a shared folder to display the shared files and folders in the folder.

5 When you're done, click the **Close** button.

Search a Domain Network

1 Click the **Start** button, and then click **Computer**.

2 Click **Network** in the Navigation pane.

3 Click the **Search Active Directory** button on the toolbar.

4 Click the **Find** list arrow, and then select the network resource you want to find.

5 Click the **In** list arrow, and then select where you want to search.

6 Specify the criteria for the search; tabs and information vary.

7 Click **Find Now**.

8 When you're done, click the **Close** button.

Viewing the Network and Sharing Center

The Network and Sharing Center provides a central location where you can view and modify network and sharing options for the computer connected to a network. From a network perspective, you can view a map of the network, view network connection status information, change the network location type (either Public or Private: Work or Home), and specify whether you want others on the network to see you, known as **network discovery**. When you connect to a network for the first time, Windows automatically detects it and asks you to choose a network location. When you change the network location, Windows automatically changes firewall settings for the type of network. In addition to viewing and setting network options, you can also turn sharing options on and off. The Network and Sharing Center visually display network maps and sharing on and off icons to make it easier to view status information.

View Network and Choose Network a Location

1. Click the **Start** button, and then click **Control Panel**.

2. Click the **Network and Sharing** icon in Small icons or Large icons view.

   TIMESAVER *Click the Network icon in the notification area, and then click Open Network And Sharing Center.*

3. In the left pane, click **Change advanced sharing settings**.

4. Click the turn on options you want for Network discovery, File and printer sharing, and Public folder sharing.

5. Click **Save changes**.

6. To specify a network location type, click the network link, click the **Home**, **Work**, or **Public**, and then click **Close**.

7. When you're done, click the **Close** button.

View a Network Map

1. Click the **Network** icon in the notification area on the taskbar, and then click **Open Network and Sharing Center**.

2. Click **See full map**.

3. Click the **Network map of** list arrow, and then select the network connection you want to view, which includes: **Local Area Connection - name** and **Wireless Network Connection - name**.

4. To open a networked device, double-click the icon.

5. When you're done, click the **Close** button.

Did You Know?

You can use the Network icon in the notification area to access commands. To see current networks, click the Network icon on the taskbar in the notification area. You can also click links to connect to a network or open the Network And Sharing Center.

You can right-click the Network icon to troubleshoot problems. Right-click the Network icon on the taskbar in the notification area, and then click Troubleshoot Problems to start the Windows Network diagnostics wizard.

For Your Information

Networking with Windows Firewall

For security purposes, Windows Firewall is turned on (the default setting) to protect your computer against security threats, such as viruses, worms, and Trojan Horses, spread over the Internet or a network. Windows 7 automatically sets Windows Firewall settings to be compatible with your network. However, you might need to make adjustments for some programs, such as Internet games, to allow them to work properly. See "Setting Up Windows Firewall" on page 136 for more information.

Viewing Network Computer Properties

Names and locations are used to identify computers on a network. The computer's name refers to the individual machine, and the computer's location refers to how the machine is grouped together with other computers. Computers anywhere on the network can be located easily through the naming hierarchy and can be addressed individually by name. You can find the name and workgroup or domain of a computer on the network by examining the system properties. Workgroups and domains are available on all Windows computers.

View Network Computer Properties

1. Click the **Start** button, and then click **Computer**.

2. Click the **System properties** button on the toolbar, and then click **Change settings**.

3. Click the **Computer Name** tab.

4. To add a computer description, type a description.

5. To change a workgroup or domain, click **Change**, specify a new name, and then click **OK**.

6. Click **OK**.

See Also

See "Running Commands" on page 46 for information on finding the IP configuration of a computer, and pinging another computer.

Viewing Network Connection Properties

A computer that uses a network must be configured so that other machines on the network recognize it. You might be responsible for configuring your computer, or that responsibility might fall to the network administrator. You can view the status of the network connection and modify some of the network settings for your computer using the Network Connections window. A network connection consists of a network adapter and three types of components: client, service, and protocol. The **client** type allows you to access computers and files on the network. The **service** type allows you to share your computer resources, such as files and printers, with other networked computers. **Protocol** is the language that the computer uses to communicate with other computers on the network, such as TCP/IP. Knowing which components are installed on your computer helps you understand the capabilities and limitations of your computer on the network.

View Network Connection Properties

1. Click the **Network** icon in the notification area on the taskbar, and then click **Open Network and Sharing Center**.

2. In the left pane, click **Change adapter settings**.

3. Double-click the network connection you want to get status information.

   TIMESAVER *In the Network And Sharing Center, you can also click Local Area Connection or Wireless Network Connection.*

4. If you have problems with your connection, click **Diagnose**.

5. To display network components installed and enabled, click **Properties**.

6. When you're done working with the components, click **OK**.

7. Click **Close**.

8. Click the **Close** button.

For Your Information

Using Network Diagnostics

If you're having problems connecting to networks or sharing files, you can use Network Diagnostics to help you identify the problem and suggest options for fixing it. Instead of calling technical support, try using Network Diagnostics first. Right-click the Network icon in the notification area on the taskbar, and then click Diagnose And Repair. Review your options, and then select the best one available. If a fix is not possible, you can report the problem to Microsoft.

Joining a Workgroup Network

Before you can set up and configure a network at home or small office, you need to physically attach the hardware so the computers can communicate. This includes installing the network cards in all the computers, connecting the computers together using cables or wireless technology, installing a modem on the host computer, turning on all computers, printers, and external modems, and establishing a connection to the Internet. A home or small office network is typically a peer-to-peer network where individual computers are organized into workgroups with a host and several clients. The host is a computer on the network who shares an Internet connection with the other client computers on the network. The host computer must be turned on whenever a client computer needs to access the Internet. To join a workgroup, you can use the Join a Domain or Workgroup wizard in System Properties. After you join, you can change the workgroup name to match the other ones in your network.

Join a Workgroup Network Using a Wizard

1. Click the **Start** button, and then click **Computer**.

2. Click the **System properties** button on the toolbar, and then click **Change settings**.

3. Click the **Computer Name** tab.

4. Click **Network ID**, and then click **Next** to continue.

5. Click the **This is a home computer; it's not part of a business network** option, and then click **Next** to continue.

6. Click **Finish**, and then restart your computer.

Change a Workgroup Network Name

1. Click the **Start** button, and then click **Computer**.

2. Click the **System properties** button on the toolbar, and then click **Change settings**.

3. Click the **Computer Name** tab.

4. Click **Change**.

5. Click the **Workgroup** option.

6. Type the workgroup name.

7. Click **OK**.

8. Click **OK**.

Joining a Domain Network

If you are not connected to a domain network, you can use the Join a Domain or Workgroup wizard (**New!**) to join a domain and create a local user account. If you already have a user account, you can use System Properties to join a domain. Before you join a domain, you need to connect your computer to a client/server network using a network adapter and network cable or wireless technology. After you connect a network adapter to your computer and start Windows 7, your computer detects the network adapter and creates a local area connection. A local area connection is the only type of network connection that Windows automatically creates. Depending on your hardware setup, your Join a Domain or Workgroup wizard options might differ.

Join a Domain Network

1. Click the **Start** button, and then click **Computer**.

2. Click the **System properties** button on the toolbar, and then click **Change settings**.

3. Click the **Computer Name** tab.

4. Click **Change**.

5. Click the **Domain** option.

6. Type the domain name.

7. Click **OK**.

8. Click **OK**.

Join a Domain Network and Create a User Account

1. Click the **Start** button, and then click **Computer**.

2. Click the **System properties** button on the toolbar, and then click **Change settings**.

3. Click the **Computer Name** tab.

4. Click **Network ID**, and then click **Next** to continue.

5. Click the **This computer is part of a business network** option, and then click **Next** to continue.

6. Click the **My company uses a network with a domain** option, and then click **Next** to continue.

7. Read the page, and then click **Next** to continue.

8. Type a user name and password.

9. Type a domain name, and then click **Next** to continue.

10. Type a computer name and domain name, and then click **Next** to continue.

11. Click the **Add the following user** option, and then click **Next** to continue.

12. Click an access user level, and then click **Next** to continue.

13. Click **Finish**, and then restart your computer.

Connecting to a Network Using a Modem

If you have a modem installed on your computer, you can use a connection wizard to set up a dial-up connection to another computer or a network. Connecting to another computer or a network is useful when you need access to information stored on another computer or a network. You only need to set up a dial-up connection to a computer or a network once. After you set up the connection, you can use the Connect to a network dialog box to select the dial-up connection and establish a dial-up connection. Windows displays a network icon in the notification area on the taskbar. You can click the icon to display information available connections, and quickly connect to or disconnect from anyone of them (**New!**).

Create a Dial-Up Connection

1. Click the **Network** icon in the notification area on the taskbar, and then click **Open Network and Sharing Center**.

2. Click **Set up a new connection or network**.

3. Click **Connect to a workplace**, and then click **Next** to continue.

4. Click **Dial Directly**, and then click **Next** to continue.

5. Type the phone number for calling the network.

6. To share this network connection, select the **Allow other people to use this connection** check box.

7. Click **Next** to continue.

8. Type user name, password and domain name.

9. Click **Connect**.

Establish a Dial-Up Connection

1. Click the **Network** icon in the notification area on the taskbar.

   ◆ Click the **down** arrow next to Dial-up and VPN, if necessary, to display the available connections.

2. Select the dial up connection, and then click **Connect**.

3. Type your assigned user name and password.

4. To save your user name and password information, select the **Save this user name and password for the following users** check box, and then click an option to specify who can use the information.

5. Click **Dial**, and then wait for the connection.

6. When you're done, click the **Network** icon, select the connection, and then click **Disconnect**.

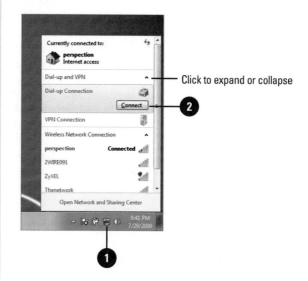

Click to expand or collapse

Did You Know?

You can delete a connection. Click the Network icon in the notification area, click Open Network And Share Center, click Change Adapter Settings, right-click the connection you want to delete, and then click Delete.

See Also

See "Changing a Dial-Up Connection" on page 380 for information on changing the settings for a dial-up connection.

Connecting to a Network over the Internet

You can create a VPN (Virtual Private Network) connection to connect to a network over the Internet. A VPN provides a secure connection between your computer and the network. The computer to which you want to connect must support a VPN and Internet connection. Before you create a connection, you need to have the name or IP (Internet Protocol) address of the VPN computer. You can use a connection wizard to set up a VPN connection. You only need to set up a VPN connection to a network once. Windows displays a network icon in the notification area on the taskbar. You can click the icon to display information available connections, and quickly connect to or disconnect from anyone of them (**New!**).

Create a VPN Connection

1 Click the **Network** icon in the notification area on the taskbar, and then click **Open Network and Sharing Center**.

2 Click **Set up a new connection or network**.

3 Click **Connect to a workplace**, and then click **Next** to continue.

4 Click **Use my Internet connection (VPN)**, and then click **Next** to continue.

5 Type the host name or IP address to the computer to which you want to connect.

6 To share this network connection, select the **Allow other people to use this connection** check box.

7 Click **Next** to continue.

8 Type user name, password and domain name.

9 Click **Connect**.

Establish a VPN Connection

1. Click the **Network** icon in the notification area on the taskbar.

   ◆ Click the **down** arrow next to Dial-up and VPN, if necessary, to display the available connections.

2. Select the VPN connection, and then click **Connect**.

3. Type your assigned user name and password.

4. To save your user name and password information, select the **Save this user name and password for the following users** check box, and then click an option to specify who can use the information.

5. Click **Connect**, and then wait for the connection.

6. When you're done, click the **Network** icon, select the connection, and then click **Disconnect**.

Click to expand or collapse

Did You Know?

What is Bluetooth wireless technology? Bluetooth technology uses radio waves to enable devices such as computers, printer, mice, or mobile phones, to communication wirelessly over a short distance. You can use Bluetooth to listen to music or use a mobile phone over wireless headphones, transfer files between laptop computers, or print to a wireless printer.

Connecting to a Wireless Network

Windows 7 provides updated wireless networking, enabling you to setup and manage wireless connections with a broad range of wireless hot spots that discover and connect to wireless networks (known as Wi-Fi). The Connection wizard makes it easy to setup a Wi-Fi network. You can quickly connect to an available wireless network with a security key or manually connect to one not recognized. As you walk through the manual process, you'll specify a network name, called the SSID (Service Set Identifier). The SSID is broadcasted from your access point (AP)—typically a wireless router—to your other wireless devices. Windows 7 also provides updated support for Bluetooth-enabled hardware devices, allowing you to take advantage of the latest wireless devices, including wireless keyboards and mice, wireless printers, and connections with cell phones and PDAs. Windows displays a network icon in the notification area on the taskbar. You can click the icon to display information available connections, and quickly connect to or disconnect from any one of them (**New!**).

Connect to an Available Wireless Network

1. Click the **Network** icon in the notification area on the taskbar.

   ◆ Click the **down** arrow next to Wireless Network Connection, if necessary, to display the available connections.

2. Select the wireless network to which you want to connect.

3. Select or clear the **Connect automatically** check box.

4. Click **Connect**.

5. Type the security key or passphrase.

6. Click **OK**.

7. When you're done, click the **Network** icon, select the connection, and then click **Disconnect**.

Click to expand or collapse

Manually Connect to a Wireless Network

1. Click the **Network** icon in the notification area on the taskbar, and then click **Open Network and Sharing Center**.

2. Click **Set up a new connection or network**.

3. Click **Manually connect to a wireless network**, and then click **Next** to continue.

4. Type the network name.

5. Specify a security type, and then specify an encryption type, if necessary.

6. Type a passphrase (point to the box and use the ScreenTip for help).

7. Click **Next** to continue.

8. Click **Connect to** or **Change connection settings**.

9. If necessary, click **Close**.

Did You Know?

You can perform a security check on your wireless network. After implementing lock down security measures, you can perform a security check. Install the free program NetStumbler available at *www.netstumber.com* onto a laptop or PDA.

Windows 7 supports 802.11n wireless connections. In addition to current support for 802.11g, Windows 7 adds support for 802.11n by which a user can plug in an 802.11n Draft 2.0 compatible wireless adapter and connect to an 802.11n Draft 2.0 compatible network. Click the Start button, click Connect To, and then point to a connection to display the Radio Type.

Setting Up a Wireless Network

If you have a wireless router or access point, you can set up your own wireless network. A router directs communication traffic between two networks, such as a home or office network and the Internet. An access point provides wireless access to a wired Ethernet network. An access point plugs into a wired router and sends out a wireless signal, which other wireless computers and devices use to connect to a wired network. During the set up process, you need to specify a network name, choose file and printer sharing options, and a passphrase (a security key) to provide secure access.

Set Up a Wireless Network

1. Click the **Network** icon in the notification area on the taskbar, and then click **Open Network and Sharing Center**.

2. Click **Set up a new connection or network**.

3. In the left pane, click **Set up a new network**, and then click **Next** to continue.

4. Wait for devices to show, select the wireless router or access point, and then click **Next** to continue. Steps vary depending on the device installation.

5. Type the Network name (SSID), and then click **Next** to continue.

6. Type a passphrase or use the one generated, and then write it down so you can use it the first time that people connect to this network.

7. Click **Next** to continue.

8. Read the screen, enable the sharing options you want.

9. Click **Close**.

Setting Up a Wireless Computer Connection

If you have two wireless computers, you can set up a connection between the two systems. During the set up process, you need to specify a network security type to keep the connection safe and a passphrase (a security key) to provide secure access. You can set the security type to Wired Equivalent Privacy (WEP), Wi-Fi Protected Access (WPA), or 802.1X authentication. WEP is a widely used network security type that uses an encrypted security key to provide a secure wireless environment. WPA improves on the security of WEP and checks to make sure the security key has not been modified. 802.1x is a server authentication security type typically used for workplace networks.

Set Up a Wireless Connection to Another Computer

1. Click the **Network** icon in the notification area on the taskbar, and then click **Open Network and Sharing Center**.

2. Click **Set up a new connection or network**.

3. Click **Set up a wireless ad hoc (computer-to- computer) network**, and then click **Next** to continue.

4. Read the screen, and then click **Next** to continue.

5. Type the network name, and then specify a security type.

6. Type a passphrase (point to the box and use the ScreenTip for help), and then write it down so you can use it the first time that people connect to this network.

7. Click **Next** to continue.

8. Read the screen, enable the sharing options you want.

9. Click **Close**.

Managing a Wireless Connection

After you setup and connect to a wireless network, you can use the Manage Wireless Networks folder to view established wireless connections, add or remove wireless networks, or change the connection order. In the Manage Wireless Networks folder, each established wireless network appears, displaying security and connectivity information. You can use buttons on the toolbar to work with the wireless network connections. If you want to view or change connection and security properties for individual wireless connections, you can use the Wireless Network Properties dialog box. You can view the wireless network name, SSID, type, and availability, and enable automatic or preferred connect options or change the security type and key.

View Wireless Connections

1. Click the **Network** icon in the notification area on the taskbar, and then click **Open Network and Sharing Center**.

2. In the left pane, click **Manage wireless networks**.

3. To add a wireless connection, click the **Add** button, and then follow the on-screen instructions.

4. Select the wireless network connection you want to modify.

5. To remove it, click the **Remove** button, and then click **OK**.

6. To change the connection order, drag the wireless connection icon to a new position.

7. When you're done, click the **Close** button.

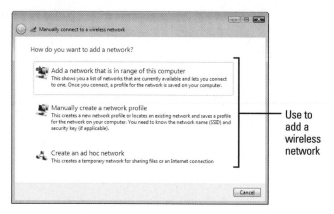

Use to add a wireless network

Display Wireless Connection and Security Properties

1. Click the **Network** icon in the notification area on the taskbar, and then click **Open Network and Sharing Center**.

2. In the left pane, click **Manage wireless networks**.

3. Right-click the wireless connection you want to view, and then click **Properties**.

4. Click the **Connection** tab.

5. Select or clear the following connection check boxes:

   ◆ **Connect automatically when this network is in range.**

   ◆ **Connect to a more preferred network if available.**

   ◆ **Connect even if the networks is not broadcasting.**

6. Click the **Security** tab.

7. To change the security type, click the list arrow, and then select the type you want.

   When you change the security type, the other options change, which you can then modify.

8. Click **OK**, and then click the **Close** button.

Mapping and Disconnecting a Network Drive

Windows networking enables you to connect your computer to other computers on the network quite easily. If you connect to a network location frequently, you might want to designate a drive letter on your computer as a direct connection to a shared drive or folder on another computer. Instead of spending unnecessary time opening the Network folder and the shared drive or folder each time you want to access it, you can create a direct connection, called **mapping** a drive, to the network location for quick and easy access. If you no longer use a mapped drive, you can right-click the mapped drive in the Computer folder and then click Disconnect.

Map a Network Drive

1. Click the **Start** button, click **Computer**, and then navigate to and select the drive or folder you want to map.

2. Click the **Map network drive** button on the toolbar, or click the **Tools** menu, and then click **Map Network Drive**.

   ◆ To show the menu, click the **Organize** button, point to **Layout**, and then click **Menu bar**.

3. Click the **Drive** list arrow, and then select a drive letter.

4. Click **Browse**.

5. Select the folder you want to connect to.

6. Click **OK**.

7. To reconnect each time you log on to your computer, select the **Reconnect at logon** check box.

8. Click **Finish**.

9. To disconnect from a mapped drive, right-click the drive in the Computer folder, and then click **Disconnect**.

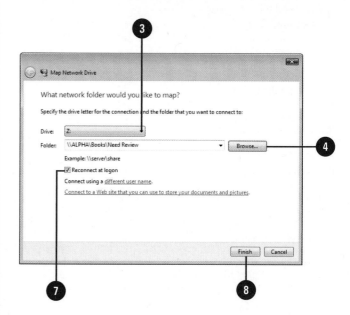

Creating a Shortcut to a Network

Instead of clicking numerous icons in the Network folder to access a network location, you can create a shortcut to the network location to provide easy access. A **shortcut** is a link that you can place in any location to gain instant access to a particular file, folder, or program on your hard disk or on a network just by double-clicking. The actual file, folder, or program remains stored in its original location, and you place an icon representing the shortcut in a convenient location, such as in a folder or on the desktop.

Create a Shortcut to a Network

① Click the **Start** button, click **Computer**, and then click **Network** in the Navigation pane.

② Right-click a network computer icon or a folder on a network computer, and then click **Create Shortcut**.

The shortcut appears on the desktop or in the folder.

③ Drag the shortcut icon to a convenient location.

Shortcut to a network

Setting Network Sharing Options

In the Network and Sharing Center you can set options to share files, printers, public folders, and media on the network. Sharing files, public folders, and printers provides a convenient way to share information and resources over a network. The sharing options allow you to share materials on a workgroup, domain, or homegroup network. After you turn on sharing options for file or public folders, you can use the Share with button on the toolbar in Windows Explorer to share your files with others on the homegroup or other networks using permissions.

Set File or Public Folder Sharing Options

1. Click the **Network** icon in the notification area on the taskbar, and then click **Open Network and Sharing Center**.

2. In the left pane, click **Change advanced sharing settings**.

3. Click the **Turn on file and printer sharing** or **Turn off file and printer sharing** option.

4. Select the Public folder sharing option you want.

   ◆ **Turn on sharing so anyone with network access can read and write files in the Public folders.**

   ◆ **Turn off Public folder sharing (people logged on to this computer can still access these folders).**

5. Click **Save changes**.

6. Click the **Close** button.

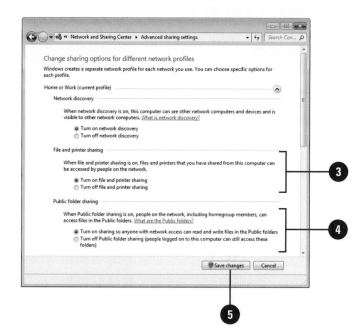

See Also

See "Sharing Folders or Files with Others" on page 92 for information on using the Shared Documents folder.

See "Streaming Media" on page 272-273 for more information on sharing media and playing music.

Setting Homegroup Sharing Options

If you have two or more computers running Windows 7 on the Home network type, you can set up and join in a homegroup (**New!**) to share files, printers, and media. You can even play music streamed from another person's computer on a homegroup using Windows Media Player. Before you can use a homegroup, you need to create one first (only workgroups). During the setup process Windows 7 creates a password, which you can view, print, and change later, for everyone to use on individual computers to join the homegroup. If you no longer want to be a part of the homegroup, you can leave it.

Set Homegroup Options

1 Click the **Network** icon in the notification area on the taskbar, and then click **Open Network and Sharing Center**.

2 Click **Choose homegroup and sharing options**.

3 If prompted, click **Create a homegroup**, select the items you want to share, click **Next**, write down the join password, and then click **Finish**.

4 Select the check boxes for the libraries and printers that you want to share.

5 To share media, select the **Stream my pictures, music, and videos to all devices on my home network** check box.

◆ Click **Choose media streaming options**, click **Allow All**, **Block All**, or select individual settings, and then click **OK**.

6 Perform any homegroup actions:

◆ **View or print the homegroup password.**

◆ **Change the password.**

◆ **Leave the homegroup.**

◆ **Start the HomeGroup troubleshooter.**

7 Click **Save changes**.

8 Click the **Close** button.

Related homegroup commands

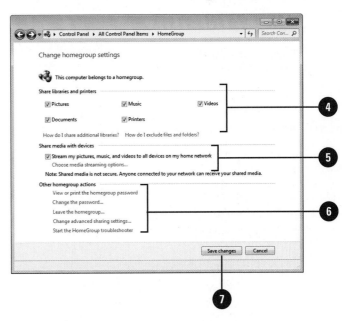

Sharing with a Homegroup

A homegroup is a home sharing network with two or more computers running Windows 7. You can join in a homegroup (**New!**) to share files, printers, and media. You can play music streamed from another person's computer on a homegroup using Windows Media Player or other networked digital media player (also called a digital media receiver), such as Xbox 360; you can access the media from a shared media folder that appears in the Network folder. Before you can view and use files from other people on your network, they need to join the homegroup. To join the homegroup, they'll need the password generated during the set up process. After you join in, you can use the Share with button on the toolbar in Windows Explorer to share your files with others on the homegroup or other network. It's important to note that any computers turned off or sleeping do not appear in the homegroup.

Join a Homegroup

1. Click the **Start** button, click **Computer**, and then click **Homegroup** in the Navigation pane.

2. Click **Join now**.

3. Select the items that you want to share on the homegroup, and then click **Next**.

4. Type the password (generated during setup), click **Next**, and then follow the remaining steps to complete the process.

5. To view files in a homegroup, click **Homegroup** in the Navigation pane.

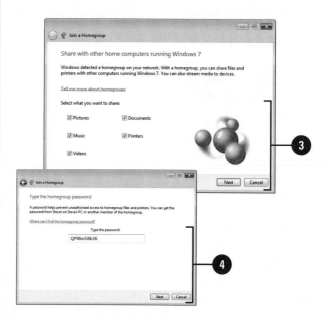

Did You Know?

Everyone can join a homegroup, not everyone can create one. You can join a homegroup in any edition, but you can only create one in Windows 7 Home Premium, Professional, or Ultimate editions connected to a workgroup using the Home network type.

Share Files and Folders

1. Click the **Start** button, click **Computer**, and then navigate to the folder location with the files or folders you want to share.

2. Click the **Share with** button on the toolbar.

  - ◆ **Homegroup (Read) or Homegroup (Read/Write).** Select to share with a homegroup using permissions.

  - ◆ **Specific people.** Select to share with a specific person.

3. Click **Homegroup** in the Navigation pane to work with shared files from other people.

4. When you're done, click the **Close** button.

Play Shared Media

1. Click the **Start** button, click **Computer**, and then click **Network** in the Navigation pane.

2. Double-click a shared media folder icon.

  Windows Media Player opens.

3. Use Windows Media Player to play the shared media files.

  - ◆ When you're finished playing music, exit Windows Media Player.

4. When you're done, click the **Close** button.

See Also

See "Streaming Media" on page 272-273 for more information on sharing media and playing music.

Music played on this computer

Music stored on this computer

Controlling a Remote Computer

You can use Remote Desktop Connection to connect to a remote computer on your network or the Internet and use the remote computer as if you were working on it. Before you can connect to a remote computer, you need to turn on the Windows 7 computer and set the option to allow users to connect remotely to the computer. Doing this provides security for the remote computer. You can allow anyone to connect to the remote computer, or you can specify users with a password. You also need to have the name or IP (Internet Protocol) address of the remote computer and the user name and password you use to log on to the computer. You can also customize settings for the remote connection, which include the display size and color depth, when to use local or remote resources, and what programs to use and options to allow. Once you connect to the remote computer, the remote desktop appears on your screen. You can use the remote desktop as if you were working at the computer.

Set Up a Remote Computer

1. Click the **Start** button, and then click **Computer**.

2. Click the **System properties** button on the toolbar, and then click **Change settings**.

3. Click the **Remote** tab.

4. Select the **Allow Remote Assistance connections to this computer** check box.

5. Click **Advanced**.

6. Specify whether you want others to remotely control this computer, and how long a remote invitation is available, and then click **OK**.

7. Select the remote desktop connection option you want.

8. Click **Select Users**.

9. Click **Add**, type user names, and then click **OK**.

   TROUBLE? *Click Examples for help with user names.*

10. Click **OK**.

11. Click **OK**.

Connect to and Control a Remote Computer

1 Establish a connection to your network.

2 Click the **Start** button, point to **All Programs**, click **Accessories**, and then click **Remote Desktop Connection**.

3 Type the name or IP address of the remote computer.

4 If available, type a user name.

5 Click **Connect**.

6 If prompted, enter the needed connection credentials.

7 Use the remote desktop as if you were sitting in front of the remote computer.

8 Click the **Minimize** or **Restore Down** button to resize the remote desktop and to display the local desktop.

9 Use the local desktop.

10 When you're done, click the **Close** button, and then click **Yes** to disconnect.

Did You Know?

You can use a wizard to setup a remote application or desktop connection. Open the Control Panel, click the RemoteApp and Desktop Connection icon in Small icons or Large icons view, click Set Up A New Connection With RemoteApp and Desktop Connections, and then follow the on-screen instructions.

Sharing an Internet Connection

If you have a home or small office network using Windows 7, you can use Internet Connection Sharing (ICS) to connect all the computers on the network to the Internet with one connection, which saves you money on multiple connections. If you have a shared dial-up Internet connection no one is using, you can change settings to have the connection end automatically, or you can manually end the connection from your computer. Windows displays a network icon in the notification area on the taskbar. You can click the icon to display information available connections, and quickly connect to or disconnect from anyone of them (**New!**).

Share an Internet Connection

1. Click the **Network** icon in the notification area on the taskbar, and then click **Open Network and Sharing Center**.

2. In the left pane, click **Change adapter settings**.

3. Right-click the Internet Network icon, and then click **Properties**.

4. Click the **Sharing** tab.

5. Select the **Allow other network users to connect through this computer's Internet connection** check box.

6. For a home network, select the adapter that connects you to the other networked computers.

7. If you want this connection to dial automatically, select the **Establish a dial-up connection whenever a computer on my network attempts to access the Internet** check box.

8. Select or clear the **Allow other network users to control or disable the shared Internet connection** check box.

9. To select specific services to share, click **Settings**, select the services you want, and then click **OK**.

10. Click **OK**.

Service settings

End an Internet Connection

1. Click the **Network** icon in the notification area on the taskbar.

   ◆ Click the **down** arrow next to Wireless Network Connection, if necessary, to display the available connections.

2. Select the connection you want to disconnect.

3. Click **Disconnect**.

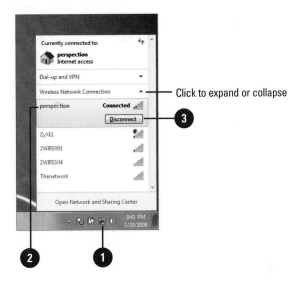

Click to expand or collapse

Did You Know?

Disable or enable a network connection. You can disable or enable a network connection by turning the network adapter for the connection off or on. To make this change, open the Network And Sharing Center, click Change Adapter Settings in the left pane, right-click the connection you want to change, and then click Disable or Enable.

See Also

See "Creating an Internet Connection" on page 135 for information on creating a new shared Internet connection using the New Connection Wizard.

For Your Information

Multihoming

Multihoming refers to a computer or a device that has connectivity to one or more networks via two or more methods, either wired or wireless. Multihoming is becoming more common, especially with the wide use of wireless devices, such as Pocket PCs and wireless connectivity on laptops. Multihoming automatically selects the route with best performance for a particular data transfer. Each route has a corresponding interface, therefore the selection of the best route also implies an interface selection for an outgoing connection.

Changing a Dial-Up Connection

After you create a dial-up connection, you can change the settings to specify how the computer creates a dial-up connection to another computer. You can change the phone number, add dialing rules, and modify redial and hang up settings. You need to log on as an administrator to change some settings for a dial-up connection. When a computer is set up to share a dial-up connection to the Internet, these settings control the connection for the network users.

Change a Dial-Up Connection

1. Click the **Network** icon in the notification area on the taskbar, and then click **Open Network and Sharing Center**.

2. In the left pane, click **Change adapter settings**.

3. Right-click the **Dial-Up connection** icon, and then click **Properties**.

4. Click the **General** tab.

5. To change the number, double-click the text box, and then type a new number.

6. To use dialing rules, select the **Use dialog rules** check box, and then specify the area and country codes.

7. Click the **Options** tab.

8. Select the check boxes for the dialog options you want, and clear the others.

9. Set the idle time you want before the dial-up connection hangs up, and any redial options.

10. Click **OK**.

See Also

See "Connecting to a Network Using a Modem" on page 360 for information on creating a dial-up connection.

Going Mobile

Introduction

You no longer have to change mobile PC related options in different places. With the Windows Mobility Center, you can change or access mobile PC related options all in one place. In the Windows Mobility Center, you can adjust volume level and power options, check your network connectivity, connect to an external display, enable presentation settings, and access the Sync Center, which helps you keep files up-to-date when you're working on different computers, such as a desktop computer and a laptop.

Keeping track of the latest versions of all your files on your desktop computer and laptop can become a problem. With the Sync Center, you can keep files (including documents, music, photos, and in some case contacts) and other information up-to-date between your computer and mobile devices, network folders, and compatible programs. The Sync Center works with offline files and keeps them in sync.

If you have a network projector at a remote location and you can connect to it, then you can operate the projector to give a presentation as if you were physically in the room. The Connect to the Network Project wizard makes it easy to establish a connection. Windows SideShow allows hardware manufacturers to build peripheral devices that you can use to view the information you need at a moments notice, such as a feed or Office PowerPoint presentation.

Windows 7 also comes standard with Tablet PC tools—Windows Journal, Tablet PC Input Panel, and Personalize Handwriting Recognition—that you can effectively use on a Tablet PC with a pen. If you have a Tablet PC or ink device, you can use the Pen and Touch and Tablet PC options to customize and personalize the way you work. If you use your Tablet PC to take notes in math or you work in an engineering or scientific profession, then you need the Math Input Panel.

What You'll Do

View the Windows Mobility Center

Control Power Options

Keep Files in Sync

Work with Offline Files

Connect to a Network Projector

View Windows SideShow

Work with Tablet PC Tools

Use the Tablet PC Input Panel

Use the Math Input Panel

Viewing the Windows Mobility Center

With the Windows Mobility Center, you can change or access mobile PC related options all in one place. You no longer have to change mobile PC related options in different places. In the Windows Mobility Center, you can adjust volume level and power options, check your network connectivity, connect to an external display, enable presentation settings, and access the Sync Center, which helps you keep files up-to-date when you're working on different computers, such as a desktop computer and a laptop. You can make an option change in Windows Mobility Center, or click the icon on a tile to open the utility in the Control Panel, where you can make additional changes.

View Windows Mobility Center

1 Click the **Start** button, and then click **Control Panel**.

2 Click the **Windows Mobility Center** icon in Small icons or Large icons view.

TIMESAVER *Click the battery meter icon in the notification area, and then click Windows Mobility Center, or press ⊞+X.*

3 Click a button or change an option for any of the following settings (options vary depending on your system):

- **Brightness** for the display.

- **Volume** for the speakers.

- **Battery Status** for power usage.

- **Wireless Network** on and off.

- **Screen Rotation** for a Tablet PC.

- **External Display** add or remove.

- **Sync Center** to keep files up-to-date.

- **Presentation Settings** on and off for giving a presentation.

4 When you're done, click the **Close** button.

Change Presentation Settings

① Click the **Start** button, and then click **Control Panel**.

② Click the **Windows Mobility Center** icon in Small icons or Large icons view.

③ Click the Presentation Settings tile icon.

④ Select or clear the **Turn off the screen saver** check box.

⑤ Select or clear the **Set volume to** check box. If you select it, drag the slider to adjust it.

⑥ Select or clear the **Show this background** check box. If you select it, select a background and specify a position.

⑦ Click **OK**.

See Also

See "Controlling Power Options" on page 384 for information on using battery power and usage.

See "Keeping Files in Sync" on page 386 for information on keeping files up-to-date on different computers.

See "Using Multiple Monitors" on page 106 for information on using more than one monitor.

See "Controlling the Volume" on page 260 for information on using the volume control.

Controlling Power Options

Windows 7 works more efficiently for longer battery life including less power use for DVD playback, automatic screen dimming, power off unused ports, and more accurate battery life (**New!**). You can change power options properties for a portable or laptop computer to reduce power consumption and maximize battery life. For example, if you often leave your computer for a short time while working, you can set your computer to go into **sleep**, a state in which your computer saves everything in memory and turns off your monitor and hard disks after being idle for a set time. If you are often away from your computer for an extended time, you can set it to go into **hibernate**, a state in which your computer saves everything in memory and to your hard disk, and then shuts down. To help you set power options, you can choose one of the power plans, modify one to suit your needs, or create your own. A **power plan** is a predefined collection of power usage settings (dim display, turn off display, put to sleep, and adjust brightness). If you want more options, you can set advanced options to define the power button (sleep, hibernate, or shut down) or other settings, such as **hybrid sleep**, which adds saving to your hard disk to sleep mode.

Select and Modify a Power Plan

1. Click the **Power** icon in the notification area, and then click **More power options**.

   - You can also click the **Power Options** icon in the Control Panel (Small or Large icons).

2. To adjust screen brightness, drag the slider (**New!**).

3. Click the power plan option you want: **Balanced**, or **Power saver**, **High performance**.

4. Click **Change plan settings** below the selected option.

5. Select an amount of time to:

   - **Dim the display. (New!)**
   - **Turn off the display.**
   - **Put the computer to sleep.**
   - **Adjust plan brightness. (New!)**

6. To restore defaults, click **Restore default settings for this plan**, and then click **Yes**.

7. Click **Save changes**.

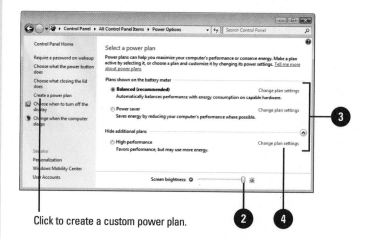

Click to create a custom power plan.

Define Power Button and Set Password Protection

1. Click the **Power** icon in the notification area, and then click **More power options**.

   ◆ You can also click the **Power Options** icon in the Control Panel (Small or Large icons).

2. In the Navigation pane, click **Choose what the power buttons does**.

3. Specify the options you want when you press the power or sleep button, or when you close the lid.

4. Select the **Require a password (recommended)** or **Don't require a password** option.

5. Click **Save changes.**

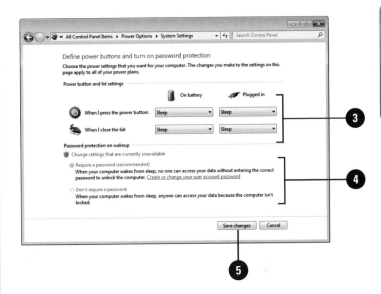

Set Advanced Options

1. Click the **Power** icon in the notification area, and then click **More power options**.

   ◆ You can also click the **Power Options** icon in the Control Panel (Small or Large icons).

2. Click **Change plan settings** below the selected power plan option.

3. Click **Change advanced power settings**.

4. Click the plus sign (+) and minus sign (-) icons to display the option you want to change.

5. Click the option list arrow, and then select a setting.

6. When you're done, click **OK**.

7. Click **Save changes.**

Keeping Files in Sync

Keeping track of the latest versions of all your files on your desktop computer and laptop can become a problem. With the Sync Center, you can keep files (including documents, music, photos, and in some case contacts) and other information up-to-date between your computer and mobile devices, network folders, and compatible programs. You can keep files in sync (short for *synchronization*) in one direction (changes on one computer get changed on the other) or in both directions (changes on both computers get changed on both). The Sync Center compares files between the two computers and then copies the latest version in the appropriate place. If the same files get changed on both computers, the Sync Center asks you to resolve it. The Sync Center also works with offline files and keeps them in sync.

Sync with a Device

1. Establish a connection between your computer and the mobile device, network folder, or program.

2. Click the **Start** button, and then click **Control Panel.**

3. Click the **Sync Center** icon in Small icons or Large icons view.

    TIMESAVER *Click the Start button, point to All Programs, click Accessories, and then click Sync Center.*

4. In the left pane, click **Set up new sync partnerships**.

5. Click the name of the device in the list of partnerships.

6. Click the **Set Up** button on the toolbar.

7. Follow the wizard instructions to select the settings and sync schedule you want. When you're done, click **Finish**.

8. To start syncing now, click the **Sync** button on the toolbar.

Sync All Offline Files

1 Click the **Start** button, and then click **Control Panel.**

2 Click the **Sync Center** icon in Small icons or Large icons view.

3 Click the **Offline Files** sync partnership.

4 If you want to sync the contents of a folder, open it up.

5 Click the **Sync All** button on the toolbar.

Sync Individual Offline Files

1 Click the **Start** button, and then click **Control Panel.**

2 Click the **Sync Center** icon in Small icons or Large icons view.

3 Click the **Offline Files** sync partnership.

4 Select the folder you want to sync.

5 To open the folder to view its contents, click the **Browse** button on the toolbar. When you're done, click the **Close** button.

6 Click the **Sync** button on the toolbar.

7 To schedule the time you want to sync this folder, click the **Schedule** button on the toolbar, and then follow the wizard instructions.

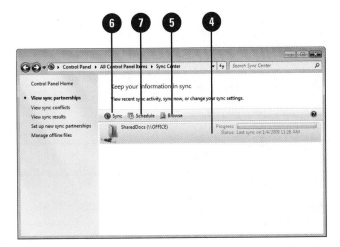

Working with Offline Files

The Sync Center works with offline files and keeps them in sync. An offline file is a copy of a network file that is stored on your local computer for use when the network connection is not available. Before you can make a network file available offline, you need to enable offline files in the Sync Center utility in the Control Panel, where you can also set disk usage, security, and network options. When you make a network file available offline, the Windows automatically creates a copy on your local computer. Whenever the network versions are not available, the Sync Center opens the offline copy and then syncs it back with the network version when the connection becomes available again.

Change Offline Files Settings

1. Click the **Start** button, and then click **Control Panel**.

2. Click the **Sync Center** icon in Small icons or Large icons view, and then click **Manage offline files**.

3. Click the **General** tab.

4. To disable or enable offline files, click the **Disable Offline Files** or **Enable Offline Files**.

5. Click the **Disk Usage** tab.

6. To change disk space allocation for offline files, click **Change Limits**, drag the slider to adjust space usage, and then click **OK**.

7. Click the **Encryption** tab.

8. Click **Encrypt** or **Unencrypt** to add or remove file security.

9. Click the **Network** tab.

10. Select the check box and specify time, if you want to automatically work offline on a slow network.

11. Click **OK**.

Make Files Available Offline

① Open the network file or folder you want to make available offline.

② Right-click the file or folder, and then click **Always Available Offline**.

TIMESAVER *Select the file or folder, and then click the Work Offline button on the toolbar.*

③ To check if you're working offline or not, open the network folder with the offline files, and check the Details pane for offline status information.

View Offline Files

① Click the **Start** button, and then click **Control Panel**.

② Click the **Sync Center** icon in Small icons or Large icons view, and then click **Manage offline files**.

③ Click the **General** tab.

④ Click the **View your offline files** button.

⑤ When you're done, click the **Close** button on the window with the offline files.

⑥ Click **OK** to close the Offline Files dialog box.

Connecting to a Network Projector

A network projector is a video projector that is connected to a wireless or local area network. If you have a network projector at a remote location and you can connect to it, then you can operate the projector to give a presentation as if you were physically in the room. The audience for the presentation needs to be in the same room as the network projector and the presentation can't be viewed over a network. To connect to a network projector, you can search for one on your network or you can enter a network or web address provided from your network administrator or the person in charge of the network projector. If the projector icon you select contains a lock, it's security-enabled and requires a password.

Connect to a Network Projector

① Click the **Start** button, point to **All Programs**, click **Accessories**, and then click **Connect to a Network Projector**.

② Click **Allow the network projector to communicate with my computer** if windows Firewall is blocking the network projector.

③ Click one of the following commands:

♦ **Search for a projector**. Select a projector from the list, and then click Next to continue.

♦ **Enter the projector address**. Type a network address. The address can be a web address (http://server.com/...) or a network path (\\server\...)

④ If the projector is security-enabled, type a projector password.

⑤ Click **Connect**.

The Network Presentation dialog box opens and then minimizes on the taskbar. The desktop temporarily resizes to accommodate custom projector resolutions.

⑥ Use the dialog box to pause and resume the presentation, or disconnect to exit the presentation.

Viewing Windows SideShow

Windows SideShow allows hardware manufacturers to build peripheral devices—such as LCD displays, remote controls, cell phones, or TVs—that can be used to view the information you need at a moments notice. Some devices are integrated into your computer, while other are separate from your computer. You can use Windows SideShow devices to check e-mail messages, view meeting schedules, or find addresses and phones numbers without having to start up your computer. To find a Windows SideShow device, check the Microsoft web site for details and look for the Windows SideShow logo on the hardware device. This innovative technology is just getting started, so new hardware will continue to expand as Windows 7 continues to grow. You install gadgets, or add-in programs to determine what information you want to gather and display using a Windows SideShow device. After you install a gadget, you can use Windows SideShow to turn it on.

View Windows SideShow

1 Click the **Start** button, and then click **Control Panel**.

2 Click the **Windows SideShow** icon in Small icons or Large icons view.

◆ You can also search for Windows SideShow in the Search box to access using Help and Support.

3 To check more gadgets, click **Get more gadgets online** in the left pane.

Your web browser opens, displaying the gadgets you want to install. Follow the online instructions.

4 Click the **Close** button to exit your web browser.

5 Click the **Close** button.

Working with Tablet PC Tools

Windows 7 comes standard with Tablet PC tools that you can effectively use on a Tablet PC with a pen. The tools are also available on a standard PC and you can use them with a mouse, but not as effectively. Windows 7 comes with three tools: Windows Journal, Tablet PC Input Panel, and Personalize Handwriting Recognition. Windows Journal allows you to handwrite notes and draw pictures that mimic a notebook pad. Tablet PC Input Panel allows you to enter text without using a standard keyboard. You use the writing pad or the character pad to convert your handwriting into typed text. You can also use the on-screen keyboard to enter characters. Personalize Handwriting Recognition (**New!**) provides writing samples and creates personalized dictionaries to help Windows recognize your handwriting more accurately.

Handwrite Journal Entries

1. Click the **Start** button, point to **All Programs**, click **Accessories**, click **Tablet PC**, and then click **Windows Journal**.

   ◆ Of first use. Click **Install** or **Cancel** to install the Journal Note Writer printer driver, which captures an image of the document.

2. Click the **Pen** button arrow on the toolbar, and then select a pen style.

3. Handwrite notes or make a drawing.

4. To make corrections, click the **Erase** button arrow, select an eraser size, and then drag to erase on the page.

5. Use many of the common tools on the toolbar and menus to create a handwritten document.

6. When you're done, click the **Save** button on the toolbar, type a name, specify a location, and then click **Save**.

7. Click the **File** menu, and then click **Exit**.

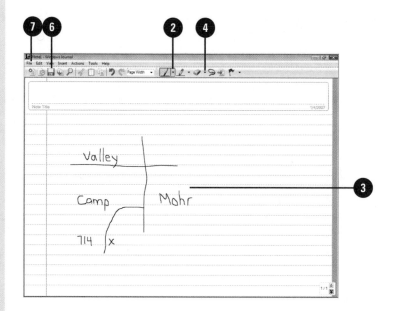

Use Personalize Handwriting Recognition

1 Click the **Start** button, point to **All Programs**, click **Accessories**, click **Tablet PC**, and then click **Personalize Handwriting Recognition**.

2 Click **Target specific recognition errors** or **Teach the recognizer your handwriting style**.

3 To set pen, flick, and handwriting options, click **Change automatic learning settings**, click a tab, select the options you want, and then click **OK**.

- ◆ **Flicks tab.** A *flick* is a quick stroke of the pen to navigate and perform shortcuts using your tablet pen. You can select options to use flicks to perform common commands and adjust the sensitivity slider.

- ◆ **Pen Options tab.** You can adjust how quickly you tap the screen when you double-tap or the distance the pointer can move between tapping when you double-tap, and then test your settings to make sure they are what you want.

4 Click the options to select the type of handwriting you want to perform.

5 Write the sentence indicated on the screen.

6 Use the **Pen**, **Erase**, and **Clear all** buttons to complete the sentence.

7 Click **Next** to continue writing some more, click **Save for later** to save it and close, or **Cancel** to exit.

8 Click **Close**.

For Your Information

Using Windows Touch

If you have a touch screen PC with multitouch capability, you can use Windows Touch (**New!**) to free yourself from your mouse and touchpad to go directly to the screen. The Start menu and taskbar icons are bigger for touch screen use, and all Windows 7 programs are touch screen ready. The common gestures are press and hold to right-click, slide two fingers apart to zoom out and back together to zoom in, flick to scroll through a page, and touch two points and rotate to turn an image.

Using the Tablet PC Input Panel

Tablet PC Input Panel allows you to enter text without using a standard keyboard. You use the writing pad to convert your handwriting into typed text or the on-screen keyboard to enter characters. Tablet PC Input Panel includes correction tools (**New!**) that allow you to correct individual letters using the character pad, delete words, split a word, and join letters. If you're not sure how to use one of the tools, a quick video is available to show you what to do.

Use the Tablet PC Input Panel

1. Open a document to insert handwriting, such as WordPad.

2. Click the **Start** button, point to **All Programs**, click **Accessories**, click **Tablet PC**, and then click **Tablet PC Input Panel**.

3. To write continuously, click the **Writing Pad** button, handwrite a message, and then click the **Insert** button.

   ◆ **Correct.** Point to the recognized text to show a selection, click it, write individual letters, and then click the Close button.

   ◆ **Delete.** Point to the recognized text to show a selection, and then drag a horizontal line through it.

   ◆ **Split.** Point to the recognized text to show a selection, and then drag a vertical line where you want the split.

   ◆ **Join.** Point to the recognized text to show a selection, and then drag a connection line between the two points.

4. To use an on-screen keyboard, click the **On-Screen Keyboard** button, and then click the keys.

5. When you're done, click the **Tools** menu, and then click **Exit.**.

Click to view videos

Character pad

Change Writing Tablet PC Options

1. Click the **Start** button, point to **All Programs**, click **Accessories**, click **Tablet PC**, and then click **Tablet PC Input Panel**.

2. Click the **Tools** menu, and then click **Options**.

3. Click the **Handwriting** tab.

4. Select the handwriting options you want:

   ◆ **Appearance.** Click the Ink thickness button, and then select a pen point thickness.

   ◆ **New writing line.** Drag the slider to specify how close to the end of the writing line you want to write before a new line appears.

5. Click the **Ink to text conversion** tab.

6. Drag the sliders to adjust the **Distance from ink** and **Length of pause** you want to convert your ink to text as you write.

7. Click **OK**.

8. When you're done, click the **Tools** menu, and then click **Exit.**.

Using Math Input Panel

If you use your Tablet PC to take notes in math or you work in an engineering or scientific profession, then you need the Math Input Panel. The Math Input Panel (**New!**) recognizes handwritten math expressions and inserts them into other programs. The program needs to support Mathematical Markup Language (MathML). Just open the document in which you want to insert your math expressions, start Math Input Panel, handwrite your math expression, and then click Insert. If you take notes in Windows Journal, you can convert your handwritten math expression to normal text that you can use in a word processing program. Simply drag the select expression directly into the Math Input Panel.

Use the Math Input Panel

1. Open the document in which you want to insert the math expression.

2. Click the **Start** button, point to **All Programs**, click **Accessories**, and then click **Math Input Panel**.

3. Handwrite the math expression you want.

   As you write, the expression appears in the recognition box. The **Write** button is selected by default.

4. To correct a letter, click the **Select and Correct** button, select a part of the expression, and then select a correction from the menu.

5. To erase the expression, click the **Erase** button, and then drag to erase it.

6. To clear the expression and start over, click the **Clear** button.

7. To undo or redo, click the **Undo** or **Redo** button.

8. Click **Insert** to place it in the open document.

Menu for Select and Correct

Printing and Faxing

14

Introduction

After you create a document or picture, or open a web page or an e-mail, you can use Windows printing options to create a hard copy. You can print files from a folder window or within a program. The Add a Printer wizard makes it easy to install a printer directly attached to your computer or connected to a network. After you send a print job to the printer, you can check the status, pause and resume the print job, or cancel it. If a printer is not working the way you want, you can change printer properties, such as a printer's computer connection or network location, sharing options, related software drivers, color management options, graphics settings, installed fonts, and other advanced settings. To customize your print jobs, you can also change printer preferences, such as orientation, page order, pages per sheet, paper size, paper tray selection, copy count, print quality, and color.

Windows also provides you with complete fax facilities from your computer. After the fax is set up, you can configure fax settings, send and receive faxes, track and monitor fax activity, and view faxes. Using Windows Fax and Scan, you can send and receive faxes, fax or e-mail scanned documents, and forward faxes as e-mail attachments from your computer. You can also change the send and receive properties for the fax to work with your phone line.

What You'll Do

Understand Printers

View Printers

Install a Printer

Specify a Default Printer

Rename or Delete a Printer

Share a Printer

Print Documents

Manage Printers and Print Jobs

Change Printer Properties and Preferences

Create an XPS Document

Understand Faxes

Set Up a Fax

Create a Fax Cover Page

Send a Fax

Manage Outgoing Faxes

Receive and Review a Fax

Change Fax Properties and Options

Understanding Printers

Although there are many different kinds of printers, there are two main categories: ink-jet and laser. An **ink-jet printer** works by spraying ionized ink on a sheet of paper. Ink-jet printers are less expensive and considerably slower than laser printers, but they still produce a good quality output. A **laser printer** utilizes a laser beam to produce an image on a drum, which is rolled through a reservoir of toner and transferred to the paper through a combination of heat and pressure. Laser printers are faster and produce a higher quality output than ink-jets, but they are also more expensive. Ink-jet and laser printers are combined with other hardware devices, such as a copier and scanner, into a multi-function device. A **multi-function device** provides common device functionality at a lower cost than purchasing each device separately. Printers are classified by two main characteristics: resolution and speed. Printer resolution refers to the sharpness and clarity of a printed page. For printers, the resolution indicates the number of dots per inch (dpi). For example, a 300-dpi printer is one that is capable of printing 300 distinct dots in a line one-inch long, or 90,000 dots per square inch. The higher the dpi, the sharper the print quality. Printer speed is measured in pages per minute (ppm). The speed of printers varies widely. In general, ink-jet printers range from about 4 to 10 ppm, while laser printers range from about 10 to 30 ppm. The speed depends on the amount of printer memory (the more the better) and the page's contents: if there is just text or the page has only one color, the ppm is in the high range, but when a page contains graphics and/or has multiple colors, the ppm rate falls to the low range.

Ink-jet printer

Laser printer

Multi-function device

Viewing Printers

After you install a printer, the printer appears in the Devices and Printers window (**New!**)—a centralized place to check and manage all devices connected to your computer—and in a program's Print dialog box, where you can view and change printer properties and personal preferences. Every installed printer on your computer is represented by an icon in the Devices and Printers window. When you select a printer icon, status information for that printer appears in the Details pane, such as number of documents to be printed, and whether the printer is ready to print. A printer icon appears in the window without a cable indicates a **local printer**, while a printer icon with a cable (not all instances) indicates a **network printer**. A local printer is a printer connected directly to your computer, and a network printer is one connected to a network to which you have access. A printer icon that appears with two heads indicates that other network users share the printer directly connected to your computer, known as a **shared printer**.

View Printer Properties

1. Click the **Start** button, and then click **Devices and Printers**.

2. Click a printer icon.

3. Click the **Close** button.

Printer status   Local printer

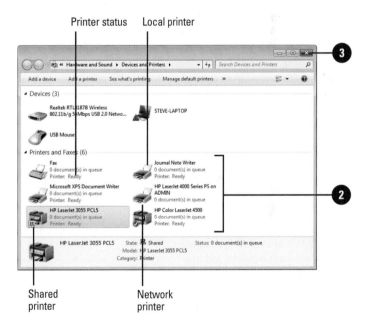

Shared printer

Network printer

Installing a Printer

To install a printer, you do not need to shut down your computer. Simply attach the printer cable to the appropriate connector on your computer, according to the manufacturer's instructions, and plug in the power cord. If you connect your printer to your computer through a USB port, Windows detects the new hardware device and installs the printer, and you are ready to print. Otherwise, you can use the Add a printer wizard in conjunction with the Found New Hardware wizard to detect and install the printer. The Add a printer wizard asks you a series of questions to help you install either a local or network printer, establish a connection, and print a test page.

Set Up a Local Printer Using the Add Printer Wizard

① Click the **Start** button, and then click **Devices and Printers**.

② Click the **Add a printer** button on the toolbar.

③ Click **Add a local printer**.

④ Select the **Use an existing port** or **Create a new port** option, and then click **Next** to continue.

⑤ Select the printer manufacturer and model, and then click **Next** to continue.

⑥ Type a printer name, and then click **Next** to continue.

⑦ Click the **Do not share this printer** or **Share this printer so that others on your network can find and use it** option, and then click **Next** to continue.

⑧ Select or clear the **Set as the default printer** check box.

⑨ To test the printer, click **Print a test page**.

⑩ Click **Finish**.

Set Up a Network Printer Using the Add Printer Wizard

1. Click the **Start** button, and then click **Devices and Printers**.

2. Click the **Add a printer** button on the toolbar.

3. Click **Add a network, wireless or Bluetooth printer**.

4. Select the printer you want to install, and then click **Next** to continue.

5. If necessary, click **Install driver** to install the printer driver.

6. If available, type a name for the printer, and then click **Next** to continue.

7. Select or clear the **Set as the default printer** check box.

8. To test the printer, click **Print a test page**.

9. Click **Finish**.

Did You Know?

You can display printer and communication ports. Click the Start button, click Devices and Printers, click the File menu, click Server Properties, and then click the Ports tab. The available ports don't have a printer name associated with it.

For Your Information

Understanding USB Ports

A **port** is the location on the back of your computer where you connect the printer cable. You can connect the cable to either a printer port, which is labeled LPT1 or LPT2, to a communications port, which is labeled COM1 or COM2, or to a Universal Serial Bus port, which is labeled USB. A printer port is called a **parallel port**, which sends more than one byte simultaneously. A communications port is called a **serial port**, which sends information one byte at a time. The USB port is a new technology that is expected to replace parallel and serial ports. A **USB (Universal Serial Bus) port** is an external hardware interface on the computer that allows you to connect a USB device. A single USB port can be used to connect up to 127 peripheral devices, such as mice, modems, and keyboards, and supports data transfer rates of 480 Mbs (480 million bits per second). USB also supports plug and play installation and **hot plugging**, which is the ability to add and remove devices to a computer while the computer is running and have the operating system automatically recognize the change.

Specifying a Default Printer

If your computer is connected to more than one printer, you can choose the default printer. The default printer is typically the printer that you use most often. However, if you use different default printers based on your location, you can set them and let Windows 7 use location-aware printing (**New!**) to automatically select the right one, which is great for laptops. When you start a print job without specifying a printer, the job is sent to the default printer. You can select a default printer in the Devices and Printers window or when you set up a new printer. The default printer displays a green circle with a check mark in the printer icon.

Select a Default Printer

① Click the **Start** button, and then click **Devices and Printers**.

② Right-click the printer icon you want to set as the default, and then click **Set as default printer**.

③ Click the **Close** button.

Current default printer

Manage Default Printers

① Click the **Start** button, and then click **Devices and Printers**.

② Click the **Manage default printers** button on the toolbar.

③ Click the **Always use the same printer as my default printer** or **Change my default printer when I change networks** option.

④ Select a network, select a printer, and then click **Add**.

⑤ To change a printer, select and change it, and then click **Update**.

⑥ To remove a printer, select it, and then click **Remove**.

⑦ Click **OK**.

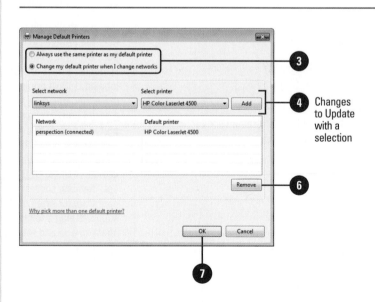

Changes to Update with a selection

Renaming or Deleting a Printer

If you have trouble identifying a printer, or if you just want to change the name, you can rename it. You rename the same way you rename a file or folder. When you rename a printer, the new name appears in the Print dialog box for all your programs. If you no longer use a printer, you can delete it. When you delete the default printer, Windows displays a warning and changes the default printer to another available printer.

Rename a Printer

1. Click the **Start** button, and then click **Devices and Printers**.

2. Right-click the printer icon you want to rename, and then click **Printer properties**.

3. Type a new name for the printer on the General tab.

4. Click **OK**.

Delete a Printer

1. Click the **Start** button, and then click **Devices and Printers**.

2. Right-click the printer icon you want to delete, and then click **Remove device**.

   TIMESAVER *You can also press the Delete key, or click the Remove Device button on the toolbar (click >> to access).*

3. Click **Yes** to confirm the deletion.

4. Click the **Close** button.

Sharing a Printer

If you have a printer connected to your computer and your computer is connected to a network, you can share your printer with other network users. Before you can share a printer, you need to turn on printer sharing in the Network and Sharing Center window, which you can accomplish by using the Sharing tab in the Printer Properties dialog box. After you share a printer, the printer icon appears with two heads in the Devices and Printers window. For security purposes, if Windows Firewall is enabled (the default setting) on the computer with the shared computer, then you need to select the File and Printer Sharing check box on the Exceptions tab in Windows Firewall for others to use the shared printer.

Share a Printer

1. Click the **Start** button, and then click **Devices and Printers**.

2. Right-click the printer you want to share, and then click **Printer properties**.

   TROUBLE? *If sharing options are not available, click the Change Sharing Options button, and then follow the instructions to turn on print sharing.*

3. Click the **Sharing** tab.

4. Select the **Share this printer** check box.

5. Type a name for the printer (eight characters recommended), or use the suggested one.

6. If other computers on the network are using different versions of Windows, click **Additional Drivers** to install other drivers for other computers, select the check boxes for the operating systems you want, and then click **OK**.

7. If prompted, insert the Windows 7 DVD into your drive or provide a driver location, and then click **OK**.

8. Click **OK**.

9. Click the **Close** button.

Printing Documents

If you have a group of documents that you want to print, you can print them all directly from a folder window without having to open each one in its program. The program needs to be installed on your computer to complete the job.

Print Documents Using the Default Printer

① Open the folder that contains the documents you want to print.

② Select the documents.

③ Click the **Print** button on the toolbar.

④ If prompted, select the options you want, and then click **Print**.

Options vary depending on the type of documents you select.

Managing Printers and Print Jobs

After you send a print job to the printer from the Print dialog box in a program, or drag files to the Printer icon in the Devices and Printers window, you can check the status. To check the status of a printer or manage multiple print jobs, you can double-click the appropriate printer icon in the Devices and Printers window or on the taskbar in the notification area. A window opens showing the **print queue**, which is the list of files to be printed. You can use this window to cancel print jobs, temporarily pause print jobs, view printer properties, and so on. If you are having problems with a printer or print job, you can **defer**, or halt, the printing process to avoid getting error messages. With deferred printing, you can send a job to be printed even if your computer is not connected to a printer. To do this, you pause printing, and the file waits in the print queue until you turn off pause printing.

Pause and Resume Printing

1 Click the **Start** button, and then click **Devices and Printers**.

2 Double-click the printer icon.

3 If a printer window opens, click the **Printer** link at the top.

4 Click the **Printer** menu, and then click **Pause Printing**.

5 To resume printing, click the **Printer** menu, and then click **Resume Printing**.

6 Click the **Close** button.

Pause a Print Job

1️⃣ Click the **Start** button, and then click **Devices and Printers**.

2️⃣ Double-click the printer icon.

3️⃣ If a printer window opens, click the **Printer** link at the top.

4️⃣ Right-click the document you want to pause, and then click **Pause**.

5️⃣ To resume the document printing, right-click the document you want to resume, and then click **Restart**.

6️⃣ Click the **Close** button.

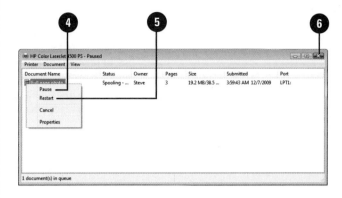

Cancel a Print Job

1️⃣ Click the **Start** button, and then click **Devices and Printers**.

2️⃣ Double-click the printer icon.

3️⃣ If a printer window opens, click the **Printer** link at the top.

4️⃣ Right-click the document you want to stop, and then click **Cancel**.

5️⃣ To cancel all documents, click the **Printer** menu, click **Cancel All Documents**, and then click Yes to confirm the cancelation.

6️⃣ Click the **Close** button.

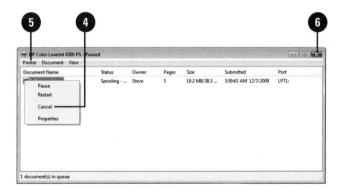

Security Alert

Displaying Printer Notification

For security purposes, if Windows Firewall is turned on (the default setting), printer notification information, such as "Ready" or "Paused," in the Devices and Printers folder is slightly delayed and your computer no longer receives other printer notifications, such as "Print job completed" or "Printer out of paper".

Changing Printer Properties

Viewing printer properties gives you information about a printer's computer connection or network location, sharing options, related software drivers, color management options, graphics settings, installed fonts, and other advanced settings, such as **spooling**. Spooling, also known as **background printing**, is the process of storing a temporary copy of a file on the hard disk and then sending the file to the print device. Spooling allows you to continue working with the file as soon as it is stored on the disk instead of having to wait until the file is finished printing.

Change Printer Device and Spooling Properties

1. Click the **Start** button, and then click **Devices and Printers**.

2. Right-click the printer icon you want to change, and then click **Printer properties**.

3. Click the **Device Settings** tab.

4. Click the plus sign (+) to expand the options you want to change.

5. Click an option link.

6. Click an option list arrow, and then select a setting.

7. Click the **Advanced** tab.

8. Click the **Spool print documents so program finishes printing faster** option.

9. Click a spooling option to specify when you want the printer to start printing your documents.

10. To keep documents in the spooler after they are printed, select the **Keep printed documents** check box.

11. To print documents that have completed spooling before other documents, select the **Print spooled documents first** check box.

12. Click **OK**.

Changing Printer Preferences

In addition to printer properties, you can also view and change personal printer preferences, such as orientation, page order, pages per sheet, paper size, paper tray selection, copy count, and print quality and color. When you change personal printing preferences from the Devices and Printers folder, the default settings are changed for all documents you print to that printer. When you change personal preferences from the Print or Page Setup dialog boxes within a program, the settings are changed for individual documents. The available printing preferences depend on the printer.

Change Printer Preferences

1. Click the **Start** button, and then click **Devices and Printers**.

2. Right-click the the the printer icon you want to change, and then click **Printing preferences**.

3. Click the tab with the option you want to change; tabs and options vary depending on the printer.

4. Change the printer preferences you want to modify.

5. Click **OK**.

6. Click the **Close** button.

Creating an XPS Document

Have you ever used Adobe Reader to view a document or created a PDF document? Well, now you can do the same type of thing with Microsoft's XPS (XML Paper Specification). With XPS, you can share files with others who don't have the same software. In addition, you can set permissions and add digital signatures to protect the document from unauthorized viewing and printing. You create an XPS document by printing it with the Microsoft XPS Document Writer printer (**New!**). The XPS Viewer—available in Windows 7—allows you to open any XPS document (**New!**). When you open a XPS document, it looks the same on the destination as it would on the source computer.

Create and View an XPS Document

1. Open the program and document you want to create as an XPS document.

2. Click the **File** menu, and then click **Print**.

3. Select **Microsoft XPS Document Writer** as your printer.

4. Click **Print**.

5. Specify a location, name the XPS document, and then click **Save**.

6. Click the **Start** button, point to **All Programs**, and then click **XPS Viewer**.

7. Click the **File** button, and then click **Open**.

8. Navigate to and select the XPS document you want to view, and then click **Open**.

9. Use the buttons on the toolbar to set and remove security permissions, add digital signatures (a electronic stamp like a written signature), print the document, and change the view percentage.

10. When you're done, click the **Close** button.

Understanding Faxes

Windows Fax and Scan is a program that allows you to send and receive faxes, fax or e-mail scanned documents, and forward faxes as e-mail attachments from your computer. From Windows Fax and Scan, you can monitor the progress of incoming and outgoing fax activity.

Before you can use Windows Fax and Scan, you need a fax device for sending and receiving faxes. The fax device can be directly attached to your computer, known as a **local fax**, or located on a network, known as a **fax server**. Windows Fax and Scan makes it easy to setup a fax device with the Fax Setup wizard. You can only connect to one local fax, however you can connect to multiple fax servers or devices on a network. To start the Fax Setup wizard and set up a fax, start Windows Fax and Scan, click Fax in the left pane, click the Tools menu, click Fax Accounts, and then click Add. In the wizard, click Connect To A Fax server On My Network, and then follow the on-screen instructions.

Once your fax is installed, you can use Windows Fax and Scan to send and receive faxes, manage incoming and outgoing faxes, and change fax device properties. You can also send faxes from a folder window or the Print dialog box in a program. When you print using a fax printer, Windows Fax and Scan starts and opens the New Fax window, where you can send a fax just like you send an e-mail message.

With the Fax Cover Page Editor, you can create and edit cover pages to use when you send a fax. The Fax Cover Page Editor is a full page editor that makes it easy to insert common fax page items, such as recipient, subject, number of pages, and message, and to format the page to create a professional look. You can also customize a few samples that come with the program.

Setting Up a Fax

If your computer has a fax modem installed, you can send and receive faxes through your computer. If you are not sure, you can use the Devices and Printers window to check if you have one installed. Using Windows Fax and Scan, you can send and receive faxes, fax or e-mail scanned documents, and forward faxes as e-mail attachments from your computer. The Fax Setup wizard helps you set up the Fax Service using a modem or a fax server. Afterwards, you can enter some personal information for the fax cover page, a phone number, and some options for the way you want to send and receive faxes.

Install a Modem

1 If necessary, attach an analog phone line to your computer, and then turn the fax on. You can't use a digital phone line to send or receive faxes.

If your computer has a built-in modem, Windows automatically detects and sets it up.

2 Click the **Start** button, and then click **Devices and Printers**.

3 Click the **Add a device** button on the toolbar.

4 Select the discovered modem device.

5 Click **Next** to continue.

6 Follow the Add a device wizard instructions to complete the installation.

Set Up for Faxing

1 Click the **Start** button, point to **All Programs**, and then click **Windows Fax and Scan**.

◆ You can also double-click the Fax icon in the Devices and Printers window to open Windows Fax and Scan.

2 In the left pane, click **Fax**.

If you're connecting to a fax device for the first time, the New Fax button starts the Fax Setup wizard.

3 Click the **New Fax** button on the toolbar.

If the wizard doesn't start, click the **Tools** menu, click **Fax Accounts**, and then click **Add**.

4 Click **Connect to a fax modem** or **Connect to a fax server on my network**.

5 Follow the wizard instructions to complete the set up; options vary depending on the fax modem you set up.

Upon completion, the New Fax window opens.

6 Click the **Close** button on the New Fax window.

7 Click the **Tools** menu, and then click **Sender Information**.

8 Enter the information you want cover pages to display.

9 Click **OK**.

Creating a Fax Cover Page

A cover page is typically a one page cover memo sent along with a fax containing the fax sender, a recipient, number of pages, a short message, and the transmission date and time. You can use the Fax Cover Page Editor to create your own cover pages or to customize cover page templates, known as common cover pages, that come with the program. You can copy and modify common cover pages without affecting the original templates. You can also edit existing cover pages and rename or delete personal cover pages as needed.

Create a Cover Page from Scratch

1. Click the **Start** button, point to **All Programs**, click **Windows Fax and Scan**, and then click the **Fax** tab.

2. Click the **Tools** menu, click **Cover Pages**, and then click **New**.

3. Click the **View** menu, and then click **Grid Lines**.

4. Click the **Insert** menu, point to **Recipient**, **Sender**, or **Message**, and then click an item.

5. Press and hold Ctrl, and then click the items you want to select.

6. Drag the items to a new location, or use the alignment buttons on the toolbar.

7. Use the formatting buttons on the toolbar to format the text.

8. Use the drawing tools on the toolbar to add shapes and lines.

9. Click the **File** menu, and then click **Save As**.

10. Type a name for the cover page.

11. Click **Save**.

12. Click the **Close** button on the Fax Cover Page Editor.

13. Click **Close**.

Copy a Cover Page Template

1. Click the **Start** button, point to **All Programs**, click **Windows Fax and Scan**, and then click the **Fax** tab.

2. Click the **Tools** menu, and then click **Cover Pages**.

3. Click **Copy**.

4. Select a common fax cover page.

5. Click **Open**.

6. Click **Close**.

Rename or Delete a Cover Page

1. Click the **Start** button, point to **All Programs**, click **Windows Fax and Scan**, and then click the **Fax** tab.

2. Click the **Tools** menu, and then click **Cover Pages**.

3. Click a cover page.

4. To rename the cover page, click **Rename**, type a new name (include the extension .cov), and then press Enter.

5. To delete the cover page, click **Delete**, and then click Yes to confirm it.

6. Click **Close**.

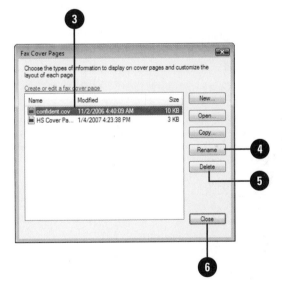

Sending a Fax

After you install and configure your fax, you can send a fax using the New Fax window. You can send a cover page fax from the Printer window or from within Windows Fax and Scan, or a document fax from a program. When you send a fax, the New Fax window opens to help you create and send a fax. When you send a document fax, the program in which you open or create the document prints it to the fax device. When you print to a fax device, Windows Fax and Scan starts and opens the New Fax window where you can send the fax.

Send a Fax

① Click the **Start** button, point to **All Programs**, and then click **Windows Fax and Scan**.

② Click the **Fax** tab.

③ Click the **New Fax** button.

④ Click the **Cover Page** list arrow, and then select a cover page.

⑤ Click the **To** button, select the recipients you want, click the **To** button, and then click **OK**.

⑥ Type a subject.

⑦ Click the **Dialing rule** list arrow, and then select a rule.

⑧ Type the message you want.

⑨ Click the **Send** button on the toolbar.

Send a Fax from a Document

1. Start the program and open or create the document you want to send as a fax.

2. Click the **File** menu, and then click **Print**.

   ◆ For a Microsoft Office 2007 program, click the **Office** button, point to **Print**, and then click **Print**.

3. Click the Fax printer as your printer.

4. Click **Print** or **OK**.

   Windows Fax and Scan opens and starts a new fax.

5. Click the **Cover Page** list arrow, and then select a cover page.

6. Click the **To** button, select a recipients you want, click the **To** button, and then click **OK**.

7. Type a subject, and any cover page notes you want.

8. Click the **Dialing rule** list arrow, and then select a rule.

9. Type the message you want.

10. Click the **Send** button on the toolbar.

Did You Know?

You can scan and fax a document.
Scan the document using a scanner, open the scanned document in a program, and then print it to the fax directly from the program.

Managing Outgoing Faxes

After you send a fax, it's sent to the Outbox folder of the Fax Console. The Outbox is a storage area for all faxes waiting to be sent, or in the process of being sent. From the Outbox, you can pause and resume faxes, restart failed faxes, and remove individual faxes as necessary. If a fax is being sent to multiple recipients, the fax for each recipient appears separately, so you can pause or delete a fax to one of the multiple recipients without affecting the others. When you change the status of a fax in the Outbox, the Status column changes to indicate the new state of the fax. Once a fax is sent successfully, it is moved to the Sent Items folder.

Cancel or Restart an Outgoing Fax

① Click the **Start** button, point to **All Programs**, and then click **Windows Fax and Scan**.

② Click the **Fax** tab.

③ Click the **Outbox** icon.

④ To cancel a fax, click the fax, and then click the **Delete** button.

⑤ To restart a failed fax, click the fax, click the **Document** menu, and then click **Restart**.

⑥ When you're done, click the **Close** button.

Did You Know?

You can't remove a fax from a remote fax printer without deleting the fax printer. Click the remote fax printer from the Printer window, and then click the Delete This Printer button on the toolbar.

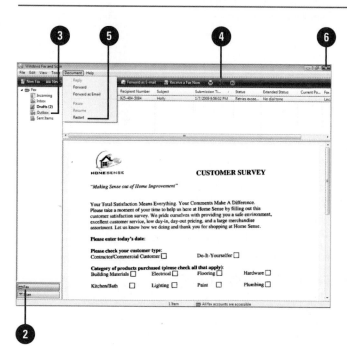

Pause or Resume an Outgoing Fax

1. Click the **Start** button, point to **All Programs**, and then click **Windows Fax and Scan**.

2. Click the **Fax** tab.

3. Click the **Outbox** icon.

4. To pause a fax, click the fax, click the **Document** menu, and then click **Pause**.

5. To resume a fax, click the paused fax, click the **Document** menu, and then click **Resume**.

6. When you're done, click the **Close** button.

View a Sent Fax

1. Click the **Start** button, point to **All Programs**, and then click **Windows Fax and Scan**.

2. Click the **Fax** tab.

3. Click the **Sent Items** icon.

4. Click the fax you want to view.

5. Review the fax information.

6. When you're done, click the **Close** button.

Receiving a Fax

If you have a phone line attached to your computer, you can set up Windows Fax and Scan to receive faxes automatically or manually. If the phone line is a dedicated fax line and set to receive faxes automatically, Windows Fax and Scan automatically stores the fax in your Inbox, just like an e-mail in your e-mail program. If the phone line is used for voice and fax calls, Windows Fax and Scan waits for you to answer the call before it receives the fax.

Receive a Fax Manually

1. When you receive a call for a fax, click to receive the call to open the Fax Status Monitor dialog box.

2. Click **Answer call**, if necessary.

3. Click **View details** to see details about the call.

4. If there are problems with the fax or if you don't want to receive it, click **Disconnect**.

Change Receive Answer Mode

1. Click the **Start** button, point to **All Programs**, click **Windows Fax and Scan**, and then click the **Fax** tab.

2. Click the **Tools** menu, and then click **Fax Settings**.

3. Click the **General** tab.

4. Select the **Allow the device to receive fax calls** check box.

5. Click the **Manually answer** or **Automatically answer after X rings** option.

6. Click the **Tracking** tab, and then select the **Received** check box.

7. Click **OK**.

Reviewing a Fax

After you receive a fax, you can use Fax Console to view, print, save, or e-mail the fax. Windows Fax and Scan informs you when a fax arrived, who sent it, how many pages were received, and the status of the job.

Review a Received Fax

1. Click the **Start** button, point to **All Programs**, click **Windows Fax and Scan**, and then click the **Fax** tab.

2. To review the status of a fax being received, click the **Incoming** icon.

3. Click the **Inbox** icon.

4. Click the fax you want to view.

5. Use the buttons on the toolbar to do the following:

   ◆ **Reply to the fax as another fax.**

   ◆ **Forward the fax as another fax.**

   ◆ **E-mail the fax as an attachment to a message.**

   ◆ **Print the fax to your printer.**

   ◆ **Delete the fax.**

6. To save the fax as a TIF file, click the **File** menu, click **Save As**, specify a name and location, and then click **Save**.

7. When you're done, click the **Close** button.

Did You Know?

You can sort faxes by a variety of different categories. In Windows Fax and Scan, click the View menu, point to Arrange By, and then select the way you want to sort. You can arrange by Fax Account, Caller ID, Subject, and Number of Pages to name a few.

Changing Fax Properties

You can change the send and receive properties for a fax device to effectively work with your phone line. You can change the number of times the the fax device tries to resend a fax. You can also change where to store a fax when you receive it. If you need to specify the use of a Transmitting Station Identifier (TSID), which is an identification sent along with a fax to identify the source, and a Called Subscriber Identifier (CSID), which is an identification sent back to the sending fax device to confirm the identity of the source, you can specify those settings as well.

Change Send Properties

1 Click the **Start** button, point to **All Programs**, click **Windows Fax and Scan**, and then click the **Fax** tab.

2 Click the **Tools** menu, and then click **Fax Settings**.

3 Click the **General** tab.

4 Select the **Allow the device to send faxes** check box.

5 To change TSID or CSID, click **More options**, type the information, and then click **OK**.

6 Click the **Advanced** tab.

7 Type the number of redialing attempts.

8 Type the number of minutes to dial again for a redial.

9 To send faxes at a specific time when discount phone charges apply, specify a start and end time.

10 Click **OK**.

Change Receive Properties

1 Click the **Start** button, point to **All Programs**, click **Windows Fax and Scan**, and then click the **Fax** tab.

2 Click the **Tools** menu, and then click **Fax Settings**.

3 Click the **General** tab.

4 Select the **Allow the device to receive fax calls** check box.

5 Click the **Manually answer** or **Automatically answer after X rings** option.

6 Click **More options**.

7 If you want, select the **Print a copy to** check box, and then select a printer.

8 If you want, select the **Save a Copy to** check box, and then select a folder.

9 Click **OK**.

10 Click **OK**.

Changing Fax Options

As you send and receive faxes, you can have fax track and notify you when events take place. For example, you can show a progress indicator when faxes are incoming or outgoing and display notifications when faxes arrive. You can also set fax options to automatically open the Fax Monitor when a fax is being sent or received and archive faxes for backup purposes.

Change Tracking Options

1. Click the **Start** button, point to **All Programs**, click **Windows Fax and Scan**, and then click the **Fax** tab.

2. Click the **Tools** menu, and then click **Fax Settings**.

3. Click the **Tracking** tab.

4. Select the check boxes in the Notifications you want.

5. Select the check boxes for the Fax Monitor you want.

6. Click **OK**.

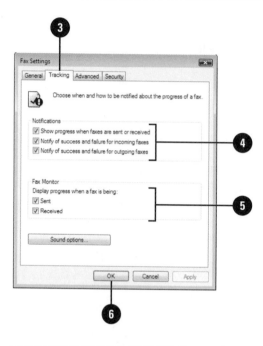

Change Archive Options

1. Click the **Start** button, point to **All Programs**, click **Windows Fax and Scan**, and then click the **Fax** tab.

2. Click the **Tools** menu, and then click **Fax Settings**.

3. Click the **Advanced** tab.

4. Click **Move Folder**, select a folder, and then click **OK**.

5. Click **OK**.

Maintaining Your Computer

Introduction

Windows 7 offers a number of useful tools for managing and maintaining routine tasks on your computer, such as installing and removing programs, and formatting, copying, and repairing disks. Windows also provides tools to find and fix disk problems, speed up disk access, and clean up disk space. By periodically finding and repairing disk errors, you can keep your files in good working condition and prevent disk problems that might cause you to lose your work. You can also schedule these tasks to run on a regular basis. If you find Windows performing sluggishly even after performing routine maintenance, you can adjust system processing and memory settings to improve performance.

Keeping your computer up-to-date is another way to keep your computer in good working condition and protect it against new and ongoing attacks over the Internet. Windows Update scans your computer for any software components or fixes (including security and high priority updates) that need to be installed and automatically or manually downloads them from the Internet. Each file that you download using Windows Update has a digital signature from Microsoft to ensure it's authenticity and security. If problems do occur, you can undo harmful changes to your computer and restore its settings, or you can use one of several startup options to help you start Windows in a safe environment with basic files and drivers where you can restore settings and fix the problems.

What You'll Do

Understand Disk File Systems

Format a Disk

Display Disk and Folder Information

Transfer Files Using a Disk

Set Disk Quota for Users

Detect and Repair Disk Errors

Optimize and Clean Up a Disk

Schedule Tasks

Add or Remove Windows Components

Install or Uninstall a Program

Update Windows

Improve Computer Performance

Boost Speed with Removable Media

Restore Computer Settings

Use Previous Versions

Start Windows When Problems Occur

Set Startup and Recovery Options

Understanding Disk File Systems

A disk must be formatted with a **file system** that allows it to work with the operating system to store, manage, and access data. Two of the most common file systems are FAT (or FAT32, which is an improvement on FAT technology) and NTFS. Disks on DOS, Windows 3.1, or Windows 98/Me computers use the FAT file system, while disks on computers running Windows NT 4.0, Windows 2000, Windows XP and later can use either the NTFS or FAT system. NTFS is a newer file system that improves on some of the shortcomings of FAT disks that make them less desirable on a network. NTFS is the preferred file system for Windows 7.

There are important differences between FAT and NTFS file systems:

FAT

When you format a disk with the FAT file system, a formatting program divides the disk into storage compartments. First it creates a series of rings, called **tracks**, around the circumference of the disk. Then it divides the tracks into equal parts, like pieces of a pie, to form sectors. The number of sectors and tracks depends on the size of the disk.

Although the physical surface of a disk is made of tracks and sectors, a file is stored in clusters. A cluster, also called an **allocation unit**, is one or more sectors of storage space. It represents the minimum amount of space that an operating system reserves when saving the contents of a file to a disk. Thus, a file might be stored in more than one cluster. Each cluster is identified by a unique number. The first two clusters are reserved by the operating system. The operating system maintains a file allocation table (or FAT) on each disk that lists the clusters on the disk and records the status of each cluster, whether it

is occupied (and by which file), available, or defective. Each cluster in a file "remembers" its order in the chain of clusters—and each cluster points to the next one until the last cluster, which marks the end of the file. The FAT and FAT32 formats provide compatibility with other operating systems on your computer, which means you can configure your computer for a dual-boot or multi-boot setup and you can backup a previous operating system.

exFAT

The exFAT file system is the next generation file system in the FAT (FAT12/16, FAT32) family. While retaining the simplicity advantages of FAT32, exFAT overcomes FAT32's 4 GB file size limit and scales up past FAT32's 32 GB formatter limit. This means you can copy files greater than 4 GB in size to an exFAT file system and format removable storage (Flash or hard disk) greater than 32 GB in capacity. In addition, exFAT is designed to enable cross operating system and cross-device (such as cameras and phones) interoperation, which will be possible as manufacturers build support for exFAT into their devices.

NTFS

NTFS features a built-in security system that does not allow users to access the disk unless they have a user account and password with the necessary rights and permissions. NTFS protects disks from damage by automatically redirecting data from a bad sector to a good sector without requiring you to run a disk-checking utility. Given the reliability and the built-in repair mechanisms of NTFS disks, only rarely do they require maintenance. This is an example of **fault tolerance**, the ability of a disk to resist damage, which is a critical issue with disks on a network computer.

Selecting a file system

NTFS supports removable Flash media, but not floppy disks, so they are formatted with a FAT. If you are running Windows on a stand-alone computer, you can choose either a FAT or NTFS, but in most cases, the file system has already been determined either by the person who originally set up the computer or by the manufacturer from whom you purchased the computer. If your computer is a client on a Windows network, it is likely that your hard disk uses NTFS. Because NTFS is more suited to network demands, such as a high level of security and resistance to system failure, network administrators format network disks with NTFS whenever possible. Sometimes, however, users on a network want or need to use a non-Windows operating system. Also, a user might need a computer that is capable of running Windows XP. The disks on that computer would then be formatted with a FAT.

NTFS disk drive

FAT32 disk drive

Formatting a Disk

Formatting a disk—including hard disks, USB flash drives and flash memory cards—prepares it so that you can store information on it. Formatting removes all information from the disk, so you should never format a disk that has files you want to keep. When you format a disk, you need to specify the certain settings; Windows has default settings recommended. Capacity is how much data the disk or partition can hold, such as the physical size, storage size, and sector size. A file system is the overall structure in which files are named, stored, and organized. NTFS, FAT, FAT32, and exFAT are types of file systems. Disk allocation unit size, or cluster size, is a group of sectors on a disk. The operating system assigns a unique number to each cluster, and then keeps track of files according to which clusters they use. If your hard disk uses a FAT file system, you can convert it to the NTFS format.

Format a Disk

1. With a disk in the drive, click the **Start** button, and then click **Computer**.

2. Right-click the drive, and then click **Format**.

3. Specify the Capacity, File system (**NTFS**, **FAT (Default)**, **FAT32** or **exFAT**), and Allocation unit size.

4. Select the **Quick Format** check box to perform a quick format, or clear the **Quick Format** check box to perform a full format and disk scan for bad sectors.

5. To use a disk to start up your computer and run MS-DOS, select the **Create an MS-DOS startup disk** check box.

6. Click **Start**, click **OK** to format the disk, and then click **OK** when it's done.

7. Click **Close**.

Convert a Disk

1 Click the **Start** button, point to **All Programs**, click **Accessories**, and then click **Command Prompt**.

2 Type **convert** *drive* : **/fs:ntfs /v**, and then press Enter.

Where *drive* is the drive letter of the drive you wanted converted to NTFS.

3 If you upgraded your computer, type **Y**, and then press Enter to delete the backup, or type **N**, and then press Enter to cancel the procedure.

4 If you're asked to force a dismount, type **N**, and then press Enter.

5 If you need to restart the system to complete the conversion, type **Y**, and then press Enter.

6 Click the **Close** button.

7 Click the **Start** button, point to the Arrow, click **Shut Down**, and then wait for the computer to restart and convert the drive.

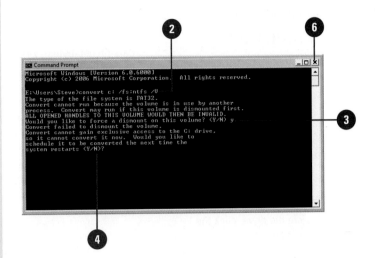

Did You Know?

You can check the format of a disk. Click the Start button, click Computer, click the disk you want to check, and then check the Details pane.

See Also

See "Detecting and Repairing Disk Errors" on page 433 for information on bad sectors.

Displaying Disk and Folder Information

As you work with files, folders, and programs, you should know the size of the disk and how much space remains available. A disk can store only a limited amount of data. Hard disks can store large amounts of data (in gigabytes), while removable disks, such as a USB flash drive or flash memory card, store smaller amounts. You can use the Properties command on a disk to display the disk size or the amount of used and free space, and to change a disk label, which is a name you can assign to a hard or removable disk. Besides checking hard disk drive or floppy disk information, you can also use the Properties command on a folder to find out the size of its contents. This can be helpful when you want to copy or move a folder to a removable disk or CD/DVD.

Determine Free Space on a Disk

1. With a disk in the drive, click the **Start** button, and then click **Computer**.

2. Click the drive, and then click the **Properties** button on the toolbar.

3. On the **General** tab, identify the amount of free space on the disk.

4. Click **OK**.

Used and free disk space

For Your Information

Understanding File Sizes

When you create a file, it takes up space on a disk. Files with text are smaller than files with graphics. The size of a file is measured in bytes. A byte is a unit of storage capable of holding a single character or pixel. It's the base measurement for all other incremental units, which are kilobyte, megabyte, and gigabyte. A kilobyte (KB) is 1,024 bytes of information while a megabyte (MB) is 1,048,576 bytes, which is equal to 1,024 kilobytes. A gigabyte (GB) is equal to 1,024 megabytes.

Transferring Files Using a Disk

You can copy files from your computer to a disk if you need to either transfer files from one stand-alone computer to another. You can also save a copy of important files to prevent losing them in the event of a power failure or a computer problem.

Copy Files to a Disk

1 With the disk in the drive, click the **Start** button, and then click **Computer**.

2 Open the folder, and then select the files you want to copy.

3 Right-click the selected files, and then point to **Send To**.

4 Click a disk from the submenu.

Copy Files from a Disk

1 With the disk in the drive, click the **Start** button, and then click **Computer**.

2 Open the disk window, and then select the files you want to copy.

3 Drag the selected files to copy the selected items.

Setting Disk Quotas for Users

If you are using a computer with multiple users, you can set up disk quotas, so a single user cannot fill the entire disk. Disk quotas are not enabled by default, so you need to turn this feature on before you can use it. You can enable and set different disk quotas for individual users. If a user exceeds the quota, you can specify whether to allow or deny disk space. If you're not sure what to set, you can create quota logs to monitor disk usage and then decide what you want to do.

Set Disk Quotas

1 Click the **Start** button, and then click **Computer**.

2 Click the drive, and then click the **Properties** button on the toolbar.

3 Click the **Quota** tab.

4 Click **Show Quota Settings**.

5 Select the **Enable quota management** check box.

6 Select the **Deny disk space to users exceeding quota limit** check box.

7 Click the **Do not limit disk usage** option or click the **Limit disk space to** option and specify the disk space limit.

8 Select either of the log event check boxes to create a record of disk usage.

9 To set specific limits for individual users, click **Quota Entries**.

 ◆ In the Quota Entries window, click the **Quota** menu, click **New Quota Entry**, and then select a user and fill in property information.

10 Click **OK**.

11 Click **OK**.

Detecting and Repairing Disk Errors

Sometimes an unexpected power loss or program error can create inaccessible file segments that take up space on a disk. The Check Disk program that comes with Windows helps you find and repair damaged sections of a disk. Check Disk can also be used to find physical disk errors or **bad sectors**. The program doesn't physically repair your media, but it moves data away from any bad sectors it finds. To keep your hard disk drive working properly, you should run Check Disk from time to time. When you run Check Disk, all files must be closed for the process to run. While the Check Disk process is running, your hard disk will not be available to perform any other task.

Check a Disk for Errors

1. Click the **Start** button, and then click **Computer**.

2. Click the drive, and then click the **Properties** button on the toolbar.

3. Click the **Tools** tab.

4. Click **Check now**.

5. Select the **Automatically fix file system errors** check box, and then select the **Scan for and attempt recovery of bad sectors** check box.

6. Click **Start**.

7. When it's done, click **OK**.

8. Click **OK**.

Did You Know?

You should run Check Disk before the Disk Defragmenter. For best results, run Check Disk to check for errors on your disk before you start the disk defragmentation process.

Optimizing a Disk

When you delete files from a disk, you create empty spaces that might be fragmented over different areas of the disk. When you create a new file on a fragmented disk, parts of the file are stored in these empty spaces, resulting in a single file that is broken into many parts, which takes longer to retrieve or store when you open or save the file. A file broken up in this way is called a **fragmented file**, which is undetectable to the user. You can use Disk Defragmenter to place all of the parts of a file in one **contiguous**, or adjacent, location. This procedure, which efficiently rearranges all of the files and unused space, is called **optimization**. Optimization makes your programs run faster and your files open more quickly. You can select disk volumes, analyze them, and set a schedule to run Disk Defragmenter on a regular basis (**New!**). While the Disk Defragmenter works, you can use your computer to carry out other tasks; however, your computer will operate more slowly.

Schedule and Defragment Disks

1. Click the **Start** button, point to **All Programs**, click **Accessories**, click **System Tools**, and then click **Disk Defragmenter**.

2. Click **Configure schedule**.

3. Select the **Run on a schedule (recommended)** check box.

4. Click the list arrows, and then specify how often, what day, and what time.

5. Click **Select disks**, select the drives you want, and then click **OK**.

6. Click **OK**.

7. To defragment disks now, select the drives you want. Press and hold Ctrl to select more than one drive.

8. To analyze your disks to determine if you need defragmenting, click **Analyze disks**.

9. Click **Defragment disks**.

10. To stop the process, click **Cancel Defragment**.

11. Click **Close**.

Cleaning Up a Disk

Cleaning up a disk involves removing unneeded files to make room for other files on your computer, which can be difficult if you don't know the significance of each file. You can use a Windows program called Disk Cleanup to clean up your hard disk drive safely and effectively. Disk Cleanup searches your drive, then lists temporary files, Internet cache files, the Recycle Bin, system files (**New!**), game related files, and unnecessary program files that you can safely delete. Disk Cleanup also gives you the option to remove Windows components and installed programs that you no longer use. You can select the types of files you want Disk Cleanup to delete. Before you select and delete files, make sure you will not need them in the future. If you have multiple users on your computer, you can specify whether to clean up only your files or all the files on the computer.

Clean Up a Disk

1. Click the **Start** button, point to **All Programs**, click **Accessories**, click **System Tools**, and then click **Disk Cleanup**.

2. If necessary, click the **Drives** list arrow, select a disk, and then click **OK**.

   Wait while Disk Cleanup calculates how much space it can free up.

3. Select the check boxes for the folders and files you want to delete.

4. To clean up only system files, click **Clean up system files**.

   Wait while Disk Cleanup calculates how much space it can free up.

5. To view the contents of a folder, click **View Files**, and then click the **Close** button.

6. To access other options to remove programs and system restore points, click the **More Options** tab.

7. Click **OK**, and then click **Yes**.

Wait while Disk Cleanup calculates disk

Scheduling Tasks

Task Scheduler is a program that enables you to schedule tasks, to run regularly, such as Disk Cleanup, at a time convenient for you. Task Scheduler starts each time you start Windows. With Task Scheduler, you can schedule a task to run daily, weekly, monthly, or at certain times (such as when the computer starts or idles), change the schedule for or turn off an existing task, or customize how a task runs at its scheduled time. You can create a basic task using the Create Basic Task wizard or a more complex task using the Create Task dialog box. Before you schedule a task, be sure that the system date and time on your computer are accurate, as Task Scheduler relies on this information to run.

Scheduled a Basic Task

1 Click the **Start** button, point to **All Programs**, click **Accessories**, click **System Tools**, and then click **Task Scheduler**.

2 In the Actions pane, click **Create Basic Task**.

3 Type a name and description for the scheduled task, and then click **Next** to continue.

4 Click a scheduled task time interval option, and then click **Next** to continue.

5 Specify a start time and a recurring interval, and then click **Next** to continue.

6 Select an action option, and then click **Next** to continue.

7 Specify the information or options related with the selected action, and then click **Next** to continue.

8 Click **Finish**.

9 To run, end, disable, or delete a task, click the **Task Scheduler Library**, select the task in the console window, and then click the command you want at the bottom of the Actions pane. To edit a task, select it, and then make changes at the bottom of the console window.

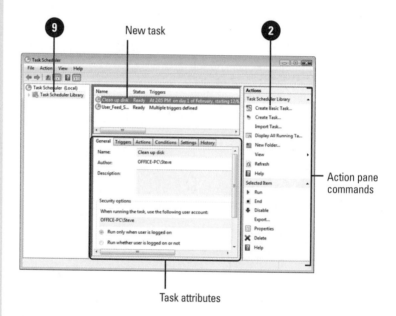

New task

Action pane commands

Task attributes

Summary of task attributes

Adding or Removing Windows Components

Windows 7 comes with a collection of components, such as Internet Explorer, Windows Media Player, Windows DVD Maker, Windows Media Center, or Solitaire, you can use to get work done and have fun on your computer. When you install Windows 7, not all the components on the installation disc are installed on your computer. You can use the the Programs and Features utility in the Control Panel to install additional components. When you install a new program on your computer, the Start menu highlights the menus you need to click to start the program. If you are no longer using a Windows component, you can remove it to save disk space.

Add or Remove a Windows Component

1 Click the **Start** button, and then click **Control Panel.**

2 Click the **Programs and Features** icon in Small icons or Large icons view.

3 In the left pane, click **Turn Windows features on or off**.

4 Click the plus sign (+) to expand a category or click the minus sign (-) to collapse a category.

A blue check box indicates that only some of the items in a component group are installed.

5 Select a check box to add the item, or clear a check box to remove an item.

6 When you're done, click **OK**.

7 If prompted, insert the Windows 7 DVD into the drive.

8 Click **OK** if prompted to restart your computer.

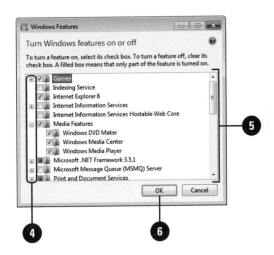

Installing or Uninstalling a Program

Windows comes with a collection of accessory programs with simple functionality. If you need more functionality, software programs are available for purchase. Before you can use a software program, you need to install it using a separate installer program. Most software programs come with their own installation program, which copies the program files to different places on your computer, some in a program folder and others in the Windows folder. When you install a new program on your computer, the Start menu highlights the menus you need to click to start the program. If you no longer use a program or a Windows update, you can remove it from your computer, which saves hard disk space. The Programs and Features utility in the Control Panel provides a faster display and shows you all the programs and/or software updates installed on your computer. Windows keeps track of all the files you install, so you should uninstall a program or system update, instead of deleting folders and files to remove it.

Install a Software Program

1. Close all running programs, and then insert the program installation disc into the drive.

   If the disc starts, the AutoPlay dialog box opens. Start the setup and follow the instructions provided to install the software.

   IMPORTANT *Only users with administrator privileges can add or remove programs.*

2. If the disc doesn't start or you're installing from a network or different drive, click the **Start** button, and then click **Computer**.

3. Double-click the CD or DVD icon with the installation set up.

4. Double-click the set up file, and then follow the installation instructions.

Start of installation

Uninstall, Change, or Repair a Software Program

1 Click the **Start** button, and then click **Control Panel.**

2 Click the **Programs and Features** icon in Small icons or Large icons view.

3 In the left pane, click **View installed updates** or **Uninstall a program** to display the software you want.

4 Click the program you want to uninstall or change.

5 Click the **Uninstall**, **Change**, or **Repair** button on the toolbar; availability varies depending on the program.

6 If prompted, click **Yes** to confirm the removal. If an uninstall program starts, follow the instructions.

7 When it's done, click **OK**, and then click the **Close** button.

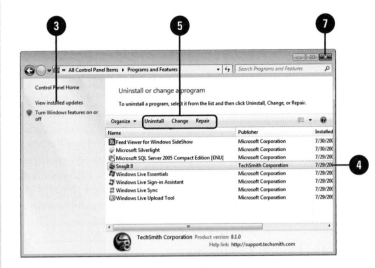

Did You Know?

You can turn the Start menu highlight off. Right-click the Start button, click Properties, click Customize, clear the Highlight Newly Installed Programs check box, and then click OK twice.

See Also

If you encounter a problem after removing a Windows update or component, see "Restoring Computer Settings" on page 444 for information on restoring Windows to a previous state using the System Restore Wizard.

Updating Windows

Microsoft continues to improve Windows 7 with new features or security fixes, known as updates. Windows Update allows you to keep your computer up-to-date with the latest system software and security updates over the Internet. You can choose to have Windows regularly check for critical updates and download them in the background (which doesn't interfere with other downloads), or you can manually select the ones you want to install using the Windows Update web site. Automatic updates occur at scheduled times or by notification acceptance. If you're busy, you can ignore/hide the update to install it later. The Windows Update web site displays express (only high priority) and custom (high priority, software, and hardware) installation update options. High priority updates are critical for your system to run properly, while software and hardware updates are optional. Windows Update confidentially scans your computer for updates that need to be installed.

Update Windows Automatically

1 Click the **Start** button, point to **All Programs**, and then click **Windows Update**.

2 In the left pane, click **Change settings**.

IMPORTANT *If you're part of a network, options are grayed out.*

3 Click the **Important updates** list arrow, and then select an option:

◆ **Install updates automatically (recommended)**, then specify a time.

◆ **Download updates, but let me choose whether to install them.**

◆ **Check for updates but let me choose whether to download and install them.**

◆ **Never check for updates (not recommended).**

4 Click **OK**, and then click the **Close** button.

5 If a Windows Update icon appears in the notification area, click the alert or icon, and then follow any instructions as needed.

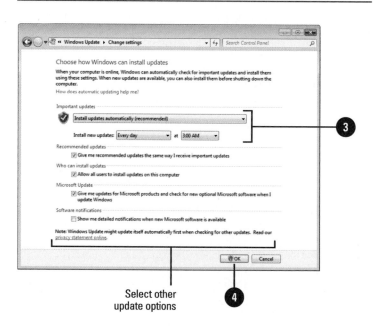

Select other update options

Update Windows Manually

1 Click the **Start** button, point to **All Programs**, and then click **Windows Update**.

2 Click **Check for updates**.

3 If you need to install any important or optional updates, click the link.

4 Select the check boxes next to the items you want to install.

5 Click **OK**.

6 Click **Install updates**.

7 If prompted, restart your computer.

Did You Know?

You can View update history. Click the Start button, point to All Programs, click Windows Update, and then click View Update History in the left pane to view the installed updates. When you're done, click OK, and then click the Close button.

You can install updates when not available or resume after an interruption. If your computer is turned off or in hibernate or sleep mode during a scheduled update, updates are installed the next time you start your computer. If you lose an Internet connection during a download, Windows Update resumes where it left off.

For Your Information

Installing Updates and Shut Down

If you set up your computer to download and receive updates automatically, and the updates are ready to be installed, the Power button on the Start menu changes to a dark red with a shield on it (shown below). When you click this button, Windows installs the updates and then shuts down your computer when installation of the updates is complete.

Improving Computer Performance

The Performance Information and Tools utility in the Control Panel provides a central location for you to determine the performance of your computer, print out a report, and access tools to increase performance. The utility analyzes your computer and provides a rating score for the critical components on your computer, which include processor, memory (RAM), graphics, gaming graphics, and primary hard disk. To help you improve performance, you can access performance related tools in the Tasks pane.

Optimize Computer Performance

1. Click the **Start** button, and then click **Control Panel**.

2. Click the **Performance Information and Tools** icon in Small icons or Large icons view.

3. Click **Re-run the assessment** to the latest information.

4. To view and print details, click **View and print detailed performance and system information**, click **Print this page**, click **Print**, and then click the **Close** button.

5. In the left pane, click links to performance improvement tools:

   ◆ **Adjust visual effects.** Set to Adjust for best performance option.

   ◆ **Adjust indexing options.** Reduce the number of folder to index.

   ◆ **Adjust power settings.** Set to use Balanced power plan.

   ◆ **Open Disk Cleanup.** Delete unnecessary or temporary files.

   ◆ **Advanced tools.** Displays additional tools, including Disk Defragmenter and ReadyBoost.

6. When you're done, click the **Close** button.

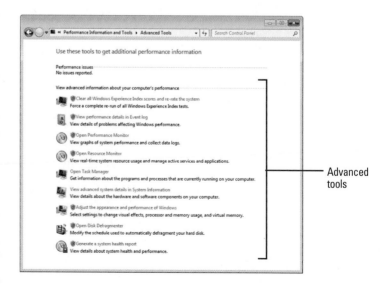

Advanced tools

Boosting Speed with Removable Media

You can use Windows ReadyBoost to speed up your computer by using disk space on certain removable media devices, such as USB flash drives. When you insert a compatible removable media device (one that uses fast flash memory), the AutoPlay dialog box opens and provides the option to use Windows ReadyBoost as a dedicated or non dedicated device (**New!**). Before you can use it, you need to turn it on and specify the amount of space you want to allocate. Windows provides a recommended space amount. In general, ReadyBoost recommends one to three times the amount of random access memory (RAM) installed on your computer for the best performance results.

Use Windows ReadyBoost

1. With removable media in the drive, click the **Start** button, and then click **Computer**.

2. Click the drive, and then click the **Properties** button on the toolbar.

3. Click the **ReadyBoost** tab.

4. Click the **Use this device** or **Dedicate this device to ReadyBoost** (**New!**) option.

5. If you want, drag the slider to specify the space to reserve for system speed.

6. Click **OK**.

7. To use ReadyBoost, remove the device, re-insert it, and then use the AutoPlay dialog box to start it.

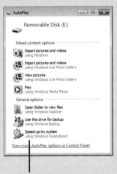

ReadyBoost in AutoPlay

For Your Information

Changing the Size of Virtual Memory

If you are running out of virtual memory (using hard disk space as RAM), you can increase the minimum size of the paging file (**a virtual memory**). The Initial size is set to installed RAM plus 300 MB and the Maximum size is set to 3 times installed RAM. To increase the size, double-click the System icon in the Control Panel, click Advanced System settings in the left pane, click the Advanced tab, click Settings (under Performance), clear the Automatically Manage Paging File Size For All Drives check box, click the drive you want, click Custom size, type a new size in the Initial or Maximum Size, click Set, and then click OK.

Restoring Computer Settings

Windows 7 is a reliable operating system, but any time you make changes to your computer, such as adding or removing software and hardware, you run the risk of causing problems with your operating system. To alleviate potential problems, you can use System Restore, a program installed with Windows 7, to undo harmful changes to your computer and restore its settings. System Restore returns your computer system, but not your personal files, to an earlier time, before the changes were made to your computer, called a **restore point**. As you work with your computer, System Restore monitors your changes and creates restore points on a daily basis or at important system events, but you can also create your own restore point at any time. If you have recently performed a system restoration, you can use System Restore to undo your most recent restoration. System Restore is turned on by default when you install Windows 7, but you can turn it off or change System Restore options for individual drives (**New!**). However, you need at least 300 MB of free space on each hard disk.

Set System Protection

1. Click the **Start** button, click **Computer**, and then click the **System properties** button on the toolbar.

2. In the left pane, click the **System protection**.

3. Select the drive you want to protect.

4. Click **Configure**.

5. Click the system protection option you want:

   ◆ **Restore system settings and previous versions of files.**

   ◆ **Only restore previous versions of files.**

   ◆ **Turn off system protection.**

6. To adjust the maximum disk space used for system protection, drag the slider.

7. To delete all restore points (this includes system settings and previous versions of files), click **Delete**.

8. Click **OK**, click **OK**, and then click the **Close** button.

Restore the System

1 Close all programs and make sure no one else is logged on to the computer.

2 Click the **Start** button, point to **All Programs**, click **Accessories**, click **System Tools**, and then click **System Restore**.

3 Click the **Recommended restore** or **Choose a different restore point** option.

4 Click **Next** to continue.

5 If you are choosing a restore point, select it, and then click **Next** to continue.

6 Review the restore point information, and then click **Finish**.

7 Wait for the system to be restored, and log on when prompted.

8 When it's done, click **OK**, and then click the **Close** button.

Create a Restore Point

1 Click the **Start** button, click **Computer**, and then click the **System properties** button on the toolbar.

2 In the left pane, click the **System Protection**.

3 Click **Create**.

4 Type a restore point name.

5 Click **Create**.

6 When it's done, click **OK**, and then click the **Close** button.

Using Previous Versions

Previous versions are shadow copies of files and folders that you back up using Backup and Restore or Windows automatically saves as part of a restore point. You can use previous versions of files to restore files that become damaged or you accidentally modify or delete. If System Protection is turned on, Windows automatically creates shadow copies of files—except Windows system files—that have been modified since the last restore point was made. You can restore individual files or complete folders. When you restore a file or folder, the current file or folder is replace by the restored one. It's important to realize that you cannot undo a restore.

Restore a File or Folder Using Previous Versions

1. Open the folder with the file or folder you want restore.

2. Right-click it, and then click **Restore previous version**.

3. Click an item in the list.

   IMPORTANT *You cannot undo a file or folder previous version restore.*

4. Click **Restore**.

   If the Restore button is not available, you cannot restore a previous version of the file or folder.

5. Click **OK**.

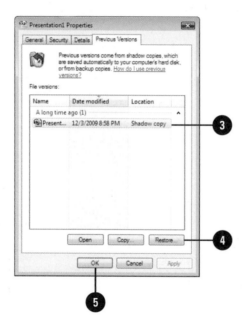

See Also

See "Restoring Computer Settings" on page 444 for information on turning on System Protection.

Starting Windows When Problems Occur

If you have a problem starting Windows, you can use one of several startup options to help you start Windows in a safe environment or use the System Recovery Options menu to restore settings and repair your computer. Safe Mode is a good place to start. If a problem does not occur when you start in Safe Mode, you can eliminate basic Windows files and drivers as possible causes of the problem. If you added a device or changed driver, you can use Safe Mode to remove the device or restore the changed driver. You can also use Choosing Last Known Good Configuration to restore settings saved when your computer was last shut down properly. Lastly, you can use Repair Your Computer.

Start Windows When Problems Occur

1. Restart your computer.

2. As your computer boots, press and hold F8.

3. Use the arrow keys to select a startup or repair option, and then press Enter.

4. If you have a dual-boot system, select the operating system you want, and then press Enter.

5. Restore any recent system changes, or remove any newly installed software that might be causing the problem.

6. Shutdown your computer.

7. Start your computer to see if it works properly.

8. If problems persist, try a different startup option, or seek assistance from a support technician.

Did You Know?

You can use Startup Repair to fix Windows 7 problems. Restart your computer with the Windows installation disc in the drive, click Repair Your Computer, select your system, click Next, click Startup Repair, and then follow the on-screen instructions.

Computer Startup Options

Option	Description
Repair Your Computer	Provides access to the System Recovery Options menu
Safe Mode	Starts with basic files and drivers and without a network connection
Safe Mode With Networking	Starts with basic files and drivers and a network connection
Safe Mode With Command Prompt	Starts with basic files and drivers and without a network connection to the command prompt
Enable Boot Logging	Starts and logs startup information in the *ntbtlog.txt* file
Enable low-resolution video	Starts using the basic VGA driver
Last Known Good Configuration	Starts using Registry settings saved at the last properly done shutdown
Directory Services Restore Mode	Restores active directory services
Debugging Mode	Starts and sends debugging information to another computer using a serial cable
Disable automatic restart on system failure	Prevents automatic reboot after a crash
Disable Driver Signature Enforcement	Allows drivers containing improper signatures to be loaded
Start Windows Normally	Starts the computer normally

Setting Startup and Recovery Options

If you installed more than one operating system on your computer (known as a **dual-boot**), such as Windows XP and Windows Vista/7, you can select the default operating system you want to use when you start up your computer. You can also specify how much time to display the list of operating systems for a dual boot before the default starts. If you have problems starting Windows, you can set options to instruct Windows what to do. You can set options to automatically restart and create a system log of events to track where the problem occurs.

Set Windows Startup and Recovery Options

① Click the **Start** button, and then click **Control Panel**.

② Double-click the **System** icon in Classic view.

③ In the left pane, click **Advanced system settings**.

④ Click **Settings** (under Startup and Recovery).

⑤ Click the **Default operating system** list arrow, and then select the operating system you want to start as default.

⑥ Select the system startup check boxes you want to use and specify the time you want to wait to select the operating system or recovery options.

⑦ Select the system failure check boxes you want to use.

⑧ Click **OK**.

⑨ Click **OK**.

⑩ Click the **Close** button.

Managing Hardware

Introduction

A **hardware device** is any physical device that you plug into and is controlled by your computer. This device can be a network or modem card that you install inside your computer. It can be a printer or a scanner that you plug into the outside of the computer. When you plug or insert a hardware device into the appropriate port or expansion slot, Windows attempts to recognize the device and configure it for you using plug-and-play technology. Plug-and-play automatically tells the device drivers (software that operates the hardware and comes with Windows 7) where to find the hardware device. After a hardware device is installed, you can change settings and options to customize the way the device works. Plug-and-play technology will recognize most any kind of hardware device, such as a mouse, modem, keyboard, game controller, laptop battery, or secondary monitor just to name a few.

All hardware devices can be managed or removed from the Control Panel. Most hardware devices are managed under the Devices and Printers folder or in the Device Manager, but some have their own program for managing them (for example, Mouse or Keyboard are located in the Control Panel).

What You'll Do

Understand Plug and Play Hardware

View Hardware Devices

Install Hardware Devices

View System Hardware Settings

Change Windows Update Driver Settings

Change Mouse Settings

Change Keyboard Settings

Change Phone Dialing Options

Change Modem Options

Manage Color

Add a Secondary Monitor

Remove Hardware Devices

Remove Plug and Play Hardware

Troubleshoot Computer Problems

Understanding Plug and Play Hardware

Windows includes **plug and play** support for hardware, making it easy to install and uninstall devices quickly. With plug and play support, you simply plug the device in, and Windows sets the device to work with your existing hardware and resolves any system conflicts. When you install a hardware device, Windows installs related software, known as a **driver**, that allows the hardware to communicate with Windows and other software applications. Plug and play tells the device drivers where to find the hardware devices. Plug and play matches up physical hardware devices with the software device drivers that operate them and establish channels of communication between each physical device and its driver. With plug and play, you can be confident that any new device will work properly with your computer and that your computer will restart correctly after you install or uninstall hardware. Microsoft recommends that you use only device drivers with the Designed for Microsoft Windows 7 logo, which have a digital signature from Microsoft, indicating that the product was tested for compatibility with Windows 7. You might need to be logged on as an administrator or a member of the Administrators group in order to install a hardware device. In order to install a plug and play device, you need to do the following:

1) Gather your original Windows 7 installation disc, the hardware device that you want to install, and the discs that come with the device, if available.

2) Turn off your computer before you physically install a hardware device, such as a network card or a sound card, inside your computer. To install a hardware device that plugs into the outside of your computer, such as a scanner, printer or other USB (universal serial bus) device, you can plug it in without turning off your computer. If your USB device uses a power cord, you need to connect the device to the power cord and turn it on before you connect the USB device to your computer.

3) Follow the manufacturer's instructions to plug the new device into your computer.

4) Turn on your computer, or start the Add Hardware utility program in the Control Panel. Windows tries to detect the new device and install the device drivers. If Windows doesn't recognize the new hardware device, the device might not be plug and play compatible or installed correctly. Turn off your computer, check the device documentation and installation carefully, and then turn on your computer again. If the device driver is not available on your computer, Windows asks you to insert into the appropriate drive the Windows 7 installation disc or the disc that comes with the device from the manufacturer. After the driver software is installed, you can disconnect and reconnect the device without taking any further action.

5) Follow the instructions on the screen until a message indicates that you are finished. Windows notifies all other devices of the new device so there are no conflicts and manages the power requirements of your hardware and peripherals by shutting them down or conserving power when you are not using them. If you are working in another program when you install or uninstall a device, plug and play lets you know that it is about to change your computer configuration and warns you to save your work.

6) Use the Safely Remove Hardware and Media Eject icon in the notification area to safely unplug or eject plug and play hardware. The Safely Remove Hardware dialog box helps you stop the device, so it's safe to remove.

Plug and play
finds new hardware

The Found New
Hardware wizard
installs the new
hardware

Safely removes
hardware

Safely Remove Hardware and Eject Media icon

Viewing Hardware Devices

If you connect an external device—typically those you plug into a USB port and add wirelessly—to your computer, Windows 7 detects and installs it using plug and play. After the device is installed, it appears in the Devices and Printers folder (**New!**). The Devices and Printers folder is a centralized place to check and manage all devices connected to your computer—such as a USB hard drives, flash drives, webcams, Bluetooth, scanners, keyboards, or mice—as well as your computer. Devices installed inside your computer—such as internal hard drives, disc drives, sound cards, video cards, RAM, and older devices—do not appear in the Devices and Printers folder; you can find these devices in the Device Manager. In the Devices and Printers folder, you can add a new wireless or network device or printer to your computer. If there is a problem with a device (indicated by a yellow warning icon), you can also start the troubleshooter to help you detect and fix the problem.

View Hardware Devices

1 Click the **Start** button, and then click **Devices and Printers**.

2 Click the **down** or **up** arrow to expand or collapse the Devices or Printers and Faxes section.

3 Click a hardware device.

4 View hardware details in the Details pane.

5 For more information about a hardware device, double-click the device icon.

6 View the hardware properties.

7 Click **OK**.

8 If you see a yellow warning icon for a hardware device, click the device, click the **Troubleshoot** button on the toolbar, and then follow the on-screen instructions to detect and fix the problem.

9 Click the **Close** button.

Installing Hardware Devices

Before you install a new hardware device, be sure to carefully read the product installation guide provided by the manufacturer. If the hardware device comes with an installation disc, it is recommended that you use the manufacturer's disc and related instructions to install the hardware. If the product documentation instructs you to perform a typical plug and play installation, turn off your computer, physically connect your hardware to your computer, and then turn on your computer again. In most cases, Windows detects your new hardware device and installs it or starts the Add a device wizard. The Add a device wizard installs hardware devices by asking you a series of questions to set up the necessary software for the new hardware device. If Windows doesn't detect the new hardware, you can start the Add a device wizard in the Devices and Printers folder and select the new hardware device to install it. You might need to be logged on as an administrator in order to install a hardware device.

Install a Hardware Device Using the Add a Device Wizard

1. If necessary, attach the hardware device you want to install according the manufacturers directions.

   If Windows doesn't detect and install it, use the Add a device wizard to complete the installation.

2. Click the **Start** button, and then click **Devices and Printers**.

3. Click the **Add a device** button on the toolbar.

4. Select the discovered device you want to install.

5. Click **Next** to continue.

6. Follow the Add a device wizard instructions to complete the installation; steps vary depending on the hardware device.

Viewing System Hardware Settings

When you install a new operating system, such as Windows 7, it is important to make sure that you are using the latest software drivers with your system hardware. If you are not using the latest software drivers, your hardware devices might not work to full capacity. You can view your system hardware using a Windows utility called the Device Manager. Device Manager provides you with a list of the hardware types, also known as **hardware classes**, which are attached to your computer. With the Device Manager, you can determine the software driver versions being used with your system hardware, update the software driver with a newer version, roll back to a previous driver version if the device fails with the new one, or uninstall a driver. After viewing your software driver version numbers, you can contact the manufacturer or visit their web site to determine the latest versions. Most manufacturers allow you to download drivers from their web sites for free. You will need to be logged on as an administrator in order to work with hardware devices in the Device Manager.

View System Hardware Settings Using the Device Manager

1. Click the **Start** button, and then click **Control Panel**.

2. Click the **Device Manager** icon in Small icons or Large icons view.

3. Click the white arrow next to a hardware category to expand it.

4. Click the device you want to view.

5. Click the **Properties** button on the toolbar.

6. To work with drivers, click the Driver tab. You can choose any of the following buttons:

   ◆ **Driver Details**. View driver details.

   ◆ **Update Driver**. Update the driver.

   ◆ **Roll Back Driver**. Roll back to a previously installed driver.

   ◆ **Disable**. Disable the driver and the device.

   ◆ **Uninstall**. Remove the driver.

7. Click **OK**.

8. Click the **Close** button.

Changing Windows Update Driver Settings

When you connect a new device to your computer, you can specify how you want Windows Update to find a software driver for the device. The default setting is to automatically check for a driver on your computer or online from the Microsoft Windows Update web site. However, if you want more control over the process, you can change it to have Windows ask you each time you connect a new device before to check for drivers or never check for drivers. You can use System Properties to specify the option you want.

Change Windows Update Driver Settings

1. Click the **Start** button, and then click **Computer**.

2. Click the **System properties** button on the toolbar.

3. In the left pane, click **Advanced system settings**.

4. Click the **Hardware** tab.

5. Click **Device Installation Settings**.

6. Select the option you want to use (**New!**).

   ◆ **Yes, do this automatically (recommended).**

   ◆ **No, let me choose what to do.**

      ◆ Always install the best driver software from Windows Update.

      ◆ Install driver software from Windows Update if it is not found on my computer.

      ◆ Never install driver software from Windows Update.

7. Click **Save Changes**.

8. Click **OK**.

9. Click the **Close** button.

Changing Mouse Settings

A mouse does not require adjustments after you plug it in and start Windows. However, you can use Mouse properties in the Control Panel to change the way your mouse works and the way the pointer looks and behaves. For the mouse, you can switch the role of the buttons, or you can change the double-clicking speed. For the mouse pointer, you can modify its appearance using a pointer scheme, increase or decrease its speed, improve its visibility with a pointer trail, or set it to be hidden when you are typing. If your button has a wheel, roll the wheel with your forefinger to move up or down in a document or on a web page.

Change Button Settings

1. Click the **Start** button, and then click **Control Panel**.

2. Click the **Mouse** icon in Small icons or Large icons view.

3. Click the **Buttons** tab.

4. To reverse the mouse buttons, select the **Switch primary and secondary buttons** check box.

5. To adjust the double-click speed, drag the slider.

6. Click **OK**.

> ## Did You Know?
>
> *You can change the mouse wheel speed.* In the Control Panel, double-click the Mouse icon, click the Wheel tab, click the Following Number Of Lines At A Time option, type a number or click the One Screen At A Time option, and then click OK.

Change Pointer Appearance

1 Click the **Start** button, and then click **Control Panel**.

2 Click the **Mouse** icon in Small icons or Large icons view.

3 Click the **Pointers** tab.

4 Click the **Scheme** list arrow, and then select a pointer scheme.

5 Click **OK**.

Change Pointer Options

1 Click the **Start** button, and then click **Control Panel**.

2 Click the **Mouse** icon in Small icons or Large icons view.

3 Click the **Pointer Options** tab.

4 To adjust the pointer speed, drag the **Motion** slider.

5 To snap the pointer to a button, select the **Automatically move pointer to the default button in a dialog box** check box.

6 To display a trail after the pointer, hide the pointer while you type, or show the pointer location, select the visibility check box you want.

7 Click **OK**.

Changing Keyboard Settings

While your keyboard should just work when you start up your computer, you can use Keyboard properties in the Control Panel to adjust the rate at which a character is repeated when you hold down a key, and the time delay before it starts repeating. You can also adjust the blink rate of the insertion point.

Change Keyboard Settings

1. Click the **Start** button, and then click **Control Panel**.

2. Click the **Keyboard** icon in Small icons or Large icons view.

3. Click the **Speed** tab.

4. To adjust the character repeat delay, drag the slider.

5. To adjust the character repeat rate, drag the slider.

6. Click **OK**.

See Also

See "Changing Language Options" on page 112 for information on changing languages and keyboard layouts.

Changing Phone Dialing Options

When phone numbers or dialing settings to an Internet Service Provider or a network change, you need to update the phone dialing options your modem uses to make a dial-up connection. You can use Phone and Modem properties in the Control Panel to add, edit, and customize phone dialing options on your computer for one or more locations. For example, you can change country, region or area codes, disable call waiting, and set up a credit card number to pay for calls. You can also set access rules for dialing local, long distance, and international calls. If you no longer use a dialing location, you can remove it.

Change Phone Dialing Options

1. Click the **Start** button, and then click **Control Panel.**

2. Click the **Phone and Modem** icon in Small icons or Large icons view.

3. Click the **Dialing Rules** tab, and then click a dialing location.

4. Click **Edit**, and then click the **General** tab.

5. Change the country/region or area code.

6. Specify the dialing rules you want.

7. If you want, select the **To disable call waiting** check box.

8. To apply area code dialing rules, click the **Area Code Rules** tab, and then click **New** to create one.

9. To use a calling card, click the **Calling Card** tab, select a calling card option, or click **New** to create your own.

10. Click **OK.**

11. Click **OK.**

Changing Modem Options

A **modem** is a hardware device that allows two computers to transmit information over a phone line. A modem translates the binary information from the computer to an analog signal (known as modulation) that can pass over the phone line. At the receiving end, another modem translates the analog signal back to binary information (known as demodulation) that can be used by the computer. If you are having problems with your modem, you can test it. With the results of the test you can consult the modem documentation or a support technician to help you fix the problem. If requested, you can change data transmission settings, such as data bits, parity, stop bits, or modulation.

Change Modem Hardware Settings

1. Click the **Start** button, and then click **Control Panel**.

2. Click the **Phone and Modem** icon in Small icons or Large icons view.

3. Click the **Modems** tab.

4. Click the modem you want to change, and then click **Properties**.

5. Click the **Modem** tab.

6. Change the maximum port speed and speaker volume.

7. Click the **Advanced** tab, and then click **Change Default Preferences**.

8. Click the **Advanced** tab.

9. Change the setting for data bits, parity, stop bits, or modulation.

10. Click **OK**.

11. Click **OK**, and then click **OK** again.

Did You Know?

You can test a modem. In Phone and Modem Options, click the Modems tab, select a modem, click Properties, click the Diagnostics tab, and then click Query Modem, wait for and view the results, and then click OK twice.

Managing Color

Color management is a system that makes sure the color you see on your display or printer is the color you want. Not all hardware displays color in the same way; each hardware device uses different characteristics, or methods, when rendering and processing color on a specific device. Even programs don't all render and process color the same way. Color Management controls the relationship between the device characteristics and the display conditions to produce the most accurate results. A color profile describes the color characteristics of a specific device. With the Color Management properties in the Control Panel, you can add or remove a color profile, associate a different color profile with a device, change the default profile, and change the color options, such as rendering intent and color space. Color profiles are typically added when you install a hardware device or software program that requires it. Windows 7 supports the standard ICC color standard and can add to it with Windows Color System.

View Color Profiles

1. Click the **Start** button, and then click **Control Panel.**

2. Click the **Color Management** icon in Small icons or Large icons view.

3. Click the **Devices** tab.

4. Click the **Device** list arrow, and then click the device you want to view.

   If a device uses a color profile, it appears in the list.

5. If you want to change the color profile, select the **Use my settings for this device** check box.

6. Use the **Add**, **Remove**, and **Profiles** buttons to modify profile associations.

7. To view all profiles on your computer or add a profile, click the **All Profiles** tab.

8. To change specific attributes and characteristics of a profile, click the **Advanced** tab.

9. Click **Close**.

Adding a Secondary Monitor

If you need more space on your desktop to work, you can add a secondary monitor to your computer. This allows you to view and work with more than one full size window on the screen at the same time. One monitor serves as the primary display while the other serves as the secondary display. You can set the multiple displays to duplicate the displays on both monitors, extend the displays over two monitors, and show desktop only on one or the other. In addition, you can set different screen resolutions and different orientation (**New!**) settings for each monitor. You can connect multiple monitors to individual video cards or to a single card that supports multiple video ports. In the Screen Resolution dialog box, you can set options for using multiple monitors. If you have a project connected to your computer, you can use Connect to a Projector (**New!**) to select secondary monitor options: Disconnect Project, Duplicate, Extend, or Projector only. You can access these options by selecting Connect to a Project in the Screen Resolution dialog box or from the Accessories submenu on the Start menu.

Set Secondary Monitor Options

1. Right-click a blank area of the desktop, and then click **Screen resolution**.

2. If the secondary monitor doesn't appear, click **Detect**.

3. Click the **Multiple displays** list arrow, and then select an option:

   ◆ **Duplicate these displays.**

   ◆ **Extend these displays.**

   ◆ **Show desktop only on 1.**

   ◆ **Show desktop only on 2.**

4. Select a monitor, if necessary.

5. Select any of the following monitor options:

   ◆ **Display.** Changes the display driver.

   ◆ **Resolution.** Changes the screen resolution; drag the slider.

   ◆ **Orientation.** Changes the screen orientation (landscape or portrait).

6. Click **OK**.

Click to select a Connect to a Projector option

Connect to a Projector options

Change the Movement
Between Monitors

1 Right-click a blank area of the desktop, and then click **Screen resolution**.

2 Click **Identify**.

3 Click the monitor icons and drag them to positions that represent how you want to move items from one monitor to another.

4 Click **OK**.

You can drag items across the primary monitor until it appears on the secondary monitor.

Change the Primary Monitor

1 Right-click a blank area of the desktop, and then click **Screen resolution**.

2 Click the monitor icon that represents the monitor you want as the primary one.

3 Select the **Make this my main display** check box.

TROUBLE? *This check box is unavailable if you select the current primary monitor.*

4 Click **OK**.

Removing Hardware Devices

If you no longer use a hardware device (not plug and play), such as a sound or modem card, or if you have an older hardware device that you want to upgrade, you need to remove the hardware device drivers and related software before you remove the physical hardware device from your computer. With the Device Manager, you can remove hardware devices and any related device drivers. Before you remove a legacy device, printing the device settings is a good idea in case you need to reinstall the device later.

Remove a Hardware Device

1. Click the **Start** button, and then click **Control Panel**.

2. Click the **Device Manager** icon in Small icons or Large icons view.

3. Click the white arrow next to the hardware category you want to expand.

4. Click the device you want to remove.

5. Click the **Uninstall** button.

6. Click **OK**.

7. Click the **Close** button.

Did You Know?

You can quickly delete a printer. Click the Start button, click Devices And Printers, right-click the printer you want to delete, click Remove Device, and then click Yes.

Removing Plug and Play Hardware

Most plug and play hardware devices, such as a USB Flash drive, can be removed and unplugged at anytime as long as the computer is not using it. However, it's not easy to know if the computer is done with it. If the Safely Remove Hardware icon appears in the notification area on the taskbar, you can use it to quickly and safely remove the hardware. If you want to remove devices more quickly, you can select an option in the Device Manager to optimize a device for quick removal.

Remove or Eject a Plug and Play Hardware Device Safely

1 Click the **Safely Remove Hardware and Eject Media** icon in the notification area on the taskbar, and then select a device.

> **TIMESAVER** *Right-click the device in the Computer window, and then click Safely Remove.*

2 If prompted, click **OK** to confirm the removal.

3 Unplug or eject the device.

Optimize Hardware for Removal

1 Click the **Start** button, and then click **Control Panel**.

2 Click the **Device Manager** icon in Small icons or Large icons view.

3 Click the white arrow next to **Disk drives** to expand it, and then select the device you want to optimize.

4 Click the **Properties** button.

5 Click the **Policies** tab.

6 Click the **Quick removal (default)** option to remove a device without the Safely Remove Hardware icon, or click the **Better performance** option to remove a device with it.

7 Click **OK**.

8 Click the **Close** button.

Safely remove hardware

Eject media

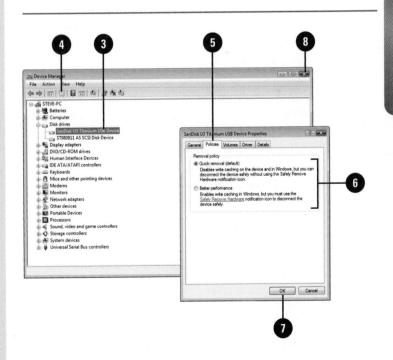

Troubleshooting Computer Problems

If you're having problems with your computer, you can use a troubleshooting wizard to help you diagnosis and fix the problem. You can access Troubleshooting (**New!**) in the Control Panel. From the Troubleshooting window, you can run troubleshooters to fix programs made for previous versions of Windows, reconfigure a hardware device, establish an Internet connection, access shared files, fix Aero desktop effects, and fix Windows Update, maintenance, and performance issues. If you need further help, you can also access and use Remote Assistance to contact someone you trust for help.

Troubleshoot Computer Problems

1 Click the **Start** button, and then click **Control Panel**.

2 Click the **Troubleshooting** icon in Small icons or Large icons view.

3 To set troubleshooting options, click **Change settings** in the left pane, set the options you want, and then click **OK**.

4 Click a link for the area you want to troubleshoot.

- ◆ **Programs.** Use to run programs made for previous versions of Windows.

- ◆ **Hardware and Sound.** Use to reconfigure a hardware device.

- ◆ **Network and Internet.** Use to fix a connect to the Internet and file sharing.

- ◆ **Appearance and Personalization.** Use to fix Aero desktop effects.

- ◆ **System and Security.** Use to fix Windows Update, maintenance, and performance issues.

5 Follow the on-screen troubleshooting wizard.

6 To use Remote Assistance to contact someone you trust for help, click **Get help from a friend** in the left pane.

7 Click the **Close** button.

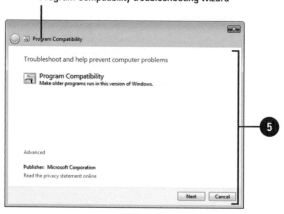

Program Compatibility troubleshooting wizard

Backing Up Your Computer

17

Introduction

It is vital that you make backup copies of the files on your computer on a regular basis so you don't lose valuable data if your computer encounters problems. The term **back up** (or **backup**, when referring to the noun or adjective) refers to the process of using a special software program designed to read your data quickly, compress it into a small, efficient space, then store it on an external medium, such as a set of disks, a network drive, or a tape cartridge.

Windows 7 includes **Backup and Restore**. Using Backup and Restore has several advantages over simply copying files to a removable disk. Your files are compressed as they are copied so that you can fit more onto a removable disk, and it splits a large file across two or more disks (saving disk space), something you cannot do with the Copy command. Also, in an emergency, Backup offers several data-recovery aids to help you locate and restore important files quickly.

If your computer system crashes and Windows cannot start, you can use System Repair disc (**New!**) and the Windows 7 installation disc, which contains the files necessary to start Windows. You can use the Startup Repair and other tools on the System Recovery Options menu to repair the problem or restore data from a backup.

What You'll Do

Create a System Repair Disc

Develop a Backup Strategy

Understand Backup Permissions

Explore Backup and Restore

Perform a Backup

Change Backup Settings

Schedule a Backup

Manage a Backup

Create a System Image

Restore Backup Files

Restore Files Using Advanced Settings

Restore Your Computer

Copy or Delete Files From a Backup

Creating a System Repair Disc

Before you start backing up of computer, you need to create a system repair disc (**New!**). If a serious error occurs with your system, you can use the system repair disc to boot your computer and provide system recovery tools to help you restore your computer. You may also need your Windows 7 installation disc. After you create a system repair disc, store it along with your Windows 7 installation disc for safe keeping. If you ever have a problem, insert the system repair disc into your disc drive, restart your computer, press a key to boot from the system repair disc, select a language setting, and then select a recovery option, which includes Startup Repair, System Restore, System Image Recovery, Windows Memory Diagnostic, and Command Prompt.

Create a System Repair Disc

1. Click the **Start** button, point to **All Programs**, point to **Maintenance**, and then click **Create a System Repair Disc**.

   ◆ You can also click **Create system repair disc** in the left pane of Backup and Restore.

2. Insert a blank DVD-R or DVD-RW disc into your disc drive.

3. Click the **Drive** list arrow, and then select a disc drive.

4. Click **Create disc**.

   Wait while Windows creates the disc.

5. Upon completion, read and following the message, and then click **Close**.

6. Click **OK**.

7. If the AutoPlay dialog box opens, click the **Close** button.

Developing a Backup Strategy

With Backup, you can back up files from a local or network hard drive to a removable disk, a CD or DVD, a network drive, or a tape drive that is attached to your computer. Before you back up files, it is a good idea to develop a backup strategy. A **backup strategy** is a method for regularly backing up your work that balances tradeoffs between safety, time, and media space. For example, if safety were your only concern, you could back up your entire hard drive every hour. But you would not have any time to work, and you would spend a fortune on backup mediums. If spending minimal time and money on backups were your only concern, you might back up only a few crucial files once a month. The best choice is a balance between the two extremes. The **backup medium** that you use to store backed up files from a hard drive is usually a set of removable disks, writeable CDs or DVDs, or a tape cartridge designed to store computer data.

Because backups take time each time you perform them, you should back up only the files that change on a regular basis; back up all of the files on your computer at less frequent intervals. For example, because software program files don't change, you can easily reinstall them from their original program CDs or DVDs, so you do not need to back them up as often as your personal document files, which might change on a daily or weekly basis. Ask yourself how much work you can afford to lose. If you cannot afford to lose the work accomplished in one day, then you should back up once a day. If your work does not change much during the week, back up once a week.

Depending on the number and size of your files and the backup device you are using, the backup can take a few minutes to a few hours to complete. If you are planning to back up large amounts of information, such as your entire hard drive, it is best to start the backup at the end of the day and use a large capacity tape or removable disk, if possible, so you do not have to swap multiple disks. When a file does not fit on a tape or disk, Backup splits the file, fitting what it can on the current disk and then prompting you to insert the next tape or disk. When you perform a backup, Backup creates a **backup set**, also known as a **backup job**, which contains the compressed copies of the files you backed up. The backup job is stored in the backup file with the .bkf extension. You can store more than one backup job in a specified backup file. An incremental backup copies only the files that have changed since your most recent normal or incremental backup. It also clears the archive attribute for each file that is backed up. Therefore, the first incremental backup after a normal backup copies all files that have changed since the normal backup, and the second incremental backup copies only those files that have changed since the first incremental backup, and so on.

Lastly, keeping your computer's clock set to an accurate time is crucial to the success of your backups and other file maintenance. When setting a backup schedule, Windows will be looking at your system's clock to commence backups. Make sure your computer's time is accurately set throughout the year to ensure proper time stamping for your backups, as well as, other file properties.

Understanding Backup Permissions

Backup Permissions

You must have certain permissions to back up files and folders. If you are an administrator or a backup operator in a local group using Windows 7, you can back up any file and folder on the computer to which the local group applies. However, if you are not an administrator or a backup operator and you want to back up files, then you must be the owner of the files and folders you want to back up, or you must have one or more of the following permissions for the files and folders you want to back up: Read, Read and Execute, Modify, or Full Control. You can also restrict access to a backup file by selecting the *Allow only the owner and the administrator access to the backup data* check box in the Backup Job Information dialog box. If you select this option, only an administrator or the person who created the backup file will be able to restore the files and folders.

To add a user to the Backup Operators group, click the Administrative Tools icon in the Control Panel (in Small icons or Large icons), and then double-click the Computer Management icon in the Administrative Tools window. This opens the Computer Management Window. Next, click the arrow next to Local Users and Groups in the console tree, click Groups in the console tree, and then double-click Backup Operators in the Details pane. Next, click Add in the Backup Operators Properties dialog box, type the domain and user name of the person you want to make a backup operator in the form \\Domain\user name, and then click OK. For

more information about using Computer Management, see Chapter 18, "Administering Your Computer."

Backup permissions

File Systems

You can back up and restore data on either a FAT or NTFS volume. In fact, you can now back up and restore (Encrypting File System) EFS encrypted files. If you have backed up data from an NTFS volume used in Windows 7, it is recommended that you restore the data to an NTFS volume used in Windows 7 instead of Windows 2000, or you could lose data as well as some file and folder features. For more information about FAT and NTFS disk file systems, see Chapter 15, "Maintaining Your Computer." For more information about EFS encrypted files, see "Encrypting Files for Safety," on page 328.

Exploring Backup and Restore

Using the Backup process in Backup and Restore (**New!**), you can pick the day, time, and how often you want to back up your files, folders, and settings. You can also specify the type of data to back up, such as documents, photos, or music. Windows 7 takes care of the rest. And you won't be interrupted while you work, because automatic data backup occurs in the background, regardless of when you've scheduled your backup. You can continue to use your computer, even when it's backing up. Easily backing up your data is only part of the story—you also need a way to get your files back where they belong if something happens to them. Using the Restore process, you can choose only what you want to restore—whether it's an individual file or even your entire system and its related settings. Windows 7 takes care of putting the files back where they were before they were lost.

Start Backup and Restore Center

1 Click the **Start** button, point to **All Programs**, point to **Maintenance**, and then click **Backup and Restore**.

2 On first use, click **Set up backup** to prepare for and backup your computer files.

- ◆ Select a backup location, and then click **Next**.

- ◆ Select options for what you want to back up, and then click **Next**.

- ◆ Review your backup settings, and then click **Save settings and run bac**k.

3 Click any of the following buttons to perform the task you want:

- ◆ **Back up now.** Back up selected files and folders. You can also click **Manage space** or **Change settings**.

- ◆ **Restore my files.** Restore selected files and folders. You can also click **Restore all users' files** or **Select another backup to restore files from**.

- ◆ **Recover system settings or your computer.** Undo recent system changes (**New!**).

4 Click the **Close** button.

Performing a Backup

The Backup process walks you through the process of backing up files on your computer. You can back up every file on your computer, or selected files and folders. Backing up your entire computer is a good idea in case you have a problem with Windows and it doesn't start properly. Typically, you back up your entire computer after you make major changes to your system and you back up changes to individual files, folders, drives, and settings on a regular schedule. During the process, you select the back up location, files and folders to backup, choose the day, time, and how often you want to back up. You can select a backup location on another drive, USB drive, writeable CDs or DVDs, or network (**New!**). While the back up takes place you can continue to use your computer, yet it may be a little slower.

Back up Files

1 Click the **Start** button, point to **All Programs**, point to **Maintenance**, and then click **Backup and Restore**.

2 On first use, click **Set up backup**, or click **Create a new, full backup** (only available for CDs or DVDs) in the left pane.

 ◆ Otherwise, click **Change settings**.

3 Select the location where you want to back up your computer.

4 To select a network location, if available, click **Save on a network**, click **Browse** to select a network, type a user-name and password, and then click **OK**.

5 Click **Next** to continue.

Click to change settings

Click to refresh drives

6 Select the **Let Windows choose (recommended)** or **Let me choose** option.

7 Click **Next** to continue.

8 If prompted, select the check boxes with the data you want to back up and clear the ones you don't want to include, and then click **Next** to continue.

9 To change the schedule, click **Change schedule**, specify an interval, and then click **OK**.

10 Confirm your backup settings, and then click **Save settings and run backup**.

◆ Otherwise, click **Save settings and exit**, and then **click Backup now**.

11 If prompted to insert a disc, insert a CD or DVD, and then click **OK**.

12 If prompted to format the disc, click **Format**.

The backup starts, displaying back up status.

13 To stop a backup, click **View Details**, click **Stop backup**, click **Stop backup** again to confirm it, and then click the **Close** button.

14 When it's done, click **Close**.

Changing Backup Settings

After you complete a back up, you can make modifications to the backup settings. You can change the backup schedule or the types of files backed up. Instead of selecting individual files and folders, the Backup process provides file types and categories for you to select. For example, you can select data for newly created users, your library folders (Documents, Music, Pictures, videos), additional locations in your personal folder, and other locations on your computer hard drives. System files, program files, temporary files, Recycle Bin files, and files on a FAT drive are never backed up. If you need to perform a manual back up, you can choose Back up now in Backup and Restore.

Change Backup Settings

1 Click the **Start** button, point to **All Programs**, point to **Maintenance**, and then click **Backup and Restore**.

2 Click **Change settings** at the bottom of the Backup section.

3 Select the location where you want to back up your computer.

4 To select a network location, if available, click **Save on a network**, click **Browse** to select a network, type a user-name and password, and then click **OK**.

5 Click **Next** to continue.

6 Select the **Let Windows choose (recommended)** or **Let me choose** option.

7 Click **Next** to continue.

8 If prompted, select the check boxes with the data you want to back up and clear the ones you don't want to include, and then click **Next** to continue.

9 To change the schedule, click **Change schedule**, specify an interval, and then click **OK**.

10 Confirm your backup settings, and then click **Save settings and exit**.

Perform a Manual Backup Using Current Settings

① Click the **Start** button, point to **All Programs**, point to **Maintenance**, and then click **Backup and Restore**.

② Click **Back up now**.

The backup starts, displaying back up status.

③ To stop a backup, click **View Details**, click **Stop backup**, click **Stop backup** again to confirm it, and then click the **Close** button.

④ When it's done, click **Close**.

Did You Know?

You can create a backup system image. If your backup drive is formatted using NTFS and has enough space, Backup and Restore creates a system image of your programs, Windows, and all drivers and registry settings. If you have problems with your hard drive, you can use the image to restore it. This automatically happens when you let Windows choose the files to backup.

Click to confirm the stop backup

Scheduling a Backup

Scheduling backups according to a backup strategy can help you perform backups on a regular basis and protect your data. Typically, late at night or on the weekends, when nobody is around, is a good time to perform backups. Backup makes it easy to schedule backups any time you want to perform them. You can schedule a backup to run once, every day, every week, or every month. If you have a back up scheduled for a certain time and you need to cancel it, you can turn off automatic back ups and then turn it back on later. And if your computer is turned off at the time the backup is scheduled to occur, the backup process will begin when you next turn on your computer.

Schedule a Backup

1. Click the **Start** button, point to **All Programs**, point to **Maintenance**, and then click **Backup and Restore**.

2. Click **Change settings** at the bottom of the Backup section.

3. Select the location where you want to back up your computer.

4. Click **Next** to continue.

5. Click **Next** to continue, and then click **Next** again if the file selection screen appears.

6. Click **Change schedule**.

7. Select the **Run backup on a schedule (recommended)** check box.

8. Click the **How often** list arrow, and then select an interval.

9. Click the **What day** list arrow, and then select a day of the week.

10. Click the **What time** list arrow, and then select a time.

11. Click **OK**.

12. Confirm your backup settings, and then click **Save settings and exit**.

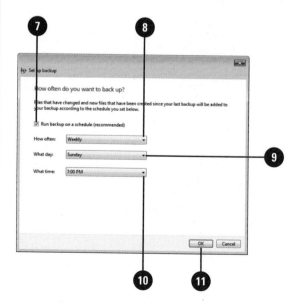

Turn Off and On Automatic Backup

1 Click the **Start** button, point to **All Programs**, point to **Maintenance**, and then click **Backup and Restore**.

2 In the left pane, click **Turn off schedule**.

The command in the left pane is removed and the Turn on schedule command appears at the bottom of the Backup section.

3 To turn on automatic backup, click **Turn on schedule**.

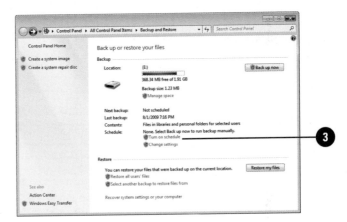

Managing Backups

After you complete a back up to a read/writeable drive (hard disk, USB, or network), you can view drive space usage, the backup location, and backup files. If you need to free up space on your drive, you can delete a backup. In addition, you can change settings for creating a system image. A disk image is an exact copy of a drive, which is useful for restoring a computer with hard drive problems.

Manage Backups

1. Click the **Start** button, point to **All Programs**, point to **Maintenance**, and then click **Backup and Restore**.

2. Click **Manage space** at the middle of the Backup section.

3. To view the drive with the backup files, click **Browse**.

4. To refresh space usage summary information, click **Refresh**.

5. Click **View backups**.

6. To delete a backup, select the backup you want to delete, and then click **Delete**.

7. Click **Close**.

8. To change settings for a system image, click **Change settings**.

9. Click **Close**.

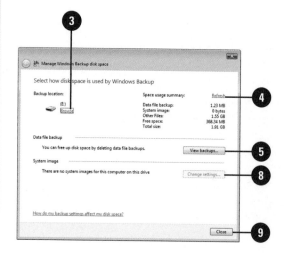

Creating a System Image

A system image is an exact copy of a drive, including Windows system files, program files, and your personal files. If you have problems with your hard drive, you can use the system image to restore it. You can create your own system image or let Windows create one for you (**New!**). If your backup drive is formatted using NTFS, has enough space, and you let Windows choose the files to backup, Backup and Restore automatically backs up your files and creates a system image of your programs, Windows, and all drivers and registry settings.

Create a System Image

1. Click the **Start** button, point to **All Programs**, point to **Maintenance**, and then click **Backup and Restore**.

2. In the left pane, click **Create a system image**.

3. Select the location where you want to back up your computer.

4. To select a network location, if available, click **Select** to select a network, type a user-name and password, and then click **OK**.

5. Click **Next** to continue.

6. Click **Start backup**.

7. If prompted to insert a disc, insert a CD or DVD, and then click **OK**.

8. If prompted to format the disc, click **Format**.

   The backup starts, displaying back up status.

Restoring Backup Files

The real value in backing up your files becomes apparent if you lose or damage some files, or need information from a document that has changed a great deal over time. You can restore a single file, several files, or an entire hard drive. Using the Restore process, you can specify which files you want to restore and where you want them to be placed. When you create a backup set, a **catalog**, or index of the backed up files, is built and stored on the backup medium. When you store the catalog on the backup medium, it speeds up the process when you want to restore the files. When you browse for folders, you won't be able to view individual files in a folder.

Restore a Backup

1. Click the **Start** button, point to **All Programs**, point to **Maintenance**, and then click **Backup and Restore**.

2. Click **Restore my files** to restore your files or click **Restore all user's files** to restore all users on your computer.

3. To browse the contents of the backup, click **Browse for files** or **Browse for folders**.

   When you browse for folder, you won't be able to view individual files in a folder.

4. To search the contents of a back up, click **Search**, type all or part of a file name, and then click **Search**.

5. To remove an item from the restore list, select it, and then click **Remove** or **Remove all**.

6. Click **Next** to continue.

7. Click the **In the original location** or **In the following location** option.

   ◆ **In the following location**. Click **Browse** to select a location. Select the **Restore the files to their original subfolders** check box.

8. Click **Restore**, and then click **Finish**.

Restore all user's files

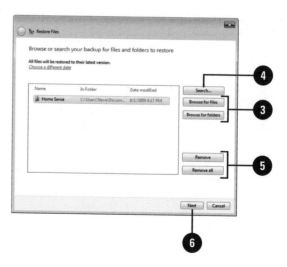

Select Files or Folders to Restore

1. In Backup and Restore, click **Restore my files**.

2. Click **Browse for files** or **Browse for folders**.

3. In the left pane, click the backup file from which you want to select files or folders.

4. Double-click the folder to navigate to the location with the files you want to restore.

5. Select the files or folders you want to restore, and then click **Add files** or **Add folders**.

6. Complete the remaining steps for the restore.

Search Files or Folders to Restore

1. In Backup and Restore, click **Restore my files**.

2. Click **Search**.

3. Type all or part of a file name.

   ◆ If you want to find all the files of a specific type, you can type a file extension to find them. For example, type BMP to find bitmap files.

4. Click **Search**.

5. Select the check boxes for the files or folders you want to restore.

6. Click **OK**.

7. Complete the remaining steps for the restore.

Restoring Files Using Advanced Settings

If you need to restore files from an older backup made on this computer or files from a back up made on a different computer, you can select additional options using an advanced restore option. The advanced options allow you to select an older backup set or one stored in a different location. You can also decide where to put the restored files. You can put them back in their original place, or select a new location. The Restore process walks you through the process, so you can restore the files and folder you want. If you are restoring files from a backup that was made on another computer, the files are stored in a folder under the user name.

Restore a Backup Using Advanced Settings

1. Click the **Start** button, point to **All Programs**, point to **Maintenance**, and then click **Backup and Restore**.

2. Click **Select another backup to restore files from**.

3. Select the backup you want to restore files from. If the backup location is not in the list, click **Refresh**.

4. To select a network location, click **Browse network location**, type a network share or click **Browse** to select it, and then click **OK**.

5. Click **Next** to continue.

6. Select the **Select all files from this backup** check box or use the **Search**, **Browse for files**, or **Browse for folders** buttons to select what you want. to restore.

7. Click **Next** to continue.

8. Click the **In the original location** or **In the following location** option.

9. Click **Restore**, and then click **Finish**.

Click to refresh list

Click to restore all files

Restoring Your Computer

To restore your computer, you can use several different methods. You can use the System Restore wizard, a system image you created earlier to recover your computer, or reinstall Windows 7. You can access these options from Backup and Restore using the Recover system settings or your computer option. Before you start the complete restore process, be sure to have your back up material available.

Restore Your Computer

① Click the **Start** button, point to **All Programs**, point to **Maintenance**, and then click **Backup and Restore**.

② Click **Recover system settings on your computer**.

③ To start the System Restore wizard, click **Open System Restore**, and then follow the on-screen instructions.

④ To restore from a system image or reinstall Windows, click **Advanced recovery methods**.

⑤ Click the advanced recovery method you want.

◆ **Use a system image you created earlier to recover your computer**

◆ **Reinstall Windows (requires Windows installation disc)**

⑥ Follow the on-screen instructions to complete the process.

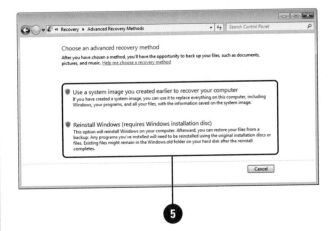

See Also

See *"Restoring Computer Settings"* on page 444-445 for more information on using the System Restore wizard.

See *"Creating a System Image"* on page 479 for more information on creating a system image.

See *"Creating a System Repair Disc"* on page 468 for more information on creating a system repair disc.

Copying or Deleting Files From a Backup

If you have a few backed up files or folders and know exactly where they are located on the back up media, you can open up the backed up media drive and navigate directly to the files and folder like any other external drive. You can use the Copy and Paste commands to copy the files and folders you need to another place on your computer. If you prefer, another method, you can also use the Copy To Folder command on the Edit menu. This method is useful when you are copying files and folder to disks, networks, and other drives. After backing up files for a while, you might find a number of unneeded backup sets accumulating in a backup file. You can delete these sets quickly and easily from the backup file within Backup. When you delete a backup set, only the backup set is deleted, but the backup file remains in the backup location. If you want to delete the backup file, drag the file icon into the Recycle Bin as you would any other Windows file.

Copy or Delete Files from the Backup

1. Click the **Start** button, and then click **Computer**.

2. Locate the drive and folder where your backup file is stored.

3. Right-click the backup file, and then click **Open**.

4. Navigate to and select the files or folders you want to copy or delete.

5. Right-click the selected files or folders, and then click **Copy** or **Delete** and click **Yes** to confirm.

6. Display the folder where you want to copy the backed up files or folders, right-click a blank area of the folder, and then click **Paste**.

Did You Know?

You can start a restore from the backup file. In Windows Explorer window, double-click the backup file, and then click Restore files.

Backup set

Catalog of backups

Administering Your Computer

Introduction

If you have purchased a computer and set it up in your home, you are that computer's administrator. Computers on a network in a company or an institution, such as at a university, are called clients. The clients are managed by one or more system or network administrators, who have the task of ensuring that the network and its services are reliable, fast, and secure. Although most network administration takes place on the server (host, as described in earlier chapters), clients must also be administered. Windows 7 includes administrative tools that make it easy to ensure that client computers are operating as they should.

You can use the administrative tools to track and view the activity on your computer. You can set up criteria for gathering event information, and then Windows automatically gathers that information for you. In the event of a problem, you can view that data to help you find and fix the problem.

When you open an administrative tool, Windows uses a two-pane view that is similar to Windows Explorer. The hierarchy of tools in the left pane of the window is called a **console tree**, and each main category of tools is called a **node**. The nodes in the console tree allow you to manage and monitor system events and performance, and make adjustments as necessary.

What You'll Do

Explore Windows Administrative Tools

Monitor Activity with Event Viewer

Manage an Event Log

Manage All Printers

Check Memory for Problems

View and Create Performance Charts

Monitor Local Security Settings

View Computer Management Tools

Manage Disks

Manage Local Users and Groups

View and Save System Information

Set System Configuration Options

Exploring Windows Administrative Tools

Windows 7 offers a set of tools that helps you administer your computer and ensure it operates smoothly. The Administrative Tools window, opened from the Control Panel, provides tools that allow you to configure administrative settings for local and remote computers. If you are working on a shared or network computer, you might need to be logged on as a computer administrator or as a member of the Administrators group in order to view or modify some properties or perform some tasks with the administrative tools. You can open User Accounts in the Control Panel to check which account is currently in use or to check with your system administrator to determine whether you have the necessary access privileges. Many Windows users won't ever have to open the Administrative Tools window, but computers on a network will probably require administrative support.

View Administrative Tools

1 Click the **Start** button, and then click **Control Panel**.

2 Click the **Administrative Tools** icon in Small icons or Large icons view.

3 When you're done, click the **Close** button.

Did You Know?

You can add Administrative Tools to the Start menu. Right-click the Start button, click Properties, click the Start Menu tab, click Customize, scroll down the list, click the Display On The All Programs Menu And The Start Menu option under System Administrative Tools, and then click OK twice.

Administrative tools

Monitoring Activity with Event Viewer

Every time you start Windows, an event-logging service notes any unusual event that occurs, such as a failed logon, the installation of a new driver for a hardware device, the failure of a device or service to start, or a network interruption. For some critical events, such as when your disk is full, a warning message appears on your screen. Most events, however, don't require immediate attention, so Windows logs them in an event log file that you can view using the Event Viewer tool. Event Viewer maintains several logs in two categories: Windows Logs and Applications and Services Logs. Windows Logs maintains three logs: System, for events logged by Windows operating system components; Security, for security and audit events (such as who logged on); and Application, for Windows program events. Applications and Services Logs maintains individual program and service logs. When you are troubleshooting problems on your computer, you can use the Event Viewer logs to monitor what activity took place.

Monitor Activities

1. Click the **Start** button, and then click **Control Panel**.

2. Click the **Administrative Tools** icon in Small icons or Large icons view.

3. Double-click the **Event Viewer** icon.

4. Click arrow next to the log category to expand it, and then click the log in which you want to monitor events.

5. Double-click an event.

6. Click the **Up Arrow** button or the **Down Arrow** button to display other events.

7. Click **Close**.

8. When you're done, click the **Close** button.

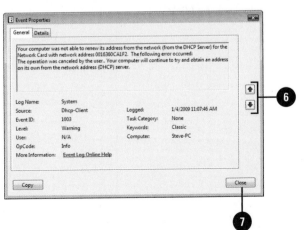

Managing an Event Log

Event logs grow in size as you work on your computer, but Event Viewer provides tools that help you view just the information you need and store the information you want to save for later. For example, you can apply a **filter** that allows you to view only events matching specified criteria, such as all events associated with a certain user. You can also search for a specific event using similar criteria. You probably don't want your active log to include events that happened long ago. With Event Viewer, you can **archive**, or save, your log periodically and then clear the archived events. Most administrators archive event logs on a regular schedule.

Sort and Filter an Event Log

1. Click the **Start** button, and then click **Control Panel**.

2. Click the **Administrative Tools** icon in Small icons or Large icons view.

3. Double-click the **Event Viewer** icon, and then select the event log you want to sort or filter events.

4. Click the **View** menu, point to **Sort By**, and then click the sort method you want.

5. In the Actions pane, click **Filter Current Log**.

6. Select the Event Level check boxes in which you want to filter.

7. Specify filter information by specific value.

8. Click **OK**.

9. When you're done, click the **Close** button.

Save an Event Log

1. Click the **Start** button, and then click **Control Panel**.

2. Click the **Administrative Tools** icon in Small icons or Large icons view.

3. Double-click the **Event Viewer** icon, and then select the event log you want to save.

4. In the Actions pane, click **Save Log File As** or **Save All Events As**.

5. Select a location for the log file.

6. Type a name for the log file.

7. Click **Save**.

8. When you're done, click the **Close** button.

Did You Know?

You can open the log file from the Event Viewer. In the Event Viewer, click Open Saved Log in the Action pane, select the log file, and then click Open.

You can find information in the Event Viewer. In the Event Viewer, click Find in the Actions pane, type what you want to find, and then click Find Next. When you're done, click Close.

You can change log settings. You can control how any log in the Event Viewer collects data by defining a maximum log size (the default is 512K) and instructing Event Viewer how to handle an event log that has reached its maximum size. In the Event Viewer, select the log you want to change, click Properties in the Actions pane, click the General tab, specify the maximum log size, select an option when the maximum size is reached, click OK, and then click the Close button.

Managing All Printers

For computers on a network running Windows 7 and Windows Server 2008 R2 or later, you can use Print Management (**New!**) to monitor print queues and get alerts when print queues stop processing print jobs. The Print Management tool allows you to work with shared printers on a network and print server from a central location. You can get status information for printers and print servers on a network and find printers that have an error by using filters. When a printer or print server needs attention, Print Management can send e-mail messages or run scripts.

Manage All Printers

1. Click the **Start** button, and then click **Control Panel**.

2. Click the **Administrative Tools** icon in Small icons or Large icons view.

3. Double-click the **Print Management** icon.

4. Click the white arrow to expand Print Management.

5. To monitor printers, expand **Custom Filters**, and then click **All Printers**, **All Drivers**, **Printers Not Ready**, or **Printers With Jobs**.

6. To work with printers, select a printer, click **More Actions**, and then click a command.

7. To work with print servers, expand **Print Servers**, select a print server, click **More Actions**, and then click a command: **Add Printer**, **Set Notifications**, or **Properties**.

8. When you're done, click the **Close** button.

Printer related commands

Print server

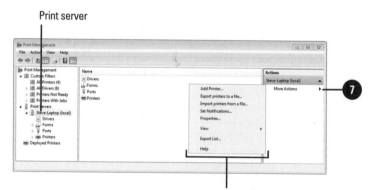

Print server related commands

Did You Know?

You can add or remove print servers. In Print Management, right-click Print Management, and then click Add/Remove Servers. To add a server, click Browse to select it, and then click Add To List. To remove a server, select it, and then click Remove.

Checking Memory for Problems

If a problem arises related to the memory on your computer, Windows automatically tries to detect it and displays an alert message, which allows you to run the Windows Memory Diagnostic. If you also suspect a memory problem, you can run the Windows Memory Diagnostic from Administrator Tools. When the memory tool starts, you can have the program restart your computer and run the memory tool immediately or run it later. While the memory tool runs, a progress bar indicates the status of the test. When the test is done, Windows restarts again. If the results indicate a problem, you should contact your computer or memory manufacturer for information about fixing the problem.

Check for Memory Problems

1. Click the **Start** button, and then click **Control Panel**.

2. Click the **Administrative Tools** icon in Small icons or Large icons view.

3. Double-click the **Windows Memory Diagnostics** icon.

4. Click **Restart now and check for problems** or **Check for problems the next time I start my computer** option.

5. Follow the on-screen instructions to complete the test.

Did You Know?

You can change registry settings. Windows 7 manages all its internal settings with a database called the **Registry**. If you are an administrator or seasoned veteran of Windows and know what you want to change in the Registry, you can fix a problem with your system or a program, or you can enhance the functionality of Windows. Click the Start button, point to Programs, click Accessories, click Run, type *regedt32*, click OK, open the folder and double-click the item you want to change, and then click OK. When you're done, click the Close button.

Viewing and Creating Performance Charts

On a daily basis, your system generates a variety of performance data, such as your computer's memory or processor use, or the amount of congestion on a device. As the system administrator, you can use the Performance tool to create charts from the data that enable you to observe how a computer's processor behaves over time. The types of performance data you monitor and record are called **performance objects**. Each performance object has a set of counters associated with it that provides numeric information. The Performance tool charts the numeric data gathered from the counters and provides graphical tools to make it easier to analyze and track the performance of your computer. Performance charts include statistics about each counter you select, but unless you know how your system should perform, these statistics might not be very meaningful. For this reason, administrators create baseline charts—charts made when the computer or network is running at a normal level. When there are problems, the administrator can create another performance chart that can be compared to the baseline chart.

View or Create a Performance Chart

1. Click the **Start** button, and then click **Control Panel**.

2. Click the **Administrative Tools** icon in Small icons or Large icons view.

3. Double-click the **Performance Monitor** icon.

4. In the left pane, click the arrow next to **Monitoring Tools**, and then click **Performance Monitor**.

5. To add counts and create a chart, click the **Add** button on the System Monitor toolbar.

6. Click the counter you want, and then click **Add**. You can continue to add other counters.

7. When you're done, click **OK**.

8. Click the **Close** button.

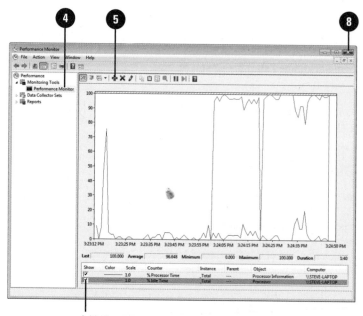

Added counter

View Resource Performance Charts

1. Click the **Start** button, and then click **Control Panel**.

2. Click the **Administrative Tools** icon in Small icons or Large icons view.

3. Double-click the **Performance Monitor** icon.

4. In the left pane, click **Performance**.

5. Click **Open Resource Monitor**.

6. Click a tab or bar (**CPU**, **Disk**, **Network**, or **Memory**) to display program specific information.

7. Click the bar again to hide the specific programs.

8. Click the **Close** button.

Performance charts

View Windows Task Manager Performance Charts

1. Right-click a blank area of the taskbar, and then click **Start Task Manager**.

   TIMESAVER *You can also press Ctrl+Alt+Del, click Task Manager, and then click Resource Monitor.*

2. Click the **Performance** tab.

3. To open the Resource Monitor, click **Resource Monitor**.

4. To view a network performance chart, click the **Networking** tab.

5. When you're done, click the **Close** button.

Monitoring Local Security Settings

Using Windows 7, you can monitor local security settings with the Local Security Settings tool to ensure that computer users are adhering to the organization's security policies. For example, you can change the way the **User Account Control (UAC)** works, including how and when Windows prompts administrators and standard users for permission to make system changes. You can also set user account and password options to require computer users to create complex passwords of a specific length and change them on a regular basis. A **complex password** contains characters from at least three of the four following categories: uppercase (A - Z), lowercase (a - z), numbers (0 - 9), and nonalphanumeric (!, $, *, etc.). In addition to setting security options, you can also **monitor**, or **audit**, the success or failure of security related events, such as account logon and logoff activities, and user account changes, which appear in the Event Viewer in the Security node.

Change UAC Policies

① Click the **Start** button, and then click **Control Panel**.

② Click the **Administrative Tools** icon in Small icons or Large icons view.

③ Double-click the **Local Security Policy** icon.

④ Click the arrow next to **Local Policies**.

⑤ Click the **Security Options** folder.

⑥ Scroll down the list, and then double-click the User Account Control policy you want to change; two common ones include:

   ◆ **Behavior of the elevation prompt for administrators.**

   ◆ **Behavior of the elevation prompt for standard users.**

⑦ Change the policy setting.

⑧ Click **OK**.

⑨ When you're done, click the **Close** button.

Behavior of the elevation prompt for administrators

Change Password Policies

1. Click the **Start** button, and then click **Control Panel**.

2. Click the **Administrative Tools** icon in Small icons or Large icons view.

3. Double-click the **Local Security Policy** icon.

4. Click the arrow next to **Account Policies**.

5. Click the **Password Policy** folder.

6. Double-click the policy you want to change.

7. Change the policy setting.

8. Click **OK**.

9. When you're done, click the **Close** button.

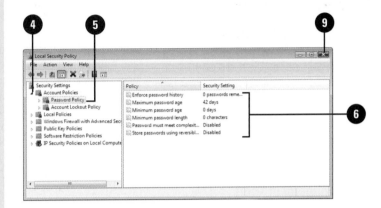

Change Audit Policies

1. Click the **Start** button, and then click **Control Panel**.

2. Click the **Administrative Tools** icon in Small icons or Large icons view.

3. Double-click the **Local Security Policy** icon.

4. Click the arrow next to **Local Policies**.

5. Click the **Audit Policy** folder.

6. Double-click the audit policy you want to change.

7. Select the **Success** and/or **Failure** check box.

8. Click **OK**.

9. When you're done, click the **Close** button.

Viewing Computer Management Tools

Computer Management consolidates administrative tools, such as Event Viewer and Performance, into a single window that you can use to manage a local or remote computer. The three nodes in the Computer Management window (System Tools, Storage, and Services and Applications) allow you to manage and monitor system events and performance and to perform disk-related tasks. Each node contains **snap-in tools**, which come in two types: stand-alone or extension. Stand-alone snap-ins are independent tools, while extension snap-ins are add-ons to current snap-ins. The selected tool appears in the right pane, and you can use the toolbars and menus that appear to take appropriate action with the tool.

View Management Tools

1 Click the **Start** button, and then click **Control Panel**.

2 Click the **Administrative Tools** icon in Small icons or Large icons view.

3 Double-click the **Computer Management** icon.

> **TIMESAVER** To open Computer Management, right-click Computer on the Start menu, and then click Manage.

4 Click the arrow next to the category you want to view.

5 Click the item you want to view.

6 Double-click the item you want to change, adjust the setting, and then click **OK**.

You can continue to change other items.

7 When you're done, click the **Close** button.

Managing Disks

The Storage node in the Computer Management window provides you with tools, such as Disk Defragmenter and Disk Management, to help you manage your disks. The Disk Management tool is a graphical tool for managing disks that allows you to partition unallocated portions of your disks into volumes. A **volume** is a fixed amount of storage on a disk. A single disk can contain more than one volume, or a volume can span part of one or more disks. Each volume on a disk is assigned its own drive letter, which is why the term volume is often synonymous with the term drive. Thus, the same physical disk might contain two volumes. Each volume can use a different file system, so you might have a single disk partitioned into two volumes, each with its own file system. You might partition a single hard disk in two different ways: first, with a single NTFS volume, and second, with one NTFS volume and one FAT volume, which can be helpful if you have a computer with two operating systems, Windows 98/Me on the FAT volume and Windows 7 on the NTFS volume.

View Disk Settings

1. Click the **Start** button, and then click **Control Panel**.

2. Click the **Administrative Tools** icon in Small icons or Large icons view.

3. Double-click the **Computer Management** icon.

   TIMESAVER *To open Computer Management, right-click Computer on the Start menu, and then click Manage.*

4. Click the arrow next to **Storage**.

5. Click **Disk Management**.

   The volumes on your computer display in the right pane.

6. Click the drive you want to modify.

7. Click the **Action** menu, point to **All Tasks**, and then click a command, such as **Format**, **Change Drive Letter and Paths**, **Mark Partition as Active**, or **Delete Volume**.

8. When you're done, click the **Close** button.

Managing Local Users and Groups

In Windows 7, you can manage the access privileges and permissions of local user and group accounts. A local user account is an individual account with a unique set of permissions, while a group account is a collection of individual accounts with the same set of permissions. You can change local user and group accounts in the Computer Management window using the Local Users And Groups tool. This security feature limits individual users and groups from accessing and deleting files, using programs such as Backup, or making accidental or intentional system-wide changes. You can create or modify a user account, disable or activate a user account, identify members of groups, and add or delete members to and from groups.

Manage Local Users and Groups

1. Click the **Start** button, and then click **Control Panel**.

2. Click the **Administrative Tools** icon in Small icons or Large icons view.

3. Double-click the **Computer Management** icon.

4. Click the arrow next to **System Tools**.

5. Click the arrow next to **Local Users and Groups**.

6. Click the **Users** or **Groups** folder.

7. Double-click the account you want to change.

8. Change the settings you want; add members if requested.

9. Click **OK**.

   You can continue to change other settings.

10. When you're done, click the **Close** button.

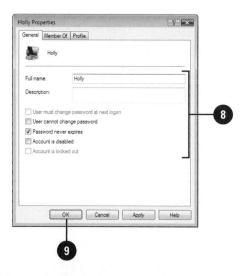

Viewing and Saving System Information

If you are having problems with Windows 7 or a program installed on your computer and can't figure out what to do, you can use System Information to locate valuable information for a support technician. For most people, the information in System Information is difficult to understand. However, if a support technician asks you for information about your system, you know where to find it. After you find the information, you can save and send it to the support technician.

View and Save System Information

1. Click the **Start** button, point to **All Programs**, click **Accessories**, click **System Tools**, and then click **System Information**.

2. Click **System Summary** to view the main information about your system.

3. Click a plus sign (+) to view a system area.

4. Click the item you want to view.

5. Click the **File** menu, and then click **Save**.

6. Select a folder.

7. Type a name for the file.

8. Click **Save**.

9. When you're done, click the **Close** button.

Did You Know?

You can display basic system information. Click the Start button, click Computer, and then click the System Properties button on the toolbar. The basic information about your computer includes system rating, processor, memory (RAM), system type, network information, and Windows activation.

Setting System Configuration Options

If you're experiencing problems with your system, you can use the System Configuration tool from Administrator Tools to help you troubleshoot and configure your computer. To help you troubleshoot your system, you can select an option to start Windows 7 with a minimal set of resources, which can help you successfully boot and narrow down the problem. After you reboot successfully, you can start to select services and startup items to add them into the equation and determine what works and what doesn't. If you need to launch an administrator tool during the process, you can do it from the Tools tab.

Change System Configuration Options

1. Click the **Start** button, and then click **Control Panel**.

2. Click the **Administrative Tools** icon in Small icons or Large icons view.

3. Double-click the **System Configuration** icon.

4. Click the **General** tab.

5. To change the way Windows starts up, click the option you want: Normal, Diagnostic, or Selective.

6. Click the tab with the options you want to change:

   ◆ **Boot.** Select options to perform a safe boot.

   ◆ **Services.** Select what services (code segments) start up.

   ◆ **Startup.** Select what programs start when Windows starts.

   ◆ **Tools.** Launch an administrator related tool.

7. When you're done, click the **OK** button.

Appendix: Installing Windows 7

Introduction

If you're upgrading to Windows 7 from a previous version of Windows, this appendix describes how to prepare and install Windows 7. The temptation is to insert the Windows 7 install disc and start the installation, but you can avoid problems by making sure your computer is ready for Windows 7. Before you install Windows 7, you need to check your computer hardware and software and make several setup decisions that relate to your computer. The Windows 7 Setup wizard walks you through the installation process.

Microsoft is continually updating and enhancing Windows 7. Instead of releasing multiple updates individually, periodically Microsoft releases an update, known as a Service Pack (SP), which provides all-in-one access to the most up-to-date drivers, tools, enhancements, and other critical updates (which were formally referred to as hotfixes). Service packs, as well as, individual updates are available free for download and installation over the Internet using Windows Update.

If you purchased a new computer that came with Windows 7 already installed on it, you can use the Windows Easy Transfer wizard to transfer the files and customized settings from your old computer to your new one.

If you have older programs that only work in Windows XP, you can use Windows XP Mode (**New!**) to install and run them in Windows 7. Windows XP Mode uses Windows Virtual PC software to provide a virtual Windows XP environment for Windows 7 Professional, Ultimate, or Enterprise users.

If you're always on the go and need to stay informed, connected, and protected, you can take advantage of Microsoft Windows Live, which is a free set of online services and specialized Web tools for Windows 7.

What You'll Do

Prepare to Install Windows 7

Install Windows 7

Update to a Windows Service Pack

Transfer Files and Settings from Another Computer

Use Windows XP Mode

Explore Windows Live

Preparing to Install Windows 7

The Windows 7 Setup wizard guides you through many of the choices you need to make, but there are some decisions and actions you need to make before you start the wizard. To ensure a successful installation, do the following:

Make sure your hardware components meet the minimum requirements. Your computer hardware needs to meet the following minimum hardware requirements to be Windows 7 PC Capability Ready:

- 1 GHz 32-bit (x86) or 64-bit (x64) processor.

- 1 GB of system memory.

- 16 GB available hard disk space.

- DirectX 9 graphics device with WDDM 1.0 or later.

Features available in specific premium editions of Windows 7, such as the ability to watch and record live TV or use Window Touch or Tablet PCs, may require additional hardware. Beyond the basic requirements, some software and hardware services, such as networking, voice and video conferencing, and sound playback, call for you to meet additional requirements; see Windows 7 documentation for specific details.

Make sure your hardware and software are compatible using the Windows 7 Upgrade Advisor. If you are running a Windows XP or Vista-based computer, you can run the Windows 7 Upgrade Advisor, which scans your computer and creates an easy-to-understand report of all known system, device, and program compatibility issues, and recommends ways to resolve them. Upgrade Advisor can also help you choose the edition of Windows 7 that best fits the way you want to use your computer. The Upgrade Advisor software is available on the Microsoft Web site at *www.microsoft.com/ windows/windows-7/get/upgrade-advisor.aspx.*

Make sure you have the required product key information. On the back of the Windows 7 DVD packaging is a unique 25-character product key, such as KFEPC-12345-MHORY-12345-IROFE, that you need to enter during the Windows 7 Setup wizard installation to complete the process. Keep the product key in a safe place, and do not share it with others. The unique product key allows you to activate and use Windows. Product activation and product registration are not the same. Product activation is required and ensures that each Windows product is not installed on more than the limited number of computers allowed in the software's end user license agreement. Activation is completely anonymous and requires no personal identification information to complete. To complete the activation process, you enter a unique 25-character product key during the Windows 7 Setup wizard installation process or when using the Activate Windows command in the System window of the Control Panel. You have a 30-day grace period in which to activate your Windows product installation. If the grace period expires and you have not completed activation, all features will stop working except the product activation feature. During the activation process, you can also register your copy of Windows 7. Product registration is not required, but completing the process ensures that you receive product update and support information from Microsoft.

Determine whether you want to perform an in-place upgrade or install a new copy of Windows 7. After you start the Windows 7 Setup wizard, you need to decide whether to upgrade your current operating system or to perform an entirely new installation, known as a **clean install**. A clean install includes completely erasing your hard drive and reformatting it with a new file system, which eliminates incompatibilities and makes your system run better. See Chapter 15, *"Maintaining Your Computer,"* for more information about file systems. Before you perform a clean install, you need to backup your files and settings on a CD, removable, or network drive before you begin. After a clean install you still need to re-install all of your programs. You can upgrade from Windows XP or Vista to Windows 7. Earlier Windows operating systems are not supported for upgrading, so those users will need to perform a clean install.

Back up your files in case you need to restore your current operating system. If you're upgrading from an earlier version of Windows or performing a clean install, you should back

up your current files so you can correct any problems that might arise during the installation. You can back up files to a removable disk, a DVD-R or DVD-RW drive, a USB drive, or another computer on your network. See Chapter 17, *"Backing Up Your Computer,"* for more information.

Make sure you have the required network information. If you are connecting to a network, you need the following information from your network administrator: name of your computer, name of the workgroup or domain, and a TCP/IP address if your network doesn't use a DHCP (Dynamic Host Configuration Protocol) server. If you are not sure whether you are connecting to a workgroup or a domain, select the workgroup option. You can always connect to a domain after you install Windows 7 Professional.

Installing Windows 7

The Windows 7 Setup wizard guides you step-by-step through the process of installing Windows 7. When the installation is finished, you are ready to log on to Windows 7. Be aware that your computer restarts several times during the installation process. Depending on the type of installation you need to perform, either upgrade or clean, you start the Windows 7 Setup wizard in different ways. If you perform an upgrade or clean install on a Windows version, you simply start your computer and insert the Windows 7 installation DVD to start the Windows 7 Setup wizard. However, if you perform a clean install on a nonsupported operating system or a blank hard disk, you need to start your computer by inserting the Windows 7 installation DVD into the DVD drive, which starts the Windows 7 Setup wizard. A clean install requires you to select additional options as you step through the wizard, but the steps are basically the same.

Install Windows 7

1. Insert the Windows 7 DVD into your DVD drive, and then start your computer, if necessary.

2. Click **Install now**.

3. Click an option whether to get important updates for installation.

4. Select the edition you want to install, and then click **Next** to continue.

5. Click the **I accept the license terms** check box, and then click **Next** to continue.

6. Click the type of installation you want: **Upgrade** or **Custom (advanced)**.

   ◆ For Custom (advanced), select a destination drive, create a partition, if necessary, and then click **Next** to continue.

7. Wait while Setup copies and installs Windows 7 on your computer. Your computer might reboot several times during this process.

8 As prompted, select the initial options you want. Options vary depending on the installation type.

- ◆ **Country, time, and keyboard.** Select a country, time, and keyboard, and then click **Next**.

- ◆ **User accounts.** Enter user account names, click **Next**, passwords, and hints to log on and share the computer, and then click **Next**.

- ◆ **Product key activation.** Type the 25-character product key, and then click **Next**.

- ◆ **Windows protection.** Select **Use recommended settings**, **Install important updates only**, or **Ask me later**.

- ◆ **Time zone, date, and time.** Select a time zone, date, and time, and then click **Next**.

- ◆ **Join wireless network.** Select a network, and then click **Next** or **Skip**.

- ◆ **Network location.** Select a network type (Home, Work, or Public).

- ◆ **HomeGroup.** Select options to create a HomeGroup, and then click **Next** or **Skip**.

9 Wait while Setup configures Windows 7 and prepares your desktop.

Did You Know?

You can check the compatibility of your computer for Windows 7. The Upgrade Advisor software is available on the Microsoft Web site at *www.microsoft.com/ windows/windows-7/get/upgrade-advisor.aspx*, then follow the online instructions.

Updating to a Windows Service Pack

Microsoft is continually updating and enhancing Windows 7. Instead of releasing multiple updates individually, periodically Microsoft releases an update, known as a Service Pack (SP), which provides all-in-one access to the most up-to-date drivers, tools, enhancements, and other critical updates (which were formally referred to as hotfixes). Service packs as well as individual updates are available free for download and installation over the Internet using the Windows Update web site. With the enhanced Windows Update web site, Microsoft makes it easy to securely download and install this important update over the Internet. After you complete the installation, turn on Automatic Updates to help you keep your computer up-to-date and secure. If you're experiencing problems with the service pack and need to reinstall it again, you can uninstall (or remove) it from your computer using Programs and Features in the Control Panel.

Download and Install a Service Pack or Other Updates

1 Click the **Start** button, point to **All Programs**, and then click **Windows Update**.

Windows connects to the Internet.

2 If prompted to install Windows Update software, click **Yes**.

3 In the left pane, click **Check for updates**, if necessary, and then wait for the update scan to complete.

4 If you need to install any important or optional updates, click the link.

5 Select the check boxes next to the service pack or any other updates you want to install.

6 Click **OK**.

7 Click **Install updates**.

8 If prompted, review the End User License Agreement, and then click **I accept the license terms** option.

9 Click **Finish**.

Windows Update downloads the updates, and then starts the installation.

10 If prompted, follow any additional installation instructions.

While updating your computer, Windows checks your system for compatibility and archives files in case of removal later.

11 Wait for the updates to be installed on your computer.

12 If prompted, click **OK** to restart your computer, and then turn on Automatic Updates.

13 Click the **Close** button as needed.

Uninstall a Windows 7 Service Pack

1 Click the **Start** button, click **Control Panel**, and then double-click the **Programs and Features** icon in Classic view.

2 In the left pane, click **View installed updates**.

> **TIMESAVER** *You can also click Installed Updates in Task pane of Windows Update.*

3 Select the service pack you want to uninstall.

4 Click **Uninstall**.

5 Click **Yes** to confirm the removal, and then follow the instructions.

6 When it's done, click **OK**.

7 Click the **Close** button.

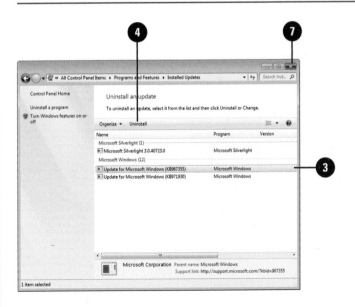

Transferring Files and Settings from Another Computer

Instead of trying to re-create Windows settings manually from an old computer (running Windows 2000, XP, or Vista) on a new Windows 7 computer, you can use Windows Easy Transfer (**New!**). If you have a removable hard drive, CD or DVD burner drives, a direct connect cable, such as an Easy Transfer Cable (a special USB cable designed for Windows Easy Transfer), or you are connected to a computer over a network, you can use Windows Easy Transfer to transfer files and settings for Windows, such as user accounts, desktop and display properties, and browser and e-mail setup options. However, it's not meant for transferring your computer programs. It's important to note that you can't transfer files from a Windows 64-bit version to a 32-bit version.

Prepare the Old Computer

1. Start Windows Easy Transfer on the old computer using one of the following methods:

   ◆ **Windows Vista/7**. Click the **Start** button, point to **All Programs**, click **Accessories**, click **System Tools**, and then click **Windows Easy Transfer**.

   ◆ **Windows XP or 2000**. Insert the Windows 7 installation disc, and then click **Transfer files and settings from another computer**.

2. Read the welcome screen, and then click **Next** to continue.

3. Click a transfer method: **An Easy Transfer cable**, **A network**, or **An external hard disk or USB flash drive**.

4. Click **My is my old computer**.

5. Follow the on-screen instructions for your selected method:

   ◆ **Easy Transfer cable**. Use the direct connect cable.

   ◆ **Network**. Use an transfer key.

   ◆ **External or USB drive**. Select files and settings to transfer, specify a password, and then save the transfer file.

6. Click **Next** to complete the process, and then click **Close**.

Transfer Files and Settings to the New Computer

① On the new Windows 7 computer, click the **Start** button, point to **All Programs**, click **Accessories**, click **System Tools**, and then click **Windows Easy Transfer**.

◆ You can also double-click the **Transfer files and settings from another computer** icon in the Getting Started window.

② Read the welcome screen, and then click **Next** to continue.

③ Click a transfer method: **An Easy Transfer cable**, **A network**, or **An external hard disk or USB flash drive**.

④ Click **My is my new computer**.

⑤ Click **I need to install it now**, **I already installed it on my old computer**, or **My old computer is running Windows 7**.

Follow the on-screen instructions to install the Windows Easy Transfer software as needed.

⑥ Read the instructions on the screen, and then click **Next**.

⑦ Follow the on-screen instructions for your selected method:

◆ **Easy Transfer cable.** Use the direct connect cable.

◆ **Network.** Use an transfer key.

◆ **External or USB drive.** Select files and settings to transfer, specify a password, and then save the transfer file.

⑧ Click **Next** to complete the process, and then click **Close**.

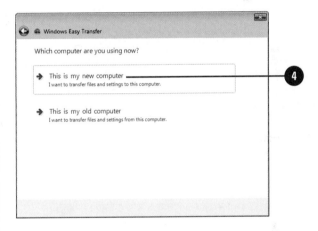

For Your Information

Viewing a Windows Easy Transfer Report

After you complete a transfer from one computer to another, you can open Windows Easy Transfer Reports to view information about the transfer. Click the Start button, point to All Programs, click Accessories, click System Tools, and then click Windows Easy Transfer Reports (**New!**).

Using Windows XP Mode

Windows XP Mode (**New!**) for Windows 7 allows you to install and run your Windows XP programs directly from Windows 7. Windows XP Mode uses Windows Virtual PC software to provide a virtual Windows XP environment for Windows 7 Professional, Ultimate, or Enterprise users. This allows you the flexibility to run many older programs. After you install your Windows XP programs, you can access them just as you would any other Windows 7 program.

Getting Prepared

Before you can use Windows XP Mode, you need to make sure your computer meets the hardware requirements (1 GHz 32 bit or 64-bit processor, 2 GB RAM, and an additional 15 GB of available hard disk space) and is compatible with the technology used by Windows Virtual PC, which requires a CPU with the Intel Virtualization Technology or AMD-V feature turned on. This feature must be enabled in the system BIOS. You can install and run a utility program to determine whether your computer is compatible, which is available on the web at *http://www.microsoft.com/windows/virtual-pc/support/configure-bios.aspx*. There is a utility for Intel-based processors and another one for AMD-based processors.

If your computer is compatible, all you need to do is download and install the Windows Virtual PC and Windows XP Mode software, which is available on the web at *http://www.microsoft.com/windows/virtual-pc/download.aspx*.

Compatible with Intel processor

Virtual Windows XP installed

Using Windows XP Mode

After you have prepared your computer to use Windows XP mode, the first thing you need to do is install your Windows XP programs. To install them in Windows XP Mode, begin by starting Virtual Windows XP from the Start menu. A Virtual Windows XP window appears, displaying a desktop for the Windows XP operating system. You install your programs just as you normally would on a computer using Windows XP; you can download software from the Web, use CDs or DVDs, or access it from a network.

After you install your Windows XP programs, you can run them in Seamless or Desktop mode. Seamless mode allows you start your Windows XP programs directly from the Windows 7 Start menu, while Desktop modes opens in a separate window (Virtual Windows XP) where you can start your Windows XP programs from the Start menu.

While you run Windows XP Mode, you can share drives, USB devices, Clipboard, and printers. This means you can cut, copy, and paste data between Windows 7 and Virtual PC and use file and printing resources.

Desktop mode

Seamless mode

Exploring Windows Live

After you install Microsoft Windows Live, you can access the Windows Live communications tools (**New!**), such as Windows Live Messenger, Windows Live Mail, Windows Live Writer, Windows Live Photo Gallery, Windows Movie Maker, and Family Safety from the Windows Live menu under All Programs on the Start menu. Windows Live Home is a personalized portal to access Windows Live online services, which also displays the Windows Live Toolbar in your Web browser. If Internet safety is important to you as a parent, you can use Family Safety in connection with Windows Live OneCare to control your children's use.

Explore Windows Live

1. Click the **Start** button, point to **All Programs**, click **Accessories**, and then click **Getting Started**.

2. Double-click the **Go online to get Windows Live Essentials** icon, and then follow the online instructions to download and install it.

3. Use links on the home page or the Windows Live Toolbar to access the available features; common ones include:

   ◆ **Windows Live Messenger.** Send and receive instant text and video messages.

   ◆ **Windows Live Mail.** Use Hotmail with different accounts to send and receive mail.

   ◆ **Windows Live Writer.** Blog pages and make posts.

   ◆ **Windows Live Photos Gallery.** Store and modify photos.

   ◆ **Windows Live Movie Maker.** Create slide shows and video files.

   ◆ **Windows Live Family Safety.** Set options to protect your computer for children's use.

   ◆ **Windows Live Toolbar.** Easy access to Windows Live programs and options.

4. When you're done, click the **Close** button.

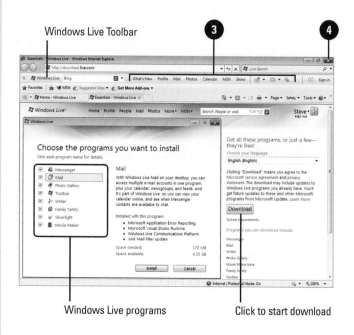

Windows Live Toolbar

Windows Live programs

Click to start download

New! Features

Microsoft Windows 7

Microsoft Windows 7 comes with new features that make your computer significantly easier and faster to use than earlier versions of Windows. Windows 7 makes it easier to use the Start menu, open files and programs, find information, and accomplish other common tasks, such as send and receive secure e-mail, browse the Internet securely, scan and view pictures, play music and videos, and change settings. Windows 7 delivers the Windows Aero user experience, Instant Searches, Explorers, Gadgets, improved Internet Explorer, Windows Media Center, and advanced security and protection.

Only New Features

If you're already familiar with Microsoft Windows Vista, you can access and download all the tasks in this book with Microsoft Windows 7 New Features to help make your transition to the new version simple and smooth. The Microsoft Windows 7 New Features, as well as other Vista to 7 transition helpers, are available on the Web at *www.perspection.com.*

What's New

If you're searching for what's new in Windows 7, just look for the icon: **New!**. The new icon appears in the table of contents and throughout this book so you can quickly and easily identify a new or improved feature in Windows 7. The following is a brief description of each new feature, and it's location in this book.

Windows 7

◆ **Action Center (p. 310, 322-323)** Action Center allows you to set the system alerts you want to see, and hide the ones you don't. If you're attention is needed, Action Center will display an icon requiring you're assistance.

◆ **Aero (p. 6-7)** Aero, available in the Home Premium, Professional, and Ultimate versions of Windows 7, makes managing your desktop a visual experience. Slick graphics and other great features such as subtle animations, glass windows, and color palettes which can be customized, all contribute to a more user friendly desktop. Place the cursor on an icon, and see a thumbnail preview, even if it's a video. If you hover over the thumbnail, it converts to a full-screen view.

- ◆ **Aero Peek (p. 7)**   Peek, also available in the Home Premium, Professional, and Ultimate versions of Windows 7, allows you to "peek" at your desktop, while various windows are open. A quick move of the cursor to the right edge of the taskbar, and open window(s) become transparent, which allows you to see the icons and gadgets on the desktop. To show just one window, point to the taskbar thumbnail, and that window becomes the primary window on the desktop.

- ◆ **Aero Shake (p. 7)**   Sometimes too many windows can make it hard to focus on the one window you need to view quickly. With a quick click of the pane and shake of the mouse, your window of the moment becomes the main focus. Click again, give the mouse another shake, and you are back to your multiple window views.

- ◆ **Backup and Restore (p. 471-482)**   Some additional improvements help keep your data safe. Now with Window 7 Professional or Ultimate editions, you can backup files to a network. With all versions, improved backups have safety copies of your folders, libraries or other drives. You control what you want Windows to backup by setting a schedule.

- ◆ **BitLocker (p. 329)**   BitLocker has been improved for Windows 7 to include BitLocker To Go. Protecting your data from loss or theft is Important in today's world. You can encrypt your entire hard drive. Once it's activated, all the files that you create, use, and save are automatically encrypted. The BitLocker To Go feature now includes all your portable storage devices.

- ◆ **Calculator (p. 45)**   Calculator performs basic arithmetic, such as addition and subtraction, functions found on a scientific calculator, such as logarithms and factorials, programmer conversion, such as Hex and Decimal, as well as functions for statistical analysis.

- ◆ **Desktop Wallpaper (p. 101)**   There are a whole host of new wallpapers in Windows 7. You can change your background to suit your day, month, or the season of the year. You can also use the new desktop slide show to show pictures, either yours or Microsoft's, for a change.

- ◆ **Device Management (p. 399, 452)**   With Windows 7, device management has all the information you need to know about your devices (cell phones, cameras, and other devices) and other equipment connected to your PC.

- ◆ **Display Monitor and Projector (p. 105-107, 462-463)**   You can also change the screen orientation (Landscape, Portrait, or flipped). If you're using a projector as an additional monitor, you can select display settings in the Screen Resolution window or on the Start menu.

- ◆ **Domain Join (p. 358-359)**   Need to connect to your office while working at home? With Domain Join, you can enter in specific network credentials through the Domain Join wizard, and you're in business.

- ◆ **Gadgets (p. 15)**   Gadgets can now be adjusted in size and location on the desktop, to make the most of the information you want to see! No longer restricted to the Sidebar, your local weather or stock news can be placed where you want to see it on your desktop.

- **Games Explorer (p. 48-49)** Windows 7 isn't all business. There's a lot of fun to be had with Games Explorer. Multiplayer, fun statistical tracking and the ability to get updates and newsfeeds makes Games Explorer a fun part of your day.

- **Getting Started (p. 4)** Getting Started continues to be where it all begins! Adding user accounts, transferring or backing up files, and personalizing Windows 7 all starts here.

- **HomeGroup (p. 8, 92, 373-375)** HomeGroup, which is available in the Home Premium, Professional, and Ultimate versions of Windows 7, allows you to create and connect your home PC's for data sharing. You can work with another feature (Libraries) to share data. Also, with HomeGroup you control the settings and the level of sharing on the PC's, and its password protected.

- **Jump Lists (p. 12-14, 26)** Ever wish you had a catalog of files that you use each day? Jump Lists are a new feature in Windows 7 that will bring you to Web sites, files, even songs, that you use each day. By right clicking on an icon on the task bar, your Jump List will appear showing the files, Web sites, or media, that you commonly use. If you have a file, Web site, or media you want to add, simply pin it to your Jump List and it will be there the next time you want it.

- **Libraries (p. 54, 58, 60-62, 90)** A library is a great new tool to sort through your entire folders, pictures, even music, stored on multiple PC's. You might have family photos that have been transferred to a laptop, and want to pull others from another PC. With Libraries, you simply set up a main folder, and can pull from various computers to show in that one Library folder. Libraries are a great tool for pictures, music, and various documents and files.

- **Location-Aware Printing (p. 402)** Now with Windows 7 Professional and Ultimate editions, your laptop automatically remembers what printer it last printed on. So, when printing to multiple printers from your laptop, Windows will remember what network and printer combination you use. So, the next time you sign into one network, it will pair that printer. Signing on at the office? You'll get your office printer as a default.

- **Magnifier (p. 125-127)** Enlarge hard to see text when running Windows 7 is one feature most of us can appreciate. The first adjustment—Full Screen Mode —will make the text larger, next you can use the Zoom feature to further magnify. You can even type text in the magnify mode to make sure that what you type or select is correct.

- **Multiplayer Games (p. 48-49)** Find yourself missing the Internet powerhouse games of Checkers, Spades, and Backgammon? Well, they're back in the Home Premium, Professional, and Ultimate versions of Windows 7. Back by popular demand, the most loved multiplayer games are back and visually enhanced to make your experience the best ever. Also included are player stats, game updates and newsfeeds.

- **Networking (p. 360-364, 378-379)** Need to connect your laptop to a network? With Windows 7 it's easy to set up your home network for your laptop to connect to, as well as, wireless networks as you are on the go. Set up networks that contain dial-up, Wi-Fi, mobile broadband, or corporate VPNs.

- ◆ **On-Screen Keyboard (p. 278)** Using Windows Touch, you can tap the letter on your on-screen keyboard that appears on your screen and be typing in no time. There is word prediction that can help speed up the process. You can also use your mouse or other hot keys to use the on-screen keyboard.

- ◆ **Paint (p. 234-235)** The drawing and painting program is improved to include a Ribbon and additional drawing/brush tools.

- ◆ **Parenting Controls (p. 48, 279, 326)** With Windows 7, you can set up a safe online environment for your kids. Time controls such as how long they can use the computer, and what time of day, along with what programs they can use all help you set the limits they need. And, with Windows Media Center, you can also block TV shows and movies based on ratings and titles.

- ◆ **Performance Improvements (p. 68-69, 78-79, 384-385, 452)** Windows 7 makes key enhancements to make your PC ready to go. The Sleep feature will sleep, resume, and reconnect in a quicker fashion based on the settings you choose. The Search feature has been enhanced to allow a fine tuning to get the information you need quicker. USB or flash drives can be set up so the read time can be even quicker. And, you can customize updates and features to run when you want them, and retrieve just the information you've set. Also, better performance than Vista, Windows 7 won't gobble up all your memory.

- ◆ **Play To Steaming Media (p. 272-273, 278-280)** The Play To feature allows you to use your PC and music on other devices (compliant with the Digital Living Network Alliance, such as your Xbox 360) or PCs around the home or office using Windows 7.

- ◆ **Private Character Editor (p. 44)** You can create your own characters, which you can insert into documents by using Character Map.

- ◆ **Power Management (p. 384-385)** With Windows 7, better usage of power will make your battery charge last longer. Efficiency with ports not in use, less background activities running while you're working, a less needy DVD playback, screen dimming, and a better battery status indicator.

- ◆ **Snap Windows (p. 16-17)** Snap provides a quick and easy resizing option for open windows. By dragging and fitting windows together using the edge of your screen, you can easily view various files.

- ◆ **Snipping Tool (p. 50)** A great new screenshot feature in the Home Premium, Professional, and Ultimate versions of Windows 7, the snipping tool allows you to snip a window, or a portion of one, to quickly and easily store it for later use, or send it along in email.

- ◆ **Sticky Notes (p. 36)** Now in the Home Premium, Professional, and Ultimate versions of Windows 7, Sticky Notes can be organized and formatted to make your experience a better one! Flip through your notes, change colors, and modify the text font to use them most effectively. If you have a touch pad or pen, Sticky Notes works with these features to provide the flexibility you need.

- ◆ **System Restore (p. 444-445, 468, 483)** In Windows 7, a potentially bad crash won't have you taking hours to restore. System Restore will bring back your files to a time when things were working fine. As you work, you can create system restore points that will be saved and used in the event of a crash.

n

- **Tablet PC and Pen (p. 393, 396)** If you don't always have a need for a mouse or a keyboard, but a pen and tablet are more your need, look no further. With the Home Premium, Professional, and Ultimate versions of Windows 7, you can now perform Tablet Math. The new Math Input Panel recognizes math expressions and can work with other programs. With shape recognition, map out and organize all you want. And with Windows 7, handwriting recognition is more accurate and supports many languages. You can have a personalized dictionary to help with many company or field specific terms.

- **Troubleshooting (p. 322, 466)** You can run troubleshooters to fix programs made for previous versions of Windows, reconfigure a hardware device, establish an Internet connection, access shared files, fix Aero desktop effects, and fix Windows Update, maintenance, and performance issues.

- **Windows Anytime Upgrade (p. 523)** Upgrading is easier than ever if you decide to move up to the next level of Windows 7. In the past, upgrading had been difficult to manage. But now with Windows 7, you can purchase one version, and if you decide you want to move up to the next level say Premium to Ultimate, that all you need to do is purchase an upgrade key from Microsoft.

- **Windows Easy Transfer (p. 508-509)** This new feature helps with the transfer of data from your old PC to your new PC or laptop. Simply use the new file explorer to select the files and folders you wish to copy over. If Windows 7 has a hard time transferring, the file will be marked and Windows 7 will move over to the next file to be transferred. At the end of the transfer process, you'll get a list of files that could not be transferred if there was a problem.

- **Windows Explorer (p. 2, 54-55, 63, 65-66, 88)**   The Navigation pane contains Favorites, Libraries, HomeGroups, Computer drives, and Networks. The available views include Extra Large, Large, Medium and Small Icons, List, Details, Tiles, and Content. Content view displays medium icons in a vertical column with date modified information.

- **Windows Firewall (p. 134, 136)** Windows Firewall has received a user-friendly update. You can fine tune your settings for each of your network profiles— Home, Work, and Public. For example, restrict incoming connections while in public places to further protect against hackers and unwanted data.

- **Windows Live Essentials (p. 166, 167-168, 240-242, 246, 248, 254, 512)** Additional features such as email, Movie Maker, photo editing, and even blogging, are an "essential" part of Windows 7. With Live Essentials, these extra applications are sure to add a personal touch. Photo and movie making, setting up and monitoring online activities, and instant messaging, all add to the Windows 7 experience.

- **Windows Media Center (p. 278-280)** Available in the Home Premium, Professional, and Ultimate versions of Windows 7, Media Center has expanded to include many of the options that we've grown to love (watch and record live TV, listed to your Playlist, view photos) and enhancements for many new ones. The Turbo Scroll feature allows you to zip to the songs and shows you love, without wading through large lists. Wonderful slide shows can be created with background music. HomeGroups is a new feature that allows sharing between PCs in the home that run Windows 7. There's even a Windows Media Center gadget for the desktop to make it easier to access and use.

- ◆ **Windows Media Player 12 (p. 256, 264-265, 272-273)** With a whole host of options, Windows Media Player 12 is sure to please. You can play music and videos, and unprotected songs from your iTunes library. Audio types such as 3GP, AVCHD, and DivX are just a few of the choices you can play. Features such as Play To allows you to use your PC, with other compatible devices in your home, or stream over the Internet from one PC to another. A new taskbar thumbnail can help you with playback controls.

- ◆ **Windows Search (p. 13, 68, 72-73)** Need to find a file and don't remember where you stored it? With Windows Search you can type in the Start Menu search box, and look up information based on your criteria. To fine tune your search, add date, file type, and other key information to narrow your search results.

- ◆ **Windows Taskbar and Start Menu (p. 8-9, 14, 24, 28, 118-121)** Taskbar improvements in Windows 7 make it easier and more user-friendly. Now you can pin your favorite programs to the Taskbar for quick retrieval, rearrange the icons the way you want to show them and you can even preview a window or close a window in a thumbnail preview. The Start menu provides a customizable Power button.

- ◆ **Windows Touch (p. 278, 393)** With the Home Premium, Professional, and Ultimate versions of Windows 7, touch screen becomes a greater reality! With the touch screen PC, you can browse papers, sites, photos, without the need for a keyboard. The Multitouch technology allows users to zoom by simply place 2 fingers and spread them apart, like you do on the iPhone. There are finger-friendly sized icons to help.

- ◆ **Windows XP Mode (p. 510-511)** With Windows 7 Professional and Ultimate, you can use all the new applications that you've recently purchased, along with the older aps that might still run on an XP platform. The XP Mode comes in a separate download and is meant to help those businesses still running on XP.

- ◆ **WordPad (p. 30, 34, 38, 40)** The word-processing program is improved to include a Ribbon, additional formatting tools, and more saving options. You can save documents in Office Open XML document (DOCX), which is for Microsoft Word 2007, OpenDocument text (ODT), which is for exchanging office documents, and Plain Text Document (TXT), which is for plain text. In addition, you can use the Paint drawing button on the Home tab to embed a new Paint object.

- ◆ **XPS Document Writer (p. 410)** You create an XPS document by printing it with the Microsoft XPS Document Writer printer. The XPS Viewer—available in Windows 7—allows you to open any XPS document.

Internet Explorer 8

- ◆ **Accelerators (p. 148)** With Accelerators in IE 8, it's never been easier to map an address, forward a link, or look up a word with an online dictionary. By highlighting the text, and then clicking the blue Accelerator icon you can then make your choice of action. The blue Accelerator icon is available with many popular online Web sites, such as Amazon, Facebook, Wikipedia, and more.

- ◆ **Address Bar (p. 140-141)** The Address Bar has been enhanced to show greater accuracy in the Web sites that you visit and use. Have you ever gone to a site and mis-typed it, only to have it come up each time you try and go to the correct site? Now you can delete it by clicking on the red X to remove the site address. You can also start typing a site that you might not remember the correct address and matches that you've recently typed will appear.

- ◆ **Automatic Crash Recovery (p. 137)** This new feature allows multiple tabs to still function, even if a Web site or add-on causes one tab to crash. IE8 will remain functional, dropping the tab. If the problem is bigger than just one tab, IE8 will be automatically reloaded so that you are returned to the pages that were originally tabbed.

- ◆ **Back Button (p. 144)** The Back button in IE8 will work the way you want it to. Instead of being brought back screen by screen, you'll be brought back to the beginning or Home page of the site.

- ◆ **Compatibility View (p. 146)** With IE8, some Web sites may not have upgraded yet and these sites may not show text properly (spacing and alignment). To see the Web site in its intended design view, you can click the Compatibility View toolbar button to easily view the site as IE7.

- ◆ **Deleting Browsing History (p. 152-155, 337)** Now you are able to save browsing history and cookies in your Favorites folder. This helps you to keep your Favorite Web sites and cookies available for viewing and use, while keeping the History folder clear.

- ◆ **Domain Highlighting (p. 140)** Have you ever gone to one Web site and before you know it, you've been transferred to another? Now with the Domain Highlighting feature, you will see the Web site domain highlighted in black, and with an easy glance at the Web address, you can see which page you are on.

- ◆ **Favorites and History Management (p. 150-153)** The Favorites bar has been enhanced to include many of the new features added with IE8. Web Slices can be added to the Favorites bar to follow data during your session. There is the One Click Add to Favorites button that can save you extra steps. You can also drag an RSS Feed to the Favorites bar. There is a Browsing History view that shows you your search and visit history for various sites. You can sort the sites by date viewed and most visited sites to help you manage data on your PC.

- ◆ **Find On Page (p. 156-157)** The Find On Page tool has been redesigned to allow you to view the page and not block the find result. With the toolbar located on the bottom of the page, your data is set for better viewing.

- ◆ **InPrivate Browsing (p. 145, 341)** Think that Web sites and data that you type is safe using another PC? They are now, thanks to InPrivate Browsing by IE8. You can activate this feature, and while typing in user ids and passwords, or account numbers and codes, this feature will NOT transfer data to cookies and store in a Web browsing history file. So feel safe while stopping in the Internet café while travelling abroad, and know that your data doesn't need to stay there after you've left.

- ◆ **InPrivate Filtering (p. 337, 344-345)** While Web sites can pull certain data that you provide to them, they can also track certain Web site activity as well. This is something that some users may not want, and with the InPrivate Filter setting located on the Safety menu, you can select to have your privacy protected.

- **Instant Search (p. 156)** The search box has been updated to better provide you with the search results you want. You can click the search result right from the menu.

- **New Tab Page (p. 142-143)** The New Tab Page helps you start your browsing and organize your results. You can add Web Slices, use InPrivate while browsing, reopen tabs that have been recently closed, and even reopen all the tabs you were viewing when you were last browsing.

- **Performance (p. 137)** IE8 now runs with an increased performance allowing Web browsing to move faster, Web sites to load more quickly, and a better response time for searches and loads.

- **Search Suggestions (p. 156-157)** With Search Suggestions, relevant data will be added to assist with the search. Simply click on a suggestion if it appears before you finish typing the entire search.

- **SmartScreen (p. 340-341)** SmartScreen is a filter developed by IE8 to help protect your PC from sites that may do more harm than good. Hackers looking to steal private or not so private information or pleas for bank account transfers to help far away victims can do more harm than good.

- **Tabbed Browsing (p. 142-143)** This feature once again helps the Web browsing experience to be more efficient and organized. Multiple sites loaded? How about a color coded system that groups similar sites. Other tab organization can open recently closed tabs, or open or close a group of tabs.

- **Visual Suggestions (p. 156-157)** Along with Search Suggestions, a visual graphic will appear as you search. Working with top search engines allows IE8 to offer a more visual search result.

- **Web Slices (p. 149)** With the new green Web Slices icon situated on the Favorites bar, you can instantly monitor the Web sites and data that you look at throughout the day. Want to follow your favorite stock? Look for the Web Slices icon to be highlighted, and you've got an update!

- **Zoom (p. 147)** With the Adaptive Page Zoom, better zoom results will leave the scroll left and right behind. The Browser will be able to "intelligently" resize the Web page so you can focus on your zoom results, while seeing the whole page.

Windows 7 Editions

Microsoft Windows 7 comes in four main editions: the Home Basic Edition for consumers; the Home Premium Edition for consumer power users; the Professional Edition for business and power users; and the Ultimate Edition for the complete package. Two other editions are available for specific needs: the Starter Edition and Enterprise Edition. The Starter Edition is for the beginning PC user and provides the most basic entry to Windows 7, which is targeted to emerging markets. The Enterprise Edition is for large corporations with advanced data protection, compatibility, and international support needs.

Microsoft Windows 7 Editions

The **Home Basic** Edition provides a basic secure entry point for using Windows 7. Windows 7 Home Basic is ideal for homes with basic computing needs like browsing the Internet, viewing photos, and the Mobility Center, while still providing a more secure environment to help protect you from harmful attacks.

The **Home Premium** Edition designed to deliver productivity, entertainment, and security for home and mobile PCs. Window 7 Home Premium adds to the basic experience by providing the Windows Aero experience, Windows Media Center for media entertainment, Windows Media Player for remote access, Tablet PC support for laptops, and premium games.

The **Professional** Edition is designed specifically to meet the needs of small businesses. Window 7 Professional modifies the Home Premium Edition by adding business networking and remote desktop access, Windows XP mode, Presentation mode in the Mobility Center, location-aware printing, and file encryption.

The **Ultimate** Edition combines every thing from all the editions into one complete package. Windows 7 Ultimate provides the power and security features needed for work, such as BitLocker and the use of different languages.

The **Enterprise** Edition lowers IT costs and risks to meet the needs of large, global organizations with complex IT infrastructures.

Windows 7 Editions

Feature	Basic	Premium	Professional	Ultimate
Max RAM (32-bit)	4 GB	4 GB	4 GB	4 GB
Maximum RAM (64-bit)	8 GB	16 GB	192 GB	192 GB
Quickly find what you need with Instant Search and Windows Internet Explorer 8	◆	◆	◆	◆
Stay connected wherever and whenever you like with Network and Sharing Center	◆	◆	◆	◆
Best choice for laptops with Windows Mobility Center support	◆	◆	◆	◆
Elegant Windows Aero desktop experience with glass-like menu bars, Windows Flip 3D, and Live Thumbnails		◆	◆	◆
Extend Windows 7 to secondary displays and devices with Windows SideShow		◆	◆	◆
Experience photos and entertainment in your living room with Windows Media Center		◆	◆	◆
Playback DVD and easily make DVDs with Windows DVD Maker		◆	◆	◆
Have more fun on your PC with premium and Internet games (Internet Backgammon, Internet Checkers, Internet Spades, and Mahjong Titans)		◆	◆	◆
Use Windows XP Mode to run Windows XP programs with Virtual PC	VPC only	VPC only	◆	◆
Create and join HomeGroup network to share files, printers, and music	Join only	◆	◆	◆
Use Multi-touch with a touch screen instead of a mouse or keyboard		◆	◆	◆
Use the Snipping Tool to capture the screen		◆	◆	◆
Use Sticky Notes to create electronic notes		◆	◆	◆
Use Windows Journal to handwrite notes using a Tablet PC and writing device		◆	◆	◆
Use Backup and Restore to create full backups to a home or business network			◆	◆
Get to the resources and applications you need to host a Remote Desktop Connection			◆	◆
Connect to company networks easily and more securely with Domain Join			◆	◆
Use location-aware printing to automatically change printers at different locations			◆	◆

Windows 7 Editions *(continued)*				
Feature	**Basic**	**Premium**	**Professional**	**Ultimate**
Use Presentation Mode in the Mobility Center			◆	◆
Protect your data files using encryption (EFS)			◆	◆
Better protect your data against loss with Windows BitLocker and BitLocker To Go				◆
Work in different languages				◆

Windows Anytime Upgrade

Upgrading is easier than ever if you decide to move up to the next level of Windows 7. In the past, upgrading had been difficult to manage. But now with Windows 7, you can purchase one version, and if you decide you want to move up to the next level say Premium to Ultimate, that all you need to do is purchase an upgrade key from Microsoft.

Windows Anytime Upgrade is now a standalone program instead of a Control Panel utility as it was in Windows Vista. You can access it from the Start menu. The Windows Anytime Upgrade program gives you two choices: god online to choose the edition of Windows that's best for you and Enter an upgrade key. Simply follow the step-by-step on-screen instructions to complete the process. It takes about 10 minutes to complete the upgrade.

1 Click the **Start** button, type **Anytime** in the Search box to locate the program, and then click **Windows Anytime Upgrade**.

2 Click **Go online to choose the edition of Windows 7 that's best for you** or **Enter an upgrade key**.

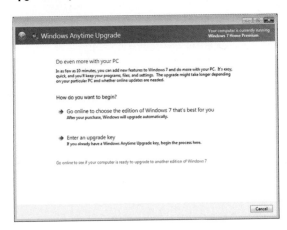

3 Enter your upgrade key, and then click **Next** to continue.

4 After the verification is complete, click **I accept** to the license terms.

5 Close any open programs, and then click **Upgrade**.

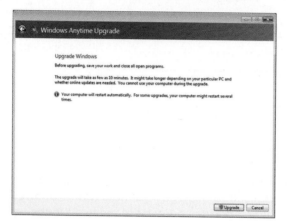

After about 10 minutes and a reboot, your upgraded version of Windows 7 appears on the screen.

Microsoft Certified Applications Specialist

About the MCAS Program

The Microsoft Certified Applications Specialist (MCAS) certification is the globally recognized standard for validating expertise with the Microsoft Office suite of business productivity programs. Earning an MCAS certificate acknowledges you have the expertise to work with Microsoft Office programs. To earn the MCAS certification, you must pass a certification exam for Microsoft Windows 7. Additional exams are available for the Microsoft Office desktop applications of Microsoft Office Word, Microsoft Office Excel, Microsoft Office PowerPoint, Microsoft Office Outlook, or Microsoft Office Access. (The availability of Microsoft Certified Applications Specialist certification exams varies by program, program version, and language. Visit *www.microsoft.com* and search on *Microsoft Certified Applications Specialist* for exam availability and more information about the program.) The Microsoft Certified Applications Specialist program is the only Microsoft-approved program in the world for certifying proficiency with Microsoft Office programs.

What Does This Logo Mean?

It means this book has been approved by the Microsoft Certified Applications Specialist program to be certified courseware for learning Microsoft Windows 7 and preparing for the certification exam. This book will prepare you for the Microsoft Certified Applications Specialist exam for Microsoft Windows 7. Each certification level has a set of objectives, which are organized into broader skill sets. To prepare for the certification exam, you should review and perform each task identified with a MCAS objective to confirm that you can meet the requirements for the exam. The MCAS objectives are available on the Web at *www.perspection.com* along with the example files for Microsoft Windows 7 On Demand.

Microsoft
Certified
Application   WIN7-1.1.1
Specialist   WIN7-2.2.1

Preparing for a MCAS Exam

Every Microsoft Certified Applications Specialist certification exam is developed from a list of objectives based on how Microsoft Office programs are actually used in the workplace. The list of objectives determine the scope of each exam, so they provide you with the information you need to prepare for MCAS certification. Microsoft Certified Applications Specialist Approved Courseware, including the On Demand series, is reviewed and approved on the basis of its coverage of the objectives. To prepare for the certification exam, you should review and perform each task identified with a MCAS objective to confirm that you can meet the requirements for the exam.

Taking a MCAS Exam

The Microsoft Certified Applications Specialist certification exams are not written exams. Instead, the exams are performance-based examinations that allow you to interact with a "live" Office program as you complete a series of objective-based tasks. All the standard ribbons, tabs, toolbars, and keyboard shortcuts are available during the exam. Microsoft Certified Applications Specialist exams for Office 2007 programs consist of 25 to 35 questions, each of which requires you to complete one or more tasks using the Office program for which you are seeking certification. A typical exam takes from 45 to 60 minutes. Passing percentages range from 70 to 80 percent correct.

The Exam Experience

After you fill out a series of information screens, the testing software starts the exam and the Office program. The test questions appear in the exam dialog box in the lower right corner of the screen.

- The timer starts when the first question appears and displays the remaining exam time at the top of the exam dialog box. If the timer and the counter are distracting, you can click the timer to remove the display.

- The counter at the top of the exam dialog box tracks how many questions you have completed and how many remain.

- If you think you have made a mistake, you can click the Reset button to restart the question. The Reset button does not restart the entire exam or extend the exam time limit.

- When you complete a question, click the Next button to move to the next question. It is not possible to move back to a previous question on the exam.

- If the exam dialog box gets in your way, you can click the Minimize button in the upper right corner of the exam dialog box to hide it, or you can drag the title bar to another part of the screen to move it.

Tips for Taking an Exam

◆ Carefully read and follow all instructions provided in each question.

◆ Make sure all steps in a task are completed before proceeding to the next exam question.

◆ Enter requested information as it appears in the instructions without formatting unless you are explicitly requested otherwise.

◆ Close all dialog boxes before proceeding to the next exam question unless you are specifically instructed otherwise.

◆ Do not leave tables, boxes, or cells "active" unless instructed otherwise.

◆ Do not cut and paste information from the exam interface into the program.

◆ When you print a document from an Office program during the exam, nothing actually gets printed.

◆ Errant keystrokes or mouse clicks do not count against your score as long as you achieve the correct end result. You are scored based on the end result, not the method you use to achieve it. However, if a specific method is explicitly requested, you need to use it to get credit for the results.

◆ The overall exam is timed, so taking too long on individual questions may leave you without enough time to complete the entire exam.

◆ If you experience computer problems during the exam, immediately notify a testing center administrator to restart your exam where you were interrupted.

Exam Results

At the end of the exam, a score report appears indicating whether you passed or failed the exam. An official certificate is mailed to successful candidates in approximately two to three weeks.

Getting More Information

To learn more about the Microsoft Certified Applications Specialist program, read a list of frequently asked questions, and locate the nearest testing center, visit:

www.microsoft.com

Index